American Propaganda from the Spanish-American War to Iraq

American Propaganda from the Spanish-American War to Iraq

War Stories

Steven R. Brydon

LEXINGTON BOOKS
Lanham • Boulder • New York • London

Published by Lexington Books
An imprint of The Rowman & Littlefield Publishing Group, Inc.
4501 Forbes Boulevard, Suite 200, Lanham, Maryland 20706
www.rowman.com

86-90 Paul Street, London EC2A 4NE, United Kingdom

Copyright © 2022 by The Rowman & Littlefield Publishing Group, Inc.

All rights reserved. No part of this book may be reproduced in any form or by any electronic or mechanical means, including information storage and retrieval systems, without written permission from the publisher, except by a reviewer who may quote passages in a review.

British Library Cataloguing in Publication Information Available

Library of Congress Cataloging-in-Publication Data

Names: Brydon, Steven Robert, author.
Title: American propaganda from the Spanish-American war to Iraq : war stories / Steven R. Brydon.
Description: Lanham : Lexington Books, [2022] | Includes bibliographical references and index. | Summary: "This book analyzes American war propaganda, beginning with the Spanish-American War and extending through the wars in Afghanistan and Iraq. Using Fisher's narrative paradigm, the author identifies and critically evaluates recurring war stories, determining whether or not they truly provided good reasons to go to war"—Provided by publisher.
Identifiers: LCCN 2021038867 (print) | LCCN 2021038868 (ebook) | ISBN 9781793626134 (cloth) | ISBN 9781793626158 (paper) | ISBN 9781793626141 (epub)
Subjects: LCSH: Propaganda, American—History—20th century. | Press and propaganda—United States—History—20th century. | United States—History, Military—20th century. | War—Public opinion.
Classification: LCC E745 .B79 2022 (print) | LCC E745 (ebook) | DDC 355.3/4—dc23
LC record available at https://lccn.loc.gov/2021038867
LC ebook record available at https://lccn.loc.gov/2021038868

This book is dedicated to the late Dr. Walter R. Fisher, decorated Marine Corps veteran of the Korean War. Dr. Fisher was my mentor and directed my PhD dissertation at the University of Southern California. His pioneering work on the role of stories in shaping human communication led to his groundbreaking "narrative paradigm." Working with him greatly enriched my life and my research.

Contents

Preface		ix
Acknowledgments		xi
1	Propaganda and Persuasion	1
2	Narratives of War	19
3	The Spanish-American War: A Splendid Little War	29
4	World War I: The War to End All Wars	49
5	World War II: The Survival War	75
6	Korea: The Never-Ending War	99
7	Vietnam: The Domino Theory Falls	129
8	The Persian Gulf War: Kicking the Vietnam Syndrome	179
9	The War on Terror: America's Forever War	205
10	Conclusion: Recurring War Stories	259
Bibliography		273
Index		295
About the Author		307

Preface

Each of us has our own story about September 11, 2001. Early that morning I was driving to work and tuned my radio to the local news station. Instead of our regular announcers, I heard a network bulletin preempting local news. There were reports of planes crashing into buildings in New York and the Pentagon. When I got to class, several of my students, who had family in New York, asked to leave. I announced that anyone who wished to leave could do so and then invited students who had been following the news to share what they had learned. Soon the campus canceled all remaining classes and time seemed to be frozen.

Initially, no one really knew what had happened or who was responsible. But it was clear that America was at war. For several years, I taught a college course in Public Opinion and Propaganda. Until 2001, I mostly focused on historical propaganda, such as that from two world wars and the Cold War. But for the first time since Pearl Harbor, we had been attacked on our own soil. I knew that what I was teaching was no longer history. The United States was about to be plunged into a conflict it did not seek and the people of this country were about to be exposed to a propaganda campaign unlike any seen in decades.

Each war has its own story. From the sinking of the *Maine* to the attacks of September 11, 2001, Americans have been repeatedly drawn into overseas conflicts, often reluctantly. On more than one occasion, America has gone to war based on what were ultimately flawed and even false narratives. In some cases, even after these stories have been refuted, many Americans continue to believe the narrative reality over empirical reality—the persistence of the belief that Saddam Hussein was hiding large quantities of Weapons of Mass Destruction, despite the failure to find them after the invasion in 2003, is but one example.[1]

Chapter 1 reviews theories about media effects, definitions of propaganda, and how it differs from other forms of persuasion. Chapter 2 approaches war propaganda from a narrative perspective. Chapters 3 through 9 focus on war stories from the war with Spain to the wars in Afghanistan and Iraq. Finally, the concluding chapter synthesizes the stories from these wars to identify recurring stories. One might reasonably ask: Have we learned anything in over a century that can help avoid repeated and costly wars? If the same basic stories are repeated throughout the history of war propaganda, then can they be critically evaluated to determine if they provide good reasons to go to war? Hopefully future conflicts will be engaged in only when supported by coherent narratives that provide valid reasons to go to war.

NOTE

1. John Stauber, "Half of Americans Still Believe in WMDs—They Saw Them on TV," *PR Watch*, August 8, 2006, https://www.prwatch.org/news/2006/08/5067/half-americans-still-believe-wmds-they-saw-them-tv.

Acknowledgments

I wish to extend my sincerest thanks to Dr. Michael Scott, my former colleague and collaborator, who provided invaluable advice on several chapters in this book. I owe a great debt of gratitude to my wife and partner, Pamela, who has proofread and provided valuable feedback throughout this process. I also extend thanks to my editor Jessica Tepper of Lexington Books, who encouraged and supported me throughout the writing of this book during the difficult time of the COVID-19 pandemic. Of course, I take full responsibility for this entire book and any errors are mine alone.

Chapter 1

Propaganda and Persuasion

It was an early weekend morning in Hawaii during the seasonably warm winter. Most folks were planning a relaxing day in the tropical sun, then came the warnings of an incoming attack, with tensions between the United States and its Asian adversary mounting, everyone feared the worst. People sought shelter or attempted to evacuate, knowing there were only minutes to react. Thirty-nine-year-old Ashly Trask quickly put her family in her car and sped to her workplace, which had concrete walls and served as a hurricane shelter. Kim Smith went to Diamond Head, where there were bunkers and tunnels in which to hide. Others in western Oahu took shelter in a parking structure, crying and huddling with their children. Was this the prelude to the December 7, 1941, attack on Pearl Harbor? No, it was an event over seven decades later, when on January 13, 2018, the Hawaii civil defense system blasted out an alert on cell phones throughout the island proclaiming that missiles were incoming. The alert added, "This is not a drill." It took nearly a half hour before the alert was acknowledged to be a mistake.[1]

The fear that Hawaii was under attack from a hostile foreign power had the ring of truth to it. December 7, 1941, proclaimed by Franklin Roosevelt as a "day which will live in infamy," came on a sleepy Sunday morning, plunging the United States into the bloodiest war in human history. The believability of a forthcoming attack in January 2018 was further enhanced by the situation facing the world at that time, with North Korea having developed and tested missiles capable of carrying nuclear warheads and reaching U.S. territory. Although the shooting war on the Korean Peninsula ended nearly seven decades ago without a peace treaty, the propaganda war has continued unabated. President George W. Bush included Korea in his Axis of Evil. President Obama warned incoming President Trump that Korea was the most urgent foreign policy threat he would face.[2] North Korean Supreme Leader Kim Jong-un, who reportedly ordered the execution of his uncle and half-brother, is portrayed as prone to horrible acts of evil. His nuclear and missile tests, along with bombastic rhetoric, are well known. In July of 2017, North Korea threatened to "strike a merciless blow at the heart of the US with our powerful nuclear hammer, honed and hardened over time."[3] This prompted President Trump to threaten "fire and fury." Undeterred, on November 29, 2017, North Korea tested an intercontinental ballistic missile, capable of reaching U.S. territory.[4] Thus, it is little wonder that two months later thousands of Hawaiians thought that they were about to become the first casualties of World War III.

This chapter will explore how our understanding of propaganda and its effects has evolved over time. First, I discuss how mass media affect public opinion. Second, I explore how our understanding of media effects has influenced perspectives on propaganda. Finally, I discuss how to recognize propaganda.

MEDIA EFFECTS

There are many ways to categorize the way media affect public opinion. The sections that follow show the evolution of our understanding of media effects and are informed by the work of Elizabeth Perse.[5]

Direct Effects

Sometimes called the "magic bullet" or "hypodermic needle" model, media were once assumed to be powerful based on "common sense" and anecdotal data. Newspaper owners bragged about their power. When confronted with the complaint from his illustrator that there was no war in Cuba, William Randolph Hearst famously wired back, "You furnish the pictures and I'll furnish the war."[6] During World War I, the Committee on Public Information's campaign to build support for the war was deemed successful by many journalists and other observers. The rise of Hitler in Germany led to a fear that master propagandists could easily manipulate a passive public.

To this day, the view that media have immense power is widely believed. Politicians rail at "fake news," convinced that the "liberal media" easily sway people. Political campaigns spend millions on advertising, believing that the right ad can swing voters' attitudes. After Vietnam, the Pentagon became convinced that the war had been lost, not in the jungle, but in the media back home, and took steps to assure that would not happen again. Yet, these assumptions don't hold up well to empirical research.

Perse argues that the direct effects model should not be completely discarded, however. When a crisis arises and the public has nowhere to go for information except the media, direct effects are more likely. During the first war with Iraq, 70 percent reported to pollsters that they were following war news "very closely." Video rentals (back in the days of Blockbuster) dropped dramatically, as people shifted from using media for entertainment to news.[7] Perse concludes, "The direct effects model may provide a good explanation for these media effects. People respond almost immediately and uniformly to media messages about crises."[8] Although direct effects may be minimal in normal times, during a wartime crisis, this model may still have utility.

Limited and Conditional Effects

World War II provided a unique opportunity for social science researchers to determine what variables made messages effective. Soldiers provided an unending source of subjects for experimental research. Much of what we know about persuasion (source credibility, primacy vs. recency, message sidedness, etc.) comes from these studies. The surprising finding was, "Although 'mass communications are extremely effective in transmitting straight information,' the wartime experiments showed 'that attitudes are very resistant to change by mass media and that personal face to face communication is often required.'"[9] This is sometimes called the *two-step flow of influence*—that the mass media may influence opinion leaders, but most people need to be persuaded by those they trust, rather than the media. Even the highly touted *Why We Fight* series of films directed by the legendary Frank Capra were found to be only minimally effective. Sproule reports, "*The Battle of Britain* (as with other films in the series) had no measurable impact on the willingness of soldiers to serve . . . ."[10] Emerging from the wartime and postwar body of social sciences was a new paradigm—the minimal or limited effects theory.

Perse proposes an expanded interpretation of the limited effects model, which she terms the *conditional effects model*, which assumes that audience characteristics influence media effects. Perse argues that "unlike the limited effects model, the conditional model holds that reinforcement effects are not the only effects. Change effects are also quite likely, but conditional on the audience."[11] As an example, depending on the media outlet selected by audience members, the effects on attitudes can differ. Operation Iraqi Freedom was justified in part on the belief that Saddam Hussein had weapons of mass destruction. As we shall see in chapter 9, which media outlet audience members selected had a profound effect on whether or not they believed such weapons had been found after the invasion. Although limited, media effects are also conditioned on audience characteristics and choices.

Cumulative Effects

As television grew in importance, researchers began to critique the limited effects model for ignoring effects that could not be easily quantified or replicated in laboratory settings. By the 1960s, television was ubiquitous and dominated by three networks that usually told the same stories. The cumulative effects model shifts the focus back to the media, rather than the audience.[12] In a world where television is pervasive, it is almost impossible to prove specific effects from a particular message or even series of messages because they are unavoidable. This view holds that the effects are so systemic and cumulative that they are easily overlooked. Examples of cumulative effects perspectives include *agenda setting*, *cultivation*, and *critical theories*.

Agenda Setting

This approach does not assume the media tell people *what* to think, but rather, what to think *about*. Its adherents contend, "By just paying attention to some issues while ignoring others, the mass media, deliberately or otherwise, may set priorities of concern within the various sectors of the public."[13] There is good evidence that this occurs during and prior to war. Anthony R. DiMaggio writes that "the media assists [sic] in setting the terms for acceptable public discourse."[14] Furthermore, he writes, "What is *not* reported determines a reporter or paper's bias just as much as what *is* reported."[15]

An important corollary to the agenda-setting hypothesis is that some types of issues are more likely to rely on media reports than others. The influence of media coverage is relatively unimportant for *obtrusive* issues compared to *unobtrusive* issues.[16] Obtrusive issues affect people's daily lives. For example, if the price of gasoline rises dramatically, drivers don't need to read about it in the newspaper to be concerned. Events that happen overseas, however, are usually unobtrusive to people in their daily lives. For example, few Americans could have found Kuwait on a map until Saddam's invasion in 1990 prompted extensive media coverage.

Cultivation Theory

In the 1970s and 1980s, there was another shift in theory and research. Baron and Davis explain that there was a move away from "questions like 'What effects do media have on society or on individuals?' . . . and 'How do people use the media?'" Instead, theorists and researchers began to focus on issues like "how cultures organize themselves, how people negotiate common meaning and are bound by it, and how media systems interact with culture to affect the latter's definition of itself."[17] Unlike the theories that dominated the social sciences in the postwar period, these theories are not based primarily on quantitative research methods.[18]

An example of this approach is *cultivation theory*, developed by George Gerbner and his associates, who write, "Television pervades the symbolic environment. Cultivation analysis focuses on the consequences of exposure to its recurrent patterns of stories, images, and messages."[19] The ubiquitous nature of TV makes it comparable to "a gravitational process."[20] For example, Gerbner and his colleagues have shown "that heavy viewers overestimate their chances of involvement in violence and their general vulnerability.... We study what exposure to violence-laden television contributes to their conceptions of the realities of their own lives."[21] One might hypothesize that portrayals of terrorism could have the same effect on viewers as violence in general.

Critical Theory

Critical theory has its roots in Marxist and neo-Marxist thought, but there are now many non-Marxists who embrace the theory. These theorists claim, "mass media are the most important instrument of twentieth-century capitalism for maintaining ideological hegemony because they provide the framework for perceiving reality."[22] Thus, like cultivation theory, critical theory is rooted in the view that the media are so prevalent that isolating their effects is almost impossible. Annabelle Sreberny-Mohammadi writes, "The ways in which the media, particularly television, select and interpret events, what they focus on and what they omit, help to define public knowledge and construct public opinion."[23] One can also see a kinship with the agenda-setting hypothesis.

Transactional Model

The transactional model is probably the most useful for studying propaganda. Perse explains, "the cognitive-transactional model is called *transactional* because both media content and audience factors are important to understanding media effects."[24] The idea is that some media content can prime consumers to activate certain mental schemas to "direct attention, perception, recall, and other reactions to environmental clues."[25] She writes, "How a news story is framed (with headlines, graphics, or introduction) influences which schema is used to interpret the information."[26] For example, during major wars such as the invasion of Iraq, cable news networks developed catchy logos and stirring music to cue audience members to focus on the upcoming story as part of a nation at war. Examples fitting the transactional model include *framing and priming*, *uses and gratification*, and the growth of *social media*.

Framing and Priming

Framing is a useful concept in understanding how people make sense of the world around them. A frame is "a specific set of expectations that are used to make sense of a social situation at a given point in time."[27] DiMaggio explains, "Framing is the means by which *an entire social reality* is constructed. The narratives adopted by use of one frame over another inevitably influence how news consumers view important issues."[28] He cites the example of "rendering the war in Iraq as a struggle against terrorism and a quest to democratize the Middle East," as clear-cut media framing.[29] Different frames can lead to very different conclusions about the wisdom and morality of a war. Closely related to framing is priming, which "affect[s] the criteria by which individuals judged their political leaders."[30] In the wake of 9/11, for example, the presidency of George W. Bush was no longer judged by how successful his domestic policies were, but rather by how well he functioned as commander-in-chief.

Uses and Gratifications

How people use media to gratify their needs is essential to understanding media effects. James W. Carey and Albert L. Krieling explain, "In sum, uses and gratifications researchers shifted the impact of mass media from the effects of producers' intentions to the effects of audiences' intentions, which are understood to depend upon sociological context and active psychological processes."[31] As an example, one might watch television purely for its entertainment value, but suppose a war appears to be on the horizon. Then people may turn to the media, not so much for entertainment, but for information about the budding crisis. The high ratings earned by cable TV outlets such as CNN and Fox as war in Iraq seemed on the horizon in 2002–2003 shows that a great many people were seeking not entertainment, but information about the upcoming battle.

Overall, this evolution of models of communication research shows that a simple one-directional model of propaganda is misguided. The transactional model, I believe, provides the best framework in which to understand the influence of propaganda on public attitudes toward going to war.

Social Media

When the wars in Afghanistan and Iraq began, social media were nonexistent. Even MySpace had not yet been created when U.S. troops entered Baghdad. Pew Research Center didn't begin tracking their use until 2005, when only 7 percent of respondents used social media.[32] By 2017, the number had reached 81 percent.[33] Since social media were not a factor during the early years of these wars, one can only speculate about their impact in future wars. What we do know is that according to W. James Potter, "The major characteristics that distinguish digital media from analog media are the fluidity across channels, the greater ability to customize messages, dispersed decision-making across more people, and ability to provide a wider range of experiences to users."[34] Clearly, social media fit the transactional model, perhaps more so than traditional mass media. Social media give all users an instant way to react—from liking to disliking to re-tweeting. Probably most relevant for the study of war propaganda are social media's interactive nature and dispersed decision-making structure. The latter "allows every user to largely bypass authorities who used to function as gatekeepers and instead create any kind of content . . . and then distribute those messages widely . . . anywhere in the world."[35] When the next war comes, it will be much more difficult for the government to control the messages people receive and far more likely that different groups of people will perceive very different realities depending on their choice of social media platforms.

PERSPECTIVES ON PROPAGANDA

Given the focus of this book on war propaganda, it is not my purpose to provide a comprehensive review of the study of propaganda. Excellent and comprehensive sources are available. I particularly recommend J. Michael Sproule's *Propaganda and Democracy: The American Experience of Media and Mass Persuasion*, which informs much of the discussion that follows.

Prior to World War I, the study of propaganda was not a major concern of theorists. However, the advent of the Great War in 1914 suddenly thrust America into a propaganda war well before it entered the shooting war in 1917. Once the war began in Europe, the British made a concerted effort to propagate their views to Americans. Reports of atrocities were featured in the highly charged Bryce Report. Sproule writes, "[I]ts effect on American public opinion in 1915 was significant. Proof positive seemingly was at hand to sustain the Allied claim that theirs was a contest of good versus evil."[36] In his highly influential work, *Public Opinion*, published in 1922, noted columnist Walter Lippmann distinguished between "the world outside and the pictures in our heads."[37] Thus, although Americans did not directly experience the European War between 1914 and the first part of 1917, thanks to largely one-sided propaganda from the Allies, they had pictures in their heads of German atrocities and the suffering of the Belgian and other European democracies. Sproule notes,

> Before the war, propaganda . . . signified chiefly the spreading of self-interested opinions through publicity. Under the influence of anti-German exposés, however, the term by 1915 had begun to take on more sinister connotations of manipulations and half-truths secretly sowed by society's avowed enemies.[38]

Once America entered the shooting war, the Committee on Public Information, headed by George Creel, embarked on a powerful campaign to support the patriotic goals of the war. Based on the apparent success of this propaganda, the notion that skilled propagandists could bend the people to their will took hold. Thus began the era of what was termed the direct effects, magic bullet, or hypodermic needle theory discussed earlier. Media were seen as so powerful that few could resist their influence. World War I seemed to offer a prime example of how propaganda could control public opinion.

After the war, it became known that much of the prowar propaganda was based on falsehoods and exaggerations. The reports of German atrocities turned out to be greatly exaggerated. Sproule writes, "American disillusionment . . . began in Europe, where the sentiment spread among American troops that atrocity stories had been false concoctions and that the Germans had behaved no worse than any other combatants."[39]

The concern about people being easily misled by propaganda led to a movement called *propaganda analysis*—the idea that if average people could be taught to recognize propaganda, then they would not be defenseless. In 1937, as war seemed to be approaching again, the Institute for Propaganda Analysis was founded. Their definition of propaganda was the *"expression of opinion or action by individuals or groups deliberately designed to influence opinions or actions of other individuals or groups with reference to predetermined ends."*[40] The Institute became best known for its list of seven propaganda techniques, with catchy titles like name-calling, glittering generalities, transfer, testimonial, plain folks, card stacking, and bandwagon.[41] However, as Hitler's power in Europe rose, the IPA became a victim of the shift in American priorities. Fighting fascism replaced identifying propaganda as the dominant concern. Sproule identifies the IPA's Achilles' heal at a time when America was preparing for war: "[E]qual treatment of propaganda rendered the IPA vulnerable to criticism that its approach was fundamentally defective for being unable to distinguish the relative moral qualities of democratic and fascist propaganda."[42] This lack of a moral distinction was evidenced in 1939 when the Institute published an analysis of Franklin Roosevelt's supposed use of propaganda. Soon the tide turned against the Institute as funds dried up and board members resigned, many to join the U.S. government's own war propaganda efforts.

If propaganda was not likely to persuade people by shooting a magic bullet at their psyches, then teaching propaganda analysis became unnecessary. Sproule views the shift from propaganda research to communication research as "what Thomas Kuhn would term a paradigmatic revolution."[43] The fall of propaganda as a term of art is shown by the decline in citing the term in *Psychological Abstracts*. By the 1950s references to propaganda were found in less than ten citations and by 1966 were totally absent.[44] Thus, for several decades, propaganda was regarded as a tired subject that had outlived its relevance to modern communication research. Sproule writes, "*Media effects* ultimately supplied the mantra that permitted communication scholars to turn away from their field's historical interest in issues of propaganda and participatory democracy."[45]

However, in the 1960s and beyond, interest in propaganda began to return, especially in the wake of revelations such as the Pentagon Papers and Watergate. The domain of mass media effects began to expand, including agenda setting, cultivation, and the like. According to Sproule, Garth Jowett and Victoria O'Donnell's 1986 book *Propaganda and Persuasion* "broke a generation's silence on comprehensive antipropaganda education . . . the likes of which had not been seen since Alfred Lee's 1952 book [*How to Understand Propaganda*]."[46] The influence of Jowett and O'Donnell's book is reflected in the publication of a seventh edition in 2019.[47] Events such as the wars with Iraq also led to a greater interest in studying propaganda, as reflected in journalist John R. MacArthur's *Second Front: Censorship and Propaganda in the 1991 Gulf War* and Nicholas Jackson O'Shaughnessy's *Politics and Propaganda: Weapons of Mass Seduction*.[48] Thus, propaganda once again became a subject of interest to academic researchers, journalists, and the general public. That raises an important issue, what exactly counts as propaganda?

RECOGNIZING PROPAGANDA

In seeking to define propaganda, one is tempted to follow the lead of Justice Potter Stewart's definition of obscenity: "I know it when I see it."[49] Where does one draw the line between propaganda and other forms of persuasion? As Downing and his colleagues admit, "The dividing line is often hard to draw."[50]

The term can be traced back to *Sacra Congregatio de Propaganda Fide* (Sacred Congregation for the Propagation of the Faith) established in 1622 by the Roman Catholic Church to propagate the faith and defeat Protestantism. Early twentieth-century definitions rested on an assumption of manipulation and deception. Harold Lasswell offered a definition in 1927 that became widely accepted: "Propaganda is the management of collective attitudes by the manipulation of significant symbols."[51] Thus, the idea of *manipulation* became integral to the definition of propaganda.

On the other hand, some practitioners of propaganda defended its use in the service of a just cause. Edward Bernays wrote, "[T]he only real difference between 'propaganda' and 'education,' really, is in the point of view. The advocacy of what we believe in is education. The advocacy of what we don't believe in is propaganda."[52] He noted, "[W]hether, in any particular instance, propaganda is good or bad depends upon the merits of the causes urged, and the correctness of the information published."[53] In a 1983 interview concerning his work with the Creel Committee in World War I he told Bill Moyers, "I think the propaganda was very effective and, as I say now, it was propaganda and not 'improperganda.'"[54] This view, therefore, comes very close to equating propaganda with persuasion. In World War II, few doubted the legitimacy of American war propaganda—after all the facts were indisputable—the United States had been attacked without warning and few villains in history could rival Hitler. Propaganda was only a concern when the Nazis and their Axis allies practiced it.

As noted earlier, Jowett and Donnell's 1986 book resurrected the study of propaganda and their definition has become widely accepted. They define propaganda as *"the deliberate, systematic attempt to shape perceptions, manipulate cognitions, and direct behavior to achieve a response that furthers the desired intent of the propagandist."*[55] In their view propaganda differs from persuasion because the latter involves not just the fulfillment of the source's goals but also that of the recipient: "Because both persuader and persuadee stand to have their needs fulfilled, persuasion is regarded as more mutually satisfying than propaganda."[56]

As widely accepted as this definition is, however, it is not without limitations. How is one to determine whether the persuader desires to fulfill only their goals or those of the persuadee? Who makes that judgment? Bernays would argue that the Creel Committee's war propaganda served the entire nation's interests not just those of the Wilson administration. Yet those who were jailed for their opposition to World War I would strongly disagree. Moreover, what if the recipients harbor objectionable goals that the propagandist exploits? A QAnon message to true believers certainly satisfies needs of both the sender and receivers. But does that mean it's not propaganda? In fact, one marker of propaganda is that it appeals to biases and prejudice. O'Shaughnessy claims that "the propagandist dramatises our prejudices and speaks to something deep and even shameful within us. Propaganda thus becomes a co-production in which we are willing participants, it articulates externally the things that are half whispered internally."[57] From a transactional view, propaganda is not simply something that a source does to a receiver. Thus, merely establishing a shared goal doesn't disqualify a message from being propaganda.

Keep in mind that direct media effects are more likely to be found in crisis situations. The attacks of September 11th were certainly a crisis. Although the first response was to attack the government that harbored bin Laden, soon Bush began pushing for war with Iraq. His father had succeeded in equating Saddam Hussein with Hitler. Thus, the forty-third president's war propaganda was conditioned by that of the forty-first. Ellul refers to this as "pre-propaganda."[58] As cultivation theory has shown, there exist myths, stories, beliefs, and prejudices cultivated for years before the actual propaganda campaign begins. The portrayal of Arabs in American media had for years been stereotyped in ways that made them easy targets for propaganda.

The definition should not be limited to official government propaganda. In fact, governments often conceal the true source of war propaganda. During the efforts of George W. Bush to promote a war with Iraq, the *New York Times* sometimes printed stories that were leaked to them by the administration. Then Vice President Dick Cheney and other administration officials quoted the very articles as supposedly independent evidence for going to war. Although it appeared to the public that the messages were from reputable and objective media sources, in reality they were from the very administration promoting the war.

In many cases, the purpose of the propagandist is clear—both Presidents Bush were seeking approval for military action against Iraq. But often the purpose is concealed or unknowable at the time. Thus, to limit one's analysis of propaganda to cases where the source is openly proclaiming a goal of war is to miss one of propaganda's most important tools—deception. For example, the war in Vietnam was escalated in response to a supposed attack on U.S. destroyers in the Gulf of Tonkin. LBJ constantly invoked the claim, "We seek no wider war," while increasing American troops to over a half-million. Had he initially announced that as his goal, it is doubtful that the propaganda underlying U.S. escalation in Vietnam would have succeeded.

Some have suggested that factual messages cannot be propaganda. Although on the surface, this might seem a reasonable limitation, propagandists have learned that facts can be powerful weapons in their arsenal. Konrad Kellen, who translated Jacques Ellul's *Propaganda*, explains this apparent paradox:

> Most people are easy prey for propaganda, Ellul says, because of their firm but entirely erroneous conviction that it is composed only of lies and "tall stories" and that, conversely, what is true cannot be propaganda. But modern propaganda has long disdained the ridiculous lies of past and outmoded forms of propaganda. It operates instead with many different kinds of truth—half truth, limited truth, truth out of context. Even Goebbels always insisted that Wehrmacht communiqués be as accurate as possible.[59]

Ellul writes, "[P]ropaganda must be based on some truth that can be said in a few words and is able to linger in the collective consciousness."[60]

Having shown problems with other definitions, one can reasonably ask what messages should be considered propaganda? O'Shaughnessy argues that we need to look at symbolism, rhetoric, and myth in ferreting out propaganda.[61] As an example, rhetorician Kenneth Burke examined Hitler's *Mein Kampf* "to discover what kind of 'medicine' this medicine-man has concocted, that we may know, with greater accuracy, exactly what to guard against, if we are to forestall the concocting of similar medicine in America."[62] Burke argues the *names* we use reveal our motives and our implicit program of action:

> To call a man a bastard is to attack him by attacking his whole line. . . . An epithet assigns substance doubly, for in stating the character of the object it at the same time contains an implicit program of action with regard to the object, thus serving as motive.[63]

As we shall see, in war after war, the enemy and even the people the United States was supposedly protecting are named in ways that convey a motive for war. For example, Germans were referred to as "Huns" in World War I. Japanese were called far worse and even American citizens of Japanese descent were rounded up and placed behind barbed wire in euphemistically named "relocation camps." Saddam was named "Hitler" in two wars, and on it goes. So we shall include in propaganda messages that use language naming a potential enemy in a biased way.

If bias is a marker of propaganda, is unintended bias excluded? According to O'Shaughnessy, Ellul "regards all biased messages as propagandist even when the biases are unconscious."[64] Some would criticize such a broad view, arguing that *intention* is essential to defining propaganda. If people were fully cognizant of their biases, then such an objection would be difficult to overcome. However, as we have learned in recent years, bias is often so built into people's psyches that they are unaware of it. In the wake of numerous killings of unarmed people of color by police, many departments around the United States have instituted training in recognizing unconscious bias. This should caution us against requiring proof of consciousness of bias before treating a message as propagandistic.

Beyond bias, what other characteristics of the message might be an attribute of propaganda? Ellul's view of propaganda includes the use of *"psychological manipulations."*[65] For example, fear appeal, appeal to prejudice, and appeals to patriotism can all be seen as potential manipulations embedded in a message. In each case, the use of such techniques is a clue that the message contains propaganda.

The channel of communication may be one of the most obvious characteristics of propaganda. The source must convey the message to as wide a population as possible. Ellul writes, "Propaganda must be total. The propagandist must utilize all of the technical means at his [*sic*] disposal—the press, radio, TV, movies, posters, meetings, door-to-door canvassing."[66] He adds that "they must *all* be used in combination. The propagandist uses a keyboard and composes a symphony."[67] Thus, our analysis must not exclude any channel of communication used to convey propaganda.

As noted earlier, the idea of a passive audience, easily manipulated by a "magic bullet" by propagandists has largely been dispelled by research. Instead, we now realize that the receivers of communication are participants in the transaction. Tony Schwartz, the creator of one of the most famous political ads of all time ("Daisy Girl" in 1964) uses the term "partipulation," not manipulation, for what he does.[68] In other words, people must participate in their own manipulation. He explains in his book *The Responsive Chord*:

> A listener or viewer brings far more information to the communication event than a communicator can put into his [*sic*] . . . message. The communicator's problem, then, is not to get stimuli across, or even to package his stimuli so they can be understood and absorbed. Rather, he must deeply understand the kinds of information and experiences stored in his audience, the patterning of this information, and the interactive resonance process whereby stimuli evoke this stored information.[69]

For the critic of propaganda, therefore, understanding the prior beliefs, attitudes, and opinions of the public is crucial to understanding propaganda. According to Ellul, people respond to "certain words, signs, or symbols, even certain persons or facts . . . . [T]he propagandist tries to create myths by which man will live, which respond to his sense of the sacred."[70] As we will see, propagandists tell "war stories" that embody people, signs and symbols, facts and even myths to move an often reluctant nation to war. To the extent that prior public opinion can be ascertained, often through public opinion polling, we can better understand how these stories resonated with the public and moved them to action.

For some writers, the distinction between propaganda and persuasion becomes almost undetectable. DiMaggio writes,

> Propaganda entails the systematic dissemination of *any* given doctrine or dogma, by *any* party, regardless of their outlook . . . . In other words, it does not, at its core require deliberate deception. Propaganda, then, is not necessarily inherently good or bad.[71]

If one accepts this definition, then it is difficult to draw a bright line between propaganda and persuasion. My view is the distinction between propaganda and persuasion lies more on a continuum, rather than there being a bright dividing line.

Based on the preceding analysis, therefore, what counts as propaganda? We will look for messages that possess *one or more* of the following characteristics. First, do they contain *false or distorted information*. Second, do the messages *omit relevant information* or introduce irrelevant appeals to the matter at hand. Third, are messages *consistent*? Fourth, do the messages misstate or ignore the possible *consequences* of the war. Finally, do messages appeal to *questionable values*, as evidenced by biased language, appeals to prejudice, or other types of manipulation. If a message contains *any* of these elements, then it should be considered as at least potentially propagandistic. In the next chapter, we will present a model of how to analyze war messages that gets to these core issues. Keep in mind, however, that not all of these characteristics are required. For example, a truthful message that is propagated for purposes of stirring hatred or violations of human rights should not be excused just because it contains elements of truth.

SUMMARY

This chapter has reviewed basic models of media effects and shown how the history of studying propaganda has evolved in light of these models. The difficulty of defining propaganda and distinguishing it from persuasion leads to a somewhat different approach. We shall look for clues that we are dealing with propaganda in terms of truth, relevance, consistency, consequences, and values. In the next chapter, we will lay out a paradigm that will guide the remainder of this book. As the opening story illustrates, in a perceived crisis, people are prone to react out of fear and readily accept what appear to be official messages, whether they are on the TV or their smart phones. Fortunately, the warning of an incoming missile attack was merely an unfortunate human error. No propaganda was intended, but the possibilities for spreading misinformation have multiplied in an era where a tweet can reach millions in mere seconds.

NOTES

1. These descriptions are based on Julia Carrie Wong and Liz Barney, "Hawaii Ballistic Missile False Alarm Results in Panic," *Guardian*, January 14, 2018, https://www.theguardian.com/us-news/2018/jan/13/hawaii-ballistic-missile-threat-alert-false-alarm.

2. David E. Sanger and William J. Broad, "Trump Inherits a Secret Cyberwar Against North Korean Missiles," *New York Times*, March 4, 2017, https://www.nytimes.com/2017/03/04/world/asia/north-korea-missile-program-sabotage.html?_r=0.

3. Zachary Cohen and Barbara Starr, "North Korea Promises Nuclear Strike on US if Regime is Threatened," CNN, July 25, 2017, https://www.cnn.com/2017/07/25/politics/north-korea-threatens-nuclear-strike-us.

4. Julia Masterson, "Chronology of U.S.-North Korean Nuclear and Missile Diplomacy," Arms Control Association, accessed January 24, 2020, https://www.armscontrol.org/factsheets/dprkchron.

5. Elizabeth M. Perse, *Media Effects and Society* (Mahwah, NJ: Lawrence Erlbaum Associates, 2001), 28–51.

6. "The Press: I'll Furnish the War," *Time*, October 27, 1947, http://content.time.com/time/magazine/article/0,9171,854840,00.html.

7. Perse, *Media Effects and Society*, 59.

8. Perse, *Media Effects and Society*, 80.

9. J. Michael Sproule, *Propaganda and Democracy: The American Experience of Media and Mass Persuasion* (New York: Cambridge University Press, 1997, 2005 edition), 216.

10. Sproule, *Propaganda and Democracy*, 200.

11. Perse, *Media Effects and Society*, 42.

12. Perse, *Media Effects and Society*, 45.

13. Sidney Kraus and Dennis Davis, *The Effects of Mass Communication on Political Behavior* (University Park: Pennsylvania State University Press, 1976), 213.

14. Anthony R. DiMaggio, *Mass Media, Mass Propaganda: Examining American News in the "War on Terror"* (Lanham, MD: Lexington Books, 2008), 42.

15. DiMaggio, *Mass Media*, 53 (italics in original).

16. Maxwell McCombs, "News Influence on Our Pictures of the World," in *Media Effects: Advances in Theory and Research*, eds. Jennings Bryant and Dolf Zillmann (Hillsdale, NJ: Lawrence Erlbaum Associates, 1994), 7.

17. Stanley J. Baron and Dennis K. Davis, *Mass Communication Theory* (Belmont, CA: Wadsworth, 1995), 285.

18. Baron and Davis, *Mass Communication Theory*, 283.

19. George Gerbner, Larry Gross, Michael Morgan, and Nancy Signorielli, "Growing Up with Television: The Cultivation Perspective," in *Media Effects: Advances in Theory and Research*, eds. Jennings Bryant and Dolf Zillmann (Hillsdale, NJ: Lawrence Erlbaum Associates, 1994), 37.

20. Gerbner, Gross, Morgan, and Signorielli, "Growing Up with Television," 24.

21. Quoted in Baron and Davis, *Mass Communication Theory*, 307.

22. Robert A. White, "Mass Communication and Culture: Transition to a New Paradigm," *Journal of Communication* 33 (Summer 1983): 291 (italics omitted).

23. Annabelle Sreberny-Mohammadi, "Global News Media Cover the World," in *Questioning the Media: A Critical Introduction*, 2nd ed. eds. John Downing, Ali Mohammadi, and Annabelle Sreberny-Mohammadi (Thousand Oaks, CA: Sage, 1995), 429.

24. Perse, *Media Effects and Society*, 49 (italics in original).

25. Perse, *Media Effects and Society*, 50.
26. Perse, *Media Effects and Society*, 46.
27. Baron and Davis, *Mass Communication Theory*, 299.
28. DiMaggio, *Mass Media*, 21 (italics in original).
29. DiMaggio, *Mass Media*, 21.
30. Shanto Iyengar quoted in DiMaggio, *Mass Media*, 42.
31. James W. Carey and Albert L. Kreiling, "Popular Culture and Uses and Gratifications: Notes Toward an Accommodation," in *The Uses of Mass Communications: Current Perspectives on Gratifications Research*, eds. Jay G. Blumler and Elihu Katz (Beverly Hills: Sage, 1974), 227.
32. Pew Research Center, "Social Media Usage: 2005–2015," October 8, 2015, https://www.pewresearch.org/internet/2015/10/08/social-networking-usage-2005-2015/.
33. W. James Potter, *Digital Media Effects* (Lanham, MD: Rowman & Littlefield, 2021), Chapter 1, loc. 426, Kindle.
34. Potter, *Digital Media*, Chapter 1, loc. 383.
35. Potter, *Digital Media*, Chapter 1, loc. 410.
36. Sproule, *Propaganda and Democracy*, 8.
37. Walter Lippmann, *Public Opinion* (New York: Harcourt Brace & Co., 1922).
38. Sproule, *Propaganda and Democracy*, 9.
39. Sproule, *Propaganda and Democracy*, 16.
40. Quoted in Sproule, *Propaganda and Democracy*, 155 (italics in original).
41. Sproule, *Propaganda and Democracy*, 135.
42. Sproule, *Propaganda and Democracy*, 156.
43. Sproule, *Propaganda and Democracy*, 224.
44. Sproule, *Propaganda and Democracy*, 217.
45. Sproule, *Propaganda and Democracy*, 227 (italics in original).
46. Sproule, *Propaganda and Democracy*, 267.
47. Garth S. Jowett and Victoria O'Donnell, *Propaganda and Persuasion*, 7th ed. (Thousand Oaks, CA: Sage, 2019).
48. John R. MacArthur, *Second Front: Censorship and Propaganda in the 1991 Gulf War*, 2nd ed. (Berkeley: University of California Press, 2004); Nicholas Jackson O'Shaughnessy, *Politics and Propaganda: Weapons of Mass Seduction* (Ann Arbor: University of Michigan Press, 2004).
49. Jacobellis v. Ohio, 378 U.S. 184 (1964), https://caselaw.findlaw.com/us-supreme-court/378/184.html.
50. John Downing, Ali Mohammadi, and Annabelle Sreberny-Mohammadi, eds., *Questioning the Media: A Critical Introduction*, 2nd ed. (Thousand Oaks, CA: Sage, 1995), 489.
51. Harold D. Lasswell, "The Theory of Political Propaganda," *The American Political Science Review* 21, no. 3 (August, 1927): 627, https://www.jstor.org/stable/1945515.
52. Quoted in Larry Tye, *The Father of Spin* (New York: Crown, 1998), 97.
53. Quoted in DiMaggio, *Mass Media, Mass Propaganda*, 23.
54. Bill Moyers, "The Image Makers," *A Walk Through the 20th Century*, April 14, 1983 [Transcript], https://billmoyers.com/content/image-makers/.

55. Jowett and Donnell, *Propaganda and Persuasion*, 22 (italics in original).
56. Jowett and O'Donnell, *Propaganda and Persuasion*, 46.
57. O'Shaughnessy, *Politics and Propaganda*, 4.
58. Jacques Ellul, *Propaganda: The Formation of Men's Attitudes*, trans. Konrad Kellen and Jean Lerner (New York: Vintage, 1973), 32.
59. Konrad Kellen, "Introduction," in *Propaganda: The Formation of Men's Attitudes*, by Jacques Ellul, trans. Konrad Kellen and Jean Lerner (New York: Vintage, 1973), v.
60. Ellul, *Propaganda*, 57.
61. O'Shaughnessy, *Politics and Propaganda*, 4.
62. Kenneth Burke, "The Rhetoric of Hitler's 'Battle,'" in *The Philosophy of Literary Form: Studies in Symbolic Action*, by Kenneth Burke (New York: Vintage, 1957), 164.
63. Burke, *A Grammer of Motives and A Rhetoric of Motives*, 57.
64. O'Shaughnessy, *Politics and Propaganda*, 20.
65. Ellul, *Propaganda*, 61 (italics in original).
66. Ellul, *Propaganda*, 9.
67. Ellul, *Propaganda*, 10 (italics in original).
68. Bill Moyers, "The 30-Second President," *A Walk Through the 20th Century*, September 19, 1984 [Transcript], https://billmoyers.com/content/30-second-president/.
69. Tony Schwartz, *The Responsive Chord* (New York: Anchor Press/Doubleday, 1974), 25.
70. Ellul, *Propaganda*, 31.
71. DiMaggio, *Mass Media*, 23 (italics in original).

Chapter 2

Narratives of War

On October 10, 1990, a fifteen-year-old Kuwaiti girl named Nayirah (her last name was withheld to protect her family) testified before the Human Rights Caucus of Congress. Saddam Hussein had invaded her country on August 2, and she was there to help convince members of Congress and the public that the United States needed to intervene. She said, in part:

> I volunteered at the al-Addan hospital with twelve other women who wanted to help as well. I was the youngest volunteer. The other women were from twenty to thirty years old. While I was there I saw the Iraqi soldiers come into the hospital with guns. They took the babies out of the incubators, took the incubators and left the children to die on the cold floor. [Crying] It was horrifying.[1]

Needless to say, the story was a bombshell. Journalist John R. MacArthur reports that six senators cited the story in support of their vote for the war, which passed by a mere five-vote margin.[2] The Persian Gulf War of 1991 rested on an underlying narrative—Saddam Hussein was another Hitler, who had invaded a helpless neighbor and then committed grievous atrocities against its citizens. Nayirah's story was but one small part of an overarching narrative told to convince the American public and Congress to go to war.

In chapter 1, we reviewed a number of approaches to understanding media effects. Ultimately, the most useful approach to this topic is the transactional model, where the source and receiver of messages are coproducers of the effects. In this chapter, we review two theories that are well suited to the study of war propaganda. Transportation theory rests on the premise that stories—both factual and fictional—can transport audiences into an experience that becomes real to them. The narrative paradigm provides a method of assessing whether a story provides good reasons to accept its values and the actions implicit in it. These theories come from very different lineages. Social psychologist Melanie Green has proposed the transportation theory to explain the effects of stories on people and has empirically tested her hypothesis and shown it to have validity. The power of the story told by Nayirah is examined in light of that theory. Walter Fisher developed his narrative paradigm based on a rhetorical approach. The narrative paradigm is applied to the Nayirah's story. Although to my knowledge Green and Fisher never met, I believe their two theories are complementary and well suited to studying war propaganda. Finally, the process for selecting artifacts for study in the following chapters is explained.

TRANSPORTATION THEORY

We've all been in the situation of reading an engrossing novel, getting lost in a movie, or listening to an engaging storyteller. It is likely that each of us has been transported, as Green suggests, to a different reality, at least for a time. Along with her colleague Timothy C. Brock, she found that narratives, both true and fictional, can transport audiences and significantly affect beliefs and evaluations.[3] Moreover, they found, "While the person is immersed in the story, he or she may be less aware of real-world facts that contradict assertions made in the narrative."[4] When reading a work of fiction this is of little concern. But when an allegedly true story advocates war, failing to compare it to real-world facts can be catastrophic. Green and Brock

> suggest that transportation into a story causes people to be less motivated (or less able) to disbelieve any particular conclusion; transported individuals are so absorbed in the story that they would likely be reluctant to stop and critically analyze propositions presented therein.[5]

Of course, stories are not just told, they are seen—whether on TV, a computer, or smart phone—and can have powerful effects. Green writes, "Story-based mental imagery may be a particularly powerful means by which narratives can influence beliefs. Visual images, or mental pictures, can be evoked by a transporting narrative or provided by a visual narrative (television, movies)."[6] Certainly, Nayirah presented a vivid word picture that transported her audience to a horrific scene and may even have caused several senators to change their vote.

Green and Philip Mazzocco applied this model to the courtroom setting in an article for the American Society of Trial Consultants.[7] One of their key findings is

Narratives . . . appear to be uniquely suited to changing opinions and beliefs which are held emotionally, and which may be resistant to other forms of persuasion. It is worth noting that emotional reactions to characters can form regardless of whether the narrative in question is fictional or factual.[8]

They posit several factors that enhance the effectiveness of narratives: Stories must be well told, immerse the hearer in realistic imagery, be well structured, heard in the right context, and the audience needs to be willing to be transported into the story.[9] It is noteworthy that almost all of these are present in Nayirah's story. She appeared to be credible storyteller, who was brought to tears by recalling the events of that day. The image of troops dumping preemies on the floor to die is unforgettable. This specific story is contextualized in a world where the president of the United States had repeatedly compared Saddam to Hitler. Many of the senators who heard her story were scheduled to face voters the next month, making it difficult to ignore her plea for action.

Transportation theory is based on the premise of a sharp dichotomy between narrative and rhetorical persuasion. The latter is seen as "a series of logical and cogent arguments in favor of a given viewpoint. In contrast, narratives describe a series of interrelated events that take place in a particular setting and typically involve one or more specific characters."[10] However, such a view depends on very narrow definitions of both narratives and rhetoric. Glenn G. Kuper writes, "The authors hail from the social psychology perspective . . . but the contributions from rhetoricians should be acknowledged. For example, Walter Fisher has developed a comprehensive theory of human communication as narration."[11] It is to that theory that we next turn.

THE NARRATIVE PARADIGM

Fisher does not draw a sharp dichotomy between narrative and rhetoric. Although not strictly a Burkean, Fisher was informed by the writings of Kenneth Burke, perhaps the most influential rhetorician of the twentieth century.[12] Burke writes that rhetoric "*is rooted in an essential function of language itself, a function that is wholly realistic, and is continually born anew; the use of language as a symbolic means of inducing cooperation in beings that by nature respond to symbols.*"[13] Although transportation theory implies that narratives are difficult to evaluate as to their validity, Fisher developed a paradigm to do just that. Fisher's thesis is "that all forms of human communication can be seen fundamentally as stories, as interpretations of aspects of the world occurring in time and shaped by history, culture, and character."[14] His narrative paradigm's primary function is to offer a way of interpreting and assessing human communication that leads to critique, to a determination of whether or not a given instance of discourse provides a reliable, trustworthy, and desirable guide to thought and action *in the world.*[15]

He distinguishes his paradigm from critical theorists, such as Habermas, who "posits persons as arguers; I see them, including arguers, as storytellers. He conceives reasons as warrants tied to claims of validity; I conceive reasons as warrants that are or entail values (good reasons)."[16] Good reasons are critical to Fisher's paradigm. He defines them as *"elements that provide warrants for accepting or adhering to the advice fostered by any form of communication that can be considered rhetorical."*[17] In applying this paradigm to war propaganda, one should ask whether the stories told in support of war supply good reasons for entering the conflict. And conversely, in analyzing anti-war propaganda, one can ask if those stories provide good reasons to oppose the war.

Fisher's paradigm also recognizes that a story is a transaction between storyteller and audience. He writes, "Viewing human communication narratively stresses that people are full participants in the making of messages, whether they are agents (authors) or audience members (co-authors)."[18] A story that has fidelity for one audience may not ring true for another. How well an audience is primed by prior experiences and beliefs to accept a given story explains why a story may persuade some people and not others. As we examine the stories that led America to war, it is vital that we understand the audiences for these stories as well as the stories themselves. The narrative that took America to war in World War II, for example, required very little elaboration—we were attacked in what Roosevelt termed a dastardly manner. Other wars have been a much harder sell, as presidents like Truman and Johnson learned when they told stories that rested on the premise that American security was dependent on events in small largely unfamiliar nations half a world away.

Let's consider how Fisher's narrative paradigm is applied in more detail. Fisher developed a two-part method for evaluating narratives.[19] First, one must assess the *coherence* or *probability* of the story. In other words, does the story make sense on its own terms? In many ways, this is similar to the conditions that Green posits make for effective storytelling. Second he asks us to examine its *fidelity* or perceived truthfulness for the audience. Green's research shows this is difficult to judge for those transported by the story to a different reality.

Fisher proposes three tests of *narrative probability*. Does the story have *argumentative or structural coherence*? Next, does the story have *material coherence*—that is does it fit with other stories that are already known? And finally, does the story have *characterological coherence*—does the action described fit with the known character of the actor? The tests of *fidelity* are equally important, and for our purposes perhaps more so. Fisher proposes five tests of narrative fidelity: *fact, relevance, consequence, consistency,* and *transcendental issue.*[20] These parallel the factors that were outlined in the last chapter as cues to look for in propaganda. *Fact* refers to whether or not the facts claimed are really true. *Relevance* is determined by whether important facts have been omitted or distorted. *Consequence* deals with what effects one could expect from adhering to the values inherent to the message. *Consistency* asks how consistent the story is with the values held by the audience and those they admire. Finally, the *transcendental issue* asks whether the values embodied in the message "constitute the ideal basis for human conduct?"[21] Fisher's narrative paradigm is not confined to stories that purport to be literally true. He writes, "Common experience tells us, however, that we do arrive at conclusions based on 'dwelling in' dramatic and literary works."[22] This is quite similar to the Green's transportation theory. To illustrate this, he applies the paradigm to fictional works such as *Death of a Salesman* and *The Great Gatsby.* As will be developed in later chapters, fictional stories, such as those told in movies and on television, can constitute powerful propaganda.

The opening of this chapter related Nayirah's story of Saddam's troops removing premature babies from their incubators and leaving them to die. This story has all the powerful components that could transport an audience to the horrific scene of what happened in that Kuwaiti hospital. Nayirah appeared to be a credible witness and was obviously so upset about her experience that it brought her to tears. President Bush was so moved by the story that five days later he referred to it in a speech: "And I heard horrible tales: Newborn babies thrown out of incubators and the incubators then shipped off to Baghdad. . . . Hitler revisited."[23] As late as 1998, he continued to recount the story in his memoir, *A World Transformed.*[24]

The story was, however, not what it seemed. Unknown to the public at the time, Nayirah was coached by a PR team before her testimony.[25] Because she testified before an informal caucus rather than a regular congressional committee, her testimony was not under oath. Finally, Nayirah was not who she seemed to be. MacArthur reveals, "Nayirah . . . is the daughter of the Kuwaiti Ambassador to the U.S., Saud Nasir al-Sabah."[26]

The story's narrative *coherence/probability* appears to be strong. The *structural coherence* of the story is straightforward—Nayirah claimed to be an eyewitness to the events she described. In terms *of material coherence,* the story fit into the broader narrative that Saddam Hussein would invade a small neighboring state without warning and his troops would steal incubators despite the loss of the life of preemies in an enemy country. Finally, *characterological coherence* was essential in selling the story. After all, by this point in promoting the war, Bush had likened Saddam to Hitler time and again. Killing babies is just the sort of thing Hitler would do. Like many war stories, the narrative coherence and probability of the incubator story was initially quite persuasive. MacArthur writes,

> [O]f all the accusations made against the dictator, none had more impact on American public opinion than the one about Iraqi soldiers removing 312 babies from their incubators and leaving them to die on the cold hospital floors of Kuwait City.[27]

When it comes to the *fidelity* of Nayirah's story, there were significant problems. Factually, in the words of NBC's John Chancellor, "It never happened."[28] Unfortunately, this was not revealed until it was too late. After the war, Dr. Mohammed Matar, and his wife, Dr. Fayeza Youssef were interviewed by ABC's John Martin. Youssef, who was in charge of obstetrics, said "No, [the Iraqis] didn't take [the babies] away from their incubator . . . ." She explained the real reason for their deaths: "No nurses to take care of these babies and that's why they died." Her husband Dr. Matar then said, "I think this is something just for propaganda."[29] The story clearly fails to meet at least two of the tests of *fidelity*. Specifically, it was not *factually* true; second, *relevant* information was concealed, namely Nayirah's connection to the ruling family and her preparation by a PR firm. On these two tests alone, the story should be classified as propaganda.

The third test of fidelity, *consequence*, is more favorable to accepting the story. Clearly, if the story had been true, the killing of babies is not the sort of thing that can be left unpunished. The fourth test, *consistency*, is more problematic. Iraq is just one of many repressive regimes in the Middle East. Why was it singled out for war, when others, such as Saudi Arabia were defended? Was it really about saving babies or, as some suggested, maintaining access to oil from the Middle East? Many of the opponents of the war rallied around the cry, "No blood for oil." Finally, the *transcendental* issue raised is not clear-cut. Given American values, one would have expected a war to bring freedom and democracy to Kuwait. In fact, that outcome was sought by coalition partner France. However, Bush's ultimate goal was to bring the ruling elite back to power. The ruling elite did not fit typical American values. For example, only China imprisoned more journalists than Kuwait.[30] If a story lacks *fidelity* because of any of these tests, it is proper to view it as propaganda and reject it as not providing good reasons for action.

This story also reveals a problem for the average citizen in evaluating the stories told in support of war. It is not particularly hard to judge the *coherence* or *probability* of a story. We do that all the time. When a "tall tale" seems too outrageous, the public is likely to reject it out of hand (although there may be segments of the public who believe even the most improbable narrative—as exemplified by the rise of QAnon). When it comes to judging the *fidelity* of a story, however, today's fragmented media environment has complicated these judgments immensely. And, as we shall see as we examine several wars, so-called objective journalists are often either censored or coopted into concealing facts inconvenient to the government's narrative. Even when some journalists attempt to expose government propaganda, they are often ignored or discounted.

Keep in mind that propaganda is transactional. Humans have a psychological need for consistency.[31] People are drawn to information that confirms their prior beliefs and consequently tend to avoid or interpret dissonant information in ways that support their underlying belief system. Facebook news feeds, Twitter, cable news, and similar sources tend to reinforce, rather than challenge the views of their users. As recent communication technologies have advanced, it has been possible to spread misleading information at an alarming rate. A study of Twitter by researchers at MIT found that false stories travel six times faster and reach 35 percent more people than true stories.[32] Of course, the possibility that false stories can be widely believed predates Twitter. In an aphorism attributed by some to Mark Twain, it is said, "A lie can travel around the world and back again while the truth is lacing up its boots."[33] In 1917, Senator Hiram Johnson famously said, "The first casualty when war comes, is truth."[34] As we shall see, wars have been fought based on stories that were later found to be highly questionable or demonstrably false. Also, when combined with military censorship, patriotic self-censorship, and organized propaganda, it becomes difficult if not impossible to challenge misstatements of fact used to promote and sustain wars.

SELECTING THE ARTIFACTS

As we look at each war, beginning with the Spanish-American War of 1898, we will not just look at discrete stories, such as Nayirah's, but rather at the larger narrative. As Susan Brewer explains, to persuade Americans to go to war, "leaders translate war aims into propaganda . . . . They seek to 'bring the whole story together in one official narrative,' as Secretary of State Dean Acheson put it in 1950."[35] It is this larger narrative that will be the focus of the following chapters. It is not just official pronouncements of government officials that are germane. In the first of the wars examined in this study, the story of sinking of the *Maine* was the critical event that galvanized public opinion in favor of the war against Spain. Would the United States have gone to war without the drumbeat of the press about the tragedy in Havana harbor? Historians continue to debate the matter, but clearly the banner headlines in Hearst's newspaper can be fairly categorized as prowar propaganda. Some wars clearly can be traced to government propaganda—the second war in Iraq would not likely have occurred without the constant effort of the Bush administration to imply Saddam had WMD and was somehow linked to 9/11. But would that have been successful without the cooperation of the mass media, which overwhelmingly bought the narrative Bush and his administration told? Would the public have been so easily persuaded to attack a nation that had not attacked the United States? Thus, I will draw my net widely—any communication telling a story supporting or opposing a war is fair game. Even those propaganda efforts that fail are worthy of study.

SUMMARY

The unique contribution of this study seeks to make to the field of propaganda studies is to combine two different, but complementary approaches to understanding narratives, one empirically based and the other founded on theories of rhetoric. Green and her colleagues have demonstrated empirically that stories in the narrow sense have the potential to change attitudes, particularly those resting on strong emotional foundations. Fisher has created a paradigm that asserts that all communication can be understood from a narrative perspective. Further he has proposed methods to judge if such narratives advance good reasons to adopt the values embraced by these narratives. These two theories fit well into the transactional model of media effects. The former provides empirical evidence for the power of stories to transport receivers into another reality, one in which contrary information is hard to absorb. The latter provides a mechanism for assessing the coherence of a story and, most importantly for our purposes, its fidelity. When a story fails at least one of the tests of fidelity—fact, relevance, consequence, consistency, or transcendental issue—then it is to be regarded as propaganda and treated as such.

Psychologist and communication theorist Paul Watzlawick writes about "the way communication creates what we call reality." He concludes,

> [T]he most dangerous delusion of all is that there is only one reality. What there are, in fact, are many different versions of reality, some of which are contradictory, but all of which are the results of communication and not reflections of eternal, objective truths.[36]

When a nation is poised to go to war, knowing which stories have the most fidelity to the reality on the ground is essential to the public making an informed decision that can have the gravest consequences.

NOTES

1. Quoted in Jack Xiong, "The Fake News in 1990 That Propelled the US into the First Gulf War," Citizen Truth, May 7, 2018, https://citizentruth.org/fake-news-1990-that-ignited-gulf-war-sympathy/.
2. John R. MacArthur, *Second Front: Censorship and Propaganda in the 1991 Gulf War*, 2nd ed. (Berkeley: University of California Press, 2004), 70.
3. Melanie C. Green and Timothy C. Brock. "The Role of Transportation in the Persuasiveness of Public Narratives." *Journal of Personality & Social Psychology* 79, no. 5 (November 2000): 701–721, https://doi: 10.1037//0022-3514.79.5.701.
4. Green and Brock, "The Role," 702.
5. Green and Brock, "The Role," 703.
6. Melanie C. Green, "Narratives and Cancer Communication." *Journal of Communication* 56 (2006): S170, https://doi:10.1111/j.1460-2466.2006.00288.x.
7. Philip J. Mazzocco and Melanie C. Green, "Narrative Persuasion in Legal Settings: What's the Story?" *The Jury Expert* 23, no. 3 (May 2011): 27–34, https://www.thejuryexpert.com/2011/05/narrative-persuasion/.
8. Mazzocco and Green, "Narrative Persuasion in Legal Settings," 28.
9. Mazzocco and Green, "Narrative Persuasion in Legal Settings," 29–30.
10. Mazzocco and Green, "Narrative Persuasion in Legal Settings," 27.
11. Glenn G. Kuper, "Review of Narrative Persuasion in Legal Settings: What's the Story?" *The Jury Expert* 23, no. 3 (May 2011): 37, https://www.thejuryexpert.com/2011/05/narrative-persuasion/.
12. As a graduate student whose dissertation was directed by Fisher, I can attest to the influence Burke had on his thinking. In fact, one of the most memorable experiences I had in my graduate studies was when Fisher invited Burke to speak to us in person.
13. Kenneth Burke, *A Grammar of Motives and A Rhetoric of Motives* (Cleveland: Meridian Books, 1962), 567 (italics in original).
14. Walter R. Fisher, "Clarifying the Narrative Paradigm," *Communication Monographs* 56 (1989): 57, https://doi.org/10.1080/03637758909390249.
15. Walter R. Fisher, *Human Communication as Narration: Toward a Philosophy of Reason, Value, and Action* (Columbia: University of South Carolina Press, 1987), 90 (italics in original).
16. Fisher, *Human Communication as Narration*, 92.
17. Fisher, *Human Communication as Narration*, 48 (italics in original).
18. Fisher, *Human Communication as Narration*, 18.
19. Fisher, *Human Communication as Narration*, 47.
20. Fisher, *Human Communication as Narration*, 108–109.
21. Fisher, *Human Communication as Narration*, 109.
22. Fisher, *Human Communication as Narration*, 158.
23. George Bush, "Remarks at a Fundraising Luncheon for Gubernatorial Candidate Clayton Williams in Dallas, Texas." October 15, 1990, accessed May 21, 2021, https://bush41library.tamu.edu/archives/public-papers/2328.
24. George Bush and Brent Scowcroft, *A World Transformed* (New York: Random House, 1998), 427.

25. John Robert Greene, *The Presidency of George Bush* (Lawrence, KS: University Press of Kansas, 2000), 124.

26. John R. MacArthur, "Remember Nayirah, Witness for Kuwait?" *New York Times*, January 6, 1992, https://www.nytimes.com/1992/01/06/opinion/remember-nayirah-witness-for-kuwait.html?searchResultPosition=1.

27. MacArthur, *Second Front*, 54.

28. Quoted in MacArthur, *Second Front*, 76.

29. MacArthur, *Second Front*, 73 (brackets in original).

30. MacArthur, *Second Front*, 234.

31. Leon Festinger. *A Theory of Cognitive Dissonance* (Stanford, CA: Row, Peterson, 1957).

32. Seth Borenstein, Associated Press, "False Stories Travel Way Faster on Twitter Than True Ones Do, Study Finds," *USA Today*, March 9, 2018, https://www.usatoday.com/story/tech/news/2018/03/09/false-stories-travel-way-faster-twitter-than-true-ones-do-study-finds/409872002/.

33. "A Lie Can Travel Halfway Around the World While the Truth is Putting On Its Shoes," Quote Investigator, https://quoteinvestigator.com/2014/07/13/truth/. Ironically, the attribution of the quotation to Mark Twain is erroneous. The origins of the quote may go as far back as Jonathan Swift.

34. Quoted in Phillip Knightley, *The First Casualty: The War Correspondent as Hero and Myth-Maker from the Crimea to Iraq*, 3rd ed. (Baltimore and London: John Hopkins University Press, 2004), vii.

35. Susan A. Brewer, *Why America Fights: Patriotism and War Propaganda from the Philippines to Iraq* (New York: Oxford University Press, 2009), 4.

36. Paul Watzlawick, *How Real is Real? Confusion, Disinformation, Communication* (New York: Vintage, 1977), xi.

Chapter 3

The Spanish-American War

A Splendid Little War

February 15, 1898, was a warm calm evening in Havana, Cuba. At anchor in the harbor was the battleship, USS *Maine*, which had been there for three weeks. It had been sent to show the flag and protect American interests as Cuban independence fighters engaged in a protracted rebellion against their Spanish colonial masters. Stories in newspapers like William Randolph Hearst's *New York Journal* and Joseph Pulitzer's *New York World* alleged that the Spanish had been merciless in their treatment of their Cuban subjects since the rebellion began in 1895. When his illustrator Frederick Remington wired Hearst "There will be no war," he famously wired back, "You furnish the pictures and I'll furnish the war."[1]

Despite deploying 190,000 troops to the island, Spain had failed to suppress the insurgents, which they outmanned five-to-one. Frustrated, Spain introduced a harsh "reconcentration" policy. Destroying their property, including livestock, the military relocated civilians to Spanish-controlled towns and many soon died from disease and mistreatment. Rebel captives were often simply shot.[2] These atrocities provided fodder for newspapers in the United States.

President McKinley was appalled by the barbarism of the Spanish, calling it not "civilized warfare," but "extermination."[3] Despite these horrific acts, McKinley was reluctant to intervene. He declared in his inaugural address that he "cherished the policy of noninterference with affairs of foreign governments." He proclaimed, "We want no wars of conquest; we must avoid the temptation of territorial aggression."[4] His critics, including the assistant secretary of the Navy and future president Theodore Roosevelt, viewed such sentiments as signs of weakness, lamenting, "McKinley is bent on peace, I fear."[5]

Then events on the night of February 15 overtook the president's cautious policy. At 9:40 p.m., an explosion came from below the waterline and rocked the *Maine*. The captain described it as "a bursting, rending, and crashing roar of immense volume, largely metallic in character. . . . There was a trembling and lurching motion of the vessel, a list to port. . . . The situation could not be mistaken. The *Maine* was blown up and sinking."[6] Two hundred and sixty men died. Newspaper stories were quick to blame the Spanish and the pressure for war intensified. Although a war that began over 120 years ago may seem irrelevant today, the seeds for America's interventionist policies of the twentieth and early twenty-first century were planted in the Spanish-American War.[7]

PRELUDE TO WAR

To understand the origins of the Spanish-American War, it's important to know what was going on in the world at that time. Several European nations were bent on expanding their empires. England reveled in the boast that the sun never set on the British Empire. They ruled nearly a quarter of the earth's land surface and a similar share of its population.[8] France, Germany, and Russia also were competing for more colonies. Sometimes nations would swap one colony for another with one of their rivals. Little concern was shown for the native inhabitants of these far-away lands. America was late to the colonial game and there were strong voices, such as Teddy Roosevelt, who thought it was time to become a colonial power. This war was fought to create an empire, despite the president's assurances that he sought no new territory.

One factor promoting the war with Spain was the rise of what became known as "yellow journalism," a term coined when Joseph Pulitzer's *New York World* published a cartoon called the "Yellow Kid."[9] The press was, of course, not alone in pushing for war with Spain over the treatment of Cubans. There were strong calls for war from leaders like Roosevelt and Sen. Henry Cabot Lodge, who saw the colonial possessions of a declining Spanish empire as ripe for the taking. However, without the pressure from the press, war might have been avoided. Historian Allen Keller concluded, "[I]t was . . . a war in which newspaper headlines and reporters' dispatches had more explosive power than the artillery on both sides."[10] He continues, "Three newspaper publishers probably had more to do with making war between the United States and Spain inevitable than all the statesmen, legislators, or military figures of both sides."[11] These newspapers used sensational stories to build readership and thus profits.[12] As media outlets from Hearst's *Journal* to CNN have learned, nothing builds an audience better than war or rumors of war.

From the earliest days of the rebellion, papers such as Hearst's *New York Journal* presented a one-sided view of the conflict, transporting readers through their stories and illustrations to horrific scenes in Cuba. Despite having no reporters in Cuba in 1895, Hearst's newspaper bylined stories as coming from Havana, although they were written in New York.[13] Both the sides burned and pillaged, but as the *New York Times* reported, "[Spanish] General Weyler drew the particular scorn of correspondents for refusing to give them access to the battlefield."[14] Stephen Kinzer, a Senior Fellow in International and Public Affairs at Brown University, explains that Hearst "published a flood of heartrending dispatches about atrocities in Cuba, some fabricated by writers and illustrators who had never been there. In the space of a couple of weeks, millions of Americans were whipped into an anti-Spanish fury."[15] A powerful example comes from a story in Hearst's *New York Journal*, accompanied by a vivid Remington illustration, showing the strip search of Clemencia Arango by male Spanish officials. She is depicted from the backside, totally naked, surrounded by men. She later admitted that she was actually searched by women, and no men were present.[16] Historian Allan Keller calls it "a *cause célèbre* that helped push America into the war that should not have come."[17] Sensationalism helped sell papers, even if stories were untrue or exaggerated.

When the USS *Maine* exploded in Havana Harbor, American's natural tendency to empathize with victims was matched with outrage against Spain. Hearst's *Journal* featured multiple headlines and a huge diagram of how the Spanish supposedly used a mine to sink the USS *Maine* (figure 3.1). Readers were transported visually to the scene of the tragic death of American sailors. After being bombarded by stories of Spain's atrocities, the story that the Spanish had planted a mine that sank the battleship had high narrative probability. Kinzer calls the story "one of the most powerfully mendacious front pages in the history of American journalism."[18]

At the time of the explosion, a naval review board concluded that a mine had caused the explosion, although it was "unable to obtain evidence fixing the responsibility for the destruction of the MAINE upon any person or persons."[19] However, the report excluded the testimony of experts who would have cast doubt on the dominant narrative. Louis Fisher of the Library of Congress writes:

> The board of inquiry did not make use of many technically qualified experts. George W. Melville, the Navy's Chief Engineer, doubted that a mine caused the explosion but was not asked for his views. He suspected that the cause of the disaster was a magazine explosion. Philip R. Alger, the Navy's leading ordnance expert, told the *Washington Evening Star* a few days after the blast that the damage appeared to come from a magazine explosion.[20]

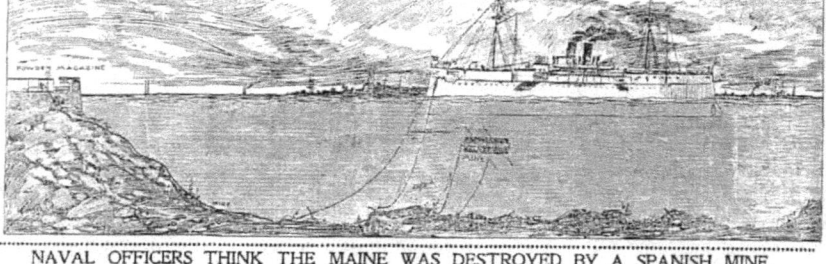

Figure 3.1 "Remember the *Maine*" became the slogan of the Spanish-American War, promoted by William Randolph Hearst in his *New York Journal*. *New York Journal*, Feb. 17, 1898.

The failure to consider a magazine explosion as the cause is surprising, given that between 1894 and 1908 over twenty fires in coalbunkers occurred on navy vessels, which under the right circumstances could cause an adjacent magazine to explode.[21] In fact, "An investigative board on January 27, 1898, warned the Secretary of the Navy about spontaneous coal fires that could detonate nearby magazines."[22]

In 1911, a new investigation ordered by President Taft concluded that a mine had sunk the *Maine*, but altered the location where it had exploded from the earlier study.[23] Ultimately, the final U.S. Navy answer came sixty-five years later. Admiral H. R. Rickover commissioned an extensive study utilizing archival information and the expertise of professional engineers. The report concluded, "The explosion was, without a doubt, a magazine explosion, since only the magazines contained sufficient explosive material to do the documented damage."[24] This remains that last official verdict from the U.S. Navy. However, a study in 1998 by Advanced Marine Enterprises (AME), commissioned by the National Geographic Society, was inconclusive, concluding, "[A] fire in the coal bunker could have generated sufficient heat to touch off an explosion in the adjacent magazine. On the other hand, computer analysis also shows that even a small, handmade mine could have penetrated the ship's hull and set off explosions within."[25] This report was controversial, as Fisher writes, "The experts who worked on the Rickover study and some analysts within AME did not accept the conclusions of the AME computer model."[26] For example, Ib Hansen, the director of the Rickover study, stated emphatically, "There was no mine under the Maine."[27] Even those who dispute Rickover's findings must admit that the initial naval report was seriously flawed due to the failure to call witnesses who supported the magazine explosion theory or to provide evidence of who was responsible for the sinking. Thus, the United States went to war with Spain without conclusive proof it was responsible for the sinking of the USS *Maine*.

The Spanish-American War provided a preview of how America would go to war in the next century and beyond. It is often triggered by outrage at heinous acts that may not have really occurred—from sinking the USS *Maine* by a Spanish mine, to attacks on destroyers in the Gulf of Tonkin, to babies thrown from incubators in Kuwait. Kinzer speaks of the implications of that long-ago war for today's world. Noting that Americans tend to feel compassion for suffering people no matter where they live, he cites a contemporary example. "We still use that today—a picture of a girl who has acid thrown in her face trying to go to school in Afghanistan makes people say we should go bomb Afghanistan, we should get rid of those horrible people."[28]

McKinley spoke to Congress on April 11, 1898. In his speech, McKinley drew a bright line between protecting Spain's colonial subjects and building an American empire, as others argued should be done. Keeping with his inaugural pledge not to seek territory or engage in wars of conquest, McKinley promised home rule and independence for both Cuba and Puerto Rico (a promise that remains unfulfilled to this day). He rejected the idea of American rule, stating, "I speak not of forcible annexation, for that can not [sic] be thought of. That, by our code of morality, would be criminal aggression."[29] He based his call for intervention on four pillars: humanitarian concerns, protection of American citizens, destruction of American commerce, and property, and the dangers to peace. Of course, the sinking of the USS *Maine* was the final event that prompted action. As McKinley put it,

> The destruction of that noble vessel has filled the national heart with inexpressible horror. Two hundred and fifty-eight brave sailors and marines and two officers of our Navy, reposing in the fancied security of a friendly harbor, have been hurled to death, grief and want brought to their homes and sorrow to the nation.

McKinley, without directly blaming the Spanish, strongly inferred their responsibility:

> In any event, the destruction of the *Maine*, by whatever exterior cause, is a patent and impressive proof of a state of things in Cuba that is intolerable. That condition is thus shown to be such that the Spanish Government can not [*sic*] assure safety and security to a vessel of the American Navy in the harbor of Havana on a mission of peace, and rightfully there.

On April 20, Congress passed a joint resolution authorizing McKinley to take steps to end the war in Cuba. Spain rejected McKinley's overtures and declared war on the United States. Congress responded with its own declaration of war on April 25.[30]

Many Cubans were suspicious of American motives. Cuban founding father José Martí wrote in an unfinished letter the day before he was killed in battle,

> I am in daily danger of giving my life for my country and duty, for I understand that duty and have the courage to carry it out—the duty of preventing the United States from spreading through the Antilles as Cuba gains its independence, and from overpowering with that additional strength our lands of America.[31]

As it turned out, Martí was prescient, as the United States continued until 1934 to assert its right to intervene in Cuba and to this day controls the Guantanamo Bay naval station.

COMMODORE DEWEY DESTROYS THE SPANISH FLEET

Prior to the declaration of war, Assistant Secretary of the Navy Theodore Roosevelt wired Commodore Dewey in Hong Kong, "In the event of declaration of war [with] Spain, your duty will be to see that the Spanish squadron does not leave the Asiatic coast, and then offensive operations in Philippine Islands."[32] Thus, even before war was declared, the United States was preparing to carry the fight with Spain across the Pacific. On May 1, Dewey, began his attack on the Spanish fleet in Manila. It took only seven hours to destroy the fleet.[33] Three war correspondents accompanied Commodore Dewey. The newsmen were hardly neutral observers, with two of them assigned to man guns on warships.[34] Dewey also cut the cable from Manila to Hong Kong, assuring that only his version of the battle would reach the outside world.[35] The war to free Cuba from Spanish control began almost 10,000 miles away, and the narrative was solidly under Dewey's control. Of course, he became an instant hero once news of his victory reached the States.

WAR STORIES FROM CUBA—THE ROUGH RIDERS

Having gotten the war it wished for, soon the press was clamoring for stories of American heroics. At the beginning of the war, the lack of press censorship was a problem with newsmen sometimes revealing sensitive information about fleet and troop movements that could help the enemy.[36] In response, Commanding General William Shafter "ordered that no dispatches be sent from Tampa without first being cleared and stamped by a censor."[37] Again, the military took control of the narrative.

As the invasion of Cuba approached, war correspondents, including such notables as novelist Stephen Crane, Richard Harding Davis, and William Randolph Hearst himself, prepared to cover the war. Roosevelt, who had resigned his position to form a group of volunteers known as the Rough Riders, realized the importance of publicizing his exploits and allowed newsreel cameramen on his ship.[38] After landing on Cuban soil, a Spanish flag was seen on a hill. Some of the Rough Riders

> raced up the hill, tore down the enemy banner, and ran up the Stars and Stripes. . . . It should be noted that the correspondents also observed the action and were quick to mention that it was Roosevelt's men who had done the deed when they filed their first dispatches.[39]

In the Battle of Las Guásimas, although General Wheeler went with the regulars, newspaper correspondents stayed with Roosevelt's troops.[40] Keller observes, "Newspaper reports of the battle . . . tended to make the Rough Riders, and Roosevelt in particular, the heroes of the engagement."[41]

Roosevelt's greatest glory came in the battle for San Juan Hill, later re-enacted for film (perhaps the first war propaganda movie).[42] In reality, the Rough Riders didn't actually take San Juan Hill, they took Kettle Hill.[43] Although 205 Americans died (along with 215 Spaniards), it was portrayed as a great victory for the Americans. Roosevelt proclaimed the victory "the great day of my life."[44] Readers were transported to San Juan Hill where Roosevelt became the war hero America seemed to need. Keller writes,

"In most of the papers back home it would have seemed that the Rough Riders were fighting the Spanish single-handed. The colonel's name was in hundreds of headlines and his picture on many a front page."[45] Roosevelt's Rough Riders, rather than Cuban rebels became the heroes. Soon the Spanish surrendered Cuba to the Americans rather than the rebels. Next to be taken was Puerto Rico, where there was no real opposition. Some villages even surrendered to reporters like Richard Harding Davis and Stephen Crane before American troops arrived.[46]

Secretary of State John Hay proclaimed, "It has been a splendid little war."[47] Kinzer called it "the most popular war in American history. Thanks to the telegraph, it was also the first one Americans were able to follow as it was being fought, reading about battles while they were still under way."[48] Thus, Americans were transported in almost real time to the scene of America's victory. As would happen often in the years to come, the changing nature of media impacted how American wars were fought as well as initiated. However, there still remained the matter of what was to become of the Philippines.

THE PHILIPPINES FALL

With Cuba under U.S. control, Spain was clearly defeated and sought peace. However, too early of a capitulation would have left the remainder of Spain's colonial empire out of America's reach. Senator Frye expressed the concern of expansionists: "The fear I have about this war . . . is that peace will be declared before we can get full occupation of the Philippines and Porto [sic] Rico."[49] The Teller Amendment guaranteed independence only for Cuba, not Spain's other colonies like Puerto Rico and the Philippines. The press joined in the call for expansion. Keller writes, "Having literally pushed the country into war, the yellow press now screamed for annexation."[50]

On August 13, the United States and Spain staged a battle designed to minimize actual casualties to establish American rule.[51] The Filipino rebels were left out of the battle. "Secretary of State Long cabled Dewey not to enter into any formal agreement with [rebel leader] Aguinaldo 'that would incur any liability to maintain their cause in the future.'"[52] The way was clear for America to take over Spain's former colonies regardless of the wishes of the native inhabitants. Of course, becoming a colonial power flew in the face of America's origin story as well as McKinley's promises. Nevertheless, he warned Filipinos that if they rejected American rule, he would use "the strong arm of authority to repress disturbance and to overcome all obstacles to the bestowal of the blessings of good and stable government upon the people of the Philippine Islands under the free flag of the United States."[53]

Although not directly a part of the war, Hawaii was annexed during this time, as it provided an important refueling station for the U.S. Navy.[54] In all, eleven million residents of Cuba, the Philippines, Puerto Rico, Guam, and Hawaii, came under American control.[55] Ironically, a war that began as a response to the colonial oppression of the Cuban people eventually allowed the United States to extend its own colonial empire halfway across the globe to the Philippines.

CUBA: COLONY OR PROTECTORATE?

The Cuban portion of the war came to a quick conclusion on July 16, with surrender by the Spanish not to the Cuban rebels, but to the United States.[56] Initially, Cubans assumed America would grant them independence, particularly in view of the Teller Amendment. Passed by Congress during the spring of 1898, it stipulated, "the United States pledged that it would never seek 'sovereignty, jurisdiction, or control over said island,' and that as soon as fighting ended Americans would 'leave the government and control of the island to its people.'"[57] However, once in control of Cuba, America proved reluctant to grant full independence. The military governor, General Leonard Wood, suggested that the United States ignore the Teller Amendment and rule indefinitely.[58] This was due, in part, to the realization that the government of an independent Cuba would include many Blacks.[59] America had a long practice of not annexing territories that were predominantly non-white.[60] For example, after the Mexican-American War in 1846–1848, when there was a talk of annexing Mexico, Sen. John C. Calhoun of South Carolina proclaimed, "We have never dreamt of incorporating into the Union any but the Caucasian race—the free white race."[61] Thus, excluding Cuba as a potential part of the United States was fully consistent with American views on race at the time.

It was not until May 19, 1902, that Cuba was finally recognized by the United States as independent, but with significant restrictions. The Platt Amendment gave the United States the power to intervene, until it was repealed in 1934.[62] The amendment also gave the United States a permanent lease at Guantanamo Bay Naval Station, which today houses prisoners in the so-called Global War on Terror.[63] Thus, although Cuba was nominally independent in 1902, it was not until over three decades later that it was officially free from the threat of U.S. intervention (although the threat was renewed with the Bay of Pigs invasion in 1961). Even after the legal threat of intervention was removed, one of its best harbors remained under perpetual U.S. control. When Fidel Castro took control of the island, the relationship with the United States became so strained it came close to igniting a nuclear war during the Cuban Missile Crisis of 1962. It was not until 2015 that diplomatic relations were resumed, although sanctions continue to this day and were strengthened under the Trump administration. There is some indication that the Biden administration may adopt a more conciliatory policy. Furthermore, over 120 years after the McKinley's promise of home rule, Puerto Rico remains an American territory without a vote in Congress or the Electoral College.

AFTERMATH: INSURGENCY IN THE PHILIPPINES

Filipinos, thinking America was about to grant them independence, wrote a constitution and assumed they would finally be free of colonial rule.[64] When it became apparent that America's goal was not to liberate the islands, an insurgency developed. By the time the Treaty of Paris, which would turn the Philippines over to the United States, was up for ratification in the Senate, the insurgency was underway. On February 4, as the Senate was preparing to vote on the treaty, two American soldiers from the Nebraska Volunteer infantry advanced into insurgent territory. A full-scale battle soon ensued, and 60 Americans and 3,000 Filipinos were killed. The *New York Times* called the battle "the insane attack of these people upon their liberators."[65] After the battle, two Democratic Senators switched sides, and the Senate ratified the treaty by only one vote.[66] Thus the battle may well have provided the impetus for America to acquire its first major colony. After the treaty was ratified by the Senate on February 6, 1899, the *New York Journal's* front page headlines juxtaposed the treaty with news of the battle: "PEACE TREATY RATIFIED/AWFUL SLAUGHTER/OUR TROOPS AT MANILA KILLED THE FILIPINOS BY THE THOUSANDS/40 AMERICANS KILLED."[67] The demonization of the enemy and glorification of American imperialism were in full swing. No declaration of war was required because the rebellion was deemed an insurrection, not a war.[68]

As Americans were to learn, it is one thing to defeat the governing power in a country and yet another to put down an insurgency from "ungrateful" natives, who viewed American forces not as liberators, but as occupiers. Initially, American military leaders thought they would only need about 5,000 troops. By February 1899, there were 20,000 with more on the way. By the end of the insurgency, American had deployed well over 100,000.[69] Just as the Spanish discovered in Cuba, defeating insurgents requires more than just military superiority.

Racial stereotyping was at the root of America's assumption of the right to rule the far-flung islands. The inherent superiority of the white race was widely accepted. Susan A. Brewer shows that this view extended to the president, who described the war "as an effort to bring Christian civilization to 'little brown brothers.'"[70] Of course, the Philippines was already a largely Christian (albeit Roman Catholic) country as a result of over three centuries of Spanish rule.

It was widely believed that the rebels would be easily defeated and that the domestic opponents of American imperialism would be silenced.[71] As it turned out, neither of those beliefs was correct. Although the rebellion would officially end in 1902, it would continue in some parts of the Philippines until 1913.[72] As the rebels switched to guerrilla tactics and became harder to suppress, domestic opposition to the war took hold. Kinzer asserts, "Not until the Vietnam era three-quarters of a century later would so many Americans rise in opposition to a foreign war."[73] Further, looking at that war, we see many of the same issues that would arise decades later in the jungles of Vietnam. The toll of the war was far more than anyone could have anticipated. In 41 months, some 120,000 American soldiers went to the Philippines. It's estimated that 20,000 Filipinos rebels were killed along with hundreds of thousands of civilians. Water buffalo, which were crucial to agriculture, were reduced by 90 percent. America lost over 4,000 lives and nearly another 3,000 were wounded. More Filipinos died during the American occupation than in over 350 years of Spanish rule.[74]

In another way, the war also foreshadowed the Vietnam War. Villages were burned, civilians were subject to reconcentration, and suspected guerrillas were tortured, employing the very techniques the United States had objected to when used by Spain. There were a great many civilian deaths, resulting not just from the fighting but also from diseases such as cholera and malaria, as well as food shortages.[75] Brewer enumerates many of the questionable ways American troops waged the war against the Filipino rebels, including torture, execution, rape, and looting. "The most effective way to punish a guerrilla fighter, explained General Robert P. Hughes, was to attack his women and children."[76] In fact, one particular method of torture was to be repeated in a modified form over 100 years later. The so-called water cure involved forcing water down the throats of prisoners to mimic drowning.[77] Not surprisingly these reports of atrocities were not easily obtained due to government censorship. Eventually, however, the stories began to emerge. According to D'Haeseleer and Peace:

> Herbert Welsh, the editor of *City and State* . . . and his assistants tracked down veterans to obtain their testimony. His efforts persuaded more journalists to report on American troops participating in torture, especially the "water cure." Anti-imperialist newspapers also seized on General Bell's reconcentration policy and compared it to [Spanish] General Weyler's. The *Chicago Public* published an item entitled "Reconcentration—Condemned by the American people in 1898, Sanctioned by the American Government in 1902."[78]

However, to the extent that American tactics were known to be cruel, they were defended as a response to the barbarism of the enemy.[79] Despite reports of American atrocities, few were disciplined and then only in minor ways. General Jacob H. Smith, who had ordered his troops to kill every person over age ten on Samar Island, faced a court-martial that ended in a mere reprimand.[80] In the end, the atrocities were whitewashed. The Senate conducted hearings in the spring of 1902. It concluded that the accusations of atrocities were largely untrue and that the Army had acted properly. The unsavory actions that were committed were deemed isolated cases and not a result of official U.S. policy.[81]

ASSESSING THE NARRATIVE

The stories of Spanish atrocities in Cuba were powerful. Remington's illustrations—such as that of a naked Clemencia Arango being searched by Spanish men—visually transported readers to the scene of their debauchery. When the *Maine* was sunk, the readers of Hearst's *Journal* were visually transported by a diagram that showed Spain's outrageous act. When McKinley endorsed the view that a mine had sunk the USS *Maine*, few could dispute the prevailing narrative. Once the war began, the Rough Riders and their leader Teddy Roosevelt were depicted as courageous heroes in print and on film. Transportation theory would indicate that the stories and pictures coming from the press would be difficult to discount.

Did the stories told to justify the war with Spain have *narrative coherence* and *probability*? Did they provide *good reasons* for going to war with Spain? Historian Allan Keller wrote in 1969, during the height of the Vietnam War, "Seventy years after the event, our war with Spain in 1898 is as difficult to justify on moral grounds as it was in the days of President William McKinley and the first President Roosevelt."[82] In particular, he calls out the lack of journalistic ethics that incited a nation to war and paved the way for the next:

> The more sensational papers carried stories of Weyler's actions that were either untrue or grossly exaggerated. . . . When stories without any foundation had Weyler's henchmen throwing Cuban rebels to the sharks, newspaper ethics touched bottom. That another generation would have to witness similar journalistic excesses, such as the charges that German soldiers were cutting the breasts off Belgian nuns, does not reduce the shame of the yellow press in the last half-decade of the nineteenth century.[83]

Regardless of one's definition, it seems clear that the exaggerated stories of Spanish atrocities, the rush to judgment about the perpetrators of the sinking of the USS *Maine*, and the racist treatment of Filipino rebels constitute propaganda. The narrative paradigm further shows how this propaganda failed to provide good reasons for war.

First, we are called to examine the *narrative coherence* of the stories that favored war. Who are the characters and how did they act? In what ways did that justify the risk to American lives and treasure? The most important clue to narrative coherence in these stories lies in their *characterological coherence*. In Cuba, the alleged villains are clear—the Spanish. They brutalize their subjects, threaten American interests, and cannot be trusted. Who are the heroes? Rather than the Cubans themselves, they are the Americans, such as Teddy Roosevelt who came to the rescue of the suffering people of Cuba. Of course, it is not enough to have villains and heroes. Certain acts are needed to move the populace from condemnation to action.

Primed by stories of Spanish brutality, it is not surprising that Americans would think them capable of unprovoked actions against innocent Americans. The sinking of the USS *Maine* provided a rallying cry for action. "Remember the *Maine*" echoed "Remember the Alamo" and foreshadowed "Remember Pearl Harbor." Pivotal events such as these are often crucial to pushing America into war. Although even the naval review board at the time could not prove the Spanish planted the mine, McKinley assured Congress and the American people that the evidence pointed to an external explosion. Because Americans already were predisposed to view the Spanish as brutal and unprincipled in their treatment of Cubans, it was a very small leap to the conclusion that they did in fact sink our ship and kill hundreds of brave American sailors.

When we attribute certain character traits to people, we expect them to act in accordance with those traits. Having been portrayed as evil and brutal, it was consistent with the perceived character of the Spanish that they would sink a ship full of innocent Americans. Attribution theory posits that we are far more likely to attribute bad actions of others to character flaws than we are for ourselves.[84] When we act in questionable ways, we are more likely to attribute actions to external circumstances. If an enemy engages in torture, that's evidence of their inherent depravity. But if American soldiers are found to have done so, it is either dismissed as a lie or attributed to a few bad apples.

Overall, the stories that prompted U.S. military action against the Spanish relied on news reports of brutality, which came to be seen as a result of the evil character of the Spanish, confirmed by an action, the sinking of the *Maine*. It took little imagination to see that the Spanish were to be blamed, either directly or indirectly, for the loss of the *Maine* and that such an event was consistent with the character they had displayed in their treatment of Cubans.

The Philippines created a different dynamic. Once the Spanish were vanquished, the original enemy was gone. How could Americans be persuaded to invest their treasure and lives to subdue a people seeking merely to control their own destiny? Again the story needed *narrative coherence*. Who are the good guys and who are the evildoers once the Spanish left? Well, the heroes are obvious—Americans who came to liberate the Filipinos from their oppressors. McKinley conveniently ignores the fact that the Filipinos wrote a constitution and sought independence. He argues that it is America's duty to govern, asking, "Can we leave these people, who, by the fortunes of war and our own acts, are helpless and without government, to chaos and anarchy, after we have destroyed the only government they have had?" His answer foreshadows future conflicts, particularly in Iraq and Afghanistan: "Having destroyed their government, it is the duty of the American people to provide for a better one."[85]

As the rebellion grew, the rebels were characterized as ungrateful and barbaric. McKinley characterized the Filipino rebels as "the liberated . . . engaged in shooting down their rescuers."[86] It is also clear that racial stereotypes played a prominent role in America's treatment of Filipinos. William Howard Taft, the first American Governor-General of the Philippines, told President McKinley, "'our little brown brothers' would need 'fifty or one hundred years' of close supervision 'to develop anything resembling Anglo-Saxon political principles and skills.'"[87] McKinley took up that theme and as Brewer claims, "His successors would apply a modified version of the 'white man's burden' to the Koreans, Vietnamese, and Iraqis."[88]

Not everyone accepted that view, and Senator George Hoar thought that Filipinos had been falsely accused of being "barbarous and savage," and having made "an unprovoked attack . . . upon our flag."[89] Mark Twain shared the suspicion that Americans had been hoodwinked:

> There must be two Americas: one that sets the captive free, and one that takes a once-captive's new freedom away from him, and picks a quarrel with him with nothing to found it on; then kills him to get his land.[90]

But could Americans really do something so cruel? Here the *narrative improbability* of Americans acting as the bad guys stood in the way of the war opponents' story. Proponents had an ace up their sleeve. To oppose the war was to attack the *character* of America's finest. McKinley linked support for his policy with support for the troops (a strategy that was to return in many subsequent American wars). He chastised his critics for proposing that our troops come home. At a homecoming speech for the Tenth Pennsylvania Regiment, he dramatically read a list of those regiments engaged in the war, with the crowd reacting with thunderous cheers.[91] Even those critical of the decision to fight the rebels in the Philippines seemed to get on board. *Harper's Weekly*, which had opposed war in the Philippines, concluded that once the country was at war, everyone needed to support the troops.[92] Again, this is a sentiment to be echoed in subsequent wars, particularly America's next great overseas adventure, World War I.

Thus, the good guys were our troops, regardless of the wisdom of the war. And although initially viewed sympathetically as victims of Spanish colonialism, once they resisted America's "liberation," the insurgents became the new evil doers—ungrateful barbarians that needed to be suppressed and civilized. After all, how could the rebels be the heroes if they were savagely killing their liberators? To save the Filipino people from themselves, the rebels had to be defeated. Nearly four years later, Theodore Roosevelt was able to declare the war over on July 4, 1902, although sporadic fighting continued until 1913.

The *fidelity* of the narratives told in support of the Spanish-American War rested on the information received by the public through the dominant medium of the day—the newspaper. These reports contained at least two flaws in terms of their fidelity. *Factually*, many of the reports were suspect or even fabricated, such as the story of Spanish men strip-searching Clemencia Arango. The report of the naval commission on the cause of the sinking of the *Maine* ignored experts who believed it was an internal explosion, not a mine. Although it took nearly eight decades to reverse that opinion, the Navy bore responsibility for fitting the facts to the narrative popular in the press rather than the reverse. Furthermore, the *relevance* of stories of Spanish atrocities in Cuba was undermined by the one-sided omission of the rebels' own misdeeds. In terms of the ingratitude of the native population in the Philippines, there was little in the way of a counternarrative, stressing their desire for independence. When the press called for war, and the leaders of the country seized on the tragic loss of American lives in Havana, it resonated with the public. Given the prior descriptions of Spanish cruelty, it is no wonder that the nation was primed for a "splendid little war." Heroes like Teddy Roosevelt and his Rough Riders were celebrated. Although eventually opposition developed to the counter-insurgency in the Philippines, that was conveniently swept under the rug. In fact, those who opposed the war were portrayed as failing to support our brave troops. Going forward, the Spanish-American War was seen as a story of American bravery and success against the barbaric Spanish and later ungrateful insurgents, who rebelled against American rule in the Philippines. America had entered a new age—a burgeoning power taking its rightful place in the world. However, the seeds of propaganda were sown for the next war, which would be anything but a "splendid little war."

NOTES

1. "The Press: I'll Furnish the War," *Time*, October 27, 1947, http://content.time.com/time/magazine/article/0,9171,854840,00.html.

2. Brian D'Haeseleer and Roger Peace, "The War of 1898 and U.S.-Filipino War," United States Foreign Policy History and Resource Guide, accessed January 30, 2018, http://peacehistory-usfp.org/1898-1899.

3. Quoted in Daniel Immerwahr, *How to Hide an Empire: A History of the Greater United States* (New York: MacMillan, 2019), loc. 1038 of 10589, Kindle.

4. William McKinley, "Inaugural Address," March 4, 1897, The American Presidency Project, https://www.presidency.ucsb.edu/node/205278.

5. Quoted in Immerwahr, *How to Hide an Empire*, loc. 1054 of 10589.

6. Quoted in Stephen Kinzer, *The True Flag: Theodore Roosevelt, Mark Twain, and the Birth of American Empire* (New York: Henry Holt and Co., 2017), [page] 32, Kindle.

7. Kinzer, *True Flag*, 4.

8. "British Empire," *Encyclopedia of Modern Europe: Europe Since 1914: Encyclopedia of the Age of War and Reconstruction*. Encyclopedia.com, updated January 31, 2020, https://www.encyclopedia.com/history/encyclopedias-almanacs-transcripts-and-maps/british-empire-1.

9. Darrell M. West, *The Rise and Fall of the Media Establishment* (Boston: Bedford/St. Martin's, 2001), 43.

10. Allan Keller, *The Spanish-American War: A Compact History* (New York: Hawthorn, 1969), 8.

11. Keller, *Spanish-American War*, 9.

12. Garth S. Jowett and Victoria O'Donnell, *Propaganda and Persuasion*, 7th ed. (Thousand Oaks, CA: Sage, 2019), 108.

13. Clifford Krauss, "The World; Remember Yellow Journalism," *New York Times*, February 15, 1998, https://www.nytimes.com/1998/02/15/weekinreview/the-world-remember-yellow-journalism.html.

14. Krauss, "The World."

15. Kinzer, *True Flag*, 32.

16. Keller, *Spanish-American War*, 20.

17. Keller, *Spanish-American War*, 19 (italics in original).

18. Kinzer, *True Flag*, 32.

19. Quoted in Louis Fisher, "Destruction of the Maine (1898)," Law Library of Congress, August 4, 2009, 1, https://www.loc.gov/law/help/usconlaw/pdf/Maine.1898.pdf.

20. Fisher, "Destruction of the Maine," 2.

21. Fisher, "Destruction of the Maine," 3.

22. Fisher, "Destruction of the Maine," 2.

23. Fisher, "Destruction of the Maine," 3.

24. H. G. Rickover, *How the Battleship Maine Was Destroyed* (Washington, DC: Naval History Division, Department of the Navy, 1976), 125, https://www.ibiblio.org/hyperwar/NHC/NewPDFs/USN/USN%20Manuals%20and%20Reports/USN.HOW%20.THE.BATTLESHIP.MAINE.WAS.DESTROYED.Rickover.pdf.

25. Thomas B. Allen, "Remember the Maine?" *National Geographic* 193, no. 2 (February, 1998): 107.
26. Fisher, "Destruction of the Maine," 5.
27. Steve Vogel, "The Maine Attraction," *Washington Post*, April 23, 1998, https://www.washingtonpost.com/archive/local/1998/04/23/the-maine-attraction/19167d57-2116-401c-922c-96cc2067349c/.
28. "Author Interview: The History of American Intervention and the 'Birth of the American Empire,'" *Fresh Air with Terry Gross*, NPR, January 24, 2018, https://www.npr.org/2017/01/24/511387528/the-history-of-u-s-intervention-and-the-birth-of-the-american-empire.
29. William McKinley, "Message to Congress Requesting a Declaration of War With Spain," April 11, 1898, The American Presidency Project, https://www.presidency.ucsb.edu/documents/message-congress-requesting-declaration-war-with-spain. All quotations from McKinley's war message are from this source.
30. Office of the Historian, Foreign Service Institute, United States Department of State, "The Spanish-American War, 1898," accessed June 21, 2021, https://history.state.gov/milestones/1866-1898/spanish-american-war.
31. José Martí, "Letter to Manuel Mercado," May 18, 1895, History of Cuba.com, http://www.historyofcuba.com/history/marti/mercado.htm.
32. Quoted in Keller, *Spanish-American War*, 40–41.
33. Keller, *Spanish-American War*, 59.
34. Keller, *Spanish-American War*, 55–56.
35. Keller, *Spanish-American War*, 60.
36. Keller, *Spanish-American War*, 93.
37. Keller, *Spanish-American War*, 93.
38. Keller, *Spanish-American War*, 113–114.
39. Keller, *Spanish-American War*, 124.
40. Keller, *Spanish-American War*, 129.
41. Keller, *Spanish-American War*, 132.
42. "The World of 1898: The Spanish American War Rough Riders," Hispanic Division of Library of Congress, https://www.loc.gov/rr/hispanic/1898/roughriders.html.
43. Kinzer, *True Flag*, 54.
44. Quoted in Kinzer, *True Flag*, 54.
45. Keller, *Spanish-American War*, 176.
46. Keller, *Spanish-American War*, 217.
47. Quoted in Kinzer, *True Flag*, 58.
48. Kinzer, *True Flag*, 49.
49. Quoted in Keller, *Spanish-American War*, 65.
50. Keller, *Spanish-American War*, 64.
51. Kinzer, *True Flag*, 65.
52. Keller, *Spanish-American War*, 224.
53. Quoted in D'Haeseleer and Peace, "The War of 1898."
54. Kinzer, *True Flag*, 45.
55. Kinzer, *True Flag*, 66.

56. Kinzer, *True Flag*, 62.
57. Kinzer, *True Flag*, 188.
58. Kinzer, *True Flag*, 190.
59. Kinzer, *True Flag*, 137.
60. Immerwahr, *How to Hide an Empire*, loc. 1248 of 10589.
61. Quoted in Immerwahr, *How to Hide an Empire*, loc. 1256 of 10589.
62. Office of the Historian, Bureau of Public Affairs, United States Department of State, "A Guide to the United States' History of Recognition, Diplomatic, and Consular Relations, by Country, since 1776: Cuba," accessed March 1, 2018, https://history.state.gov/countries/cuba.
63. Lily Rothman, "Why the United States Controls Guantanamo Bay," *Time*, January 22, 2015, http://time.com/3672066/guantanamo-bay-history/.
64. Kinzer, *True Flag*, 112.
65. Quoted in Kinzer, *True Flag*, 118–119.
66. Daniel A. Miller (producer, writer, and director), *Crucible of Empire*, PBS Video [Transcript], 1999, accessed May 6, 2021, https://www.pbs.org/crucible/frames/_journalism.html.
67. Quoted in Kinzer, *True Flag*, 126.
68. D'Haeseleer, and Peace, "The War of 1898."
69. Kinzer, *True Flag*, 129, 225.
70. Susan A. Brewer, *Why America Fights: Patriotism and War Propaganda from the Philippines to Iraq* (New York: Oxford University Press, 2009), 8.
71. Kinzer, *True Flag*, 139.
72. David Halberstam, *The Best and the Brightest* (New York: Modern Library, 2001), [page] 164, Kindle.
73. Kinzer, *True Flag*, 142.
74. Kinzer, *True Flag*, 225.
75. Office of the Historian, Foreign Service Institute, U.S. Department of State, "The Philippine-American War, 1899–1902," accessed March 6, 2018, https://history.state.gov/milestones/1899-1913/war.
76. Brewer, *Why America Fights*, 40.
77. D'Haeseleer and Peace, "The War of 1898."
78. D'Haeseleer and Peace, "The War of 1898."
79. D'Haeseleer and Peace, "The War of 1898."
80. Brewer, *Why America Fights*, 42.
81. D'Haeseleer and Peace, "The War of 1898."
82. Keller, *Spanish-American War*, vii.
83. Keller, *Spanish-American War*, 18.
84. Fritz Heider, *The Psychology of Interpersonal Relations* (New York: Wiley, 1958).
85. William McKinley, *Speeches and Addresses of William McKinley* (New York: Doubleday & McClure, 1900), 174, Google Books, https://play.google.com/books/reader?id=iOh2AAAAMAAJ&hl=en&pg=GBS.PP1.
86. McKinley, *Speeches*, 189.

87. National Parks Service Presidio of San Francisco, "The Philippine War - Suppressing An Insurrection," accessed March 15, 2018, https://www.nps.gov/prsf/learn/historyculture/the-philippine-war-suppressing-an-insurrection.htm.
88. Brewer, *Why America Fights*, 8.
89. Quoted in Brewer, *Why America Fights*, 39.
90. Quoted in Brewer, *Why America Fights*, 39.
91. Brewer, *Why America Fights*, 34–35.
92. Brewer, *Why America Fights*, 38.

Chapter 4

World War I
The War to End All Wars

The man who would become Kaiser William (Wilhelm) II was the first-born grandchild of Queen Victoria of Britain. One would have expected Britain and Germany to be allies. Not only did they have an historical common enemy in France, the blood ties between the English royal family and the German Emperor should have guaranteed a faithful alliance. However, it turns out that although he adored his grandmother, Wilhelm had a very different attitude toward the rest of his family, sometimes calling them "the damned family."[1] He even called his uncle King Edward VII "Satan."[2] When Queen Victoria celebrated her eightieth birthday on May 24, 1899, the Kaiser was furious—he was not invited. Writing to his grandmother three days later, he wrote "Now you will understand, dear Grandmama, why I so ardently hoped to be able to go over for your birthday. . . . I can assure you that there is no man more deeply grieved and unhappy than me!"[3] In early January 1901, as Queen Victoria lay dying, the uninvited Kaiser broke off a celebration of the bicentenary of the Kingdom of Prussia and rushed to his grandmother's side, despite opposition within his own country. The Kaiser made it clear that he would favor an alliance with Britain. At a luncheon given in his honor on the day he departed England, he stated, "We ought to form an Anglo-German alliance, you to keep the seas while we would be responsible for the land."[4] Ironically, as Barbara Tuchman points out, "The Kaiser always wanted an agreement with England if he could get one without seeming to want it."[5] Yet, a little over a decade later, the two countries were bitter rivals in what was, until World War II, the most destructive conflict in human history.

Understanding how such a promising alliance turned into an apocalypse is the subject of much research and controversy. It is beyond my purpose to try to explain the underlying causes of this tragic war—particularly because American involvement came nearly three years into the conflict. However, the broad outline of the origins of the war is helpful to understanding how the United States was drawn into a conflict, which on the surface did not directly involve it.

Despite his statements about an alliance with Britain dominating the sea while Germany dominated the land, the Kaiser was an enthusiastic proponent of building a strong German fleet. As Pulitzer Prize winner Robert Massie documents, an arms race between the Royal Navy and the German fleet became a costly and dangerous contest from 1905 to the outbreak of the war in 1914.[6] At the same time, a British-German alliance failed to emerge for a variety of reasons. The Germans began to feel threatened by Russia and France. Russia, in particular, presented a problem, since it was allied with ethnic Slavs, specifically Serbia. Germany's ally, Austria-Hungary ruled the Slavic provinces of Bosnia, Herzegovina, and Montenegro. Many Serbians sought to unite with them. Belgrade, the capital of Serbia was a hotbed of propaganda, which was distributed in the Slavic portions of Austria-Hungary. Thus, Germany's alliance with Austria-Hungry put it in direct conflict with the Serbian-Russian alliance. Further leading Germany to feel isolated was the alliance of France with Russia. Thus, Germany feared a two-front war should it come to Austria's defense in a war with Serbia and its ally Russia.[7]

Meanwhile, Britain shifted its attention to Germany rather than its traditional enemy, France. The German naval build-up threatened Britain's superiority at sea—which was the foundation of its empire, on which the sun never set. Knowing that the German navy would attack the north of France from the English Channel, the British were compelled to not only match but also exceed Germany's naval construction. Although no formal alliance was made with France, an understanding, called an entente, was established. France came to believe that it would not be left to its own devices should the Germans declare war. Further, Belgium was protected under the 1839 Treaty of London signed by all the major European powers. Should Germany attack France through Belgium, Britain would have a treaty obligation to intervene. Unfortunately, Germany's preferred path to defeating France led through Belgium.[8] Thus, the table was set for a conflict, the likes of which the world had never seen. As Tuchman put it, "Europe was a heap of swords piled as delicately as jackstraws; one could not be pulled out without moving the others."[9]

In June 1914, the heir to the Austrian throne, Archduke Franz Ferdinand, visited Sarajevo, the capital of Bosnia, which had been annexed by the Austrian-Hungarian Empire in 1908. Sunday, June 28, 1914, was St. Vitus's Day, the anniversary of the 1389 Battle of Kosovo, a day of great importance to all Serbs.[10] Seeking to show his goodwill, he dispensed with the normal level of security. Yet, the Archduke knew his visit could be dangerous, remarking prophetically when his car overheated, "Our journey starts with an extremely promising omen. Here our car burns, and down there they will throw bombs at us."[11]

That morning the Archduke proceeded in his motorcade, seeing smiling faces, flags, and his own portrait in windows along the way. Suddenly, a bomb was hurled at his car, but instead it landed under a trailing car. Two men were wounded and the bomb thrower apprehended. The Archduke was visibly shaken and angry, complaining, "One comes here for a visit . . . and is welcomed by bombs."[12] To avoid a repetition of the attack, a different route was planned for his return. Unfortunately, the driver of the lead car was confused about the route and took a wrong turn. This caused the driver of the Archduke's car to stop momentarily, giving nineteen-year-old Garilo Princip a clear shot at his target. He first shot Ferdinand's wife, Sophie, causing the Archduke to say, "Sophie! Sophie! Don't die! Stay alive for our children!"[13] However, soon both were dead and their bodies were taken to the ballroom where, ironically, a reception had been planned. The assassin was one of several Bosnians recruited in Serbia to promote the independence of the Slavs from Austrian rule. They were supplied with pistols and bombs in Belgrade by an organization known as the Black Hand. Although the Serbian government itself was not involved in the plot, it was clear Serbia would pay a dear price for the deaths of the future emperor and his wife.

The origins of the Great War are complex and continue to be debated over a century later. However, it is clear that the assassination of Franz Ferdinand was the spark that ignited the flammable continent of Europe. Austria, aligned with Germany, demanded satisfaction from Serbia. It produced a list of demands, most of which were patently unreasonable, threatening war if they were not met. Serbia's ally Russia was drawn into the conflict. Russia's ally France was attacked by Germany. The German generals assumed that by attacking France first, they could subdue it within six weeks, enabling their army to turn its full attention to Russia. However, to assure a quick victory, the German war plan required that they invade France through Belgium, which drew Great Britain into the war, due to the Treaty of London guaranteeing Belgium's neutrality. Soon the Central Powers of Germany and Austria-Hungary waged war against the Allies of France, Great Britain, and Russia. As Bismarck had predicted, "Some damned foolish thing in the Balkans" led to war.[14]

AMERICAN "NEUTRALITY"

For nearly three years, the United States remained on the sidelines, although its neutrality had a decided tilt toward the Allied Powers. Since American weapons and supplies could reach allied nations, but not Germany due to a British blockade, it is not surprising that so-called neutrality was hardly neutral in its effect. As historian Michael Kazin explained on the 100th anniversary of U.S. entry into the war, neutrality was one of the great myths surrounding the Great War:

> [T]he federal government did little to prevent U.S. businesses from selling goods and lending money to Britain and France. . . . Meanwhile, the Royal Navy was blockading the North Sea, making it all but impossible for American firms to do business with Germany—a disparity Wilson complained about briefly and only in the mildest terms.[15]

Many Americans opposed entering the war. As a nation of immigrants, many from countries at war with one another, there was no one side that appealed to everyone. Substantial German-American populations were unlikely to support the Allies; Irish immigrants had no love for England. British Admiral Jacky Fisher complained,

> The Yankees are dead set against us . . . . Only ¼ of the population of the United States are what you may call natives; the rest are Germans, Irish, Italians and the scum of the earth! [A]ll of them hating the English like poison.[16]

Kazin writes: "Until April 1917, this formidable coalition of idealists—or realists—did much to keep the nation at peace."[17] President Wilson realized that, as a nation of immigrants drawn from all sides in the conflict, picking any one side would have jeopardized his chances for re-election.

As the Great War began, Wilson was ostensibly a proponent of self-determination. Helping one side in the Great War would have meant endorsing one group of colonial powers over another. In reality, of course, the United States provided aid primarily to the Allies, supplying them with arms and money to fight against the Central Powers. But direct involvement in the war would have created great difficulties for Wilson. At the onset of the war, Wilson stressed America's commitment to neutrality: "The people of the United States are drawn from many nations, and chiefly from the nations now at war." He proclaimed, "The United States must be neutral in fact, as well as in name, during these days that are to try men's souls. We must be impartial in thought, as well as action, must put a curb upon our sentiments, as well as upon every transaction that might be construed as a preference of one party to the struggle before another."[18] Even William Randolph Hearst, who helped bring America the war against Spain, encouraged the United States to stay out of Europe's war.[19] The anti-war song, "I Didn't Raise My Boy to Be a Soldier!" became a hit in 1915.[20]

Given these considerations and facing a difficult re-election bid, Wilson maintained U.S. neutrality until he went before Congress on April 2, 1917, to ask for a declaration of war, less than a month after his second inauguration March 5. This delay was despite efforts of many to push the nation to intervene. Theodore Roosevelt, for example, was harshly critical of Wilson's neutrality, accusing him of "culpable weakness and timidity."[21] For Wilson, it was a difficult balancing act between preparing for possible war, placating those who thought him too timid, and satisfying the peace activists who were essential to his re-election.

The years between the war's outbreak and the re-election of Wilson were marked by a variety of conflicting impulses. The National Security League, founded by industrialists like Cornelius Vanderbilt, sought conscription and a larger army. On the other side, peace activists, such as Senator Robert La Follette and his wife, Belle, pushed for a peace conference. Wilson tried to placate both sides, as Geoffrey Wheatcroft writes, "Even as 1917 began, and Wilson continued to meet with Belle La Follette's WPP activists, it was clear that the country was now headed into the conflict."[22]

Although nominally neutral, the United States continued to supply Britain with the materials of war, while allowing it to blockade German sea-lanes, starving the Central Powers of the resources they needed to fight the war. In some ways, the eventual involvement of America resulted from a great naval battle in May 1916. The German fleet engaged the larger British fleet off the coast of Denmark in the battle of Jutland. Although the Germans sank more ships and killed more British sailors than they lost, they were unable to break the British blockade. After failing to do so, the Germans turned to unrestricted submarine warfare, including attacks on passenger ships. Ultimately, this violation of international law was what finally prompted the United States to join the war, thus insuring Allied victory.[23]

Significantly, one of Great Britain's first acts of war was to cut the transatlantic cable, cutting off direct communication from Germany and allowing Britain to dominate the propaganda reaching the United States.[24] The percentage of news about Europe coming from Germany was cut from 30 to 4 percent, allowing Britain to dominate the front pages of U.S. newspapers with its narrative about the war.[25] Much of the propaganda coming from Britain focused on alleged German atrocities. Lord James Bryce, former ambassador to the United States, headed a committee that released a report based on over a thousand stories from Belgian refugees alleging German atrocities. Among the horrendous examples, "German officers and men had publicly raped twenty Belgian girls . . . eight German soldiers had bayoneted a two-year old child, and . . . another sliced off a peasant girl's breasts in Malines."[26] According to J. Michael Sproule, the report was based on testimony that had two fundamental flaws: the witnesses were not cross-examined and there's a natural human tendency to make oneself a hero. Sproule personally examined thirty depositions, and found most were hearsay, not real eyewitness testimony.[27] At the time, Sproule reports, "[I]ts effect on American public opinion in 1915 was significant. Proof positive seemingly was at hand to sustain the Allied claim that theirs was a contest of good versus evil."[28] After the war, the report was fully discredited when "a Belgian commission of enquiry in 1922 . . . failed markedly to corroborate a single major allegation in the Bryce report."[29] This, of course, came long after the war was over.

The United States was the main target of British propaganda, as its leaders knew they would eventually need U.S. help to defeat the Germans. According to Phillip Knightley, they "knew that the public was not convinced by logic but seduced by stories."[30] Knightley adds, "British efforts to bring the United States into the war on the Allied side penetrated every phase of American life, from the pulpit to the classroom, from the factory to the office."[31]

Of course, U.S. "neutrality" was hardly perceived that way by the Central Powers. That led to U-boats torpedoing ships they believed to be supplying the Allies. On May 7, 1915, the Germans sank the passenger ship *Lusitania* off the coast of Ireland, strengthening the hand of those seeking U.S. involvement in the war. Kazin reports,

> [N]ewspapers devoted their front pages to such heart-breaking details as the corpses of drowned mothers with babies clinging to their breasts. . . . *The Nation* . . . compared the perpetrators to "wild beasts, against whom society has to defend itself at all hazards."[32]

Historian Arthur Stanley Link claims the sinking

> represented an important turning point in American opinion in general. . . . It converted some pro-Allied extremists in the United States into active interventionists . . . . By so doing it marked the dividing line between the time when there was no organized and vocal sentiment for American participation and the time when that sentiment existed in substantial measure.[33]

Although it took almost two more years for the United States to enter the conflict, this event was a key story that fed the prowar propaganda machine.

Wilson threatened to break diplomatic relations if the Germans sank another ship with Americans on board.[34] When he addressed a joint session of Congress on April 19, 1916, he claimed the high moral ground:

> But we cannot forget that we are in some sort and by the force of circumstances the responsible spokesmen of the rights of humanity, and that we cannot remain

silent while those rights seem in process of being swept utterly away in the maelstrom of this terrible war.[35]

The Germans were temporarily deterred from such further attacks, pledging on May 4 that U-boats would warn unarmed civilian ships before torpedoing them and would attempt to rescue crew and passengers.[36] Thus, at least for the time being, American entry into the war was delayed. Of course, the sinking of the *Lusitania* eventually became, like the explosion of the *Maine*, a seminal event that propelled the United States into war.

THE 1916 CAMPAIGN—HE KEPT US OUT OF WAR

As the election of 1916 approached, Wilson knew he was in for a very close race. It was important to his re-election that he steer a careful course between the peace movement and those who wanted to enter the war in Europe. The Democratic Party Platform stated, "We commend to the American people the splendid diplomatic victories of our great President, who has preserved the vital interests of our Government and its citizens, and kept us out of war."[37] Thus "He kept us out of war" became the rallying cry for the president's re-election campaign.[38]

At the same time, was Wilson actually preparing for war? As Democrats were praising Wilson for keeping the United States out of war, the president marched in a preparedness parade in Washington, D.C., carrying a large American flag.[39] Further, he and his allies in Congress were laying plans for an expanded military and draft. The National Defense Act, signed June 3, almost doubled the size of the army, gave Wilson the power to federalize the National Guard, and authorized a draft.[40] So the seeds of war were sown even as he campaigned as the peace candidate—a process to be repeated by later presidents. Biographer A. Scott Berg alleges that Wilson probably was planning to go to war all along:

> And then in a startling soul-baring moment, the President told [his Secretary] Tumulty that maintaining his impartiality during the last thousand days of war had been a terrible ordeal. "From the beginning I saw the utter futility of neutrality, the disappointment and heartaches that would flow from its announcement," he confessed, "but we had to stand by our traditional policy of steering clear of European embroilments."[41]

Wilson won a narrow victory by only twenty-three electoral votes. His success may have been due, at least in part, to carrying ten of the twelve states where women (who tended to be more anti-war) could vote.[42] Included in those states was California, which he carried by a mere 4,000 votes.[43]

WILSON PREPARES THE COUNTRY FOR WAR

After the election of 2016, events began to overtake the president and his efforts to keep the United States out of the war. In a speech delivered on January 22, 1917, Wilson told members of Congress that the war must end in "a peace without victory." He explained,

> Victory would mean peace forced upon the loser, a victor's terms imposed upon the vanquished. It would be accepted in humiliation, under duress, at an intolerable sacrifice, and would leave a sting, a resentment, a bitter memory upon which terms of peace would rest, not permanently, but only as upon quicksand.[44]

Unfortunately, as Lorraine Boissoneault points out:

> In the end, Wilson's idealism and the crusading anti-war parties in the U.S. couldn't save the country from getting sucked into the conflict. On January 30, just one week after Wilson's speech, Germany announced unrestricted submarine warfare, meaning U.S. merchant and passenger ships would once again be targeted by German U-boats. Wilson responded by severing diplomatic relations with Germany, but still hesitated to ask Congress to declare war.[45]

Unlimited German submarine warfare began on February 1.[46] Berg claims that the new German policy made war inevitable in Wilson's mind. Wilson's private secretary Joseph Tumulty brought him the bulletin announcing the new German policy, and watched the president's reaction. "Wilson turned gray, his lips tightened, and his jaw locked. Placing the paper back in Tumulty's hand, Wilson quietly said, 'This means war. The break that we have tried to prevent now seems inevitable.'"[47]

When informing Congress about his decision to break diplomatic relations, he promised restraint:

> We do not desire any hostile conflict with the Imperial German Government. We are the sincere friends of the German people and earnestly desire to remain at peace with the Government which speaks for them. We shall not believe that they are hostile to us unless and until we are obliged to believe it . . . . We wish to serve no selfish ends.[48]

Wilson pointedly distinguished between the people of Germany and their leaders. As has happened in innumerable conflicts, one side often claims to be fighting the adversary's leaders, not the people. Yet, it is the people who die in conflict, rarely the leaders.

Wilson was still publicly reluctant to ask for a declaration of war. Kazin notes, "Wilson also knew it would take more than just the threat of attacks on U.S. ships and passengers to convince most Americans that the moment for intervention had come."[49] On February 26, 1917, the president addressed a joint session of Congress. After detailing the effects of the German submarine warfare on commerce, including the sinking of two U.S. ships, Wilson stated, "We can only say, therefore, that the overt act which I have ventured to hope the German commanders would in fact avoid has not occurred." However, he stressed, "there may be no recourse but to armed neutrality . . . ."[50] Although a Senate filibuster prevented the arming of the ships proposal from passing, Wilson simply acted on his own.[51] Further, outrage at the filibuster led to the adoption of the cloture rule, allowing two-thirds of the Senate to end debate.[52]

Two days after Wilson's speech, the infamous Zimmerman Telegram appeared. The coded telegram from the German foreign minister was sent to his ambassador to Mexico "who was to encourage President Carranza to ally with Germany and to invite Japan to do the same. In return Mexico would not only receive financial reward but could also reclaim Texas, New Mexico, and Arizona."[53] Newspapers sounded the alarm: The *New York Times* proclaimed, "Germany Seeks an Alliance Against US; Asks Japan and Mexico to Join Her; Full Text of Her Proposal Made Public." The *Washington Post* sounded the alarm, "German Plot to Conquer U.S. With Aid of Japan and Mexico Revealed."[54]

By the time of Wilson's second inaugural on March 5, the man who "kept us out of war" was preparing to do just the opposite. As he addressed the nation, he stressed,

> We are provincials no longer. The tragic events of the thirty months of vital turmoil through which we have just passed have made us citizens of the world. There can be no turning back. Our own fortunes as a nation are involved whether we would have it so or not.

Thus, he called upon the nation to come together:

> United alike in the conception of our duty and in the high resolve to perform it in the face of all men, let us dedicate ourselves to the great task to which we must now set our hand. For myself I beg your tolerance, your countenance and your united aid.[55]

Even as Wilson waited to formally declare war, the Germans were providing the proverbial straw that broke the back of neutrality. On March 18, it was announced in the press that three unarmed U.S. ships had been sunk and fifteen men had died.[56] On April 1, the first armed American ship was sunk.[57] Kazin argues that by that point Wilson had already made the decision to go to war: "Perhaps he had purposely misled the public, Congress, and his own appointees when he had so recently described armed neutrality as the last, best chance to preserve the peace."[58] But in any case, purposefully or not, the die was cast and America was about to enter the "Great War."

WAR IS DECLARED

On April 2, 1917, one day after the first armed American vessel was sunk, Wilson addressed the Congress to ask for a declaration of war. Less than six months after being re-elected on the slogan, "He kept us out of war," Wilson was prepared to do just the opposite. In his address Wilson outlined German alleged atrocities, which were an important aspect of the prowar propagandist's arsenal:

> Vessels of every kind . . . have been ruthlessly sent to the bottom without warning and without thought of help or mercy for those on board, the vessels of friendly neutrals along with those of belligerents. Even hospital ships and ships carrying relief to the sorely bereaved and stricken people of Belgium . . . have been sunk with the same reckless lack of compassion or of principle. . . . Property can be paid for; the lives of peaceful and innocent people can not [sic] be. The present German submarine warfare against commerce is a warfare against mankind.[59]

He placed the blame for these acts on the Kaiser's government, not on the German people, stating, "We have no feeling towards them but one of sympathy and friendship." Further, he described the purpose of the war as a

> fight thus for the ultimate peace of the world and for the liberation of its peoples, the German peoples included: for the rights of nations great and small and the privilege of men everywhere to choose their way of life and of obedience. The world must be made safe for democracy.

These were themes to be repeated in future wars—that we have no quarrel with the people (be it Korea, Vietnam, or Iraq) and that we seek no conquest or territory. In addition, with a large German-American population, Wilson was careful not to antagonize them. Of course, that didn't stop subsequent war propaganda from demonizing the "Huns." As Brewer points out, "To fit the role of the enemy, the Germans, although white and Christian, became dehumanized barbarians called Huns, after the fifth century Mongolian invaders led by Attila."[60] Ironically, it was the Kaiser himself who characterized his troops during the Boxer Rebellion in China as the "Huns of Attila."[61]

Another tactic used by Wilson foreshadowed war messages from his successors, declaring that America was already at war:

> I advise that the Congress declare the recent course of the Imperial German Government to be in fact nothing less than war against the Government and people of the United States; that it formally accept the status of belligerent which has thus been thrust upon it, and that it take immediate steps not only to put the country in a more thorough state of defense but also to exert all its power and employ all its resources to bring the Government of the German Empire to terms and end the war.[62]

In addition, Wilson laid the groundwork for domestic actions to root out spies and others who might subvert the war effort. Citing, among other evidence, the Zimmerman telegram, he stated:

> One of the things that has served to convince us that the Prussian autocracy was not and could never be our friend is that from the very outset of the present war it has filled our unsuspecting communities and even our offices of government with spies and set criminal intrigues everywhere afoot against our national unity of counsel, our peace within and without our industries and our commerce.[63]

It is noteworthy that he named the enemy as "Prussian," not German, a moniker that carried connotations of aggressive militarism.

Finally, the fundamental premise of his speech was that only democracies can be counted on to be peaceful. This is a theme that would be repeated many times by his successors, most recently George W. Bush, who sought to remake the Middle East in a democratic mold. Wilson's theme was neatly summed up in one phrase, "The world must be made safe for democracy." By definition, the Central Powers were anti-democratic. Wilson's speech achieved its goal, with the Senate voting for war 82 to 6 and the House by a similarly overwhelming margin of 373 to 50.[64] He signed the declaration on Good Friday, April 6.[65] The United States was now at war.

As the war progressed, Wilson sought to define America's war objectives in the most favorable and unselfish ways. On January 8, 1918, he delivered to Congress his famous fourteen points for ending the war. He stressed that America entered the war so that the world would "be made safe for every peace-loving nation which, like our own, wishes to live its own life, determine its own institutions, be assured of justice and fair dealing by the other peoples of the world as against force and selfish aggression."[66] Among the points he called for were open covenants of peace, without private side agreements; freedom of navigation; removal of trade barriers; reduction of armaments; resolution of colonial claims "based upon a strict observance of the principle that in determining all such questions of sovereignty the interests of the populations concerned must have equal weight with the equitable claims of the government whose title is to be determined"; a fair adjustment of borders for all the nations involved; and perhaps most importantly, "[a] general association of nations must be formed under specific covenants for the purpose of affording mutual guarantees of political independence and territorial integrity to great and small states alike."

WAR PROPAGANDA/SILENCING DISSENT

Once war was declared, the Wilson administration realized that it would need an effective propaganda campaign to persuade the public to support the war. After all, they had just re-elected him as a peace candidate a few months earlier. Just as important, dissent against the war needed to be silenced. These dual goals led to the creation of the Committee on Public Information (CPI), headed by George Creel. As Mock and Larson's definitive study of the CPI revealed, "America was not unified when war was declared. The necessary reversal of opinion was too great to be achieved overnight."[67] The CPI was ultimately successful in mobilizing opinion in support of the war. Mock and Larson write, "What the Committee did do was to codify and standardize ideas already widely current, and to bring the powerful force of the emotions behind them."[68] The CPI accomplished this based on the work of Harold Lasswell.[69] Recall from chapter 1 that "manipulation of significant symbols" was a key part of Lasswell's definition of propaganda.[70] Mock and Larson write, "The use of symbols assumed greater and greater importance, and a number of the CPI divisions were concerned exclusively with symbol-manipulation."[71] Brewer put it this way: "To mobilize the nation in 1917, the Committee on Public Information embarked on a 'vast enterprise in salesmanship.' Propagandists extolled American greatness and condemned German barbarism by using sensational stories of atrocity, which were later discredited."[72]

The CPI had numerous domestic divisions, including news (which issued thousands of press releases), film, and the Four-Minute Men.[73] There were also foreign divisions, including wireless and cable services, a foreign press bureau, and the foreign film division, all dedicated to spreading the Wilsonian views of the war throughout the world.[74] Kazin writes, "Never before had the federal government created a propaganda agency whose sole aim was to make an altruistic, near messianic case both to its citizens and to the wider world."[75]

An example of the wide reach of the propaganda campaign was the Four-Minute Men program. With an estimated one million speeches, reaching a total audience of 400 million, these speakers were spread throughout the entire nation, speaking primarily at movie houses, but also at numerous other gathering places, such as churches and labor unions.[76] The name came from the four minutes it took to change movie reels, providing them the opportunity to speak.[77] Mock and Larson write,

> Wherever an American might be, unless he lived the life of a hermit, it was impossible to escape the ubiquitous Four-Minute Men. Judging from the estimated theater and movie audience in the fall of 1918, they must have reached several million daily.[78]

Their messages were patriotic, of course, explaining the draft, selling bonds, and encouraging patriotic actions on the home front. But they also told stories of atrocities, as this passage from an illustrative speech reveals:

> Prussian "Schrecklichkeit" (the deliberate policy of terrorism) leads to almost unbelievable besotten brutality. The German soldiers . . . were often forced against their wills, they themselves weeping, to carry out unspeakable orders against defenseless old men, women, and children, so that "respect" might grow for German "efficiency." For instance, at Dinant the wives and children of 40 men were forced to witness the execution of their husbands and fathers. Now, then, do you want to take the slightest chance of meeting Prussianism here in America?[79]

Once again, the enemy was described as Prussian, not German. German soldiers, with whom German-Americans might identify, were forced *against their wills* into unspeakable acts. Add in the fear appeal that such atrocities might be inflicted upon Americans, and the speech, which was intended as a model for Four-Minute Men, was propaganda at its purest.

Not only was government propaganda unprecedented, popular culture joined the fight. "I Didn't Raise My Boy to Be a Soldier" was replaced by George M. Cohan's patriotic "Over There."[80] The press, although supposedly only subject to "voluntary censorship," was in fact constrained from publishing articles critical of the war. After agreeing to voluntary censorship, the press was subjected on April 16, a mere ten days after the declaration of war, to this warning from President Wilson that any of the following were treasonous: "The performance of any act or publication of statements or information which will give or supply, in any way, aid and comfort to the enemies of the United States."[81] Soon the passage of the Espionage Act and other regulations put the press on notice that they needed to be careful about what they published. By May the CPI published "Regulations for the Periodical Press of the United States during the War."[82] The regulations divided news into three categories: dangerous (such as publishing troop movements), questionable, and finally routine, which comprised most stories. Those stories in the questionable category were subject to the approval of the CPI. Many news organizations encouraged their readers to report violations of these regulations, creating an atmosphere of surveillance. Thus, while avoiding the rigid censorship practiced by the enemy powers, it is clear that strong pressures to conform to the government line pervaded the printed press. Despite these rules, critical articles did appear.[83] Of course, such stories were in the minority, as Mock and Larson point out that Creel "could afford to overlook unimportant details in a small number of papers because all the rest of the press was pounding out an anvil chorus of patriotism under the direction of the CPI."[84] Some 20,000 columns per week were attributed by Creel to CPI materials.[85]

Pictorial propaganda was ubiquitous during the war, much of it from the CPI. The cover of this volume depicts Uncle Sam declaring, "I WANT *YOU* FOR U.S. ARMY," probably the most well known and positive propaganda poster of the war. Yet, Berg notes, "A year later, the American posters turned ugly (figure 4.1), depicting Germans as slobbering apes carrying off Lady Liberty."[86] As transportation theory would predict, visualizing the horrors of the enemy helps transport audiences to the scene of the story. In addition to posters, the CPI produced about fifty million pamphlets.[87]

Films were also a staple of war propaganda, vividly transporting audiences to the war. Berg points out,

> The film industry produced feature films centering on the war that grew increasingly brutal in their portrayal of the enemy. Lon Chaney starred in *The Kaiser, the Beast of Berlin*. In the *Heart of Humanity*, Erich von Stroheim played a brutal "Hun" who attempts to rape a nurse before throwing a baby out a window. D. W. Griffith himself produced a wartime epic, about young lovers in France torn apart by the war and reunited by killing a sadistic German rapist.[88]

The Kaiser is named here as a "beast," a word with powerful connotations. As Kenneth Burke argued, naming is a powerful force for persuasion. It is also worth noting that the Hun throwing the baby out the window foreshadows accusations (later proven untrue) that Saddam's soldiers tossed babies from their incubators in Kuwait. Young lovers torn apart by war is a common theme, as seen in the World War II classic *Casablanca*. Even in its earliest days, film served as war propaganda. And, of course, moviegoers were also the recipients of regular propaganda presentations from the Four-Minute Men.

Figure 4.1 The portrayal of the German soldiers as beasts became a staple of World War I propaganda. *Poster by Harry R. Hopps, 1918. Source: Image courtesy of the Library of Congress.*

In addition to prowar propaganda, the administration strove to suppress dissent. It is ironic that Wilson viewed the war as one to make the world safe for democracy, while at the same time suppressing First Amendment rights to freedom of speech and the press. Kazin writes, "Once the United States chose to enter the fray, the president, with the aid of the courts, prosecuted opponents of the war with a ferocity neither his defenders nor his adversaries had expected."[89] Most notable is the Espionage Act passed less than ten days after war was declared, that made it a felony to "willfully obstruct the recruiting or enlistment service of the United States."[90]

Kazin also laments the spying on U.S. citizens in the name of security:

> The surveillance state was also launched during the First World War . . . The Bureau of Investigation (later renamed the FBI) took charge of enforcing the Espionage and Sedition Acts; Military Intelligence hired undercover agents to report on the "subversive" activities of black and radical organizations.[91]

Targets of this spying included citizens who protested the war, encouraged others to do the same, and particularly Black and radical groups.

Once war was declared, especially after passage of the Espionage Act, not only was it dangerous for ordinary citizens to criticize the war, even those in Congress who had opposed the war were unwilling to speak out against it.[92] More than 24 million men registered for the draft, and by the end of the war, nearly four million had entered the ground armed forces.[93] Nevertheless, there was significant resistance to conscription. In fact, a higher percentage of men resisted the draft during the First World War than during Vietnam. Some 3 million failed to register. Further, over 300,000 of those who had registered failed to show up for induction or subsequently deserted.[94]

More restrictive than the Espionage Act was the Sedition Act, passed in May 2018. Under the latter act, people could be indicted for "disloyal, profane, scurrilous, or abusive language."[95] Socialist and five-time presidential candidate Eugene Debs received a ten-year prison sentence for a speech delivered on June 16, 1918.[96] As Sproule describes it, "Debs spoke of the irony of free speech suppressed by a nation allegedly fighting for democracy." Debs proclaimed, "I'd rather be a free soul in jail than a coward on the street." Sproule adds, "Debs might have been more careful about what he wished for."[97] Indeed, he was forced to conduct his fifth and final campaign for president from prison. In another example of suppression of dissent run amok, Robert Goldstein, the producer of a movie that censors found objectionable, *The Spirit of '76*, was sentenced to ten years in prison.[98] His offense—in telling the story of the American Revolution, English soldiers, now our allies, were portrayed as engaging in a brutal massacre. Mock and Larson argue that Creel and his committee, although it lacked official censorship power, "enjoyed censorship power which was tantamount to direct legal force, although this was energetically denied by the Committee during the war."[99]

Conscientious objectors were often the object of derision, even from ministers, who according to Sproule often allowed their congregations to "heap condemnation upon conscientious objectors."[100] One of the great heroes of the war, Sgt. Alvin York, who won the Medal of Honor, initially registered as a conscientious objector.[101] Making someone who initially opposed the war into a hero enhanced the narrative that all patriots should support the war, even those with religious objections.

THE LEGACY OF THE GREAT WAR

The story of the Great War and the U.S. role in it shaped the American views on involvement in the world, particularly European nations, for the next two decades. A key factor in the story was that the United States had saved democracy from the tyranny of the Germans and their allies. How accurate was this interpretation? How much difference did America make to the war effort? By the end of its first year of involvement, less than 200,000 American troops were on the continent.[102] Nevertheless, America's brief foray into the war was decisive. Kazin writes, "In the end, it was the ever-increasing number of American soldiers, as much as the intense combat they waged, that made the difference. . . . 50,280 Americans lost their lives in combat."[103]

One might think America's role as the savior of democracy would encourage future such endeavors, but the result was quite the opposite. Wilson's League of Nations, which was the key to his goal of making the Great War the "War to End All Wars," was ineffectual, especially because the United States did not become a member. Also, Wilson's hope for fair treatment of colonies and of a peace not built on retribution was abandoned. At Versailles, Wilson acquiesced to punishing treatment of the Central Powers, while Britain and France kept their colonies. As Kazin puts it, "The 'Wilsonian moment' soon passed."[104] He adds, "[T]he way the Great War ended touched off nearly thirty years of genocide, massacres, and armed conflict between and within nations."[105] Eric Hobsbawm, refers to the period between 1914 and the end of the World War II as "An Age of Catastrophe."[106] John Keegan claims, "The Second World War was the continuation of the First, and indeed it is inexplicable except in terms of the rancours and instabilities left by the earlier conflict."[107]

Most Americans eventually came to believe that the Great War had been a mistake. Of course, no polls exist to demonstrate whether or not the public fully supported the war in the first place. However, Gallup found that by 1937, 70 percent of respondents believed it had been a mistake for the United States to enter the war.[108] According to Michael Beschloss, "Asked by the Gallup Poll why the U.S. had entered World War I, people replied most frequently that their country had been 'the victim of propaganda and selfish interests.'"[109] Brewer notes, "In the 1920s, investigations exposed much of the wartime atrocity propaganda as fabrication, leaving many convinced that propaganda meant lies."[110] It is little wonder that 73 percent supported a constitutional amendment that would have prohibited the nation from entering a war without a national referendum, unless it was attacked.[111] A May 1941 poll showed 80 percent opposed to the United States voluntarily joining the World War II.[112] As we will see in the next chapter, the story of how the United States had been sucked into a costly and unnecessary European conflict seriously constrained what Franklin Roosevelt could do to aid the democracies of Europe as World War II raged. It further constrained his 1940 re-election campaign. It took Pearl Harbor to get the United States into the next war. Eventually, World War II became the archetypical narrative—the good war fought by the greatest generation—while World War I receded into the fog of collective memory.

The story of World War I and how the United States became involved is one of the more puzzling in history. Tyler Cowen writes: "If you don't quite follow how a single assassination, which was not even seen as so important the day it occurred, triggered the death of so many millions, and the destruction of so much of Europe, that is exactly the point."[113] As German Chancellor Otto von Bismarck prophetically stated, "You know where a war begins but you never know where it ends."[114]

In addition, the Great War's effects remain to this day. Kazin writes in the *New Republic* that the war

> initiated thirty years of bloodletting on an unprecedented scale and planted the seeds for civil conflicts that continue to rage today. Witness the fate of the Sykes-Picot Treaty, the secret pact drawn up in 1916 by diplomats from Britain and France that mashed together Shiites, Sunnis, and Kurds in a new nation called Iraq.[115]

Decisions made over a century ago in secret, which ignored religious and ethnic divisions, have turned the Middle East into a constant source of conflict.

ASSESSING THE NARRATIVE

The first question to ask is if the stories told to justify United States entry into World War I had narrative *probability*. Consider first, *characterological coherence*. Who are the key characters and how did they act? The villains are clear—the Prussians and their leader, the Beast of Berlin, not the German people themselves. The British dominated the propaganda that reached the United States, thanks to the cutting of the Atlantic cable. Thus, atrocity stories were widely circulated, transporting Americans to the battlefield seen from only one point of view. Recall the Four-Minute Man speech that stressed that the German soldiers were forced to commit horrific acts. Naming the enemy as Prussian, not German, and the use of the term "Hun" were both designed to demonize the enemy, while distinguishing him from the average German, in a nod to the large German-American population.

The *structural coherence* of the story was again dominated by British propaganda. The acts of the German U-boats fit the narrative perfectly and reinforced the evil character of the German government. Newspaper reports of the sinking of the *Lusitania* vividly transported readers to the awful scene of carnage. This was a key event that paved the way for seeing the Kaiser and his military leaders as "beasts." Once unlimited U-boat activity resumed, the prior acts of sinking civilian ships created a situation that could only lead to more loss of innocent life. Finally, the *material coherence* of the story was enhanced when the Zimmerman telegram provided the final proof of the Kaiser's duplicity. Overall, the case for war was presented as a coherent narrative.

Assessing the *fidelity* of the narrative was almost impossible for Americans due to wartime censorship and the cutting of the Atlantic cable. The public was hampered by the absence of a counternarrative, largely as a result of both overt and self-censorship. The threat of prison and the actual imprisonment of men like Debs left the public with no real alternative to Wilson's narrative. Lacking reliable public opinion polling during the time of the war, it is difficult to know whether the public largely believed the dominant narrative or was simply unable to express its discontent. One indication of an undercurrent of opposition is the surprising finding that there was more resistance to the draft in World War I than in Vietnam. After the war, when the truth became known about the lack of *factual fidelity* of the Bryce Report, the result was to stigmatize propaganda for years to come. Thus, although the factual inaccuracy of the propaganda unleashed during World War I was concealed until after the war, it nevertheless impacted the nation two decades later when Europe again erupted in war.

One of Wilson's biggest challenges in terms of fidelity was dealing with the issue of *narrative consistency*. Having run on a peace platform, Wilson was surprisingly successful in pivoting to a war narrative. To do so, he stressed that American motives were pure—we sought no territorial conquest as had occurred in the Philippines and Puerto Rico. One key argument that likely did have fidelity was that due to German submarine warfare, we were already at war. Wilson was only declaring what already was.

To complete the pivot from the man who kept us out of war to a wartime president, Wilson needed to appeal to *transcendental issues*. Having been a peace candidate, he reframed the conflict as "the war to end war." He also appealed to what is the fundamental core of American values—democracy. The U.S. entry was making the world safe for democracy. Clearly, these were issues that would resonate, even with those who initially opposed the war. As with the tests of fact, however, the fidelity of the Wilsonian narrative crumbled in the face of postwar events. The *consequence* of his failure to achieve his goals at the Paris conference helped sow the seeds for opposition to engaging in the next world war. In time, most Americans felt they had been duped by propaganda into entering the war, which left Franklin Roosevelt hamstrung in his attempts to aid Britain. Allowing colonies to remain in the hands of their European masters gave lie to the promise of Wilson's Fourteen Points, which had stressed self-determination for all peoples, including those in European colonies. Ho Chi Minh (then known as Nguyễn Ái Quốc) was a young man living in Paris during the Paris Peace Conference in 1919.[116] He brought a petition asking for autonomy, not full independence, but no one from the victorious Allied powers, including the United States would meet him.[117] The consequence of that failure would not be clear until a half century later in Indochina.

What can we conclude about the narrative spun about World War I? First, Wilson may well have been disingenuous in his re-election campaign, as indicated by his confession to Tumulty. Although World War I was portrayed as thrust upon us, it is likely that the United States would have eventually been drawn in due its continued support of the Allies. Because of censorship and the lack of scientific public opinion polls at the time, we will never know if the propaganda campaign really convinced most Americans of the war's necessity. But there are certainly indications, such as the draft refusal rate, that the war was not as widely approved of as Wilson might have claimed. Most significantly, the postwar revelations of the flaws in narrative fidelity created a public suspicious of prowar propaganda preceding Pearl Harbor. Had the United States not been attacked, one suspects that Roosevelt would have had a very hard time selling the public and Congress on joining that war.

NOTES

1. Robert K. Massie, *Dreadnought: Britain, Germany, and the Coming of the Great War* (New York: Ballantine Books, 1991), 106.
2. Barbara Tuchman, *The Guns of August* (New York: MacMillan, 1962), 2.
3. Massie, *Dreadnought*, 258–259.
4. Massie, *Dreadnought*, 303.
5. Tuchman, *The Guns*, 5.
6. Massie, *Dreadnought*.

7. Massie, *Dreadnought*, 844–845, cites German Ambassador Lichnowsky relaying an eerily accurate prediction of how this would occur: "Sir Edward Grey said that he wished above all that there might be no repetition of . . . 1909 [i.e. the Bosnian Crisis]," the Ambassador reported on the eve of the London Conference.

> For he was convinced—and this sentence he twice repeated with special emphasis—that Russia would not a second time beat a retreat but would rather take up arms. . . . If a European war were to arise through Austria's attacking Serbia, and Russia, compelled by public opinion, were to march . . . rather than again put up with a humiliation like that of 1909, thus forcing Germany to come to the aid of Austria, France would inevitably be drawn in *and no one could foretell what further developments might follow* [emphasis Lichinowsky's]. Brackets supplied by Massie.

8. Tuchman, *The Guns*, 17.
9. Tuchman, *The Guns*, 18.
10. Richard Preston, "First World War Centenary: The Assassination of Franz Ferdinand, As It Happened," *Telegraph*, June 27, 2014, https://www.telegraph.co.uk/history/world-war-one/10930863/First-World-War-centenary-the-assassination-of-Franz-Ferdinand-as-it-happened.html.
11. Preston, "First World War."
12. Massie, *Dreadnought*, 858–859.
13. Massie, *Dreadnought*, 859.
14. Tuchman, *The Guns*, 71.
15. Michael Kazin, "Five Myths About World War I," *Washington Post*, April 6, 2017, https://www.washingtonpost.com/opinions/2017/04/06/06a8bcae-1597-11e7-9e4f-09aa75d3ec57_story.html?utm_term=.03a04afe0839.
16. Quoted in Massie, *Dreadnought*, 426.
17. Michael Kazin, *War Against War: The American Fight for Peace, 1914–1918* (New York: Simon & Schuster, 2017), [page] xiv, Kindle.
18. Woodrow Wilson, "Message to Congress, 63rd Cong., 2d Sess., Senate Doc. No. 566," August 19, 1914, 3–4, accessed February 23, 2020, https://wwi.lib.byu.edu/index.php/President_Wilson%27s_Declaration_of_Neutrality.
19. Kazin, *War Against War*, 22.
20. Kazin, *War Against War*, 38.
21. "The Great War," Part I, PBS, July 3, 2018, [Transcript], https://www.pbs.org/wgbh/americanexperience/films/great-war/#transcript.
22. Geoffrey Wheatcroft, "The War to End All Wars: The Ardent But Flawed Movement Against World War I," *Nation*, October 5, 2017, https://www.thenation.com/article/the-war-to-end-all-wars/.
23. Andrew Lambert, "Jutland: Why World War I's Only Sea Battle Was So Crucial to Britain's Victory," *The Conversation*, May 27, 2016, http://theconversation.com/jutland-why-world-war-is-only-sea-battle-was-so-crucial-to-britains-victory-59415.
24. Daniel Immerwahr, *How to Hide an Empire: A History of the Greater United States* (New York: Farrar Straus & Giroux, 2019), loc. 4872 of 10589, Kindle.

25. J. Michael Sproule, *Propaganda and Democracy: The American Experience of Mass Media and Mass Persuasion* (New York: Cambridge University Press, 1997), 6.

26. Phillip Knightley, *The First Casualty: The War Correspondent as Hero and Myth-Maker from the Crimea to Iraq*, 3rd ed. (Baltimore and London: John Hopkins University Press, 2004), 88.

27. Sproule, *Propaganda*, 8.

28. Sproule, *Propaganda*, 8.

29. Knightley, *The First Casualty*, 88.

30. Knightley, *The First Casualty*, 89.

31. Knightley, *The First Casualty*, 129.

32. Kazin, *War Against War*, 59.

33. Arthur Stanley Link, *Wilson: The Struggle for Neutrality, Vol. 3* (Princeton, NJ: Princeton University Press, 1947), 373, https://hdl-handle-net.mantis.csuchico.edu/2027/heb.01547, EPUB.

34. Kazin, *War Against War*, 105.

35. Woodrow Wilson, "Message Regarding German Actions," April 19, 2016, accessed February 27, 2020, https://millercenter.org/the-presidency/presidential-speeches/april-19-1916-message-regarding-german-actions.

36. Kazin, *War Against War*, 108.

37. Kazin, *War Against War*, 112.

38. Charles G. Cogan, "He Kept Us Out of War," *The World Post* [Huffington Post], Updated November 15, 2013, https://www.huffingtonpost.com/dr-charles-g-cogan/he-kept-us-out-of-war_b_3931495.html.

39. Kazin, *War Against War*, 114.

40. Kazin, *War Against War*, 117.

41. A. Scott Berg, *Wilson* (New York, G. P. Putnam's Sons, 2013), 438. Joseph Patrick Tumulty was Wilson's Secretary, essentially his Chief of Staff.

42. Kazin, *War Against War*, 133.

43. "Election of 1916: Now Just Two Parties, But Same Results as 1912," United States History, accessed December 7, 2018, https://www.u-s-history.com/pages/h888.html.

44. Woodrow Wilson, "Address of the President of the United States to the Senate," January 22, 1917, accessed February 23, 2020, https://wwi.lib.byu.edu/index.php?title=Address_of_the_President_of_the_United_States_to_the_Senate&oldid=8374.

45. Lorraine Boissoneault, "What Did President Wilson Mean When He Called for 'Peace Without Victory' 100 Years Ago?" Smithsonian.com, January 23, 2017, https://www.smithsonianmag.com/history/what-did-president-wilson-mean-when-he-called-peace-without-victory-100-years-ago-180961888/.

46. Kazin, *War Against War*, 144.

47. Berg, *Wilson*, 423.

48. Woodrow Wilson, "President Wilson's Address to Both Houses of Congress in Joint Session," February 3, 1917, accessed February 23, 2020, https://wwi.lib.byu.edu/index.php/President_Wilson%27s_Address_to_Both_Houses_of_Congress_in_Joint_Session,_February_3,_1917.

49. Kazin, *War Against War*, 147.
50. Woodrow Wilson, "Message Regarding Safety of Merchant Ships," February 26, 1917, UVA Miller Center, accessed February 26, 2020, https://millercenter.org/the-presidency/presidential-speeches/february-26-1917-message-regarding-safety-merchant-ships.
51. Kazin, *War Against War*, 171.
52. Kazin, *War Against War*, 171.
53. Berg, *Wilson*, 425.
54. Quoted in Kazin, *War Against War*, 164.
55. Woodrow Wilson, "Second Inaugural Address," March 5, 1917, UVA Miller Center, accessed February 26, 2020, https://millercenter.org/the-presidency/presidential-speeches/march-5-1917-second-inaugural-address.
56. Kazin, *War Against War*, 172.
57. Kazin, *War Against War*, 174.
58. Kazin, *War Against War*, 173.
59. Woodrow Wilson, "War Message to Congress," April 2, 1917, aaccessed December 1, 2019, https://wwi.lib.byu.edu/index.php/Wilson's_War_Message_to_Congress. All quotations from the speech are from this source.
60. Susan A. Brewer, *Why America Fights: Patriotism and War Propaganda from the Philippines to Iraq* (New York: Oxford University Press, 2009), 47.
61. Tuchman, *The Guns*, 7.
62. Wilson, "War Message."
63. Wilson, "War Message."
64. Kazin, *War Against War*, 182–183.
65. Kazin, *War Against War*, 185.
66. Woodrow Wilson, "President Wilson's Fourteen Points," January 9, 1918, accessed February 27, 2020, https://wwi.lib.byu.edu/index.php/President_Wilson%27s_Fourteen_Points.
67. James R. Mock and Cedric Larson, *Words that Won the War: The Story of The Committee on Public Information 1917–1919* (Princeton: Princeton University Press, 1939), 4, http://www.archive.org/details/wordsthatwonwars00mockrich.
68. Mock and Larson, *Words that Won the War*, 10.
69. Mock and Larson, *Words that Won the War*, ix.
70. Harold D. Lasswell, "The Theory of Political Propaganda," *The American Political Science Review* 21, no. 3 (August, 1927): 627, https://www.jstor.org/stable/1945515.
71. Mock and Larson, *Words that Won the War*, 65.
72. Brewer, *Why America Fights*, 10.
73. Mock and Larson, *Words that Won the War*, 68–73.
74. Mock and Larson, *Words that Won the War,* 73–74.
75. Kazin, *War Against War*, 188.
76. Mock and Larson, *Words that Won the War*, 125.
77. Brewer, *Why America Fights*, 63.
78. Mock and Larson, *Words that Won the War*, 125.
79. Mock and Larson, *Words that Won the War*, 123.

80. Kazin, *War Against War*, 260.
81. Mock and Larson, *Words that Won the War*, 78.
82. Mock and Larson, *Words that Won the War*, 81.
83. Mock and Larson, *Words that Won the War*, 88.
84. Mock and Larson, *Words that Won the War*, 89.
85. Mock and Larson, *Words that Won the War*, 90.
86. Berg, *Wilson*, 452.
87. Sproule, *Propaganda and Democracy*, 10.
88. Berg, *Wilson*, 451–452.
89. Kazin, *War Against War*, xv.
90. Kazin, *War Against War*, 205.
91. Kazin, *War Against War*, xviii.
92. Kazin, *War Against War*, 223.
93. John Keegan, *The First World War* (New York: Vintage, 2012), 373.
94. Kazin, *War Against War*, 208–209.
95. Kazin, *War Against War*, 245.
96. Kazin, *War Against War*, 246.
97. Sproule, *Propaganda and Democracy*, 1–2.
98. Mock and Larson, *Words that Won the War*, 147–148.
99. Mock and Larson, *Words that Won the War*, 20.
100. Sproule, *Propaganda and Democracy*, 12.
101. Kazin, *War Against War*, 266.
102. Kazin, *War Against War*, 260.
103. Kazin, *War Against War*, 262.
104. Kazin, *War Against War*, 276.
105. Kazin, *War Against War*, xv.
106. Eric Hobsbawm, *Age of Extremes: The Short Twentieth Century 1914–1991* (London: Abacus, 1994, 1995), 6, http://libcom.org/files/Eric%20Hobsbawm%20-%20Age%20Of%20Extremes%20-%201914-1991.pdf.
107. Keegan, *The First World War*, 423.
108. Kazin, *War Against War*, 280.
109. Michael Beschloss, *Presidential Courage: Brave Leaders and How They Changed America 1789–1989* (New York: Simon & Schuster, 2007), 158.
110. Brewer, *Why America Fights*, 85.
111. Beschloss, *Presidential Courage*, 158.
112. Clive Ponting, *1940: Myth and Reality* (Chicago: Ivan R. Dee, Inc., 1990), 198.
113. Tyler Cowen [Bloomberg], "Middle East Resembles the Situation before World War I," *Japan Times,* April 16, 2018, accessed April 16, 2018, https://www.japantimes.co.jp/opinion/2018/04/16/commentary/world-commentary/middle-east-resembles-situation-world-war/#.WtUqldPwaRs.
114. Quoted in Massie, *Dreadnought*, 76.
115. Michael Kazin, "If the U.S. Had Not Entered World War I, Would There Have Been a World War II?" *New Republic*, July 6, 2014, https://newrepublic.com/article/118435/world-war-i-debate-should-us-have-entered.

116. Maggie Bria, "What Did the 1919 Paris Peace Conference Have to Do with the Vietnam War?" Bria Historica, March 30, 2017 and June 4, 2018, accessed June 3, 2020, https://briahistorica.com/2017/03/30/what-did-the-1919-paris-peace-conference-have-to-do-with-the-vietnam-war/.

117. Neil Sheehan, *A Bright Shining Lie: John Paul Vann and America in Vietnam* (New York: Random House, 1988, Modern Library, 2009), [page] 147, Kindle.

Chapter 5

World War II
The Survival War

It was 7:53 a.m. on a Sunday morning on the Hawaiian island of Oahu. Moored in the harbor were 130 vessels of the U.S. Seventh fleet, including ninety-six warships, eight of which were battleships, seven lined up on Battleship Row.[1] Without warning, 420 Japanese planes from six aircraft carriers some 230 miles offshore attacked the vulnerable fleet.[2] Marine Corporal E. C. Nightingale described what happened that morning on the *Arizona*: "At approximately eight o'clock on the morning of December 7, 1941, I was leaving the breakfast table when the ship's siren for air defense sounded. Having no anti-aircraft battle station, I paid little attention to it. Suddenly I heard an explosion." Soon he was on deck and "saw Second Lieutenant Simonson lying on his back with blood on his shirt front. I bent over him and taking him by the shoulders asked if there was anything I could do. "Nightengale realized, " he was dead, or so nearly so that speech was impossible. Seeing there was nothing I could do for the Lieutenant, I continued to my battle station." As Corporal Nightingale finally left the doomed ship, he described the scene: "The bodies of the dead were thick, and badly burned men were heading for the quarterdeck, only to fall apparently dead or badly wounded." Ultimately he found himself in the water and eventually made it to shore, surviving to tell the tale of that horrible day.[3] The attack was devastating—2,403 dead, 188 destroyed planes, and 8 damaged or destroyed battleships.[4] The *Arizona* sank to the bottom never to be raised again and became a permanent memorial. Those who have visited it cannot help but be transported back to that terrible Sunday in 1941.

The story of how America was drawn into World War II is about far more than just the attack on Pearl Harbor, which brought a reluctant America into the worldwide conflagration. Just over two decades after the "War to End All Wars" the nations of Europe and the Far East were drawn into another World War. By the late 1930s, the bulk of Americans believed that the Great

War had been a mistake.[5] The United States once again claimed neutrality. As Franklin Delano Roosevelt sought an unprecedented third term in office, he was careful to stress his opposition to involvement in the war, short of an attack on the United States.

Perhaps the seminal moment in the run-up to World War II was the agreement signed by British prime minister Neville Chamberlain at Munich on September 30, 1938. After handing over part of Czechoslovakia to Hitler, Chamberlain declared that they had achieved "peace in our time."[6] U.S. Ambassador Joseph Kennedy was a supporter of Chamberlain and the Munich Pact and tried to persuade Roosevelt to keep the United States out of Europe's war.[7] Unfortunately, "peace in our time" was short-lived. Germany invaded Poland in September of 1939, engulfing Europe in its second major war in just over two decades. Thus, the narrative became an article of faith—appeasing a dictator like Hitler only emboldened him to pursue even more aggression.

1940 PRESIDENTIAL CAMPAIGN

With Europe and the Far East at war, the question of U.S. involvement was one of the defining issues of the 1940 election. Roosevelt was mindful of how Wilson had run for re-election on the slogan, "He kept us out of war," and then only a few weeks after taking the oath of office asked Congress for a Declaration of War. American public opinion was running strongly against getting involved in another world war, and thus Roosevelt knew he needed to convince Americans he was not planning to do what Wilson had done.

Because of this concern, the Democratic Party Platform specifically promised that the United States would not get involved in foreign wars, *except in case of attack*, a condition Roosevelt added. As he pointed out, "If someone attacks us, it isn't a foreign war, is it?"[8] In the last week of the campaign, Roosevelt pledged, "I have said this before, but I shall say it again and again and again: *Your boys are not going to be sent into any foreign wars!*"[9] In fact, in a subsequent speech, he made an even bolder claim, "Your President says this country is not going to war."[10] That, of course, was a pledge he could not keep. Roosevelt won the popular vote by 54.7 percent to Willkie's 44.8 percent and enjoyed an Electoral College landslide of 449 to 82.[11] The popularity of his anti-intervention rhetoric was evident in a Gallup poll taken shortly after his re-election. Eighty-eight percent indicated that they would vote in a national referendum to stay out of war.[12]

Although publicly proclaiming that the United States would stay out of the war in Europe, Roosevelt was aiding Great Britain. In fact, in 1939 he began secretly corresponding with Winston Churchill, who was not yet prime minister, but whom he knew from his time as assistant secretary of the Navy during the Great War.[13] Despite much public opposition, once the war in Europe began, Roosevelt used a variety of methods, such as Lend-Lease, to aid the allies. Roosevelt explained the program in terms everyone could understand—what to do if a neighbor's house was on fire. He wouldn't say, "My garden hose cost me fifteen dollars; you have to pay me fifteen dollars for it." Rather, he would "want my garden hose back after the fire is over."[14] The president even met with Churchill prior to the U.S. entry into the war.[15]

At the same time that Roosevelt was promising to keep America out of the war in Europe, Great Britain was engaged in an extensive propaganda campaign to change America's predominately isolationist public opinion. Nicholas Cull writes, "From the eve of the German invasion of Poland to the moment of Japan's attack on Pearl Harbor, the British government mounted a concerted effort to draw the United States into the war."[16] Cull concludes that British propaganda was eventually successful in shifting American public opinion. Although Roosevelt had to restrain his pro-British inclinations prior to the 1940 election, he used his bully pulpit to build support for the British cause. However, Cull reports, "Roosevelt remained a prisoner of American public and Congressional opinion."[17] Even a U-boat sinking an American destroyer on October 31, 1941, was not sufficient to propel America into a war as happened in 1917.[18]

Japan presented a different problem. Until July of 1939, the main source of Japanese war materials was the United States.[19] Roosevelt became concerned about the threat Japan posed to the colonial possessions of the British, French, and Dutch, and thus imposed a severe embargo, banning oil, gas, iron, and steel exports, which the Japanese badly needed.[20] Although the Japanese were engaged in negotiations with the United States, they were preparing their surprise attack. Roosevelt was not unaware of this danger. Secretary of War Henry Stimson recorded in his diary that the president knew that "the Japanese are notorious for attacking without warning," and the task was "how to maneuver them into firing the first shot without too much danger to ourselves."[21] Of course, the attack on Pearl Harbor proved far more disastrous than could have been foreseen.

The United States knew Japan might well launch a surprise attack, but its leaders assumed it would be on Philippines. As Michael E. Ruane writes on the seventy-seventh anniversary of the attack:

> Tensions between Japan and the United States were at the boiling point. The United States suspected that the Japanese were up to something, but it didn't know what or where. It looked as if an attack could come in the area of the Philippines.[22]

Later conspiracy theories developed, implying that the United States knew that the attack on Pearl Harbor was coming, but allowed it to happen to justify going to war with Japan. An extensive investigation by the judge advocate debunked the theory. In fact, the clustering of planes and ships at Pearl Harbor was designed to thwart sabotage, which was viewed as the more likely threat.[23]

"A DATE WHICH WILL LIVE IN INFAMY"

The day after the attack on Pearl Harbor, Roosevelt laid out the case for a Declaration of War against Japan. He began quite directly: "Yesterday, December 7, 1941—a date which will live in infamy—the United States of America was suddenly and deliberately attacked by naval and air forces of the Empire of Japan."[24] It is noteworthy that Roosevelt changed the original text from "world history" to "infamy."[25] Roosevelt clearly understood the importance of capturing the emotional impact of the sudden attack from the *Empire* of Japan.

After describing how the United States had been in peace talks with Japan as it was obviously preparing its attack, he acknowledged the severe damage and loss of lives from the attack and suggested a pattern of attacks that could threaten the continental United States. He noted that there had been reported torpedo attacks on U.S. ships between Hawaii and San Francisco. To reinforce the threat, he listed one after another the places Japan had attacked, transporting the audience to the scene of Japanese aggression:

> Yesterday the Japanese government also launched an attack against Malaya.
> Last night Japanese forces attacked Hong Kong.
> Last night Japanese forces attacked Guam.
> Last night Japanese forces attacked the Philippine Islands.
> Last night the Japanese attacked Wake Island.
> This morning the Japanese attacked Midway Island.[26]

Rather than merely listing each victim of Japanese attacks, he used a parallel construction focusing on how they had *attacked* each and every location. Finally, after expressing a resolute commitment to defeat the enemy and gain "absolute victory," Roosevelt invoked much the same language as did Wilson—emphasizing that a state of war already existed and that he was asking Congress not to initiate a war, but to recognize that one already existed: "I ask that the Congress declare that since the unprovoked and dastardly attack by Japan on Sunday, December 7, a state of war has existed between the United States and the Japanese Empire." The use of the adjective "dastardly" carried a strong connotation of the evil intent of the Japanese "empire," which was in stark contrast to the American democracy that was living peacefully.

Unlike Wilson, he failed to distinguish between the government of the enemy and its people. Hermann Stelzner points out, "Roosevelt's treatment of the Japanese *people* is quite different from Wilson's treatment of the German *people*."[27] Wilson went to great pains to point out they were not the enemy; Roosevelt made no such effort. This is likely because, although Americans of German descent were widespread in the United States in 1917, in 1941, there were few Japanese Americans, who were mostly clustered on the west coast. The blurring of the lines between the enemy of Japan and Japanese people helped set the stage for one of the most shameful chapters in American history, the internment of Americans of Japanese ancestry, including those born into citizenship.

Missing from the speech were references to the other Axis powers— Germany and Italy. However, three days later Hitler and Mussolini relieved Roosevelt of the need to initiate action against them. They declared war on the United States on December 11. Declarations of war against Germany and Italy passed without debate, with only one dissenting vote.[28]

The reaction of the American people was overwhelmingly supportive of the president and U.S. entry into the war. A Gallup poll "taken following the bombing showed an unprecedented 97 [percent] support for war. Not even the 9/11 attacks 60 years later produced such unanimity (support for the so-called War on Terror peaked early at 89 percent)."[29] Another Gallup poll in early 1942 showed 84 percent approving of FDR's performance compared to only 9 percent disapproving.[30]

Although history has come to know the conflict as World War II, Roosevelt sought to give it a new name that would not echo Wilson's war. He proposed calling it "the Survival War." He declared in the spring of 1942, "That is what it comes pretty close to being—the survival of our civilization."[31] Kenneth Burke has argued, "naming" is one of the most powerful tools a rhetorician possesses.[32] Thus, to name this war the "Survival War," would give it gravity far beyond previous wars.

OFFICIAL WAR INFORMATION (PROPAGANDA)

Unlike many other American wars, World War II didn't require a major effort to persuade Americans initially to support the war. After all, the nation had been subjected to a dastardly surprise attack. Japan's allies then declared war on the United States. So unlike the sinking of the *Maine* or U-boat attacks on the high seas, the importance of winning was clear. Even if the name didn't stick, it was in fact a war for survival.

As with World War I, a department was created to carry out war propaganda. It was named the Office of War Information, propaganda having acquired a decidedly negative connotation. As Becky Little reports:

> The United States was about six months into World War II when it founded the Office of War Information (OWI). Its mission: to disseminate political propaganda. The office spread its messages through print, radio, and film—but perhaps its most striking legacy is its posters. With bright colors and sensational language, they encouraged Americans to ration their food, buy war bonds, and basically perform everyday tasks in support of the war effort.[33]

One of the most famous posters, which emphasized the importance of the contributions of women to the war effort, showed an iconic image that came to be known as "Rosie the Riveter" (see figure 5.1.).

Although the posters may have been ubiquitous, it is the use of film and radio that distinguishes World War II from earlier conflicts. Films had played a limited role in World War I, but by the onset of the next war, they were a dominant part of American life. Some 60 million Americans went to the movies every week.[34] Radio also played an important role, including the fireside chats of President Roosevelt.

The most obvious use of film was in direct propaganda. Frank Capra's *Why We Fight* series was the most notable effort. Mark Harris called it "the single most important filmed propaganda of the war."[35] However, as pointed out in chapter 1, the series fell short of the Pentagon's objectives. The films did increase viewers' knowledge, but served mostly to reinforce already existing attitudes. One surprising finding was that as time passed after viewing the films, viewers' attitudes began to change, a phenomenon that came to be known as the sleeper effect.[36] With most Americans already supportive of the war, reinforcing existing attitudes and increasing information were useful to the war effort.

In an interview with Bill Moyers, Capra explained the purpose of the first part of the series, *Prelude to War*:

> My specific aim was to show the difference between our method of living, our thinking about our families and so forth, and the enemy's. The enemy was out to destroy, destroy anybody they didn't agree with. We were trying to mind our business over here, send our kids to school. And we weren't thinking of any war. We don't want any part of any war. That's where we were.[37]

Capra insisted the writers of the narration for the episodes should make them "clear enough for a child to understand."[38] After seeing German propaganda films such as Leni Riefenstahl's *Triumph of the Will*, Capra hit on the idea to

Figure 5.1 This poster, which came to be known as "Rosie the Riveter," was part of a campaign to encourage women to take part in the war effort. *Source*: Poster created by the War Production Co-ordinating Committee of the United States. Image courtesy of World Digital Library, Library of Congress.

use their own propaganda films against them. "Let's let them [the American soldiers] see only their stuff. We make nothing. We shoot nothing. But we use their own stuff as propaganda for ourselves. Let them see. Let them see the guys. Let them see these guys."[39] Although the seven-part series was originally intended just for American troops, it was eventually shown to civilians in theaters as well. It has been described as a masterpiece.[40] Despite the unity of Americans after Pearl Harbor, the government realized that prior to the attack, support for American involvement was slim, as revealed in a Gallup poll released just before Pearl Harbor, showing that only 52 percent thought U.S. war with the Axis was inevitable.[41] The seven individual episodes each dealt with distinct topics. The first, *Prelude to War*, presented the war's origins. Later episodes dealt with specific topics, including the rise of the Nazis, the fall of Poland and France, and so on. By the end of the war in Europe, over fifty-four million Americans had seen the series.[42]

Although Capra supposedly just wanted to "tell the truth," there were notable instances of racism, especially in dealing with the Japanese. According to John Dower, in Capra's 1945 installment *Know Your Enemy—Japan*, "The audience was told that the Japanese resembled 'photographic reprints off the same negative.' Visually, this was reinforced by repeated scenes of a steel bar hammered by a forge." The film also "provided ample scenes of regimented activity that confirmed the impression of a race lacking in any individual identity."[43] The negative portrayal of the Japanese as a race, as opposed to the focus on European enemy leaders Hitler and Mussolini, is significant in understanding the treatment of Japanese Americans.

THE WAR CORRESPONDENT

Phillip Knightley's comprehensive study of war correspondents from the Crimean War through Operation Iraqi Freedom, reveals that in World War II, reporters were essentially on the same team as the military. As Supreme Allied Commander Dwight Eisenhower said famously, "Public opinion wins wars."[44] Although subject to censorship, American reporters were patriotic and unlikely to submit stories that undermined the war effort. In some cases, reporters even took part in military actions. Many carried weapons, and several were awarded medals, including a Silver Star to AP reporter, Vernon Haughland. Another, Marguerite Higgins, helped liberate Dachau. Leonard Mosley actually dropped behind German lines by parachute.[45] Thus, it is fair to say that reporters were actually part of the military's propaganda machine. As Canadian reporter, Charles Lynch said, "We were a propaganda arm of our governments. . . . by the end we were our own censors. We were cheerleaders."[46]

In fact, it is possible that censorship actually improved reporter's access to what was really happening in the war. Drew Middleton, who was a correspondent in both World War II and Vietnam told Knightley,

> As long as all copy was submitted to censors . . . people in the field, from generals down, felt free to discuss top secret material with reporters. On three trips to Vietnam I found generals and everyone else far more wary of talking to reporters precisely because there was no censorship.[47]

One aspect of reporting that created a paradox was when the true extent of German atrocities was revealed after the liberation of concentration camps. Although there had been reports of Germans killing large numbers of Jews as early as 1942, these stories tended to not be believed because the World War I propaganda about the Huns and their atrocities turned out to be false. Knightley writes, "The disastrous effect of the Allied atrocity propaganda of the First World War was now fully realised."[48] Even the revered Edward R. Murrow was forced to confront skepticism about Nazi horrors as he attempted to transport his audience over the radio, pleading with them "to believe what I have said about Buchenwald."[49]

POPULAR MOVIES

Hollywood was sympathetic to the allies, even before Pearl Harbor. Prior to the war, Hollywood had produced numerous films that portrayed the Germans and Japanese as potential enemies. Among the films were *Confessions of a Nazi Spy*, *Beast of Berlin*, and *The Great Dictator*, Chaplin's satirical portrayal of Hitler. Robert Fyne writes, "So in the broadest terms, December 7 did not surprise most Hollywood producers. . . . By war's end, this high-powered industry . . . delivered approximately four hundred motion pictures that in one form or another were outright propaganda films."[50]

Many of the commercial films were demonstrably war films, such as *Guadalcanal Diary*, *Thirty Seconds Over Tokyo*, and *Flying Tigers*.[51] There were also films that on the surface were not war propaganda, but subtly reinforced the more explicit propaganda with their stories. One example is the iconic love story told in *Casablanca*, set in the days just before Pearl Harbor, and based on a play by Murray Bennett and Joan Alison. Although many might regard the movie as just a love story, it actually had a clear anti-Nazi message. As do Robert Fyne and J. Michael Sproule, I consider the film a skillfully crafted example of propaganda.[52] Apparently the playwright did as well. The *New York Times* wrote, "Mr. Burnett went to German-occupied Vienna in the summer of 1938 to help Jewish relatives smuggle out money. He returned to the United States with the idea for an anti-Nazi play."[53] The movie vividly transports the audience back to a world before Pearl Harbor, when many did not take the Nazi threat seriously.

In the movie, Rick makes a statement that, while literally true (given the time difference between Casablanca and New York), also speaks to the state of America just before Pearl Harbor. He says, "I'd bet they're asleep in New York. I'd bet they're asleep all over America." And at one point, resistance leader Victor Laszlo sums up why the Nazis cannot succeed: "What if you killed all of us? From every corner of Europe, hundreds, thousands would rise up to take our places. Even Nazis can't kill that fast." Finally, consider the words Rick speaks to Ilsa as she is about to board the plane out of Casablanca with Laszlo, "It doesn't take much to see that the problems of three little people don't amount to a hill of beans in this crazy world."[54] The story of Rick's sacrifice of his beloved Ilsa would likely have resonated with the girlfriend, wife, mother, or sister at home, thinking of her own loved one who might never come back from war.

Popular American movies were harsher in their portrayal of the Japanese enemy than the Germans. Fyne writes:

> Hollywood portrayed the Japanese foes as sadistic, inhuman, bestial animals, a nation of fanatics lacking compassion, dignity, or decency, happy to kill American prisoners of war, torture civilian workers, or rape captured nurses. Frequently called monkeys, rodents, rats, or snakes, these Orientals—like the epithets used to describe them—required immediate extermination. For the German enemy, however, different criteria prevailed. . . . This European foe, for the most part, resembled a clown, buffoon, or simpleton.[55]

After the war, Hollywood produced a plethora of movies about the war, which came to define the story of World War II. In the years immediately following the war, films such as 1949's *Sands of Iwo Jima* inspired the nation.[56] By the time of the stalemated Korean War, Hollywood harkened back to the glory days of World War II. Fyne notes,

> With its January 1953 opening date—a time when many Americans feared the Korean War could escalate into a deadly conflagration with the Soviet Union—*Above and Beyond* reaffirmed the popular 1941 propaganda song's slogan, "We Did It Before and We Can Do It Again."[57]

From the mid-1950s to the late 1960s, "Hollywood continued to turn out an array of photodramas that in one shape or another recalled the World War II glory days."[58] Even as Vietnam raged, movies recalling the heroic fighters of World War II continued. After the Vietnam War, Hollywood continued to harken back to the powerful stories of America's "Greatest Generation."[59] Notable examples include *Saving Private Ry*an and *Flags of Our Fathers*. Dramatic stories of heroism and clear-cut good vs. evil define the World War II movie. Subsequent wars have lacked the moral certitude of that war. The contrast between wars in places such as Korea and Vietnam, compared to the clear-cut fight for survival in World War II, placed subsequent wars at a distinct propaganda disadvantage.

RADIO

The 1930s and 1940s brought a new medium into American homes. Although previous presidents had used radio in a limited way, Roosevelt was particularly adept at using it to transport American people to his fireside. Although only 42 percent of Americans had radio in their homes in 1932, by the eve of the war in 1937 the number had risen to nearly 90 percent.[60] Two days after Pearl Harbor, Roosevelt spoke to the nation in one of his patented "Fireside Chats," bracing the nation for a long and difficult conflict. He labeled the enemy "gangsters," and charged that they "have banded together to make war upon the whole human race." This clearly implies that they are something other than human. He continued, transporting listeners to the battlefield:

> The Japanese have treacherously violated the longstanding peace between us. Many American soldiers and sailors have been killed by enemy action. American ships have been sunk; American airplanes have been destroyed. The Congress and the people of the United States have accepted that challenge. Together with other free peoples, we are now fighting to maintain our right to live among our world neighbors in freedom, in common decency, without fear of assault.[61]

Throughout the war, according to Beschloss, "Roosevelt gave repeated press conferences and speeches and spoke on radio, informing Americans about the current state of battle, both good and alarming."[62]

Americans had already been prepared for the horrors of war by radio reporting from groundbreaking journalist Edward R. Murrow, who transported his audience to wartime London. By September 1940, London was under constant air attack from Germany's "blitz." As Bob Edwards put it,

> Murrow brought World War II into the living rooms of American homes. Rarely had people heard the sounds of actual war unless they had fought in one themselves. To hear the shooting along with Murrow's outstanding reporting was something new and exciting.[63]

Just as with film, Americans had a clear warning of what was to come, even before the attacks on Pearl Harbor.

In addition to the president's speeches and the reports of the war from the field, Americans were subject to direct radio propaganda. All four radio networks carried the Office of Facts and Figures program "This is War." According to James Spiller, these programs "wove dry statistics on military production and conscription into moving tales of global war and national mobilization."[64]

PORTRAYING THE GERMANS

As the war in Europe was ending, the full extent of German atrocities became known. On January 27, 1945, Soviet troops entered the Auschwitz concentration camp in Poland. About 7,000 survivors remained as the Nazis fled. Overall, more than six million Jews were murdered by the Nazis in their concentration camps, some 1.1 million just at Auschwitz.[65] As survivors gathered for the seventy-fifth anniversary of the liberation of Auschwitz on January 27, 2020, many chastised the civilized world for ignoring their plight during the Nazi occupation. As survivor Batsheva Dagan, 95, said, "Where was everybody? . . . Where was the world, who could see everything and yet did nothing to save all those thousands?"[66] After the war, of course, the full extent of Nazi cruelty became painfully obvious. The photos, films, and testimony of survivors were concrete evidence of their evil. Films, such as *Schindler's List*, transport viewers back to the Holocaust. Works of literature, such as Anne Frank's diary and Elie Wiesel's *Night*, have become classics. Thus, one must ask, given the depravity of the Nazis, why was that not a staple element of American and Allied war propaganda?

Garth Jowett and Victoria O'Donnell claim, "One of the most controversial problems facing historians examining World War II is why the issue of the treatment of German concentration camp victims received such little public acknowledgment until almost the end of the war."[67] Because Americans had learned that the portrayal of German atrocities in World War I had been exaggerated, they were likely skeptical of claims of new atrocities. Also, one cannot discount the strain of anti-Semitism in America, a problem that persists to this day. Finally, the attack on Pearl Harbor became the dominant storyline justifying American involvement in the war. Thus, the Japanese became the main villains in the story. Although the Germans had declared war on the United States, they had not directly attacked it. A public that was skeptical of U.S. involvement in a war in Europe was probably not receptive to anti-German propaganda at the outset of hostilities.

PORTRAYING THE JAPANESE

The Japanese were singled out for propaganda with racial overtones. As noted above, Roosevelt charged that they had made war on the whole of humanity, implying they were not human. Capra portrayed them in his *Why We Fight* series as a race lacking individual identity. Of course, it was Japan that attacked the United States, but that alone does not seem sufficient to explain the level of racial stereotyping directed at the people of Japanese descent.

During the war, Japanese were often the subject of offensive slurs and were characterized as rats and baboons.[68] Another persistent image was of Japanese as monkeys or bats.[69] *Collier*'s magazine showed Japanese as a vampire bat ready to drop a bomb on Pearl Harbor.[70] Comparing their dehumanized portrayal with the portrayal of the European enemies shows that the

Japanese were singled out for such racist stereotyping. A Marine speaking to war correspondent John Hersey in 1942 summed up this difference starkly: "I wish we were fighting against Germans. They are human beings, like us—But the Japanese are like animals."[71] Neil Sheehan writes, "The market-research pollsters in the Treasury Department discovered that advertising that relied on racist hate propaganda against the Japanese sold more war bonds than anti-German hatemongering."[72]

Japanese Americans were treated quite differently than those with German or Italian roots. Although some 10,000 Italian immigrants were relocated from areas deemed sensitive, they were largely noncitizens or first-generation immigrants without citizen children. Former Defense Secretary Leon Panetta, whose grandfather was forced to move from Monterey to San Jose, writes, "As a civil rights issue, it paled next to the treatment of the Japanese and Japanese Americans, 110,000 of whom were interned for most of the war."[73] The internment of well over 100,000 Japanese Americans, most of whom were citizens, is now regarded as one of the most shameful episodes in American history. But at the time, it was treated as a necessity of war. Tomoko Mukawa, a Japanese student studying in the United States, explored the narratives told about the Japanese American internment, both to the public at large and to the inmates of the camps. In her thesis, Mukawa examined two types of artifacts—the ironically named camp newspaper, the *Manzanar Free Press*, and several articles written for public consumption by officials from the camp and other non-inmates.[74]

In focusing on a pictorial edition of the newspaper, published September 10, 1943, Mukawa found that five major themes emerged: Life is normal; life is good; the inmates are pioneers and settlers; Manzanar is beautiful and blessed by nature; and Manzanar is not a prison camp.[75] To illustrate normalcy, consider how inmates describe their lives in the *Manzanar Free Press*:

> We work and play and enjoy. It is much different in its environmental factors than the average home but the human elements, emotions, and satisfactions are the same. To us it is even more—it is our struggle to prove that Democracy is practical, possible and probable when your home is where you lay your heart as well as your hat.[76]

Notice that the patriotic theme of democracy is prominently featured. The project director, Ralph P. Merritt, praises the inmates for "their pioneering spirit."[77] An article titled "Memories of Manzanar" describes the camp in almost poetic terms:

> The blue-purple haze veiled over the Inyo mountains moments before sunrise, eye-catching to those hardy few early risers—. The hush of summer's

evening-tide after the sun dips behind the Sierra; and the arched panoply of the rugged blue-black etched by the craggy mountain ranges against the sky, a veritable back drop for an impressionistic stage drama—.[78]

The camps are anything but prisons. Ironically, Manzanar is even called "Shangri-La."[79] Patriotic Japanese Americans tend their victory gardens, much as do those outside the camps.[80] The residents are well cared for, in fact, receiving "good substantial food of a quality and quantity comparable to that available to the general public."[81]

How did the internal propaganda compare with messages directed to the public at large? Not surprisingly, they were quite similar in their themes. In her analysis of magazine articles, Mukawa found themes of opportunity, responsibility, and democracy. The internees were portrayed as pioneers and volunteers, who were recipients of opportunities and living normal lives.[82]

The line between Japanese American citizens and immigrants without citizenship was blurred. As the internment program was just getting underway, *Business Week* in July 1942 referred to "American-born and foreign-born Japanese . . . ."[83] This leads Mukawa to conclude, "It seems that whether one is American born or born elsewhere, Japanese are Japanese, after all."[84] Other stories describe incidents of violence where protestors spoke in Japanese.[85]

Camp Public Relations Director Robert Brown refers to the inmates as volunteers and pioneers, writing, "They feel safe and protected, and for this protection the vast majority are openly grateful."[86] One of the more interesting features of the external propaganda was the attempt to make life in the camp appear almost better than life outside. The opening line for the article in *Business Week*, states, "Big West Coast market shifts as 100,000 Japanese, two-thirds of them American citizens, are relocated. Housed, clothed and fed by government, they are also paid for project work."[87] The article notes that they don't have to pay rent and that they are referred to not as internees, but evacuees, diminishing their hardship. In fact, *Business Week* featured a photo of happy children standing in line at an ice cream and candy stand. So, while Americans outside the camps sacrificed their sons and husbands, dealt with rationing, blackouts, and other war hardships, the internees lived an easy life on the taxpayer's dollar, which of course was far from reality.

There was also an effort to diminish the patriotism and sacrifice of the inmates. Carey McWilliams, Chief of Immigration and Housing for the State of California, wrote,

> [E]vacuation provides an opportunity to democratize the Japanese communities themselves, for it can definitely be geared to an educational program. The first generation were never encouraged to become citizens . . . . But the evacuation

program now provides the opportunity to correct a serious mistake in national immigration policy.[88]

McWilliams supports reintegrating Japanese back into society, but leaves some room for doubt, writing "*If* we assume then that the Japanese are to remain with us as citizens after the war . . . ."[89] The *Business Week* article notes that as far as what happens after the war, "The WRA [War Relocation Administration] figures that the problem isn't theirs right now."[90] Public Relations Director Brown suggests that the camps actually made the inmates soft, writing, "Fathers shake their heads and say that the lack of competition, the government created jobs, will cause their boys to become soft and lazy and ill fit them for the hard work that must come 'when this is over.'"[91] This patronizing attitude is reminiscent of the way "our little brown brothers" were portrayed during the Spanish-American war and the suppression of the Filipino rebellion.

In sum, the propaganda associated with the relocation camps emphasized how well treated the internees were, how they were protected and coddled, although they were, after all, merely Japanese, who needed to be educated about democracy. Even those residing in the camps were subjected to propaganda that characterized them as pioneers and volunteers, doing their part to help the war effort. What is today regarded as one of the most shameful events in American history was at the time portrayed as a normal part of the war effort that was not only accepted by the internees, but actually welcomed. In retrospect, how did the forced internment of thousands of American citizens become normalized? Jeanne Wakatsuki Houston explains in her epic autobiography *Farewell to Manzanar*, "Three years of wartime propaganda—racist headlines, atrocity movies, hate slogans, and fright-mask posters—had turned the Japanese face into something despicable and grotesque."[92] It is symptomatic of this demonization that it was not until 1952 that Japanese immigrants were allowed to become citizens.[93]

THE WAR ENDS

America's objective was the unconditional surrender of all the Axis Powers. Even after Germany had been defeated, forcing Japan to capitulate was expected to take another year and a half and some half million American lives according to President Truman's *Memoirs*.[94] At the Potsdam conference July 17–August 2, 1945, Truman met Churchill and Stalin. One of Truman's major objectives was to enlist the support of the Soviet Union in defeating Japan. At the Yalta conference, February 4–11, 1945, Roosevelt had gained a pledge from Stalin that he would enter the war within three months of

Germany's surrender. Truman explains the urgency of the Soviet's entering the war against Japan:

> There were more than a million Japanese deployed in China and ready to carry on war for an indefinite time there. We were eager for the Russians to get into the war with Japan because of their border with China and their railway connections with Europe.[95]

Although the United States had developed the atomic bomb, no one knew for certain if it alone would induce Japan to surrender unconditionally, which was the U.S. goal. Truman told Stalin about a tremendous new weapon, although he didn't mention the specifics. Stalin seemed unsurprised, and it later was discovered that the Soviets had known about the effort to develop the bomb for some time.[96]

That the invasion of Japan would be costly in lives and time was a foregone conclusion. Charlton Ogburn, Jr., a military intelligence officer, recalled that "surrender was excluded from the Japanese ethos."[97] No Japanese unit had ever surrendered. In addition to the two-and-half-million regular troops in the Japanese homeland, every male between seventeen and sixty and every female between seventeen and forty-five was conscripted to defend against the expected invasion. Russian help was viewed as essential.

On July 26 an ultimatum was issued from Potsdam, offering the Japanese one last chance to surrender before "they may expect a rain of ruin from the air, the like of which has never been seen on this earth."[98] As Truman recounts,

> On July 28 Radio Tokyo announced that the Japanese government would continue to fight. There was no formal reply to the joint ultimatum . . . . There was no alternative now. The bomb was scheduled to be dropped after August 3 unless Japan surrendered before that day.[99]

On August 6, the *Enola Gay* dropped the first atomic bomb on Hiroshima, initially killing tens of thousands of people and many more in subsequent days from radiation. Truman issued another threatening statement: "We are now prepared to obliterate more rapidly and completely every productive enterprise the Japanese have above ground in any city."[100] Japan continued to refuse to surrender. On August 9 two more blows were delivered to Japan. The Russians entered the war bringing a million troops into Manchuria and another atomic bomb was dropped, this time on Nagasaki.[101] Finally, Japan knew it was beaten. As Truman recounts, "This second demonstration of the power of the atomic bomb apparently threw Tokyo into a panic, for the next morning brought the first indication that the Japanese Empire was ready to surrender."[102]

In retrospect, many have questioned the use of the atomic bomb—was it moral to kill so many civilians in such a brutal way and usher in an era of potential world annihilation? However, it becomes clearer why Truman felt justified in ordering the bombing when it is weighed against the potential loss of American lives in taking the Japanese homeland. Further, as indicated earlier in this chapter, the demonization of the Japanese enemy was a fundamental part of the story of the war. Not only had the Japanese attacked Pearl Harbor without warning while in the midst of negotiations with the United States, they had engaged in numerous wartime atrocities, including the Bataan death march, killing of American POWs, and even the beheading of an American POW, seen in newspapers shortly after the Germans surrendered.[103] As Truman wrote in his *Memoirs*,

> The final decision of where and when to use the atomic bomb was up to me. Let there be no mistake about it. I regarded the bomb as a military weapon and never had any doubt that it should be used.[104]

After the atomic bombs were dropped on Hiroshima and Nagasaki, there was an effort to conceal the devastation caused by the new weapon. The southern part of Japan was closed to the media. The head of the Manhattan Project, Major General Leslie Groves stated, "This talk about radio-activity is so much nonsense."[105] He even invited reporters to the site of the atomic bomb tests, although the presence of Geiger counters and shields on their shoes, along with warnings not to bring anything from the site, probably didn't really support the general's message.

The first reports to reveal the dangers of radiation sickness came from a British source, the *Daily Express*, which reported that "thirty days after the first atom bomb destroyed the city and shook the world, people are still dying . . . from something which I can only describe as the atomic plague."[106] The American public was enlightened to the horrors of atomic war by a full issue of the *New Yorker* in August 1946 devoted to the reporting from Hiroshima by John Hersey. Hersey managed to get to Hiroshima in early 1946. When he returned to New York, he produced a 30,000-word tome that used the stories of six survivors to show the devastation caused by the bomb and its radioactive aftermath. William Langewiesche writes of Hersey's reporting:

> Afterward, as part of a clampdown on information—an extension of routine wartime censorship—little mention of realities on the ground was allowed by American authorities . . . . And so what? In the United States the hatred for the Japanese far exceeded that of the hatred for the Germans . . . . Days after the bombings a Gallup poll found that 85 percent of Americans approved of the

attacks, and another survey, made after the war, indicated that 23 percent wished that more such weapons had been dropped before the Japanese surrender.[107]

Some to this day believe that his descriptions helped the world avoid nuclear holocaust for three-quarters of a century by personalizing and graphically showing how devastating such weapons were, effectively transporting readers to ground zero.

ASSESSING THE NARRATIVE

There was no denying the savage attack on Pearl Harbor. Photos, films, and vivid news reports transported virtually every American to the scene of the disaster. The story told to justify United States' entry into World War II had *narrative coherence* and *probability*. In terms of the *characters* in the story, the Japanese were the most obvious villains. Their "dastardly" attack on Pearl Harbor was, in Roosevelt's telling, totally unprovoked. Unlike World War I, where only the leaders were initially demonized, Roosevelt made no distinction in his war speech between the leaders and their people. The Germans and Italians, on the other hand, were not so much demonized, but rather portrayed as victims of their rulers—Hitler and Mussolini. In fact, Hitler was even portrayed as a comic figure in Disney cartoons and Charlie Chaplin's *Great Dictator*. Thus, the villains in this story are the Nazis and Fascist leaders and the Japanese people.

The event that led to the war was an unambiguous surprise attack on a Sunday morning, no less. Unlike so many American wars where the events leading to war were sometimes contrived or misconstrued, this event could not be denied; its *narrative probability* and *fidelity* were absolute. Hence, there was almost unanimous approval of the Declaration of War (one pacifist member of the House voted no) and the 97 percent approval of going to war in public opinion polls. The motives of enemies were conquest and domination, America was motivated by pure self-defense. It was a war, in Roosevelt's terms, for survival. Unlike Wilson, no one could reasonably accuse Roosevelt of deception in his campaign promises. After all, he had explicitly excluded "if attacked" from his promise to stay out of the war. Even when attacked by Japan, he refrained from calling for war in Europe until the German and Italian governments declared war on the United States.

The character of Americans fighting the war was portrayed as pure and innocent, yet courageous. Americans were minding their own business, had no interest in getting into another European War (viewing it largely as a mistake), and were attacked. Although Capra's *Why We Fight* series sought to gave American boys a reason to fight, in reality, very little convincing was needed. This perhaps explains why the series reinforced rather than changed attitudes. And once the war began, American soldiers showed what they were made of—as portrayed by the likes of John Wayne. Even poor Rick in *Casablanca* sacrificed the love of his life to help save the world. The other characters in the story were the American people who stayed at home. From Rosie the Riveter to the Gold Star families of fallen GIs to the average person who saved ration coupons and planted a victory garden, the American people were all part of the war effort. Given that 16 million people served in the military in the war, it was a rare family that did not have someone close to them in the service. It was not just a war fought "over there," it was fought in the homeland as well.

Looking ahead to future wars, the most significant aspects of the narrative's *structural coherence* were how the war began and how it ended. The appeasement of Hitler came to be viewed as the great mistake that led to war. Understanding the story of World War II drives our understanding of the Cold War and the hot wars that ensued—Korea and Vietnam. The narrative that Chamberlain's efforts to appease Hitler at Munich emboldened him to launch his war drove a narrative that the world must stand up to ruthless dictators bent on conquest. The war ended with the full and unconditional surrender of all the Axis Powers. Japan, after being twice bombed by the newly developed A-bomb, made a full surrender on the deck of the battleship *Missouri* in Tokyo bay. Thus, the definition of "victory" came to be one of total and complete defeat of the enemy—something the United States was hard-pressed to replicate in its future wars.

After the defeat of the Axis powers, a new enemy appeared—America's former ally, the Soviet Union. The narrative soon developed that the Communists were bent on world domination, just as Hitler had been. Thus, the lesson of Munich was learned, perhaps too well. Do not appease them—challenge them any time it appears that Communism is moving into a new part of the world. After China fell to the Reds, the narrative became even more powerful. Something had to be done to stop the spread of godless Communism and therefore save the world. It is ironic that Ambassador Joseph Kennedy, who tried to stop Roosevelt from entering World War II, saw his son declare in his inaugural address, "[W]e shall pay any price, bear any burden, meet any hardship, support any friend, oppose any foe to assure the survival and the success of liberty."[108] Even as late as 1991, World War II veteran, George H. W. Bush, drew on a comparison of Saddam Hussein to Hitler to justify American intervention in the Persian Gulf. And, his son, George W. Bush would label Iraq part of the "Axis of Evil," recalling the Axis Powers of World War II. Thus, the story of World War II shaped American policy for the remainder of the twentieth century and into the first years of the twenty-first.

As the story of World War II is told and retold, it stands out as the "good war"—forced upon a reluctant nation, bringing the entire country together to sacrifice, and ultimately resulting in complete victory over the enemies. In terms of the World War II model of how the story of a war ends, subsequent wars fell far short of unconditional surrender. The standard of victory in World War II has proved impossible to achieve in the postwar world.

NOTES

1. J. Owen, "Pearl Harbor Ships on the Morning of the Attack," Pearl Harbor Visitors Bureau, October 12, 2012, https://visitpearlharbor.org/pearl-harbor-ships-on-december-7th/.

2. Caroline Redmond, "'It Was War': 33 Photos of the Pearl Harbor Attack That Changed History Forever," *ATI* [All That's Interesting], published December 7, 2018, updated February 28, 2019, https://allthatsinteresting.com/pearl-harbor-attack-pictures.

3. "Attack at Pearl Harbor, 1941," Eyewitness to History, www.eyewitnesstohistory.com, 1997, accessed October 11, 2019, http://www.eyewitnesstohistory.com/pfpearl.htm.

4. "Attack at Pearl Harbor."

5. Michael Kazin, *War Against War: The American Fight for Peace, 1914–1918* (New York: Simon & Schuster, 2017), [page] 291, Kindle.

6. History.com editors, "Hitler Appeased at Munich," History, last updated July 28, 2010, https://www.history.com/this-day-in-history/hitler-appeased-at-munich.

7. Michael Beschloss, *Presidential Courage: Brave Leaders and How They Changed America 1789–1989* (New York: Simon & Schuster, 2007), 159.

8. Quoted in Beschloss, *Presidential Courage*, 173.

9. Quoted in Beschloss, *Presidential Courage*, 188 (italics supplied by Beschloss).

10. Quoted in Beschloss, *Presidential Courage*, 189.

11. Editors of Encyclopaedia Britannica, "United States Presidential Election of 1940," *Encyclopedia Britannica*, October 29, 2019, https://www.britannica.com/event/United-States-presidential-election-of-1940.

12. Michael Beschloss, *Presidents of War* (New York: Crown, 2018), [page] 391, Kindle.

13. Beschloss, *Presidential Courage*, 159.

14. Quoted in Beschloss, *Presidents of War*, 376.

15. Beschloss, *Presidents of War*, 379.

16. Nicholas John Cull, *Selling War: The British Propaganda Campaign Against American "Neutrality" in World War II* (New York: Oxford, 1995), 3, Adobe Digital Edition.

17. Cull, *Selling War*, 200.

18. "1941: Germany and Italy Declare War on U.S.," *BBC On This Day*, accessed May 25, 2019, http://news.bbc.co.uk/onthisday/hi/dates/stories/december/11/newsid_3532000/3532401.stm.

19. Phillip Knightley, *The First Casualty: The War Correspondent as Hero and Myth-Maker from the Crimea to Iraq*, 3rd ed. (Baltimore and London: John Hopkins University Press, 2004), 295.

20. Beschloss, *Presidents of War*, 380.

21. Quoted in Beschloss, *Presidents of War*, 381.

22. Michael E. Ruane, "The U.S. Was Looking for the Enemy Near Pearl Harbor—But It Was Looking in the Wrong Direction," *Washington Post*, December 7, 2018, https://www.washingtonpost.com/history/2018/12/07/us-was-looking-enemy-near-pearl-harbor-it-was-looking-wrong-direction/?utm_term=.106d476a76d3.

23. Brian Dunning, "Why was Pearl Harbor so Vulnerable?" *Reader's Digest*, May 2019, 104–105.

24. Franklin D. Roosevelt, "Address by the President," *Congressional Record—House*, December 8, 1941, 9519–9520, https://www.govinfo.gov/content/pkg/GPO-CRECB-1941-pt9/pdf/GPO-CRECB-1941-pt9-9-2.pdf. All quotations from the speech are from this source.

25. "December 8, 1941—Franklin Roosevelt asks Congress for a Declaration of War with Japan," accessed May 25, 2019, http://docs.fdrlibrary.marist.edu/tmirhdee.html.

26. Roosevelt, "Address by the President."

27. Hermann G. Stelzner, "'War Message,' December 8, 1941: An Approach to Language," *Speech Monographs* 33, no. 4 (1966): 431, https://doi.org/10.1080/03637756609375508 (italics in original).

28. "1941: Germany and Italy declare war on U.S."

29. "'Why We Fight'—America's World War Two Propaganda Masterpiece," *Military History Now*, November 21, 2014, https://militaryhistorynow.com/2014/11/21/why-we-fight-americas-world-war-two-propaganda-masterpiece/.

30. Beschloss, *Presidents of War*, 393.

31. Quoted in Beschloss, *Presidents of War*, 394.

32. Gregory Hansen, "Kenneth Burke's Rhetorical Theory within the Construction of the Ethnography of Speaking," *Folklore Forum* 27, no. 1 (1996): 52, https://scholarworks.iu.edu/dspace/bitstream/handle/2022/2207/27(1)%2050-59.pdf?sequence=1.

33. Becky Little, "Inside America's Shocking WWII Propaganda Machine," National Geographic, December 19, 2016, https://news.nationalgeographic.com/2016/12/world-war-2-propaganda-history-books/.

34. Mark Harris, *Five Came Back: A Story of Hollywood and the Second World War* (New York: Penguin Press, 2014), 58.

35. Harris, *Five Came Back,* 113.

36. Stanley J. Baron and Dennis K. Davis, *Mass Communication Theory* (Belmont, CA: Wadsworth, 1995), 131.

37. Bill Moyers, "WWII: The Propaganda Battle," *A Walk Through the Twentieth Century,* May 9, 1984, [Transcript], https://billmoyers.com/content/wwii-propaganda-battle/.

38. Harris, *Five Came Back*, 131.
39. Moyers, "WWII."
40. "'Why We Fight'—America's World War Two Propaganda Masterpiece."
41. "'Why We Fight'—America's World War Two Propaganda Masterpiece."
42. "'Why We Fight'—America's World War Two Propaganda Masterpiece."
43. John W. Dower, *War without Mercy: Race and Power in the Pacific War* (New York: Pantheon Books, 1993), 19, https://hdl-handle-net.mantis.csuchico.edu/2027/heb.02403, EPUB.
44. Quoted in Knightley, *The First Casualty*, 344.
45. Knightley, *The First Casualty*, 345–346.
46. Quoted in Knightley, *The First Casualty*, 364.
47. Quoted in Knightley, *The First Casualty*, 345.
48. Knightley, *The First Casualty*, 359–360.
49. Knightley, *The First Casualty*, 360.
50. Robert Fyne, *Long Ago and Far Away: Hollywood and the Second World War*, (Lanham, MD, The Scarecrow Press, 2008), 3.
51. Fyne, *Long Ago*, 5.
52. Fyne, *Long Ago*, 6 and J. Michael Sproule, *Channels of Propaganda* (Bloomington, IN: ERIC Clearinghouse on Reading, English, and Communication, 1994), 242, https://files.eric.ed.gov/fulltext/ED372461.pdf.
53. Aljean Harmetz, "Murray Burnett, 86, Writer of Play Behind 'Casablanca,'" *New York Times*, September 29, 1997, https://www.nytimes.com/1997/09/29/arts/murray-burnett-86-writer-of-play-behind-casablanca.html.
54. Michael Curtiz, dir., *Casablanca* (Burbank, CA: Warner Home Video, 1999) DVD.
55. Fyne, *Long Ago*, 5–6.
56. Fyne, *Long Ago*, 31.
57. Fyne, *Long Ago*, 40.
58. Fyne, *Long Ago*, 48.
59. Tom Brokaw, *The Greatest Generation* (New York: Random House, 1998).
60. Margaret Biser, "The Fireside Chats: Roosevelt's Radio Talks the White House Speaks to America," The White House Historical Association, August 19, 2016, https://www.whitehousehistory.org/the-fireside-chats-roosevelts-radio-talks.
61. Franklin D. Roosevelt, "Fireside Chat 19: On the War with Japan," Miller Center, University of Virginia, December 9, 1941, https://millercenter.org/the-presidency/presidential-speeches/december-9-1941-fireside-chat-19-war-japan.
62. Beschloss, *Presidents of War*, 433.
63. Bob Edwards, "Edward R. Murrow Broadcast from London (September 21, 1940)" Added to the National Registry, 2004, http://www.loc.gov/static/programs/national-recording-preservation-board/documents/murrow.pdf.
64. James Spiller, "This is War! Network Radio and World War II Propaganda in America," *Journal of Radio Studies* 11, no. 1 (June 2004): 55, https://doi.org/10.1207/s15506843jrs1101_6.
65. Ishaan Tharoor, "75 Years after Auschwitz's Liberation, The Ghosts of the Past Loom Large," *Washington Post*, January 27, 2020, https://www.washingt

onpost.com/world/2020/01/28/75-years-after-auschwitzs-liberation-ghosts-past-loom-large/.

66. Tharoor, "75 Years."

67. Garth S. Jowett and Victoria O'Donnell, *Propaganda and Persuasion*, 7th ed. (Thousand Oaks, CA: Sage, 2019), 240.

68. Erin Steuter and Deborah Wills, *At War with Metaphor: Media, Propaganda, and Racism in the War on Terror* (Lantham, MD: Lexington Books, 2008; PB edition 2009), 45.

69. Steuter and Wills, *At War with Metaphor*, 46.

70. Steuter and Wills, *At War with Metaphor*, 46–47.

71. Steuter and Wills, *At War with Metaphor*, 46.

72. Neil Sheehan, *A Bright Shining Lie: John Paul Vann and America in Vietnam* (New York: Random House, 1988, Modern Library, 2009), [page] 53, Kindle.

73. Leon Panetta with Jim Newton, *Worthy Fights: A Memoir of Leadership in War and Peace* (New York: Penguin Press, 2014), 14.

74. Tomoko Mukawa, "Making the Unacceptable Seem Acceptable: Narrative Rhetoric and the Japanese American Internment of World War II" (Master's thesis, California State University, Chico, 1999).

75. Mukawa, "Making the Unacceptable Seem Acceptable," 46–47.

76. "Hanging My Hat in Manzanar," *Manzanar Free Press*, (Manzanar, CA), Sep. 10 1943, 16, https://www.loc.gov/item/sn84025948/1943-09-10/ed-1/.

77. Robert P. Merritt, "The Spirit of Manzanar," *Manzanar Free Press* (Manzanar, CA), Sep. 10, 1943, 2, https://www.loc.gov/item/sn84025948/1943-09-10/ed-1/.

78. "Memories of Manzanar," *Manzanar Free Press,* (Manzanar, CA), Sep. 10 1943, 2, https://www.loc.gov/item/sn84025948/1943-09-10/ed-1/.

79. Mukawa, "Making the Unacceptable Seem Acceptable," 39, 41.

80. Mukawa, "Making the Unacceptable Seem Acceptable," 46.

81. "Camp Food Quality Comparable to the Average Standards," *Manzanar Free Press,* (Manzanar, CA), Sep. 10 1943, 8, https://www.loc.gov/item/sn84025948/1943-09-10/ed-1/.

82. Mukawa, "Making the Unacceptable Seem Acceptable," 69.

83. "Business in Evacuation Centers," *Business Week*, July 18, 1942, 19.

84. Mukawa, "Making the Unacceptable Seem Acceptable," 55.

85. "What Happened at Manzanar," *Common Ground* 3, no. 3 (Spring 1943): 84–85, https://www.unz.com/print/CommonGround-1943q1-00083/.

86. Robert L. Brown, "Manzanar—Relocation Center," *Common Ground* 3, no. 1 (Autumn 1942): 31, https://www.unz.com/print/CommonGround-1942q3-00027/.

87. "Business in Evacuation Centers," 19.

88. Carey McWilliams, "Japanese Evacuation: Policy and Perspectives," *Common Ground* 2, no. 4 (Summer 1942): 71. https://www.unz.com/print/CommonGround-1942q2-00065/.

89. McWilliams, "Japanese Evacuation," 67 (italics added).

90. "Business in Evacuation Centers," 21.

91. Brown, "Manzanar," 31.

92. Jeanne Wakatsuki Houston and James D. Houston, *Farewell to Manzanar* (Boston: Houghton Mifflin, 1973, 2002 edition), [page] 127, Kindle.

93. Jane Hong, "Immigration Act of 1952," Densho Encyclopedia, accessed February 29, 2020, https://encyclopedia.densho.org/Immigration%20Act%20of%201952/.

94. Harry S Truman, *Memoirs, Vol. 1: Year of Decisions* (Garden City, NY: Doubleday, 1955), 416–417.

95. Truman, *Memoirs, Vol. 1*, 229.

96. David McCullough, *Truman* (New York: Simon & Schuster, 1992), 442–443.

97. Quoted in McCullough, *Truman*, 438.

98. Truman, *Memoirs, Vol. 1*, 422.

99. Truman, *Memoirs, Vol. 1*, 421.

100. McCullough, *Truman*, 455.

101. McCullough, *Truman*, 457.

102. Truman, *Memoirs Vol. 1*, 426.

103. McCullough, *Truman*, 439.

104. Truman, *Memoirs Vol. 1*, 419.

105. Quoted in Knightley, *The First Casualty*, 329.

106. Quoted in Knightley, *The First Casualty*, 329.

107. William Langewiesche, "The Reporter Who Told the World about the Bomb," *New York Times*, August 4, 2020, https://www.nytimes.com/2020/08/04/books/review/fallout-hiroshima-hersey-lesley-m-m-blume.html.

108. John F. Kennedy, "Inaugural Address," John F. Kennedy Presidential Library and Museum, January 20, 1961, accessed April 17, 2019, https://www.jfklibrary.org/learn/about-jfk/historic-speeches/inaugural-address.

Chapter 6

Korea

The Never-Ending War

June 25, 1950, began with a rainy summer morning in Korea. Just before dawn the North Korean People's Army (NKPA) began heavy artillery shelling around the routes leading to the South Korean capital of Seoul. T-34 tanks came next, followed by masses of infantry. The Republic of Korea (ROK) forces were thoroughly outnumbered, out maneuvered, and lacked weapons to stop the tanks. Gen. Matthew Ridgway writes, "It was as if a few troops of Boy Scouts with hand weapons had undertaken to stop a Panzer unit."[1] President Harry Truman was spending what he expected to be a relaxing weekend with family in Independence, Missouri. A bit after 10:00 p.m., while sitting in his library, he received a phone call from his secretary of state, Dean Acheson, who told him "I have very serious news. The North Koreans have invaded South Korea."[2] In his *Memoirs*, he recalls his state of mind at the time:

> I recalled some earlier instances: Manchuria, Ethiopia, Austria. I remembered how each time that the democracies failed to act it had encouraged the aggressors to keep going ahead. Communism was acting in Korea just as Hitler, Mussolini, and the Japanese had acted .... If this was allowed to go unchallenged it would mean a third world war, just as similar incidents had brought on the second world war.[3]

The U.S. reaction came quickly. Truman, who did not hesitate in making a decision, ordered "U.S. air and sea forces to give the ROK government troops cover and support."[4] Around 11:30 the next morning, Acheson called Truman again to report that the UN Security Council had been called into emergency session. Not expecting the North Koreans to honor any resolution from the United Nations, Truman determined that he needed to return to Washington,

D.C. On the way, he was notified that the UN Security Council had voted 9–0 to call for a cessation of hostilities and withdrawal of North Korean troops. Because they were boycotting the Security Council due to its refusal to seat Red China, the Soviet Union could not veto the resolution.[5]

The *New York Times* portrayed the attack of that day as an extension of Soviet aggression. The lead paragraph read, "The Russian-sponsored North Korean Communists invaded the American-supported Republic of South Korea today and their radio followed it up by broadcasting a declaration of war."[6] Later in the article, the link to the Soviets was emphasized: "United States officials, however, have said that Washington would hold the Soviet Union responsible for the actions of the North Korean government under the Soviet puppet Kim Il Sung."[7] There was nothing to suggest that the conflict might be a civil war between the two Koreas. Ridgway points out that the initial response of the American citizenry was subdued. "I believe the majority of our citizens . . . thought of the Korean outbreak as hardly more than a bonfire that would be extinguished soon enough."[8] Of course, that wishful thinking was soon proven wrong. The NKPA offensive was swift and effective and by June 28 the South Korean capital of Seoul had fallen.

June 25, 1950, is a date forgotten by most Americans. Unlike December 7 or September 11, there are no commemorations marking the beginning of a war that would claim over 33,000 American lives.[9] It took over three years to sign an armistice and nearly seven decades later the Korean Peninsula remains technically at war. Today, a nuclear-armed North Korea poses a threat to world peace. Despite repeated efforts to negotiate a nuclear-free Korean Peninsula, as of this writing, the threat that a conflict there could escalate into Armageddon remains real.

THE COLD WAR AND CONTAINMENT

The Korean War, or as President Harry S. Truman called it, "police action," has roots in how World War II ended and the ensuing Cold War. Korea had been dominated by Japan after the Sino-Japanese war of 1894–1895 and was annexed in 1910. At the Cairo conference in 1943, Roosevelt, Churchill, and Chiang Kai-sheck agreed that Korea would be free and independent after the war. At Yalta, Stalin and Roosevelt agreed to a three-power trusteeship, including the United States, U.S.S.R., and China. According to Truman, Roosevelt in his discussion with Stalin "cited the Philippines as an example of how long it might take Korea to become prepared for full self-government. The islands had required forty years; perhaps Korea might be ready in twenty or thirty years."[10] Of course, as we saw in chapter 3, the long delay in the Filipino independence was due to colonial ambitions and paternalistic racism toward our "little brown brothers," rather than their inherent inability to govern themselves.

After the unconditional surrender of Japan on September 2, 1945, its occupation of the Korean Peninsula ended. In April 1948, Korea was divided at the 38th parallel, with the United States to the south and the Soviet Union in the north.[11] This militarily indefensible demarcation was chosen arbitrarily by a couple of low-ranking officers at the Pentagon, Col. Dean Rusk and another young officer, Charles Bonesteel.[12] Rusk would go on to become secretary of state under Presidents Kennedy and Johnson, and played a crucial role in the Vietnam War. Much like Germany, Korea became a divided country, with diametrically opposed political systems. To the south, the ROK was established with American support. To the north, the Democratic People's Republic of Korea (DPRK) was aligned with the Communist Soviet Union and eventually China.

The terms *Cold War* and *containment* came to define the postwar era. However, the architect of America's policies, Harry S. Truman, didn't like either term. In his *Memoirs*, he refers to the term Cold War as inaccurate.[13] Furthermore, he claims that his policy was "mistakenly called . . . containment."[14] Despite Truman's objections, these have become the accepted terminology for the postwar era. Interestingly, the Truman Library and Museum online actually has a "Timeline of the Cold War," thus ignoring its namesake's preference.[15] The timeline marks the Cold War as beginning at the Yalta Conference held from February 4–11, 1945, as Germany was nearing defeat and the Soviets were establishing control in Eastern Europe. Within a year, Stalin declared that communism and capitalism were incompatible and by March 1946, Winston Churchill had proclaimed the Soviet occupation of Eastern Europe an "Iron Curtain."

With the Russians gaining more and more territory in Eastern Europe and threatening Greece and Turkey, the president addressed a joint session of Congress on March 12, 1947. The immediate issue was aid to Greece and Turkey. More historic was his declaration, "I believe that it must be the policy of the United States to support free peoples who are resisting attempted subjugation by armed minorities or by outside pressures."[16] As Truman reveals in his *Memoirs*, he changed the wording of the speech from his speechwriters' "should" to "must." Truman writes that he "wanted no hedging in this speech. This was America's answer to the surge of expansion of Communist tyranny."[17] What came to be known as the Truman Doctrine dominated American foreign policy from the late 1940s through the fall of the Soviet Union in 1991. Truman writes, "This was, I believe, the turning point in America's foreign policy, which now declared that wherever aggression, direct or indirect, threatened the peace, the security of the United States was involved."[18] How American security was at stake in a faraway land of no military importance can only be understood as part of this larger narrative of the Cold War.

By 1948, the Soviets had taken over Czechoslovakia. Communism appeared to be on the march. Sooner or later the United States and the Soviets were bound to clash if the Truman Doctrine were to be followed. The anticipated direct clash of the two major postwar powers came on June 24, 1948, when the Soviets blockaded Berlin. Situated in East Germany, Berlin was a divided city and the United States and its allies asserted their right to remain in West Berlin and bring in supplies. How to do so in the face of a blockade without starting a war with Russia was Truman's dilemma. Thus, he ordered a full-scale airlift to West Berlin on June 26.[19] The airlift was successful in ending the blockade by May 1949. Turkey and Greece remained free, and NATO was established, with its famous Article V guaranteeing that an attack on one member would be considered an attack on all. The situation in Europe seemed to have stabilized, with Truman halting, but not reversing, Soviet expansion. Thus, it is not altogether surprising that the Communists turned to a different part of the world to extend their ideology and influence. Furthermore, the United States was about to lose its exclusive possession of the most powerful weapon ever created. Although Russia wasn't expected to get the A-bomb until 1952, by September of 1949, radiation was detected that indicated Russia had set off an atomic explosion sometime in late August.[20] The Cold War suddenly had the potential to become very hot.

The first loss to Communism in Asia came in October 1949, when Mao Zedong forced the Nationalists, led by Chiang Kai-shek, off the mainland and established the People's Republic of China. Why didn't the United States do more to stop the fall of China? "In the end, of course, Chiang was defeated by loss of support among his own people," Truman writes, adding that once the military began to defect, even using U.S. supplied weapons against them, "I decided to cut off further shipments to China."[21] Chiang was forced to retreat to what was then known as Formosa (now Taiwan). Nevertheless, the United States continued to recognize the Nationalists as the legitimate government of China and opposed what was called Red China taking its seat on the UN Security Council.

The dual successes of the Communists, both in developing the atomic bomb and in taking over China led to panic. Senator Joseph McCarthy made the most of this when he claimed in early 1950 that the State Department was heavily infiltrated by Communist spies and sympathizers. Speaking in Wheeling, West Virginia, he waved a sheet of paper and claimed there were 205 employees of the State Department known by the secretary of state to be Communists. Over the next few weeks, the number fluctuated, but the hysteria continued unabated.[22] Although he never provided any proof, McCarthy become a dominant figure in the so-called Red Scare that led to blacklisting, loyalty oaths, and the destruction of reputations for many innocent people.

Thus, the scene was set for the next chapter in the Cold War narrative. Communists had taken over China, developed the atomic bomb, and allegedly infiltrated the U.S. government. Truman had declared that Communist expansion threatened American security, no matter where it took place. It was as if Communism were a deadly virus, that if not stopped would infect the rest of the free world. It is little wonder that the next step in the Cold War would be anything but cold. It is obvious why, in retrospect, Truman disliked the term. Michael Beschloss writes that Stalin

> took notice when President Truman declined to employ the US military in an effort to keep China from falling to Mao Zedong's Communists. Stalin was also told by some Soviet intelligence officials that Truman did not consider it crucial enough to defend South Korea by military force.[23]

FAILURE TO ASSURE SOUTH KOREA'S SECURITY

Once the division of Korea at the 38th parallel was established, the Russians began treating it as a permanent border, rather than as a temporary dividing line.[24] By September 1947, the Russians called for a removal of all occupying troops by the first months of 1948.[25] The Joint Chiefs of Staff (which included Gen. Eisenhower) made it clear in a memorandum that keeping American troops in Korea served no military purpose, writing that "from the standpoint of military security, the United States has little strategic interest in maintaining the present troops and bases in Korea . . . . [Should war break out] our present forces in Korea would be a military liability."[26] By August 15, 1948, the United States recognized the ROK headed by strongman Syngman Rhee and on September 9, the Soviets recognized the DPRK, thus formalizing the 38th parallel as a permanent border. By the end of 1948, the Soviets withdrew their troops, leaving behind the North Korean "People's Army." By June 29, 1949, all but about 500 U.S. troops were withdrawn, based on the opinion of Gen. MacArthur that South Korea's security forces were adequate for its defense.[27] Of course, this turned out to be tragically wrong.

In a speech in January of 1950, Secretary of State Dean Acheson described the perimeter of U.S. interests in the Pacific and notably left out Korea.[28] After Acheson's speech North Korean leader Kim Il Sung sought and received Soviet and Chinese support for invading the south, although Stalin insisted that direct assistance should come from China, not Russia.[29] How important was that speech in encouraging Stalin to approve Kim's request? Historian John Lewis Gaddis claims the speech "significantly reshaped Stalin's thinking on the risks of war with the United States in east Asia."[30] On the other hand, General Matthew Ridgway, who eventually took command of the forces in Korea, exonerates Acheson: "It is a gross and misleading simplification to lay the blame for the outbreak of the Korean War upon Dean Acheson's public 'writing off' of Korea as beyond our defense perimeter. He was merely voicing an already accepted United States policy."[31] Ridgway goes on to point out that while the United States left a poorly trained and underequipped army in the ROK, the Russians left the North Koreans with far superior military forces. They had large quantities of modern weapons, including tanks and aircraft. Their forces far outnumbered those in the South and were well trained and thoroughly indoctrinated by the Communists.[32]

Despite the superiority of the North Korean troops, the exclusion of Korea from the American defense perimeter was deeply rooted in the belief that the next war would be an atomic war and that the Communists were not ready to risk such a war. Thus, the United States ignored intelligence reports received just six days prior to the invasion that there were "extensive troop movements" and evacuation of civilians just north of the 38th parallel.[33] This was viewed as a Communist bluff—not a prelude to war.

Beschloss argues that the muted reaction to the Korean invasion led to the American public not being prepared for what was to follow:

> For weeks after sending US armed forces into Korea, Truman gave no extended explanation of his action to the American people. . . . This was a mistake. By entering a war to save a regime most Americans knew nothing about, in a theater from which he had previously withdrawn US troops, he had left much of the public puzzled, asking why, only five years after winning a global war, the American goliath was bogged down in a struggle against North Koreans.[34]

UN "POLICE ACTION"

Truman's actions in the days following the invasion were designed to slow the progress of the attack and send a strong message to the Communists that they could not simply take whatever they wanted. He endeavored to develop a strategy that would parry their thrust without embroiling the globe in a third world war. MacArthur was authorized to use American ground forces to support the ROK. The Seventh Fleet was sent to the Strait of Formosa to protect Chiang Kai-shek's Chinese Nationalists from an attack by Red China. Truman also sought to strengthen the defense of the Philippines and increase aid to the French in Indo-China.[35]

One of the key differences between the Korean conflict and the wars discussed in the preceding chapters is that Truman did not seek formal congressional approval or a declaration of war. Beschloss notes, "Truman's refusal—and the willingness of Congress and the courts to put up with it—established a dangerous excuse for every later President to avoid asking the House and Senate for war declarations."[36] In fact, no American war since World War II has involved a formal declaration of war, and numerous military actions have occurred without congressional approval.

After meeting with several key congressional leaders, Truman issued a statement outlining American actions being undertaken under the auspices of the UN resolution:

> The attack upon Korea makes it plain beyond all doubt that communism has passed beyond the use of subversion to conquer independent nations and will now use armed invasion and war. It has defied the orders of the Security Council of the United Nations issued to preserve international peace and security. In these circumstances the occupation of Formosa by Communist forces would be a direct threat to the security of the Pacific area and to United States forces performing their lawful and necessary functions in that area.[37]

Truman's statement established the basic narrative that would guide his policy for the remainder of his term. First and foremost, this was not a conflict among the Korean people themselves. There was no acknowledgment that it was in any way a civil war. Rather, this was presented as a clear-cut case of Communist aggression. He did not argue that Korea was a direct threat to national security, but rather that should the hostilities spread to Formosa, it would become such a threat. In addition, by utilizing the framework of the United Nations, America was not standing alone. At his first press conference after the invasion, on June 29, he repeatedly said, "We are not at war." When asked by a reporter if this was a "police action," he replied, "That is exactly what it amounts to."[38]

For Truman,

> the one purpose that dominated me in everything I thought and did was to prevent a third world war. One of the events that has cast a shadow over our lives and the lives of peoples everywhere has been termed, inaccurately, the "cold war."[39]

The Korean conflict was no isolated bonfire, easily extinguished, as Ridgway believed most Americans thought. Rather, it was part of a broader story of a life-and-death struggle between the free world and the tyranny of Communism. That Americans broadly supported Truman's initial response is apparent from public opinion polls, reaching 77 percent approval in a Gallup Poll in July 1950.[40]

MACARTHUR'S INCHON MIRACLE

The South Korean and UN forces were badly outnumbered and unprepared. By August, they had been pushed into a small portion of the southeastern Korean Peninsula known as the Pusan perimeter. It was clear that the UN forces were in dire straits. They were successful in holding off several North Korean attempts to break through the perimeter. Despite inflicting severe causalities on the Communists and as well as some civilians, there was no easy way for them to regain the initiative.

In an effort to go on the offensive and keep the UN forces from being forced into the ocean, General MacArthur developed one of the most daring military operations ever attempted. The Inchon landing was conducted over the objections of most of his staff, including General Ridgway, who writes,

> Almost before the rest of us fully comprehended that our nation was at war, MacArthur had begun to plan the amphibious enveloping movement . . . that would hit the enemy where he least looked for a blow, would sever his supply lines, and trap him between anvil and hammer. While others thought of a way to withdraw our forces safely, MacArthur planned for victory.[41]

On September 15, some 70,000 men in 262 ships landed at Inchon, an almost impossible feat given the harsh conditions. There was a tidal variation of about 30 feet, which limited the landing window to only six hours. The channel was narrow, and there were defensive sites along the way. However, MacArthur was counting on the element of surprise, knowing that the area was not well defended by the NKPA, which was concentrating on assaulting the UN forces in Pusan.[42] In merely eleven days, Seoul was recaptured. The Eighth Army broke out of the Pusan Perimeter and by October 1, the United Nations was back at the 38th parallel. As McCullough writes, "Seldom in military history had there been such a dramatic turn in fortune."[43]

GOVERNMENT AND MEDIA PROPAGANDA

Initial press coverage of the war was subject to only voluntary censorship. There were early press reports of political executions by the South Koreans, including those of women and children.[44] Such negative reporting led General MacArthur to impose censorship on December 21. Those who violated the rules faced expulsion, as United Press reporter Peter Webb learned when he reported the death of an American general.[45] Phillip Knightley explains, "[I]t was now forbidden to make any criticism of the allied conduct of the war or 'any derogatory comments' about United Nations troops or commanders."[46]

The net result, according to Knightley was that "the prospect of the Korean War's being reported fully and truthfully receded rapidly . . . Not one major daily newspaper opposed the war."[47] The lack of the truthful reporting was confirmed by UP's Robert Miller, who said in 1952, "We are not giving them the true facts about Korea," adding that some stories "were pure fabrication."[48]

With a compliant media, the Truman administration did not feel the need to create a new office to propagandize the war. Rather, they chose to run the campaign from the White House. With his reputation for saying "the buck stops here," Truman became the embodiment of the war propaganda campaign.[49] Television, although still not present in the majority of homes, soon became a big part of the campaign. The heads of CBS and NBC had been involved in the Office of War Information and their public affairs programs, such as *Meet the Press*, relied primarily on government representatives as guests.[50] Programs such as *Battle Report—Washington* on NBC and *The Facts We Face* on CBS were produced in collaboration with the White House; the State Department worked with CBS on *Diplomatic Pouch*.[51] On the latter show Secretary of State Acheson portrayed the Cold War as a fight "between civilization and barbarism."[52]

Although no Frank Capra appeared to create a propaganda masterpiece, the movie industry was enlisted to support the war. *Why Korea*, produced by Twentieth Century Fox, was released in early 1951 and won an Oscar for best documentary. It tied the Korean War to past aggression, including Japan in Manchuria, Mussolini in Ethiopia, and Russia in Finland. Koreans were portrayed as happy with their supposedly democratic government (which of course was not the case). The storyline was that if we didn't fight them over there, we'd have to fight them here. Some theater owners resisted showing the film, doubting that people would pay to see such propaganda.[53] Nevertheless, until other events changed the narrative, the propaganda campaign seemed to be working well.

NORTH TO PYONGYANG AND THE YALU

It is one of the great unknowns of history what would have happened had the UN stopped at the 38th parallel and negotiated a ceasefire. Truman's objective of stopping Communist aggression might have been met and hundreds of thousands of lives saved. On the other hand, the North might have refused a ceasefire, regrouped, and attacked again. Buoyed by their success, the UN forces under MacArthur continued to move north. Truman authorized him to "extend his operations north of the parallel and to make plans for the occupation of North Korea."[54] This order included the caveat that he was not to extend ground operations north should the Communist Chinese or Soviets intervene. By September 27, MacArthur was further ordered to pursue "the destruction of the North Korean Armed Forces."[55] This was a dramatic change in the original purpose of stopping Communist aggression. The Chinese were alarmed and Foreign Minister Chou En-lai warned that if the UN crossed the 38th parallel, China would intervene, but Washington viewed the threat as a bluff.[56]

By October 19, the Eighth Army had taken the North Korean capital of Pyongyang and within a week the ROK Army had reached the Yalu River bordering China. When Truman met with MacArthur on Wake Island (figure 6.1) on October 15, he was assured privately that "victory was won in Korea" and that the Chinese Communists would not attack. He also told Truman that he believed resistance would end by Thanksgiving.[57] After their private meeting, MacArthur proclaimed at a public meeting that "if the Chinese tried to get down to Pyongyang, there would be the greatest slaughter."[58] Polls showed that most Americans thought the war was nearly over and in a November 26 television broadcast, David Brinkley declared that our troops would be "out of the fox-holes by Christmas."[59] Yet the war was soon to take an unexpected turn.

Figure 6.1 President Harry S. Truman meets General Douglas MacArthur for the first time on Wake Island on October 15, 1950. MacArthur assured Truman the war in Korea was almost over. *Source: Photo courtesy of Harry S. Truman Library & Museum. (Accession number 69-1199)*

"Home by Christmas" was to morph into a stalemate that lasted over two and a half more years, and continues to threaten renewed hostilities to this day.

CHINA INTERVENES

Contrary to MacArthur's assurances, the Chinese became involved in the war in far more than a token way. In late 1950, it was known by U.S. intelligence that Chinese troops were in Korea helping the North Koreans. MacArthur estimated there were around 30,000, but didn't think it was significant.[60] The architect of the miracle at Inchon developed a plan to end the war in one overwhelming attack. On the day after Thanksgiving, November 24, MacArthur began a "massive comprehensive envelopment" of the enemy, which he hoped would "get the boys home for Christmas." Four days later, the hoped for victory had turned sour. The Chinese had attacked with a massive force of 260,000.[61] By December 15, the U.S. Eighth Army and the ROK Army had withdrawn below the 38th parallel. On that date, Truman spoke to the American people declaring a national emergency and calling on each American "to put aside his personal interests for the good of the country."[62] The *New York Times* reported on December 28 that the United States had suffered a total of 33,878 casualties, including 5,870 dead.[63] Further, the *Times* reported that 450,000 enemy troops were in Korea and 1,350,000 were in the battle area or on the way.[64] By January 4, Seoul was once again evacuated.[65] In less than two months, all of the gains from the offensive north of the 38th parallel were erased, and it was clear that the "police action," was becoming a true war.

Although public support for the defense of Korea was initially quite high, reaching 77 percent in July of 1950, it dropped by some 25-percentage points after the Chinese intervention, where it remained for most of the rest of the war.[66] John E. Mueller's analysis of public opinion polls on the Korean and the Vietnam Wars reveals that the decline in support was directly related to the level of American causalities: *"In each war, support is projected to have started at much the same level and then every time American causalities increased by a factor of 10 . . . support for the war dropped about 15 percentage points."*[67] Unlike Vietnam, where casualties were low for a long time, in Korea within a few months American losses started to mount quickly, thus eroding public support more precipitously. By January 1951, a Gallup poll found that 49 percent of respondents thought the war was a mistake and in February Truman's approval rating dropped to 26 percent.[68]

One might ask, as did many Americans and many of our troops, what are we fighting for? After all, it's doubtful most Americans could find Korea on a map prior to the war. And even the Joint Chiefs of Staff (JCS) had declared the peninsula unimportant to American strategic military interests. One of the more interesting attempts to explain the war was written by General Ridgway. One January 21, 1951, he sent all personnel under his command answers to two questions: "Why are we here?" and "What are we fighting for?" To the first question, his answer was simple and what one might expect from a career military officer, "We are here because of the decisions of the properly constituted authorities of our respective governments."[69] In other words, we are good soldiers and we follow orders. The answer to the second question, however, reflected the fundamental narrative of a fight to save civilization. The battle was about

> whether the rule of men who shoot their prisoners, enslave their citizens, and deride the dignity of man, shall displace the rule of those to whom the individual and his individual rights are sacred . . . . In the final analysis, the issue now joined right here in Korea is whether Communism or individual freedom shall prevail.[70]

However, South Korea is misleadingly portrayed as a place where individual freedom was respected. In reality, South Korea's strongman Rhee was corrupt and ruthless. When the war began, some 14,000 people were held as political prisoners, and when Seoul was retaken from the North Koreans, executions of political opponents increased dramatically.[71] Thus, the freedom versus tyranny narrative lacked fidelity to the actual nature of the South Korean regime.

The freedom versus tyranny dualism was evident in news coverage as well. In early 1951, a young Marine corporal questioned the war and in a letter to his father, who forwarded it to the State Department. The *New York Times* characterized the letter writer as "a disturbed and questioning young Marine Corps corporal, bitterly critical of United States foreign policy."[72] Secretary of State Dean Acheson wrote back, responding, that the war was happening "because some distant and shadowy figures in the Kremlin, controlling millions of people far from them" had been behind the attack. He characterized them as "monstrous" and "evil."[73] Thus, the war was set in the context of good versus evil. As the *Times* reported, the letter was persuasive and the corporal responded "that Mr. Acheson's letter 'has convinced me,' adding 'I definitely think we ought to be in Korea.'"[74] Thus, only a bitter or disturbed person dared question the Cold War narrative, and once the truth was explained to him, his objections were resolved.

Framed, not as a defense of a single nation of Korea, but rather as part of a wider global struggle against Communism, this narrative resonated with the troops and the public. As Mueller found in his analysis of public opinion polls, it made a significant difference how the question was framed. Adding a reference to "Communist invasion," increased support from 15 to 20 percentage points, compared to similar questions that asked if the respondent approved of the effort to "defend South Korea."[75] Given the anti-communist hysteria of the early 1950s, including Joe McCarthy's wild charges, it's not surprising that framing the narrative in terms of Communism versus freedom initially enhanced the persuasiveness of the government's narrative.

TWO NARRATIVES CLASH: VICTORY OR LIMITED WAR?

Truman's narrative held within it the seeds of its own destruction. There was a fundamental contradiction in seeking to limit the war at the same time that Communism was portrayed as an existential threat. If the Communists were the embodiment of evil, why would the United States just want to "contain" rather than defeat them? This contradiction was further aggravated as atrocity stories began to emerge. The official Army Handbook, for example, claimed the enemy had "the Oriental disregard for human life."[76] The same attitude toward the North Koreans was found in the domestic media. Suicidal waves of North Korean troops just kept coming. The *Washington Post* quoted an American soldier describing the attacks, "For every ten we killed another ten came charging over the hill to replace them."[77] The *New York Times* reported that seven American soldiers held as prisoners had been executed by the side of a road, shot in the face, their hands tied behind their backs.[78] Later in the war, North Koreans were accused of brainwashing American POWs, whose forced confessions to war crimes were used for propaganda.[79] In short, the North Korean Communists were portrayed as the embodiment of evil. So how could it be sufficient to just contain them north of the 38th parallel?

This contradiction played out in dramatic form in the dispute that eventually led to the firing of General MacArthur. Truman sought to stop Communist expansion, while at the same time avoiding a global war. This limited objective made it difficult to explain the continued sacrifice and loss of life as the war continued well past the promise of "home by Christmas." Once the Chinese intervened in large numbers, MacArthur sought to take the fight to mainland China, asserting, "There is no substitute for victory."[80] As General Ridgway explains,

> When MacArthur spoke of victory, he did not mean merely victory in Korea . . . .What he envisaged was no less than the global defeat of Communism . . . . His plan therefore entailed the very considerable risk of igniting World War III.[81]

MacArthur did not just present his opinions to Truman and the JCS. Through a series of public statements he clashed with administration policy, despite repeated warnings to not do so publicly. On March 24, 1951, MacArthur released a statement that Truman saw as the final act of insubordination. It stated,

> The enemy, therefore, must by now be painfully aware that a decision of the United Nations to depart from its tolerant effort to contain the war to the area of Korea, through an expansion of our military operations to its coastal areas and interior bases, would doom Red China to the risk of imminent military collapse.[82]

MacArthur suggested using atomic weapons and laying down a barrier of radioactive waste along the border to prevent additional Chinese infiltration into Korea.[83] Truman complicated the issue, implying in a press conference on November 30, 1950, that he might use the A-bomb in Korea. In considering the weapons we might use in Korea, a reporter asked, "Will that include the atomic bomb?" Truman replied, "That includes every weapon that we have." Asked a follow-up question, "Did we understand you clearly that the use of the atomic bomb is under active consideration?" the president reiterated, "Always has been. It is one of our weapons."[84] Although the answer was later walked back by the White House, the United Press wire had already released the story, proclaiming, *"President Truman said today that the United States has under consideration use of the atomic bomb in connection with the war in Korea."* Other news services and papers followed suit.[85]

It is not hard to understand the general public's confusion. On the one hand, Truman was advocating a limited war to contain Communism, but not to attack its base. Mainland China was off-limits. The beloved hero of World War II and architect of the Inchon miracle proposed a strategy of victory. He would liberate North Korea and punish Red China for its aggression. A nation that had just come off the resounding defeat of the Nazi and Japanese war machines, having used the most powerful weapon in history, appeared to be hamstringing a military genius for no good reason.

On April 11, 1951, MacArthur and the world learned that Truman had fired him. Public reaction was overwhelmingly negative. A Gallup poll found that 69 percent of the respondents backed MacArthur. When Truman threw out the first pitch on opening day, he was roundly booed.[86] MacArthur, on the other hand, received a hero's welcome upon his return to the United States. Speaking to a joint session of Congress on April 19, he was greeted by a standing ovation. He recounted his frustration with the administration:

I called for reinforcements, but was informed that reinforcements were not available. I made clear that if not permitted to destroy the build-up bases north of the Yalu; if not permitted to utilize the friendly Chinese force of some 600,000 on Formosa; if not permitted to blockade the China coast . . . and if there were to be no hope of major reinforcements, the position of the command from the military standpoint forbade victory. . . . War's very object is victory—not prolonged indecision. In war, indeed, there can be no substitute for victory. There are some who for varying reasons would appease Red China. They are blind to history's clear lesson. For history teaches with unmistakable emphasis that appeasement but begets new and bloodier war.[87]

It was a powerful rebuttal to the narrative proposed by the administration, which saw the Korean War as the antithesis of appeasement. To MacArthur, the failure to take the war to the Communists in China was appeasement. The Communists were bent on world conquest and unless the United States stood up to them, it would be Hitler at Munich all over again, only this time with atomic weapons. When one of the most revered and celebrated military leaders of his generation sought the support he claimed he needed for victory, he was denied. How to create a narrative to support a limited war became increasingly difficult for Truman. The public clearly sided with MacArthur. In a sense, the choice was victory or leave. Stalemate was not an option.

McCullough describes the public's frustration with the war:

America didn't fight to achieve a stalemate, and the cost in blood had become appalling. . . . According to the latest figures, there were more than ten thousand Americans dead, another fifty thousand wounded or missing in action. The country wanted it over. MacArthur at least offered victory.[88]

Reminding the public of the contrast with World War II, the award-winning documentary television series, *Victory at Sea*, ran from October of 1952 through April of 1953.[89] The celebration of America's mighty sea power, accompanied by the stirring score of Richard Rogers, visually transported viewers back to the scene of some of its greatest victories. Most of the films made during the Korean War were about World War II, not Korea. A few, such as *One Minute to Zero* and *The Glory Brigade* were made about Korea. One of the most interesting films, *The Steel Helmet*, made without Department of Defense assistance, raised doubts about the U.S. role in Korea, ending with the prophetic title card, "There is no end to the story."[90]

Television was beginning to gain traction in America. Although only 9 percent of Americans had TVs in their homes in 1950, that number rose considerably by 1953.[91] Thus, television began to impact the public's perception of the war. In late 1952, Edward R. Murrow hosted a "Christmas in Korea" program that showed the war's devastation and allowed troops to send greetings home.⁹² Of course, TV also helped promote the anticommunist crusade of McCarthy, until Murrow exposed him in 1954. And MacArthur's "Old Soldiers Never Die," speech was viewed by millions thanks to television.

TRUCE TALKS

A year into the Korean War, Truman was under pressure from all sides. Those who supported MacArthur's position wanted to expand the war to China. On the other hand, there was a movement toward seeking a truce. On June 1, the secretary general of the UN, Trygve Lie, proposed a ceasefire. On June 7, Secretary of State Acheson concurred. On June 23, Russian Representative to the UN Jacob Malik also proposed starting talks. Two days later, China's *People's Daily* endorsed Malik's proposal.⁹³ Truman spoke on June 25, 1951, one year after the start of the war, to a group in Tullahoma, Tennessee. He responded to his hawkish critics with a striking analogy, "They want us to play Russian roulette with the foreign policy of the United States—with all the chambers of the pistols loaded." Instead of expanding the war, he said, "We are ready to join in a peaceful settlement in Korea now, just as we have always been. But it must be a real settlement which fully ends the aggression and restores peace and security to the area and to the gallant people of Korea."⁹⁴ Thus, all of the major parties seemed to be pushing in the direction of a ceasefire preserving the status quo. Truce talks began on July 10, yet, an armistice took over a year to achieve and nearly seven decades later there is no peace treaty.

One of the biggest obstacles to a truce was South Korean President Syngman Rhee, who proclaimed on repeated occasions that he would accept nothing less than a united Korea. Nevertheless, Truman reports that substantial progress was made between November 1951 and January 1952.⁹⁵ Then a vexing problem arose over the return of POWs. Truman complained that the North Koreans refused to allow Red Cross inspection of their camps. On January 1, the UN side proposed that all *willing* prisoners of war should be returned. The key difference was that the Communists wanted *all* prisoners returned, which meant that North Korean soldiers who did not wish to return to Communist rule would have to be forcibly repatriated. Given the portrayal of Communists as brutal, Truman was adamant, "We will not buy an armistice by turning over human beings for slaughter or slavery."⁹⁶ The *coherence* of Truman's narrative was flawed—how could Communists be allowed to rule millions in the North, while denying the return of a few thousand POWs to their home country.

While the war in Korea was dragging on, with neither side approaching victory, truce talks stalled and were adjourned on October 8. Truman's public approval ratings continued to plummet. By December 1951, his job approval had reached a startling low of 23 percent.[97] Although future presidents were limited by the Twenty-Second Amendment to two terms, Truman was exempted from the limitation and could have sought another term. Nevertheless, he announced on March 29, 1952, that he would not do so.[98] Thus, the nation was faced with a choice of two paths on the future of the country and the war in Korea. Having declined to run again, Truman's public approval was no longer the deciding factor.

EISENHOWER PROMISES TO "GO TO KOREA"

The Democrats chose Illinois Governor Adlai Stevenson as their nominee when the man whom many Democrats preferred, Dwight Eisenhower, spurned their party's overtures, declaring that he was a Republican. Ike, as he was commonly known, was the military hero responsible for D-Day and the ultimate defeat of Hitler in Europe. The hero of the Pacific theater, MacArthur was not a candidate, but for Americans who wanted someone who knew how to win a war, there was no contest—Ike was their man.

At this point, the Korean War had dragged on for more than two years, costing over 25,000 American lives. Challenged by Truman to present a plan to end the war in Korea, Ike responded on October 24, "I shall go to Korea."[99] One of the greatest military commanders in history made this ambiguous promise and convinced millions of Americans to "like Ike." Eleven days later, on November 4, America overwhelmingly voted him into the White House.

Shortly after the election, Ike fulfilled his promise to go to Korea and see for himself what was happening. He was briefed by the JCS at the Pentagon before departure and presented only two options: indefinitely continue the fighting or seek an all-out victory with concomitant casualties. The president-elect rejected both options.[100] Upon returning from Korea to Pearl Harbor on December 14, Eisenhower spoke to the press: "We face an enemy . . . whom we cannot hope to impress by words, however eloquent, but only by deeds—executed under circumstances of our own choosing."[101] Eisenhower biographer Jean Edward Smith concludes that this statement was an implied threat of escalation—even to the extent of using atomic weapons.[102] In 1984 formerly classified documents were released that confirmed Eisenhower had considered using nuclear weapons in Korea.[103] There is dispute among historians as to whether or not the Communists were made aware of the threat of nuclear weapons, but Eisenhower's public pronouncements made it clear he was willing to use greater force in resolving the conflict.

THE ARMISTICE—NO PEACE TREATY

Although Eisenhower was motivated to end the Korean War, little progress could be made while Stalin lived. The Soviet leader relished tying down American forces in Asia while he was free to pursue his goals elsewhere in the world. When on March 5, 1953, Stalin died, the United States saw an opportunity to seek peace with a new Soviet leader. On April 16, Eisenhower delivered a major foreign policy address laying out a vision for a more peaceful world:

> Every gun that is made, every warship launched, every rocket fired . . . signifies, in the final sense, a theft from those who hunger and are not fed . . . Is there no other way the world may live?

He then called upon the new leaders of the U.S.S.R. to

> turn the tide of history. A world that begins to witness a rebirth of trust among nations *can* find its way to a peace that is neither partial nor punitive. . . . *The first great step along this way must be the conclusion of an honorable armistice in Korea.*[104]

On April 26, 1953, truce talks were resumed. The issue of repatriation of prisoners was resolved by agreeing to allow those prisoners who rejected repatriation to be turned over to a neutral international organization made up of representatives from Czechoslovakia, Poland, Sweden, Switzerland, and India. South Korean President Rhee initially opposed the armistice because it did not provide for a unified Korea. Eisenhower pressured him to comply, writing,

> It is my profound conviction that . . . acceptance of the Armistice is required . . . . We would not be justified in prolonging the war with all the misery that it involves in the hope of achieving, by force, the unification of Korea.[105]

On June 18, Eisenhower went so far as to threaten Rhee with the total withdrawal of American troops and financial assistance. Rhee held out until July 12 when he finally publicly agreed to the armistice, which was signed on July 27 at 10:12 in the morning Korean time. Eisenhower then issued a statement on what was July 26 in Washington: "And so at long last the carnage of war is to cease and the negotiations at the conference table to begin."[106] Although Rhee capitulated and agreed to the armistice, no representative of his nation signed it.[107] The negotiations for a permanent peace treaty were not productive. No peace treaty was ever agreed to and the peninsula still remains technically at war.

Once the truce was signed, the public's reaction was somewhat unexpected. Fewer people actually found the war "worth fighting" than had done so during the war itself, with 62 percent in the NORC poll believing it was not worth the fight in August 1953. Yet, by the last few months of 1953, support for the war had risen, and by 1956 a majority of Americans finally agreed that the Korean War was "worth fighting."[108]

WAR CRIMES AND ATROCITIES

It is fairly predictable that in any war, both sides will tell a narrative that accuses the other of war crimes and atrocities. The Korean War was no exception. Americans were accused without proof of using germ warfare against North Koreans.[109] Reports of North Korean Communist atrocities begin to emerge in early July 1950.[110] The U.S. Senate Committee on Government Operations appointed a subcommittee to investigate these allegations, and it produced a report in January 1954. In part, the committee reported:

> The evidence before the subcommittee conclusively proves that American prisoners of war . . . were beaten, wounded, starved, and tortured; molested, displayed, and humiliated before the civilian populace and/or forced to march long distances without benefit of adequate food, water, shelter, clothing, or medical care to Communist prison camps, and there to experience further acts of human indignities.[111]

As an example of North Korean war crimes, the committee cited the Hill 303 massacre, where over forty U.S. troops were shot with their hands tied behind their backs. In another case, five American airmen were killed by North Koreans, who punctured them repeatedly with sharpened bamboo sticks. Overall, the report claimed there had been 5,639 deaths resulting from war crimes by the North Koreans.[112] The impact of the report was enhanced by the inclusion of numerous gruesome photos, which visually transported readers to the scene of North Korean atrocities. The man responsible for forming the subcommittee was none other than anti-communist crusader Joseph McCarthy. Thus, the atrocities reported in this report were propaganda designed to further fuel the fears of the threat posed by Communism.

Of course, in any war, there are usually misdeeds on both sides, even if they are never prosecuted as war crimes. There were reports of American soldiers committing questionable acts. *Time-Life* writer Robert Osborne wrote about America soldiers firing on civilian refugees, who they thought might actually be the enemy in disguise. Osborne called these shootings the "utmost savagery."[113] Edward R. Murrow visited Korea in August 1950. He recorded a program that was to be broadcast on radio claiming that American troops had burned villages in Korea, leaving their inhabitants with nothing. CBS refused to run the broadcast, but when Murrow returned he produced a program questioning America's ability to understand the plight of Asians who were impoverished and seeking change.[114]

It was not until over four decades later that the true extent of American misconduct became known. An Associated Press investigation told of the massacre of hundreds of South Korean civilians under a railroad bridge at No Gun Ri in July 1950:

> In interviews . . . ex-GIs speak of 100, 200 or simply hundreds dead. . . . American soldiers, in their third day at the warfront, feared North Korean infiltrators among the fleeing South Korean peasants, veterans said. . . . American commanders had ordered units retreating through South Korea to shoot civilians as a defense against disguised enemy soldiers, according to once-classified documents found by the AP. . . . "We just annihilated them," said ex-machine gunner Norman Tinkler of Glasco, Kan.[115]

Of course, by the time the true extent of the massacre became public, the Korean War was a "forgotten war," and those who had been involved in the massacre were old men. No one considered taking any kind of punitive action against them.

No matter who did the killing, whether it fell within the rules of civilized warfare or not, the Korean War was one of the costliest "limited" wars in history. The total price to the United States was 35,574 killed (including nonhostile), 103,284 wounded, 7,667 missing, and $67 billion. Estimated South Korean deaths were 217,000 military and 1,000,000 civilians. Estimated North Korean deaths were 406,000 military and 600,000 civilians. China suffered an estimated 600,000 military deaths.[116] It you add these numbers together, they approach three million lives sacrificed in a war that basically ended in a tie. The Korean Peninsula on both sides of the 38th parallel was laid to waste. Some 635,000 tons of bombs and over 32,000 tons of napalm were dropped on Korea.[117] In addition to the millions who died, millions more become refugees. As the Korean War receded into history, few remembered it or memorialized those who fought and died. It took forty-five years from the onset of the war for a Korean War Memorial to be built and opened to the public—long after the more famous Vietnam War Memorial was built. However, forgotten or not, the echo of the Korean War has continued to reverberate through the decades, and is still heard to this day.

KOREA'S NUCLEAR THREAT IN THE TWENTY-FIRST CENTURY

In the nearly seven decades since the end of hostilities in Korea, the Korean Peninsula has continued to be a source of tension. On numerous occasions, the peninsula has threatened to become the scene for yet another hot war. For example, on January 23, 1968, North Koreans captured the USS *Pueblo*, a U.S. intelligence vessel, while it was allegedly in international waters off the coast of Korea. After torturing the captive sailors, the North Koreans forced "confessions" from members of the crew. Eventually, the crew was released after the U.S. agreed to admit it had intruded into Korean waters. Further incidents with the Communist North included the downing of a U.S. intelligence aircraft that resulted in the death of thirty-one Americans.[118] Although an original signatory to the armistice that ended the war, North Korea announced in March of 2013 that it was repudiating the armistice. This was not the first time it had issued such a threat. But the tenuous nature of the peace between the two Koreas was clearly illustrated by this announcement.[119]

The most threatening development by far is the North's acquisition of nuclear weapons and the missiles capable of delivering them. As early as January 1994, the CIA reported that North Korea might have produced its first nuclear weapons. In October 2006, the North Koreans conducted an underground nuclear test yielding an estimated 5–15 kilotons. This was followed by several other tests, culminating on September 3, 2017, with a test generating 100 kilotons of explosive power, indicating that it may have been an H-bomb, as North Korea had claimed. On August 8, 2017, North Korea announced it was planning to test four intermediate-range missiles that could reach as far as Guam. In response the next day, President Donald Trump threatened "fire and fury." Even more threatening to the United States, on November 29, 2017, North Korea launched an intercontinental ballistic missile, capable of reaching U.S. territory.[120]

Bob Woodward writes,

> Trump's policy of maximum pressure on North Korea included not only draconian economic sanctions but also an unprecedented personal rhetorical assault on Kim, threatening 'fire and fury' and nuclear obliteration in scores of tweets and public remarks. The third element was military pressure.[121]

Not surprisingly, the United States and North Korea came very close to open conflict. Woodward, who recorded a number of interviews with President Trump, asked him directly how close we had come to war. He relates the conversation in his book *Rage*:

> "So, hard question, President Trump," I said. "I understand we really came close to war with North Korea." "Right. Much closer than anyone would know. Much closer. You know. He knows it better than anybody," he said, referring to Kim.[122]

According to Woodward, "Kim told CIA director Pompeo the same in their first meeting—that he was ready to go to war. 'We were very close,' Kim told Pompeo."[123] That the confrontation de-escalated was in no small part due to Trump's developing friendship with Kim. Woodward, who was given copies of their mutual correspondence, writes, "His relationship and letters with North Korean leader Kim Jong Un outlined in detail here were not by the foreign policy establishment playbook. But as Trump says repeatedly we had no war. That was an achievement."[124]

All of this nuclear and missile development led to round after round of sanctions from the UN. By early 2018, attempts at de-escalating the tensions began, with the North and South resuming negotiations, and the North Koreans participating in the Olympics under a unified Korean flag. In June 2018, Trump became the first sitting American president to meet with the leader of North Korea. North Korea suspended further nuclear tests and limited missile tests to shorter-range missiles. Trump canceled joint U.S.-South Korean military exercises. Both sides appeared to have stepped back from the "fire and fury" threats of the previous year.

In February 2019, Trump and Kim met again in Hanoi, but the meeting ended abruptly without any agreements being signed. In June, Trump visited the demilitarized zone and staged a brief photo-op with Kim, becoming the first American president to step briefly across the line into North Korea. Nevertheless, talks stalled and by December North Korea threatened to send the United States a "Christmas gift," although ultimately nothing happened.[125] But it was clear that nearly seven decades after the armistice, the war in Korea, remains never-ending. Former Secretary of Defense Bob Gates sees Trump as having accomplished no more than his predecessors. He writes, "For all the rhetoric and photo opportunities of the three summit meetings, by mid-2019, Trump had made no more progress toward North Korean denuclearization than had his three predecessors."[126]

As the United States and most of the rest of the world seek to pressure Kim into giving up his nuclear weapons, James D. Fearon, professor of Political Science at Stanford University, argues these threats have the opposite effect.

Despite assurances that the United States seeks no regime change in North Korea,

> Kim knows that this is cheap talk. If the opportunity for regime change arose, there is no way that the United States (and South Korea) could make a credible promise not to support opposition to Kim. . . . What is puzzling is that the Trump administration seems to think that threats and coercion . . . can work to get Kim to agree to stop his missile program in a verifiable way. . . . But threats and coercion just reinforce Kim's sense that his safety—from the United States and China—requires a working nuclear weapons capability.[127]

Ironically, the very threats and sanctions taken by the United States and others to pressure the North Koreans into abandoning their nuclear weapons, actually makes them more determined to keep them.

With the election of Joe Biden as president, the relationship with North Korea remains unsettled. On his campaign website Biden's policy was vague: "In North Korea, President Biden will empower our negotiators and jumpstart a sustained, coordinated campaign with our allies and others, including China, to advance our shared objective of a denuclearized North Korea."[128] On Veterans Day 2020, President-elect Biden chose to visit a Korean War Memorial, which some have interpreted as a signal to the North Koreans that American policy would remain firm.[129] North Korea's response has been to announce an increase to its nuclear forces, building more missiles for its arsenal.[130] Thus, the "bromance" between Kim and Trump will likely be replaced by a more adversarial relationship and a continuing propaganda war.

ASSESSING THE NARRATIVES

Using Fisher's tests of *coherence* and *fidelity*, the narratives Truman used to justify the U.S. involvement in the Korean War fell short on both counts. The story lacked *structural coherence* in terms of Korea being essential to national security. Not only had Dean Acheson publically excluded Korea from the U.S. defense perimeter, even the JCS and MacArthur argued against keeping substantial numbers of troops there. The United States had pulled out almost all its troops. Why would it do that if Korea were essential to national security? As far as the public was concerned, the greatest threats from Communism were in Europe. In terms of *material coherence*, if Communism were a threat in Asia, why were Chiang and his Chinese Nationalists abandoned? In terms of *characterological coherence*, Kim Il Sung was not a person well known to the U.S. population, thus not easily demonized. Atrocity stories about the North Koreans did appear and were subsequently publicized by a subcommittee appointed by Joseph McCarthy. But it was difficult to demonize a race, such as the Koreans, when the United States was fighting with troops from the same racial group. Perhaps Stalin, then, was the villain. While Truman argued that Stalin was behind the attacks, there was only an indirect link. It was not as if Russians had crossed into Korea. And until the ROK troops reached the Yalu, the Chinese presence was hidden.

Initially, Truman had to shift from the usual arguments used to support U.S. involvement—that its military security was threatened—to a more complicated narrative. June 25, 1950, was not on a par with December 7, 1941, or even the sinking of the *Maine* or *Lusitania*. He was forced to rely on the Truman Doctrine—that the United States needed to defend free people from Communist aggression wherever it occurred. Given the anti-communist hysteria of the 1950s, this was his best storyline. At the outset, when the conflict was presented as a "police action," it worked. The public support for the commitment of American troops was strong. However, the analogy to "cops on the beat" broke down when the Chinese responded with human wave attacks and pushed America back—meaning the troops would not be home by Christmas. As Mueller showed, when American casualties grew, public support declined.

Further complicating Truman's dilemma was that once Chinese intervention forced UN troops back below the 38th parallel, MacArthur presented a diametrically opposite narrative. Most Americans sided with the war hero and believed that wars are fought to be won. No one wants to "die for a tie."[131] If the Communists are savages and civilization is threatened by their aggression, how could Truman justify letting them keep North Korea? Once peace talks began, Truman held up a truce because he refused to force unwilling POWs back to the savagery of the North Korean Communists. How then could he simultaneously justify letting them control the lives of millions of North Koreans?

With respect to *narrative fidelity*, Truman's story faced a big obstacle. The United States had the atomic bomb, but refused to use the ultimate weapon as it had against Japan. Although Truman suggested in a press conference he was considering its use, he quickly walked back that threat. Americans had to ask, however, if we could beat Hitler and Japan, why can't we beat Kim? In World War II, the result was unconditional surrender, but in Korea, it was to keep the status quo. MacArthur was revered as a military genius and Truman fired him. What exactly was the reason for fighting a "limited war" in Korea, rather than a war for victory as MacArthur proposed and as he had achieved in the Pacific? As Susan Brewer put it, this is a dilemma that future presidents would also face: "[H]ow to persuade Americans that they were fighting for the highest stakes in a limited war in a small faraway country about which they knew nothing."[132]

During the 1952 campaign, although he was not a candidate for re-election (which at 23 percent approval was a lost cause), Truman made a speech attacking critics of the war, including the Republican nominee. One month before the election and prior to Ike's "go to Korea" promise, Truman spoke in Oakland, California, in defense of his policy in Korea. He sought to transport his listeners to a world where the Communists won in Korea:

> The best explanation I know as to why we are in Korea was given by Capt. James Jabara of Wichita, Kansas, who had been fighting there in our Air force. He put it very, very simply. "We are fighting in Korea," he said, "so we won't have to fight in Wichita."
>
> He is right. We are fighting in Korea so we won't have to fight in Wichita, or in Chicago, or in New Orleans, or on San Francisco Bay.[133]

It is no surprise General Eisenhower was elected and Korea became a "forgotten war." Truman's story, this analysis shows, didn't meet the fundamental tests of *narrative coherence* and *fidelity* for the American public. Part of the problem was the constant shift in the story. From a "police action," that would be over by Christmas, to a battle to liberate the entire Korean Peninsula, to a retreat to the 38th parallel, and finally a stalemate that left the Communists in control, the story just didn't ring true. Finally, Truman's argument that if we didn't fight them in Korea, they'd soon be in Wichita, didn't resonate with Americans. The Korean "police action" was hardly a survival war on a par with World War II.

Unfortunately, "fight them over there instead of here," became the rallying cry that would lead to another Asian war, this time in Vietnam. As we will see in chapter 7, actions taken by Truman in 1950 began an involvement in Indo-China that was to evolve into what, until Afghanistan, was the longest war in American history. Truman announced increased military assistance and a military mission to help France fight the Communists in Indo-China on June 27, 1950.[134] Although Truman did not use the term "domino theory" (Eisenhower is credited with the first usage of the phrase), that was what he was suggesting by saying we were fighting in Korea instead of Wichita. Like Korea, the war in Vietnam, although initially receiving wide public support, eventually became unpopular and convinced another president not to seek re-election. It is perhaps telling that one of the most popular movies of the Vietnam era was *M*A*S*H,* which was set in Korea.

NOTES

1. Mathew B. Ridgway, *The Korean War* (Garden City, NY: Doubleday and Co., 1967), 17.

2. Harry S. Truman, *Memoirs, Vol. 2: Year of Trial and Hope* (Garden City, NY: Doubleday, 1956), 332.
3. Truman, *Memoirs, Vol. 2*, 333.
4. Ridgway, *The Korean War*, 23.
5. David McCullough, *Truman* (New York: Simon & Schuster, 1992), 777 and Truman, *Memoirs*, 334–335.
6. United Press, "War is Declared by North Koreans; Fighting on Border," *New York Times*, June 25, 1950, 1, https://nyti.ms/3z5DQ59.
7. United Press, "War is Declared," 21.
8. Ridgway, *The Korean War*, 23.
9. Michael Beschloss, *Presidents of War* (New York: Crown, 2018), [page] 487, Kindle.
10. Truman, *Memoirs, Vol. 2*, 316–317.
11. Ridgway, *The Korean War*, 7.
12. McCullough, *Truman*, 785–786.
13. Harry S. Truman, *Memoirs, Vol. 1: Year of Decisions* (Garden City, NY: Doubleday, 1955), x.
14. Truman, *Memoirs, Vol. 2*, 290.
15. "Timeline of the Cold War," Truman Presidential Library and Museum, accessed January 12, 2020, https://www.trumanlibrary.gov/public/TrumanCIA_Timeline.pdf.
16. Harry S. Truman, "Special Message to the Congress on Greece and Turkey: The Truman Doctrine," March 12, 1947, Harry S. Truman Library and Museum, accessed January 14, 2020, https://www.trumanlibrary.gov/library/public-papers/56/special-message-congress-greece-and-turkey-truman-doctrine.
17. Truman, *Memoirs, Vol. 2*, 105.
18. Truman, *Memoirs, Vol. 2*, 106.
19. Truman, *Memoirs, Vol. 2*, 123.
20. Truman, *Memoirs, Vol. 2*, 306.
21. Truman, *Memoirs, Vol. 2*, 91.
22. "McCarthy Says Communists Are in State Department," History.com, last updated July 17, 2019, accessed January 14, 2020, https://www.history.com/this-day-in-history/mccarthy-says-communists-are-in-state-department.
23. Beschloss, *Presidents of War*, 443.
24. Truman, *Memoirs, Vol. 2*, 317.
25. Truman, *Memoirs, Vol. 2*, 324.
26. Truman, *Memoirs, Vol. 2*, 325.
27. Truman, *Memoirs, Vol. 2*, 328–329.
28. McCullough, *Truman*, 777.
29. John Maggio (writer and producer), *Korea: The Never Ending War*, PBS Video, 2019.
30. Quoted in Beschloss, *Presidents of War*, 443.
31. Ridgway, *The Korean War*, 10.
32. Ridgway, *The Korean War*, 9–11.
33. Ridgway, *The Korean War*, 12–13.

34. Beschloss, *Presidents of War*, 462.
35. Truman, *Memoirs, Vol. 2*, 337.
36. Beschloss, *Presidents of War*, 488.
37. Harry S. Truman, "Statement by the President on the Situation in Korea," June 27, 1950, Harry S. Truman Library and Museum, accessed January 15, 2020, https://www.trumanlibrary.gov/library/public-papers/173/statement-president-situation-korea.
38. McCullough, *Truman*, 782.
39. Truman, *Memoirs, Vol. 1*, x.
40. John E. Mueller, "Trends in Popular Support for the Wars in Korea and Vietnam," *The American Political Science Review* 65, no. 2 (June, 1971): 361, https://doi.org/10.2307/1954454.
41. Ridgway, *The Korean War*, 33.
42. "Inch'ŏn landing," *Encyclopaedia Britannica*, September 8, 2019, https://www.britannica.com/event/Inchon-landing.
43. McCullough, *Truman*, 798.
44. Phillip Knightley, *The First Casualty: The War Correspondent as Hero and Myth-Maker from the Crimea to Iraq*, 3rd ed. (Baltimore and London: John Hopkins University Press, 2004), 374–375.
45. Knightley, *The First Casualty*, 376.
46. Knightley, *The First Casualty*, 377.
47. Knightley, *The First Casualty*, 379.
48. Quoted in Knightley, *The First Casualty*, 386.
49. Susan A. Brewer, *Why America Fights: Patriotism and War Propaganda from the Philippines to Iraq* (New York: Oxford University Press, 2009), 152.
50. Brewer, *Why America Fights*, 154.
51. Brewer, *Why America* Fights, 154–155.
52. Brewer, *Why America Fights*, 155.
53. Brewer, *Why America Fights*, 163.
54. Truman, *Memoirs, Vol. 2*, 359.
55. Truman, *Memoirs, Vol. 2*, 360.
56. McCullough, *Truman*, 799.
57. Truman, *Memoirs, Vol. 2*, 365–366.
58. Truman, *Memoirs, Vol. 2*, 366.
59. Brewer, *Why America Fights*, 158.
60. McCullough, *Truman*, 814.
61. McCullough, *Truman*, 815.
62. Truman, *Memoirs, Vol. 2*, 428.
63. Associated Press, "U.S. Casualties Rise in Korea to 33,878," *New York Times*, December 28, 1950, 11, https://nyti.ms/34OCJsP.
64. Lindesay Parrott, "M'Arthur Reports 450,000 of Enemy Are Now in Korea," *New York Times*, December 28, 1950, 1–2, https://nyti.ms/3fRhlt4.
65. Ridgway, *The Korean War*, 254–255.
66. John E. Mueller, "Trends," 361.
67. Mueller, "Trends," 366 (italics in original).

68. Brewer, *Why America Fights*, 162–163.
69. Ridgway, *The Korean War*, 264.
70. Ridgway, *The Korean War*, 264–265.
71. Knightley, *The First Casualty*, 374.
72. Walter H. Waggoner, "Acheson Tells Bitter Marine to Have Faith in U.S. Ideals," *New York Times*, March 4, 1951, 1, https://nyti.ms/3ikzHV5.
73. Waggoner, "Acheson Tells Bitter Marine," 5.
74. Waggoner, "Acheson Tells Bitter Marine," 1.
75. Mueller, "Trends," 359.
76. Brewer, *Why America Fights*, 142.
77. McCullough, *Truman*, 788.
78. McCullough, *Truman*, 788.
79. Garth S. Jowett and Victoria O'Donnell. *Propaganda and Persuasion*, 7th ed. (Los Angeles: Sage, 2019), 245–246.
80. Truman, *Memoirs, Vol. 2*, 446.
81. Ridgway, *The Korean War*, 145.
82. Truman, *Memoirs, Vol. 2*, 441.
83. McCullough, *Truman*, 832, 835.
84. Harry S. Truman, "The President's Press Conference," November 30, 1950, Harry S. Truman Library and Museum, accessed January 20, 2020, https://www.trumanlibrary.gov/library/public-papers/295/presidents-news-conference.
85. McCullough, *Truman*, 822 (italics in original).
86. McCullough, *Truman*, 848.
87. Douglas MacArthur, "Address of the General of the Army, Douglas MacArthur," *Congressional Record—House*, April 19, 1951, 4124–4125, https://www.govinfo.gov/app/details/GPO-CRECB-1951-pt3/GPO-CRECB-1951-pt3-18-1.
88. McCullough, *Truman*, 847.
89. "Victory at Sea," IMDb, accessed January 22, 2020, https://www.imdb.com/title/tt0046658/
90. Brewer, *Why America Fights*, 173.
91. Brewer, *Why America Fights*, 154.
92. Brewer, *Why America Fights*, 173.
93. Truman, *Memoirs, Vol. 2*, 455–456.
94. Harry S. Truman, "Address in Tullahoma, Tenn., at the Dedication of the Arnold Engineering Development Center," June 25, 1951, Harry S. Truman Library and Museum, accessed January 21, 2020, https://www.trumanlibrary.gov/library/public-papers/138/address-tullahoma-tenn-dedication-arnold-engineering-development-center.
95. Truman, *Memoirs, Vol. 2*, 459–460.
96. Truman, *Memoirs, Vol. 2*, 460.
97. McCullough, *Truman*, 873.
98. Truman, *Memoirs, Vol. 2*, 488, 492.
99. Jean Edward Smith, *Eisenhower in War and Peace* (New York: Random House, 2012), 547.
100. Smith, *Eisenhower*, 557.

101. Smith, *Eisenhower*, 561.
102. Smith, *Eisenhower*, 561.
103. Bernard Gwertzman, "U.S. Papers Tell of '53 Policy to Use A-Bomb in Korea," *New York Times*, June 8, 1984, http://www.nytimes.com/1984/06/08/world/us-papers-tell-of-53-policy-to-use-a-bomb-in-korea.html.
104. Smith, *Eisenhower*, 575 (italics in original).
105. Quoted in Ridgway, *The Korean War*, 269.
106. Smith, *Eisenhower*, 577.
107. "Korean War," Encyclopaedia Britannica, January 3, 2020, accessed January 22, 2020, https://www.britannica.com/event/Korean-War.
108. Mueller, "Trends," 360, 374.
109. Brewer, *Why America Fights*, 171.
110. Senate Subcommittee on Korean War Atrocities. *Korean War Atrocities*, January 11, 1954, 2, https://www.loc.gov/rr/frd/Military_Law/pdf/KW-atrocities-Report.pdf.
111. Senate Subcommittee on Korean War Atrocities, *Korean War Atrocities*, 3.
112. Senate Subcommittee on Korean War Atrocities, *Korean War Atrocities*, 14.
113. Brewer, *Why America Fights*, 157.
114. Brewer, *Why America Fights*, 157.
115. Sang-Hun Choe and Charles J. Hanley, "Ex-GIs Tell AP of Korea Killing Associated Press Writers," *Washington Post Archives*, September 30, 1999, https://www.washingtonpost.com/wp-srv/aponline/19990930/aponline010625_000.htm.
116. "Korean War Fast Facts," CNN, last modified June 10, 2019, accessed December 2, 2019, https://www.cnn.com/2013/06/28/world/asia/korean-war-fast-facts/index.html.
117. Brewer, *Why America Fights*, 174.
118. "USS *Pueblo* Captured," History.com, July 20, 2010, last updated January 22, 2020, https://www.history.com/this-day-in-history/uss-pueblo-captured.
119. Rick Gladstone, "Threats Sow Concern Over Korean Armistice," *New York Times*, March 9, 2013, https://www.nytimes.com/2013/03/10/world/asia/threats-sow-concerns-over-korean-armistice.html.
120. Julia Masterson, "Chronology of U.S.-North Korean Nuclear and Missile Diplomacy," Arms Control Association, January, 2020, accessed January 24, 2020, https://www.armscontrol.org/factsheets/dprkchron.
121. Bob Woodward, *Rage* (New York: Simon & Shuster, 2020), [page] 72, Kindle.
122. Woodward, *Rage*, 184.
123. Woodward, *Rage*, 82.
124. Woodward, *Rage*, 388.
125. Masterson, "Chronology."
126. Robert M. Gates, *Exercise of Power: American Failures, Successes, and a New Path Forward in the Post-Cold War World* (New York: Alfred A. Knopf, 2020), loc. 5822 of 7416, Kindle.
127. James D. Fearon, "The Big Problem with the North Koreans Isn't That We Can't Trust Them. It's That They Can't Trust Us," *Washington Post*, April 16, 2017,

https://www.washingtonpost.com/news/monkey-cage/wp/2017/08/16/the-big-problem-with-north-korea-isnt-that-we-cant-trust-them-its-that-they-cant-trust-us/.

128. "The Power of America's Example: The Biden Plan for Leading the Democratic World to Meet The Challenges Of The 21st Century," accessed November 7, 2020, https://joebiden.com/americanleadership/.

129. Donald Kirk, "One of Biden's First Acts as President-Elect Was to Antagonize Kim Jong Un," Daily Beast, November 16, 2020, https://www.thedailybeast.com/one-of-joe-bidens-first-acts-as-president-elect-was-to-antagonize-kim-jong-un?source=articles&via=rss.

130. Choe Sang-Hun, "Kim Jong-un Vows to Boost North Korea's Nuclear Capability as Leverage With Biden," *New York Times*, January 8, 2020, https://www.nytimes.com/2021/01/08/world/asia/kim-nuclear-north-korea.html.

131. Brewer, *Why America Fights*, 174.

132. Brewer, *Why America Fights*, 145.

133. Harry S. Truman, "Address in the Oakland Auditorium," October 4, 1952, Harry S. Truman Library and Museum, accessed January 15, 2020, https://www.trumanlibrary.gov/library/public-papers/279/address-oakland-auditorium.

134. Truman, *Memoirs, Vol. 2*, 339.

Chapter 7

Vietnam

The Domino Theory Falls

On July 8, 1959, thirty-seven-year-old Army Major Dale Buis and a few of his buddies from the eight-man U.S. Military Assistance and Advisory Group (MAAG) in Bien Hoa, Vietnam, gathered to watch a movie, *The Tattered Dress*, starring Jeff Chandler and Jeanne Crain. They met in the gray stucco mess hall of their residential compound some 20 miles north of Saigon. As Master Sergeant Chester Ovnand flipped on the lights to change reels on the movie projector, Communist guerrillas fired their submachine guns at the Americans. Buis and Ovnand were killed along with two South Vietnamese guards and a young boy. The rest were saved when Major Jack Hallet turned out the lights and one of the guerrillas blew himself up trying to throw a homemade bomb.[1] These were the first deaths among members of the MAAG, which were introduced into Vietnam in 1950 to aid the French in subduing Communist fighters led by Ho Chi Minh.[2] Buis and Ovand are considered the first American deaths of the Vietnam era and their names are engraved on the Vietnam Memorial (figure 7.1).[3]

On July 8, 1959, no one suspected America was about to embark on a nearly sixteen-year conflict that would end with evacuations from the American embassy roof in Saigon. President Dwight Eisenhower had warned Americans that allowing the Communists to win in Southeast Asia would cause neighboring nations to fall like "a row of dominoes."[4] Ike's predecessor Truman had told Americans that unless they fought the Communists in Asia, they'd end up fighting them in Wichita. Yet today, over four decades after the first domino fell in Vietnam, the Soviet Union is no more and most Americans could probably find items in their homes that are stamped "Made in Vietnam." It turns out the dominoes didn't fall, even though Vietnam became the first war that America lost.

Figure 7.1 The Vietnam Veterans Memorial has the names of over 58,000 Americans who died in the Vietnam War era. It is the most visited memorial site in Washington, D.C. *Source*: U.S. Army photo by Sgt. Ken Scar. Image courtesy of the U.S. Army Reserve.

Unlike World War II, it is difficult to establish a precise date which will live in infamy for the Vietnam War. In his analysis of public opinion polling, John E. Mueller dates the beginning of the Vietnam War to mid-1965, as U.S. involvement escalated.[5] Others date its inception to the incidents in the Gulf of Tonkin on August 2 and 4, 1964, which led to a resolution by Congress giving presidents the authority to escalate the war.[6] Finally, some trace the beginning of the war as far back as 1950, as reflected in the title of George C. Herring's book: *America's Longest War: The United States and Vietnam, 1950–1975.*

PRELUDE TO WAR

Regardless of when the American war in Vietnam is thought to have begun, tracing the U.S. role in French Indochina can go as far back as the end of World War I. While in Paris, President Wilson ignored requests for Vietnam to be granted autonomy.[7] Indochina remained under French control until it was taken over by the Japanese during World War II. After World War II, Ho Chi Minh beseeched the American government to support independence for his countrymen. On September 2, 1945, Ho issued a Vietnamese declaration of independence to a crowd of half a million people in Hanoi, beginning with the same words as Thomas Jefferson used in 1776. American planes flew over the assembly, which the Vietnamese took as a sign of support, although the flights were a mere coincidence.[8] The Truman administration ignored Ho's request to turn Indochina into a protectorate like the Philippines.[9] Instead, America supported the French colonialists. It is ironic that a nation founded by revolution against a colonial power would support colonialists against independence-seeking people.

In early 1950, Truman provided aid to France in its war to retain its colonies in Indochina. In addition to over $133 million in financial aid, the United States sent the first MAAG advisers in 1950.[10] Truman feared that if the United States did not provide aid to France, it would lack the resources to aid the efforts in Western Europe to prevent Soviet aggression. Aid to France became part of the larger strategy of containing Communism throughout the world, which was the keystone to the Truman Doctrine. Understanding why the United States sided with the French rather than the independence-seeking Vietnamese requires an appreciation of the power of anti-communism at the time. China had fallen to the Reds, Joseph McCarthy was gaining power, and Truman's foreign policy was anchored in stopping the expansion of Communism. No distinction was made among the Soviets, Chinese, or Vietnamese. A Communist was a Communist and that was all that mattered. The appeasement of Hitler at Munich foreshadowed what could happen if Communists were not stopped in Indochina.[11] However, according to Neil Sheehan, "The Vietnamese got no assistance from Moscow, because Stalin was not interested in furthering their revolution."[12] The policy to aid France in keeping its colonies was continued under the Eisenhower administration. A total of $2.6 billion in aid was provided between 1950 and 1954.[13]

By 1954, the French were unable to defeat the insurgents known as the Viet Minh led by Ho Chi Minh. In March and April, the Viet Minh laid siege to the French fortress at Dienbienphu. France begged Eisenhower for air support, but he refused. He was undoubtedly influenced by General Mathew Ridgway, who was serving as Army Chief of Staff. He cautioned against U.S. involvement, predicting that such a war would require half a million to a million troops and 100,000 draftees per month.

> Instead of being like the Korean War it would really be more like a larger and more costly version of the Philippine insurrection, a prolonged guerrilla war, native against Caucasian, which lasted from 1899 to 1913 and which had been politically very messy.[14]

Also notable among those opposed to U.S. intervention was a young Massachusetts Senator, John F. Kennedy, who said U.S. aid could not defeat "an enemy of the people which has the support and covert appeal of the people."[15]

France, outnumbered and exhausted, surrendered on May 7.[16] The Geneva Accords ending France's colonial rule were signed July 21, 1954.[17] Vietnam was split in two, with the North controlled by the Viet Minh. The agreement specified that "the military demarcation line [17th parallel] is provisional and should not in any way be interpreted as constituting a political or territorial boundary."[18] Reunification was to occur after elections in the summer of 1956 supervised by an international commission. The Accords were less than satisfactory to all parties and both the United States and South Vietnam declined to sign. Moreover, the National Security Council (NSC) saw them as a "disaster," and recommended using "all available means" to undermine the North Vietnamese, including paramilitary groups that crossed the Demilitarized Zone (DMZ) to engage in sabotage and psychological warfare.[19]

The government of South Vietnam left by the French colonialists was headed by Ngo Dinh Diem, a staunchly anti-communist nationalist, who was Catholic in a largely Buddhist country.[20] Diem and the Americans knew that Ho Chi Minh would likely win the scheduled elections. Even Eisenhower admitted that a free election would likely give Ho 80 percent of the vote and control of the entire country.[21] Surprisingly, the Soviets and Chinese "tacitly conspired to cancel the elections" as well.[22] Refusing to hold the reunification elections, Diem held a referendum and claimed to have won with over 98 percent of the vote.[23] South Vietnam, known officially as the Republic of Vietnam (RVN), became a separate country. Contrary to the intent of the Geneva Accords, the United States set upon a mission of nation building, seeking a strong anti-communist bastion south of the 17th parallel.[24]

In reviewing this history, there are two competing narratives. On the one hand is the story of patriotic nationalists who sought to free their country from colonial rule, only to find their nation divided into two parts, one of which was basically an American colony. The narrative that America was simply replacing the French colonialists resonated with much of the Vietnamese population. The other narrative fell into the well-established Cold War story: Ho was a Communist and therefore obviously a puppet of the Soviets. Given the prevailing American narrative that monolithic Communism was bent on world domination, Eisenhower and his successors felt compelled to support an anti-communist bulwark in Southeast Asia. As David Halberstam points out, several events shaped this narrative:

> The first event was the hardening of the Cold War as tensions in Europe grew; the second was the fall of China . . . These events, coupled with the Korean War and the coming of Senator Joseph McCarthy, would markedly change the American perceptions of international Communism.[25]

Stopping the Communists at the 17th parallel became a fundamental part of America's containment narrative. By early 1956, the United States had taken over training of the Army of the Republic of Vietnam (ARVN). Between 1955 and 1961, the United States gave South Vietnam over $1 billion in aid and by the end of the decade more than 1,500 advisers assisted the government.[26]

Although Ike was the first to explicitly compare the region to a row of dominoes, he was not alone. Senator Kennedy, who had opposed aiding the French, soon shifted to embracing the domino theory. In 1956 the future president stated,

> Vietnam represents the cornerstone of the Free World in Southeast Asia, the keystone to the arch, the finger in the dike. Burma, Thailand, India, Japan, the Philippines and obviously Laos and Cambodia are among those whose security would be threatened if the Red Tide of Communism overflowed into Vietnam.[27]

As in previous wars, enemy brutality was fundamental to the narrative. The Geneva Accords permitted Vietnamese to move across the 17th parallel for resettlement in either the North or South. A U.S. Navy Task Force was given one year to move refugees, primarily Catholics, from the North to the South. Dr. Tom Dooley, who provided medical aid to the refugees, published a best-selling book, *Deliver Us from Evil*, which told gruesome stories of Communist atrocities.[28] Dooley wrote, "The Communists have perfected the techniques of torture, inflicting in one moment pain on the body and in the next pain on the mind." In one example, his powerful language transported readers to the scene of Communist brutality when he told of what happened to a priest who had escaped from the Communist Viet Minh.

> His head was matted with pus and there were eight large pus-filled swellings around his temples and forehead. . . . This particular priest had also been punished for teaching 'treason.' His sentence was a Communist version of the Crown of Thorns, once forced on the Saviour of Whom he preached.[29]

The *Los Angeles Times* later reported that these stories were likely fabricated:

> None of Dooley's correspondence, official or personal, describes the atrocities, that, in his book, he attributes to the communists. There are no corroborating accounts in the war diaries kept by Navy commanders nor in anything Dooley wrote during the operation.[30]

Nevertheless, Dooley's book became a best seller and popularized the story that North Vietnamese Communists were savages.

The Catholic Diem repressed his opponents, particularly Buddhists, comprising four-fifths of the population. Diem's repression was initially successful in suppressing dissent, but also created fertile ground for a revolution. In the spring of 1959, the North Vietnamese government established a secret force to move supplies and men into South Vietnam. By September 1960, the party approved armed struggle in the South, and in December founded the National Liberation Front (NLF). The North concealed its role, hoping that the NLF would appear to be indigenous to the South.[31] Some questioned the extent to which the insurgency in the South was indigenous, although a National Intelligence Estimate in October 1961 found that from 80 to 90 percent of the Viet Cong (as the NLF was called by the Americans) were locals rather than infiltrators from the North.[32]

THE TORCH IS PASSED

As the "torch was passed" to a new president, Kennedy made clear that he would be a Cold Warrior committed to protecting the free world from Communism. On January 20, 1961, he addressed the nation and the world, promising that "we shall pay any price, bear any burden, meet any hardship, support any friend, oppose any foe to assure the survival and the success of liberty."[33] The narrative was clear—the United States would do whatever was necessary to stop Communism. Defending South Vietnam clearly fit into that narrative, which resonated with the American public still steeped in Cold War rhetoric.

After he was elected, JFK ramped up military spending and termed Communist insurgencies "an international disease."[34] The new president faced a deteriorating situation in Vietnam. Seeing it as a keystone in America's efforts to stop Communist expansion, he was determined to meet the challenge, including engaging in covert activities in Vietnam.[35] In November 1961, Kennedy increased U.S. advisers beyond the numbers allowed in the Geneva Accords. Although many of the advisers were involved in combat along with their Vietnamese counterparts, Kennedy denied that fact.[36] Because the South Vietnamese Army was largely ineffective, Kennedy continued to increase the number of Americans in Vietnam to 11,300 by the end of 1962.[37] However, Halberstam writes, "Soon the only tangible result of the great American build-up was that the Vietcong were capturing better weapons."[38]

The war was becoming Americanized, although the public was kept in the dark. This represented a fundamental change in the U.S. mission. "Project Beefup" greatly increased America's role in Vietnam, including enlarging its military assistance, which was renamed from MAAG to MACV—Military

Assistance Command, Vietnam. Kennedy began the use of defoliants (including the notorious Agent Orange). Like presidents to follow, Kennedy deceived the public about the true extent of American involvement. When the press learned of the truth, the response in Saigon was to tighten restrictions on the media.[39]

As in Korea, one of the stories widely told about Vietnam was that the United States was close to victory. In April 1963 the head of the MACV, General Paul D. Harkens, told top officials in Honolulu that the war could end by Christmas.[40] On October 2, 1963, Secretary of Defense Robert McNamara and Chairman of the Joint Chiefs of Staff Gen. Maxwell Taylor reported after visiting Vietnam that the war was going well, a thousand Americans would be home by Christmas, and all troops would be out by the end of 1965.[41] Such optimism resulted from relying on reports from the military leadership, which were at odds with the conditions on the ground.

In reality, the situation in Vietnam continued to deteriorate. The undo optimism was partly the result of the ARVN avoiding battles that could result in casualties and American officers telling the brass what they wanted to hear. American military advisers, such Lt. Col. John Paul Vann, the subject of Neil Sheehan's Pulitzer Prize winning book, *Bright Shining Lies*, were frustrated by the incompetence of the ARVN commanders. Vann realized "that few of the regulars or territorials knew how to adjust the sights of their rifles and carbines well enough to hit a target, let alone a guerrilla."[42] Frustrated by the incompetence of the South Vietnamese army, Halberstam reports, "The Americans in Vietnam . . . had come up with a slogan to describe the ARVN promotion system: 'Fuck up and move up.'"[43] John R. MacArthur writes,

> In Halberstam's Vietnam there appear to have been two competing teams. One team was made up of older military officers and diplomats . . . and it insisted that things were going fine and the Vietcong were losing. . . . Another team was made up of younger army officers, like . . . Vann, and junior CIA agents, who knew the Vietcong was actually winning.[44]

Neither team challenged the basic narrative that the Communists had to be contained in Vietnam or Southeast Asia would fall like a row of dominoes. The disparagement of their South Vietnamese counterparts reflected an attitude of superiority by the American military. Asians, even those allied with America, were simply not as competent as the predominantly Caucasian U.S. forces.

The Catholic Diem put severe restrictions on the 80 percent of the population who practiced Buddhism and banned their religious observances.[45] In June a Buddhist monk, Quang Duc, set himself on fire at a major Saigon intersection to protest Diem's oppressive tactics.[46] The images of the monk on fire transported people around the world to a Vietnam far different than what America had portrayed. Diem's sister-in-law, Madame Nhu, made things worse when she referred to such immolations as "barbeques."[47] As the protests expanded, Diem's forces responded with a vengeance. In the early morning on August 20, they attacked pagodas in several cities, including Saigon and Hue.[48] Well over a thousand monks and nuns were arrested, many wounded and several killed. Sheehan reports, "[T]he great statue of Buddha in Hue's main Tu Dam Pagoda was smashed."[49] In October, Diem stepped up his oppression, going after students, first in college, then high school, and finally elementary schools, which were all closed.[50]

Given the widespread oppression by the regime, Diem and his brother Ngo Dinh Nhu became an obstacle to American policy in Vietnam. After all, it was difficult to make the case that the United States was defending freedom when the government it supported brutalized its people. Any doubt that the United States treated the government as its client was removed when it supported a coup that resulted in the assassination of Diem and his brother. When Diem learned he would not have American support, he resigned and escaped with his brother. They were soon captured and brutally murdered.[51] H. R. McMaster claims,

> The Diem coup marked a turning point in the Vietnam War. . . . By March the Viet Cong would control between 40 and 45 percent of the land of South Vietnam, up from less than 30 percent before the coup.[52]

The coup not only failed to solve the problem of leadership in Vietnam, it led to even more instability due to a series of coups leading to ten different governments in the next twenty months.[53] Thus, the U.S. succeeded only in further destabilizing the South Vietnamese government and undermining any remaining legitimacy.

Kennedy's own assassination occurred only three weeks after the coup that led to Diem's murder. It is unknowable what Kennedy would have done about Vietnam had he lived. In his 1995 retrospective, former Secretary of Defense Robert McNamara writes, "I think it highly probable that, had President Kennedy lived, he would have pulled us out of Vietnam."[54] But, of course, Kennedy did not live to implement whatever policy he had envisioned for Vietnam. Halberstam reflects on the situation at the time of JFK's death:

> He had escalated the number of Americans there to 16,900 at the time of his death, with more than 70 dead (each dead American became one more rationale for more dead Americans); more important, he had markedly escalated the rhetoric and the rationale for being there.[55]

Rather than a remote colonial war on the periphery of American national interest, the conflict in Vietnam became a test case of how the United States would respond to so-called wars of national liberation.

LBJ TAKES THE REINS

After the death of Kennedy, Vice President Lyndon Johnson assumed the presidency and the challenge of what to do about Vietnam. In his folksy way, LBJ complained that he was in the same situation as a catfish who "grabbed a big juicy worm with a right sharp hook in the middle of it."[56] With Diem gone, at first the North faced difficulties motivating its allies in the South. In December 1963, the North ramped up its efforts, including adding its own forces to the struggle. Johnson was committed to saving the South Vietnamese from the Communists. A memorandum issued by the NSC stated that "the central objective of the United States" was to help the South Vietnamese "to win their contest against the externally directed and supported communist conspiracy."[57] This policy continued the narrative that South Vietnam was the key to containing Communist expansion. Untold was the story that the Vietnamese people might prefer the other side in a civil war.

The situation on the ground in South Vietnam only worsened. Catholics and Buddhists were bitter enemies. The junta that overthrew Diem was ineffective. In late January 1964, it was overthrown by Gen. Nguyen Khanh.[58] In Washington, Johnson was focused primarily on his domestic program, which was stalled in Congress. Vietnam was a distraction that he feared could derail his agenda. He also was fearful that losing Vietnam to the Communists would ruin his chances for election in his own right. As he said in his own colorful way, if he lost the battle there, his political opponents would "push Vietnam up my ass every time."[59]

Early in 1964, in response to the deteriorating situation in Vietnam, LBJ replaced Harkins with General William Westmoreland and over the next nine months, increased the so-called advisers to 23,300. He also expanded covert operations in North Vietnam, including commando raids. However, these efforts did little to help the South Vietnamese cause. Estimates were that by spring 1964 the NLF controlled over 50 percent of the population and 40 percent of the territory.[60]

During the early years of the Johnson administration, dealing with the media in South Vietnam presented a challenge. On the one hand, the Johnson administration couldn't afford to alienate them. On the other, LBJ didn't want negative or critical stories to dominate the coverage. Thus in 1964 the administration launched a public relations program ironically named "Operation Maximum Candor."[61] Its twin goals of promoting the war and providing accurate information were inherently incompatible. The ploy failed to satisfy those reporting on the war. As William Tuohy of the *Los Angeles Times* complained, "We're drowning in facts here, but we're starved for information."[62] The official briefings became so obviously misleading that reporters called them the "Five O'Clock Follies."[63]

THE GULF OF TONKIN INCIDENTS

The incidents in the Gulf of Tonkin can be traced back to LBJ's decision to intensify covert actions against the North, a program called 34A.[64] This included commando raids and naval shelling of North Vietnam's coastal military installations.[65] On August 2, the destroyer USS *Maddox* was engaged in electronic spying in support of these covert actions. The USS *Maddox* actually fired first and was attacked by North Vietnamese torpedo boats responding to South Vietnamese bombardment of the North Vietnamese island of Hon Me the previous evening.[66] The torpedo boats were forced to retreat and at least one was damaged. President Johnson did not retaliate, perhaps realizing the North had been provoked. Stanley Karnow writes,

> Since no Americans had been hurt, he told his staff, further action was unnecessary . . . . He instructed his spokesmen to play down the matter, so that the initial Pentagon press release . . . did not even identify the North Vietnamese as having been involved.[67]

Two days later, on the night of August 4, the USS *Maddox* and USS *Turner Joy* reported being attacked off the coast. The two destroyers had been sent within eight miles of the North Vietnamese coast and four miles of offshore islands. Karnow writes, they "were effectively being used to bait the Communists."[68] Secretary of Defense McNamara phoned Johnson, "[W]e just had word by telephone from Admiral Sharp that the destroyer is under torpedo attack."[69] On the other hand, a flash message from Capt. John J. Herrick, commander of the *Maddox*, cast doubt on the attack: "Review of action makes many reported contacts and torpedoes fired appear doubtful. Freak weather effects on radar and overeager sonar men may have accounted for many reports. No actual visual sightings by *Maddox*."[70] Despite the confusion over what had actually happened, Michael Beschloss writes,

> McNamara discovered that someone . . . had leaked to the press that there has been a new attack in the Gulf of Tonkin. With the cat out of the bag, it would be very difficult for the administration . . . to withhold the proposed retaliation

against North Vietnam without subjecting LBJ to election-year charges of cover-up and cowardice.[71]

Thus, Johnson ordered retaliatory air strikes against North Vietnamese targets. As LBJ put it, "I didn't just screw Ho Chi Minh . . . . I cut his pecker off."[72]

Future Vice Admiral and POW James Stockdale was a pilot with a bird's eye view of the whole incident. He later wrote that "the *Joy* was firing at 'targets' the *Maddox* couldn't track on sonar, and the *Maddox* was dodging 'torpedoes' the *Joy* couldn't hear on sonar."[73] Within a few days, even Johnson apparently had doubts, telling an assistant, "Hell, those dumb-stupid sailors were shooting at flying fish."[74] Karnow writes, "Subsequent research by both official and unofficial investigators has indicated that with almost total certainty that the second Communist attack never happened."[75] Stockdale later called it "a tragic way to commit a nation to war."[76]

Until 1995, McNamara had publicly professed that the second attack had *probably* occurred. In 1995, he went to Vietnam to meet with his former adversaries.[77] The *Washington Post* reported, "But after meeting with [Gen. Vo Nguyen] Giap . . . McNamara said . . . that 'I am absolutely positive' the second attack never took place."[78] The alleged second attack became the impetus for passing the Gulf of Tonkin Resolution. McNamara admits that "the Johnson administration in any case would have probably sent to Congress the same resolution . . . it had already been drafted by the State Department in May."[79]

Given the confusion about the attack, it's difficult to claim that the administration deliberately lied, but it clearly did not tell the whole truth. Prior to speaking to the nation, LBJ spoke with his opponent, Barry Goldwater, who expressed support for retaliation, thus taking a major issue away from the Republican. In speaking to the nation just before midnight, Johnson laid out his case that there had been "open aggression on the high seas" by the North Vietnamese, failing to acknowledge that they were responding to covert attacks on their territory. Finally, he repeated a phrase that had become his mantra, "We still seek no wider war."[80]

The Gulf of Tonkin Resolution authorized "all necessary measures to repel any armed attacks against the forces of the United States and to prevent further aggression."[81] It was, as Nicholas Katzenbach called it, a "functional equivalent of a declaration of war."[82] Congressional approval was overwhelming, with the Senate voting 88-2 and the House unanimously. One of the two Senators who opposed the resolution, Wayne Morse, called it "another sinking of the Maine."[83] He had been secretly tipped off by someone at the Pentagon that the USS *Maddox* was gathering intelligence rather than on a routine patrol. The source also suggested "there was a hell of a lot of confusion" about the attacks on August 4.[84] But Morse's concerns were ignored. LBJ's Harris poll standing jumped thirty points to 72 percent, a classic example of the rally-around-the-flag effect.[85] In addition, he took the issue away from Goldwater, who could no longer portray him as soft on Vietnam. McNamara later admitted the congressional resolution was seriously misused:

> The fundamental issue of Tonkin Gulf involved not deception but, rather, misuse of power.... Congress did *not* intend to authorize without further, full consultation the expansion of U.S. forces in Vietnam from 16,000 to 550,000 men.[86]

The attacks in the Gulf, real or imagined, proved pivotal in allowing Johnson to fundamentally change the U.S. role in Vietnam. During the period from taking office until July 1965, Johnson turned the relatively small commitment of financial aid and military advisers into a large-scale effort to save South Vietnam from the Communists, involving the United States in a land war in Asia. How the United States made that transition is a story that is now well known. But at the time, much was concealed from the American people and their representatives in Congress.

It is clear that both Johnson and McNamara soon had serious misgivings about the prospects of winning in Vietnam, but were trapped in their own narrative and hid their reservations from the public. A subsequent attack in the Gulf on September 18 received a very different response. As the *New York Times* reported the next day, "Two United States destroyers fired upon, and presumably hit what they took to be four or five hostile targets today in the Gulf of Tonkin."[87] Yet, the United States took no retaliatory action and didn't even identify the attackers as North Vietnamese. White House tapes of Johnson's conversations with McNamara show that the president had doubts about the most recent incidents and perhaps the earlier ones. After McNamara reports the apparent attacks, President Johnson shows his distrust of the military brass and raises a number of questions about whether the attacks actually happened:

> JOHNSON: Now Bob, I have found over the years that we see and we hear and we imagine a lot of things in the form of attacks and shots and people running at us and I think it would ... make us very vulnerable, if we conclude that these people were attacked and we're merely responding and it develops that just wasn't true at all. And I think that we outta check that very very carefully. And I don't know why in the hell sometime or other they can't be sure that they're being attacked.... I have been watching and listening to these stories for 30 years before the Armed Services Committee and we're always sure we've been attacked and a day or two later we're not so damned sure and day or two more we're sure it wasn't, didn't happen at all.... *'Cause you just came in a few*

weeks ago that they damn near launched an attack on us and they fired on us. And when we got through all the firing we concluded that maybe they hadn't fired at all.[88]

The significance of this conversation is twofold. First, Johnson was reluctant to automatically take the word of the military that it had been attacked again and apparently had been skeptical of their claims for years. Second, he clearly states that a few weeks ago he'd been told of attacks that may well have not occurred, which can only refer to the Gulf of Tonkin attacks of August 4.

ESCALATION

After the Gulf of Tonkin incident, South Vietnam strongman Khanh cracked down on dissidents, leading to large protests. He was forced to resign and the situation bordered on anarchy. Johnson realized that this was not the time to increase American involvement. Furthermore, escalation would have been an unwise move for the peace candidate, who was portraying Goldwater as a risky choice who could plunge the United States into war. Like so many presidential candidates before him, Johnson portrayed himself as the best man to keep the United States out of a wider war. His campaign became famous for its "Daisy Girl" television ad, which transported viewers to a world where a little girl counting flower pedals morphs into a mushroom cloud. Although Goldwater's name is not mentioned, the ad clearly implied that electing him would risk plunging the world into a nuclear war. Johnson further portrayed himself as a peace candidate in a speech at Akron University on October 21. He promised that "we are not about to send American boys 9 or 10,000 miles away from home to do what Asian boys ought to be doing for themselves."[89] Yet, he was secretly planning to do just that. According to McMaster, in a private conversation he promised JCS Chairman Earle Wheeler "to do something" postelection.[90] Fulfilling that promise after he was elected to a full term, Johnson began bombing the North. Although some in the military wanted more aggressive bombing, Johnson was swayed by his civilian advisers to pursue a policy of graduated response. Only one advisor objected to the bombing. George Ball, Undersecretary of State, prophetically warned, "Once on the tiger's back we cannot be sure of picking the place to dismount."[91]

Johnson's decisions to escalate the war between January 28 and July 28, 1965, were critical in turning the conflict into an American ground war. After Khanh was deposed, the flamboyant Vice Air Marshall Nguyen Cao Ky assumed power. Ky was known as a daring pilot who dressed in purple jumpsuits accessorized with pearl-handled revolvers.[92] The scene was set for a more aggressive air campaign against the North in an effort to prop up the South Vietnamese government. McMaster writes, "The president . . . needed an incident to which the United States could respond with military force."[93] The incident occurred with attacks on American barracks at Pleiku in February, which cost eight American lives and wounded more than 100.[94] On February 13, the Viet Cong attacked another barracks in Qui Nhon and Johnson ordered continuous bombing of the North.[95] He failed to publicly announce this new policy. McNamara admits, "All of this occurred without adequate public disclosure or debate, planting the seeds of an eventually debilitating credibility gap."[96]

Why did Johnson make such a momentous decision? LBJ was haunted by the backlash that Truman faced after the loss of China to the Communists and he pledged, "I am not going to lose Vietnam. I am not going to be the President who saw Southeast Asia go the way China went."[97] Operation Rolling Thunder began on March 2, 1965. It would last for three years and exceed the bombs dropped on Europe in World War II.[98] The bombing had far-reaching implications. McNamara reflects,

> Wars generate their own momentum and follow the law of unanticipated consequences. Vietnam proved no exception. . . . Rolling Thunder not only started the air war but unexpectedly triggered the introduction of U.S. troops into ground combat as well.[99]

McNamara laments, "We were sinking into quicksand."[100]

The introduction of ground troops was originally cast as simply a protective measure for American bases to support the bombing of the North. The first Marines landed at Danang on March 8. Rather than doing so inconspicuously as the South Vietnamese government preferred, they landed in full combat gear, greeted by Vietnamese girls with flowers.[101] By June the strategy changed from merely providing security to search and destroy missions that would commit the United States to full-scale combat.[102] This change in mission was kept from the public and Congress. Johnson also scrupulously avoided calling up the reserves. Doing that would have put the United States on a war footing, endangered his Great Society program, and removed a haven for those, like George W. Bush and Dan Quayle, seeking to avoid the draft.

In March, John McNaughton, who was an assistant to McNamara, assigned a percentage weight to each of the reasons for sending troops to Vietnam: Seventy percent to avoid the humiliation of an American defeat; 20 percent to keep Vietnam and nearby countries out of Chinese control; and 10 percent to give the people of South Vietnam freedom and a better way of life.[103] Yet, these were not the publicly expressed reasons for the war, at least not in that order.

Publicly, President Johnson laid out a time-tested narrative justifying his actions when he spoke at Johns Hopkins University on April 7, 1965. South Vietnam was the victim of North Vietnam's aggression. The Communists had committed terrible atrocities, which he enumerated, including assassination, kidnapping, strangling of women and children, sneak attacks on villages, and terrorist attacks in large cities. But America was not in Vietnam just to help the innocent victims of brutal aggression. Containing Communism, particularly the Chinese, put the defense of Vietnam squarely in America's interest. Johnson said,

> The rulers in Hanoi are urged on by Peking. This is a regime which has destroyed freedom in Tibet, which has attacked India, and has been condemned by the United Nations for aggression in Korea. It is a nation which is helping the forces of violence in almost every continent. The contest in Vietnam is part of a wider pattern of aggressive purposes. . . . Let no one think for a moment that retreat from Viet-Nam would bring an end to conflict. The battle would be renewed in one country and then another. The central lesson of our time is that the appetite of aggression is never satisfied.[104]

This narrative resonated with a population that had lived through a World War that was believed to have been encouraged by appeasement at Munich, as well as a Cold War, a hot war in Korea, and the Cuban missile crisis. That the Vietnamese Communists were simply pawns of the Chinese and Soviets was taken as a given by an administration and public that was largely ignorant of Vietnamese history.

Johnson faced foreign policy challenges beyond those in Vietnam. On April 28, 1965, he sent American troops to the Dominican Republic to prevent a feared Communist takeover and another Cuba in the Caribbean. He used this crisis as an excuse to obtain further funding for defense, including the war in Vietnam. His narrative was a familiar one—we need to support the troops. Johnson warned that failure to quickly pass the bill, "means to deny and delay . . . support . . . to those brave men who are risking their lives . . . in Viet-Nam."[105] As other presidents before and after him would do, Johnson made supporting the war about the brave troops fighting overseas. Even if one disagreed with the policy, supporting the troops was the litmus test of patriotism.

Unlike McKinley, Wilson, and Roosevelt, Johnson led the nation to war without a formal Declaration of War. Unlike Truman, he was not able to intervene under the auspices of the United Nations, as the Soviets would have vetoed such a resolution. Although the Gulf of Tonkin Resolution provided Johnson a legal pretext for his escalation, it is unlikely that those who approved it contemplated an open-ended commitment to ground combat in the jungles of Vietnam. Herring explains the deception: "Johnson thus took the nation into war in Vietnam by indirection and dissimulation. . . . The administration never publicly acknowledged the shift from reprisals to 'sustained pressures.'"[106] Despite Johnson's efforts to conceal the true purpose of his escalation, some started to question the policy, including the *New York Times* and a number of senators. Teach-ins were held on university campuses, and 12,000 students protested in April in Washington, D.C.[107]

In April and June 1965, Johnson increased the air war and the number of troops. He authorized the military to use American troops in combat with or without their South Vietnamese counterparts. This represented a new level of American commitment—assuming a significant burden in the fighting and dying. Yet, Johnson continued to conceal the extent of America's commitment. He only publicly revealed 50,000 of the 100,000 troops immediately deployed. Furthermore, he secretly approved another 100,000 to be sent in 1966.[108] These decisions were crucial in committing the United States to a long, costly, and divisive conflict. As Marine Commandant Wallace Green stated in May 1965, the American mission had truly changed in Vietnam: "I told them to find the Vietcong and kill 'em. That's the way to carry out their mission."[109] The change in mission was finally affirmed publicly by a low-level State Department spokesperson, Bob McCloskey, prompting the *New York Times* to editorialize, "The American people were told by a minor State Department official yesterday that, in effect, they were in a land war on the continent of Asia."[110]

WAR OF ATTRITION

The essence of General Westmoreland's strategy was to use his new troops to conduct a war of attrition. By depriving the Viet Cong of their population base, he hoped to stop the replenishment of their forces. The American strategy became search and destroy. Further, the United States engaged in heavy bombing of hamlets believed to shelter the Viet Cong. The so-called "strategic hamlet" program relocated many South Vietnamese from their villages to supposedly secure villages. This was similar to the reconcentration strategy employed against Filipino rebels after the Spanish-American War. Given that they were no longer on their ancestral land where their relatives were buried, this undermined support for the South Vietnamese government among villagers. Free-fire zones were established in large parts of the country, killing many civilians along with Viet Cong. Lacking clear battle lines and territories to conquer, the measure of battlefield success became unreliable and inflated "body counts."[111] The U.S. military also ravaged the South Vietnamese countryside from the air. McNamara reveals that from 1965 to 1967 twice the tonnage was dropped on the South as the North.[112] In addition to bombs, over 100 million pounds of defoliants, like Agent Orange, were sprayed over the countryside, destroying about half of the timberland in South Vietnam. The motto of those dropping the chemicals was "Only You Can Prevent Forests."[113]

Such bombing actually was counterproductive. Sheehan writes, "Vann denounced as cruel and self-defeating the indiscriminate bombing and shelling of the countryside which the U.S. high command was conducting to try to deprive the Vietnamese Communists of their population base."[114] Much of the rice land was lost, free-fire zones proliferated, 825 tons of bombs were dropped per day, and defoliants such as Agent Orange were used to destroy almost 850,000 acres. By 1968 the annual death toll of civilians had reached 85,000.[115] Not only were bombs dropped, the United States engaged in "Zippo Jobs" on Vietnamese villages. Sheehan writes,

> The first Vietnamese peasant homes to be burned by U.S. troops were put to the torch by the Marines in several hamlets near Da Nang on August 3, 1965. Morley Safer of CBS filmed the burnings and shocked millions of Americans who watched the network's evening news.[116]

The strategy of attrition actually worked against the Americans. According to calculations by Lieutenant General Victor H. "Brute" Krulak, the Communists had

> a probable military manpower pool of about 2.5 million men. If one accepted the current official "kill ratio" . . . 10,000 Americans and 165,000 Saigon soldiers would have to die in order "to reduce the enemy [manpower] pool by only a modest 20 percent."[117]

The war of attrition was more likely to affect American resolve than the reverse. Sheehan writes, "The Hanoi leaders believed that if they killed and wounded enough American soldiers over a period of time they would 'erode our national will and cause us to cease our support of the GVN.'"[118] Even Henry Kissinger argued before he joined Nixon's administration that the enemy could sustain higher casualties than the United States and thus a strategy of attrition was doomed.[119]

PROWAR PROPAGANDA

The story of how appeasement failed in stopping Hitler haunted McNamara and his colleagues. McNamara explains the impact of World War II and the Cold War on his generation's alarmist view:

> We had lived through appeasement at Munich . . . the Soviet takeover of Eastern Europe . . . the Cuban Missile Crisis . . . and most recently Communist Chinese statements that the South Vietnam conflict typified "wars of liberation," which they saw spreading across the globe.[120]

LBJ also held fast to this narrative. McMaster writes, "LBJ concluded that to withdraw from Vietnam would be the equivalent of British Prime Minister Chamberlain's appeasement of Hitler at Munich."[121]

In a press conference on July 28, 1965, Johnson attempted to answer the question asked in a letter by the mother of a soldier in Vietnam, "Why?" LBJ explained using many of the same narratives used by his predecessors:

> The answer, like the war itself, is not an easy one, but it echoes clearly from the painful lessons of half a century. Three times in my lifetime, in two World Wars and in Korea, Americans have gone to far lands to fight for freedom. We have learned at a terrible and a brutal cost that retreat does not bring safety and weakness does not bring peace. . . . But we must not let this mask the central fact that this is really war. It is guided by North Viet-Nam and it is spurred by Communist China. Its goal is to conquer the South, to defeat American power, and to extend the Asiatic dominion of communism.
>
> Nor would surrender in Viet-Nam bring peace, because we learned from Hitler at Munich that success only feeds the appetite of aggression. The battle would be renewed in one country and then another country, bringing with it perhaps even larger and crueler conflict, as we have learned from the lessons of history. . . . We just cannot now dishonor our word, or abandon our commitment, or leave those who believed us and who trusted us to the terror and repression and murder that would follow.[122]

Here, in a nutshell is the basic narrative for supporting the war. We are fighting because we are defending freedom, just as we did in two World Wars and Korea (although the people of South Vietnam were hardly free). We are defending them against the threat of monolithic Communism, which seeks to engulf all of Southeast Asia—the row of dominoes that would fall. The mother who wrote Johnson was the wife of a World War II veteran and Johnson drew a direct analogy between the two wars. His reference to Hitler and the appeasement at Munich called out the terrible costs of that mistake. Peace would not come in our time if we did not honor our commitments. To do so would not only bring dishonor but also would lead to massacres and murders—the very type of atrocities that we'd seen in World War II. So to preserve freedom, stop Communism, avoid appeasement, preserve our national honor, and prevent atrocities, we had to fight.

This press conference not only laid out the case for Vietnam, but it also provided much of the material for the Department of Defense's 1965 propaganda film, *Why Vietnam*.[123] Far less polished than Frank Capra's *Why We Fight* series, it presented the case for American soldiers to fight and die in a far-off land. Interspersed throughout with clips of Johnson, McNamara, and Rusk, it used scenes of combat, casualties, and children whose lives were disrupted by war. It was accompanied by a soundtrack that was ominous when presenting the enemy and uplifting when portraying Americans helping the beleaguered Vietnamese. The narrative began with Hitler and Chamberlain at Munich, followed by Mussolini conquering Ethiopia. Next came Korea, where we learned according to LBJ that "aggression unchallenged is aggression unleashed." The film presented a one-sided history of the conflict, neglecting to mention that the United States and South Vietnam thwarted the scheduled reunification elections. Instead, South Vietnam was portrayed as the victim of brutal aggression from the Communist North. A map showed all the neighboring countries that would fall if the Communists won, visualizing the domino theory. The film characterized American forces as advisers, concealing their combat role. It is only near the film's end that the narrator admits that Marines were finally being sent into combat for the *first* time since Korea, contradicting the pictures of wounded American soldiers shown early in the film's chronology.

The film portrayed the Gulf of Tonkin attacks as if they all really occurred, and misleadingly asserted that the United States had never struck against the North until after those attacks. Throughout the film, the mantra, "We seek no wider war" is repeated, as is the linkage of Hanoi and Red China, as if they were one. The word "terror" is repeatedly applied to the Viet Cong and North Vietnamese. Near the end of the film, as pictures are shown of American flag-draped coffins, the narrator asserts, "If freedom is to survive in any American hometown, it must be preserved in such places as South Vietnam."

The film was but a small part of the Pentagon's prowar propaganda. Sen. William J. Fulbright investigated the Pentagon's lavish propaganda campaign. By late 1969 the Defense Department was spending almost $28 million a year on propaganda compared to one-tenth of that amount a decade earlier. Among the propaganda tactics were speeches and appearances by military leaders promoting the war, production of films about Vietnam and Communism, which Fulbright alleged "distort[ed] key facts," and five television camera crews in Vietnam that were making films with "a propaganda rather than a journalistic thrust."[124] One military propaganda effort was the "Big Picture" program of 30-minute films made available to the general public through a large number of television stations. Seventeen of the fifty-five programs produced in the prior two years dealt with Vietnam.[125] Fulbright adds, "I would point out that the material dealing with Vietnam understandably presents only the positive side of our presence—a situation not completely consistent with today's newspaper reporting from that country."[126]

In addition to films, the Pentagon provided speakers, who Fulbright alleged violated Army regulations by advocating the government's war policy, rather than simply providing facts. For example, Major General R. G. Ciccolella gave a speech in which he dramatically repeated the domino theory narrative:

> The outcome of the war in Vietnam is vital not only to the free nations of Asia, but to those of western Europe as well. . . . If we fail in South Vietnam, if the forces of communism win, then . . . . the free Asian nations will be the targets and the victims of Communist armed aggression.[127]

The General also misled his audience about the military situation on the ground: "On the battlefields of South Vietnam, we have not failed. Insofar as the military aspects of this war are concerned, the Communists have been defeated." Fulbright concludes based on this and numerous other examples, "We are talking about military men using their position and their ability to travel around the country as a public relations tool designed to promote support of a political activity on which there is profound difference of opinions."[128]

Despite all the expense and efforts to promote the war, Caroline Page's analysis of American war propaganda from 1965 to 1973, found it suffered from four flaws: The remoteness of Vietnam, the length of the struggle, the repressive nature of the South Vietnamese governments, and the secrecy of the U.S. escalation of the war. She writes, "The American administration was caught in a trap of its own making."[129]

VIETNAM BECOMES A QUAGMIRE

Initially, the public was largely supportive of Johnson's actions after Tonkin and Pleiku. Keep in mind that most Americans were convinced that Communism was an existential threat and they lived with the haunting memory of the Cuban Missile Crisis. The United States supposedly had been attacked in international waters; it was defending freedom in South Vietnam; there was little reason to doubt that it would prevail. After all, this was the nation that defeated the combined forces of Hitler, Hirohito, and Mussolini in less than four years. Surely it could defeat a rag-tag bunch of guerrillas in the jungles of Vietnam. Yet, within a couple of years, the United States was bogged down in a quagmire. After sending over 500,000 troops, dropping more bombs than it had in World War II, and spending billions, the light at the end of the tunnel seemed no closer.[130] The air war cost the United States over nine dollars for each dollar's worth of damage to North Vietnam and captured U.S. airmen became propaganda tools for the Communists. Some Americans began to question the morality of dropping so many bombs on a small, impoverished nation.[131]

One question that is often raised is why the United States didn't go all out for a decisive victory in Vietnam. Some, including Barry Goldwater, had suggested using nuclear weapons. LBJ was fearful of another Korea or worse—that the Chinese and even the Soviets might be drawn into the conflict, which could escalate uncontrollably, risking nuclear war. VanDeMark writes,

> This fear of crossing the "flash point"—of sparking a direct confrontation between the nuclear superpowers—troubled LBJ constantly. . . . The images of Chinese armies surging across the Yalu and of nuclear brinkmanship in the Caribbean haunted him as fully as Chamberlain's protestation of "peace in our time."[132]

Johnson's policies soon encountered growing opposition. By 1966 and 1967 protestors outside the White House were chanting "Hey, hey, LBJ, how many kids have you killed today."[133] As protests ramped up, however, many Americans rallied around their president and rejected what were perceived as radical, unwashed, and unpatriotic "hippies." Combined with other major social divisions of the 1960s, the war helped fuel the most turbulent time in American history since the civil war. A poll taken in August of 1967 showed the stark divisions in national opinion: 24 percent favored seeking total victory, 37 percent wanted a negotiated peace, and 34 percent wanted the United States out of Vietnam as soon as possible.[134]

Johnson was not moved by the protests. To the contrary, he believed that the peace movement was undermining public support of the war. He authorized CIA surveillance in an effort to prove its leaders were Communists. LBJ also organized propaganda efforts such as the supposedly independent "Committee for Peace with Freedom in Vietnam," and the White House "Vietnam Information Group."[135] McMaster notes,

> In response to the growing opposition, LBJ redoubled his effort to prevent leaks and to conceal deepening American involvement in the war. . . . He said that those who publicly opposed his Vietnam policy and journalists who speculated about it disregarded "our soldiers who are dying" in Vietnam.[136]

To improve the public's perception of the war, and no doubt to enhance his own re-election chances, Johnson's administration pursued a propaganda strategy called the "Progress Campaign" in September of 1967. General Wheeler assured the public and Congress that within two years, the South

Vietnamese would be able to take over the fight.[137] At the same time as optimistic reports were being made to the public, the members of the press in South Vietnam were growing more skeptical. General William Sidle, who had taken over the Office of Information, made sure that when the press interviewed troops in the field, they were monitored by officers who encouraged soldiers to present an optimistic picture of the war.[138] Despite sometimes less than positive reporting on the war, Johnson's propaganda campaign seemed to be successful, as polling showed that about half the respondents thought the United States was "making progress" by late 1967. In November, General Westmoreland constantly used that word in an interview on CBS.[139] In a November 21 speech at the National Press Club in Washington Westmoreland assured the audience, "We have reached an important point when the end begins to come into view."[140] The strategy was, in McGeorge Bundy's words, "Emphasize the 'light at the end of the tunnel' instead of battles, deaths, and danger."[141]

Some have called Vietnam the first television war. Unlike prior wars, which the public read about in newspapers, heard about on radio, or saw in newsreels at the movie theater, audiences were transported to Vietnam right from their living rooms. It is true Korea was covered on TV, but in 1950 only 9 percent of homes had television. Even by 1953, barely a third of households owned one. By 1962, however, 90 percent of Americans lived in homes with TV and by 1968, only about one in twenty was without a television.[142]

Prior to 1968, it was difficult for television to provide the kind of vivid combat footage that came later in the war. This was because the equipment was heavy and bulky and the use of film required developing it in Tokyo and transmitting it to New York via satellite. At that time television coverage was more likely to increase viewers' support for the war than the reverse. A poll in July 1967 found 83 percent of respondents more prowar after watching TV reports. War coverage was not typically combat footage, but interviews with clean-cut American soldiers, who would give answers to why they were fighting that echoed the administration's storyline. As one soldier put it, "Better to be fighting the Communists here than fighting them back in San Diego."[143]

By October 1967, McNamara did not share the military's optimism. He was pessimistic about the prospects of winning and told the president that it was "impossible to win the war militarily."[144] He suggested Johnson remove him and Dean Rusk from the cabinet. His memoir reflects his frustration, "I could see no good way to win—or end—an increasingly costly and destructive war."[145] McNamara writes, "It became clear then, and I believe it is clear today, that military force—especially when wielded by an outside power—just cannot bring order in a country that cannot govern itself."[146] Of course, his opinion was kept from the American public and Congress. Furthermore, McNamara reveals that the consequences of losing in Vietnam were greatly exaggerated. In the fall of 1967, a secret memo from Director of Central Intelligence Dick Helms revealed that "the CIA's most senior analysts believed we could have withdrawn from Vietnam without any permanent damage to U.S. or Western security."[147]

In South Vietnam itself, a change of leadership was again needed. The Ky government conducted elections in September 1967 for a constituent assembly to draft a new constitution. Ky stepped aside under America pressure and agreed to accept the vice presidency under the presidency of General Nguyen Van Thieu. The ticket was elected with a large turnout. Despite questions about the legitimacy of the elections, including banning of candidates who were Communists or "neutralist sympathizers" and charges of last-minute fraud, Herring claims they still were not "as corrupt as critics charged nor as pure as Johnson claimed."[148]

THE TET OFFENSIVE

As 1967 turned to 1968, an election year, Vietnam was no longer a minor issue. Beschloss writes, "In January 1968, the President told Congress in his State of the Union that the enemy in Vietnam had been defeated 'in battle after battle.'"[149] Soon, however, the administration's optimistic predictions of success were undermined by what happened during Tet, the Vietnamese New Year. On January 31, 1968, the NLF launched coordinated attacks from the DMZ to the southern tip of Vietnam. Their attacks included thirty-six provincial capitals, all but one of the five major cities, and capitals in sixty-four districts, not to mention fifty hamlets.[150] Although the Tet offensive was costly for the NLF, which lost up to 40,000 lives, it was also costly for the U.S and South Vietnam, which lost 1,100 and 2,300 troops, respectively. Around 12,500 civilians died and a million were made refugees.[151] Television stories about the fighting, including gruesome images, made a mockery of the administration's optimistic projections about the war, expanding what came to be widely known as the credibility gap. One of the most shocking images was of the chief of the national police shooting a captive rebel in the head. Viewers of the nightly news were transported into the conflict. The story they saw dramatically contradicted the one coming out of Washington. The so-called most respected man in America, CBS News Anchor Walter Cronkite, reported on February 27, "It seems now more certain than ever that the bloody experience of Vietnam is to end in a stalemate.... To say that we are mired in stalemate seems the only reasonable, yet unsatisfactory conclusion." This alarming statement shocked LBJ, who is reported to have said, "If I've lost Cronkite, I've lost Middle America."[152]

After the Tet offensive, television coverage began to sour on the administration's narrative. Not only did the coverage dominate the evening newscasts, but it also often brought the savageness of the war directly into the living room right about dinnertime. It was not just Walter Cronkite who changed his views about the war after Tet. Prior to the offensive, coverage had been fairly neutral and even favorable. But after Tet it became quite critical. Herring writes, "Vietnam was the first television war, to be sure, and it is possible that the nightly exposure to violence contributed to public war-weariness."[153]

Colin Powell, who served two tours in Vietnam, points out the significance of Tet: "Judged in cold military terms, the Tet offensive was a massive defeat for the Viet Cong and North Vietnam." However, that meant little in the overall picture. Powell quotes military theorist Carl von Clausewitz:

> If you want to overcome your enemy, you must match your effort against his power of resistance, which can be expressed as the product of . . . the total means at his disposal and the strength of his will.[154]

A defeat in the strictly military sense was transformed into a political victory for the Viet Cong. The administration's story that the war was being won, and there was light at the end of the tunnel suddenly lacked any semblance of narrative fidelity once viewers were able to see for themselves what was happening in South Vietnam.

On the ground in Vietnam, the post-Tet period was exceptionally violent. Historian Ronald Spector, subtitled his book about that time "The Bloodiest Year in Vietnam."[155] Critics sarcastically suggested that the light at the end of the tunnel was an oncoming train. On February 7, the United States bombed and demolished the town of Ben Tre. That action led to one of the most infamous statements about the war. A major was quoted saying, "It became necessary to destroy the town to save it."[156] It was also during this period that one of the most horrific events of the war occurred. On March 16, 1968, American forces led by Lt. William Calley entered the village of My Lai and killed everything in sight, murdering 504 people, including old men, women, and children. The incident was covered up at the time and the official story was only that 128 enemy soldiers had been killed. However, a helicopter gunner who had been recently discharged wrote to officials demanding an investigation, which led to Calley's arrest in September 1969.[157] Although the story was not told publicly until 1969, once known, it became a major black mark on the American war effort.

The effects of the Tet offensive were devastating for Johnson. Between November 1967 and March 1968, public approval of LBJ's conduct of the war fell from 40 percent to 26. By March, 78 percent didn't believe the United States was making progress in the war. Senator Eugene McCarthy challenged Johnson for the nomination. Although he didn't defeat Johnson, he won 42 percent of the votes in the March 12 New Hampshire primary, shocking the president.[158] Soon Senator Robert F. Kennedy joined the battle for the nomination as an anti-war candidate. On March 31, President Johnson again addressed the nation on Vietnam and concluded his address with an announcement that had been a closely held secret, "I shall not seek, and I will not accept, the nomination of my party for another term as your President."[159]

The country was not only being torn apart by the war. Racial tensions reached a climax when Martin Luther King Jr. was assassinated on April 4 in Memphis. Riots soon followed in many cities. King had become a harsh critic of the war in which African Americans, who comprised 11 percent of the overall population, suffered a quarter of all deaths.[160] Blacks were more likely to oppose the war than whites by a wide margin. In 1968, polling showed that 37 percent favored withdrawal compared to 23 percent for whites, and they were only about half as likely to support escalation (20–39 percent).[161] Kennedy, the best hope for antiwar Democrats, was shot on June 5 after winning the California primary and died the next day. Thus, a deeply divided party faced a difficult battle in the election of 1968 in a badly divided nation. After a long, divisive primary and even more divisive convention in Chicago, where police beat anti-war protestors, the Democrats nominated Vice President Hubert Humphrey, who entered the race too late to compete in the primaries.

Johnson began to pursue a diplomatic, rather than exclusively military strategy in Vietnam. He only added 13,500 troops in March, well short of what had been requested. He brought General Westmoreland home. Peace talks finally opened in Paris in May, although they quickly stalled.[162] In late October, Johnson halted bombing, trying to move the peace talks forward and hoping to boost Humphrey's chances of winning. South Vietnam's government was not cooperative, preferring to wait for a new administration that it believed would be more favorable to their interests.

Saigon had good reason to assume that Republicans would be more favorable to their side. We now have proof that Nixon actively sought to undermine the peace talks. John A. Farrell, author of *Richard Nixon: The Life*, found proof in the Nixon Library archives of the so-called "Chennault affair," named after the back channel to Saigon's government, Anna Chennault. Farrell writes:

> It wasn't until after 2007, when the Nixon Presidential Library finally opened Haldeman's notes to the public, that I stumbled upon a smoking gun . . . four pages of notes his brush-cut aide had scrawled late on an October evening in 1968. "![*sic*] Keep Anna Chennault working on SVN," Haldeman wrote, as Nixon barked orders into the phone. They were out to "monkey wrench" Johnson's election eve initiative, Nixon said. And it worked.[163]

After Nixon won, the South Vietnamese finally agreed to participate in the peace talks, which were further delayed by a dispute about the shape of the table.[164]

NIXON PROMISES "PEACE WITH HONOR"

Richard M. Nixon, who made his political reputation as a hardline anti-communist crusader, took over the presidency after winning a narrow victory over Humphrey and third-party candidate George Wallace. During the campaign, Nixon allowed the media and public to believe that his "secret plan" would end the war, a plan he later admitted never existed.[165] By 1969, roughly 60 percent of Americans thought the war had been a mistake, but a narrow majority disapproved of the anti-war protestors' tactics.[166] Nixon realized that the old narratives had failed. He adopted a two-prong strategy—reduce American casualties by turning over more of the war to the Vietnamese and attack the protesters and "liberal" media as unpatriotic. Nixon embraced an idea proposed by Vann—de-Americanization (which was renamed Vietnamization). Neil Sheehan writes of Nixon, "He intended to do what Vann wanted—purchase time from the American public with U.S. troop withdrawals while continuing the war by using the Vietnamese on the Saigon side to fight it."[167] Vietnamization, however, was not without a tragic cost in American lives. Close to 21,000 Americans died during Nixon's tenure and a third of all casualties occurred during that time.[168]

Nixon had harshly criticized the Johnson administration's war efforts and promised to bring "peace with honor" to Vietnam. Herring points out that this promise was a subterfuge, designed to conceal his real goal: "Although disguising it in the rhetoric of 'peace with honor,' the Nixon administration persisted in the quixotic search for an independent, non-Communist Vietnam."[169] Although the Cold War narrative still drove Nixon privately, the public narrative shifted to seeking an honorable peace. Nixon even coined an oxymoronic slogan, calling Vietnam "a war for peace."[170]

In May 1969, Nixon announced the withdrawal of 25,000 American troops. His attempts to force North Vietnam to agree to a settlement failed, and as the peace talks stalled, his public approval ratings started to fall.[171] Thus, Nixon leaked plans for massive attacks against the North, all the while pledging not to "be the first American President to lose a war."[172] His close adviser, H. R. Haldeman, revealed that Nixon threatened to use nuclear weapons, calling it "the Madman Theory . . . . We'll just slip the word to them that, 'for God's sake, you know Nixon's obsessed about Communism . . . and he has his hand on the nuclear button.'"[173] Although he didn't actually turn to nuclear weapons, Nixon ordered massive secret bombing of Cambodia, dropping over 100,000 tons of bombs in fifteen months.[174]

Rather than hold frequent press conferences (he held only thirty-nine as compared to 193 by Eisenhower and 132 by LBJ) Nixon made use of the bully pulpit of the Oval Office address. All networks routinely carried these live, allowing Nixon a way to get his unfiltered message to the people.[175] Nixon gave a major speech on November 3 to explain his policy to the nation. He put the issue this way, "The great question is: How can we win America's peace?"[176] He warned of a bloodbath if we pulled out and explained his policy of Vietnamization:

> For the South Vietnamese, our precipitate withdrawal would inevitably allow the Communists to repeat the massacres which followed their takeover in the North 15 years before.
>
> —They then murdered more than 50,000 people and hundreds of thousands more died in slave labor camps.
>
> —We saw a prelude of what would happen in South Vietnam when the Communists entered the city of Hue last year. During their brief rule there, there was a bloody reign of terror in which 3,000 civilians were clubbed, shot to death, and buried in mass graves.

Nixon also used the speech to criticize the peace movement, recalling,

> In San Francisco a few weeks ago, I saw demonstrators carrying signs reading: "Lose in Vietnam, bring the boys home." . . . But as President of the United States, I would be untrue to my oath of office if I allowed the policy of this Nation to be dictated by the minority who hold the point of view and who try to impose it on the Nation by mounting demonstration [sic] in the street.

Instead, he appealed to "the great silent majority of my fellow Americans." He added, "North Vietnam cannot defeat or humiliate the United States. Only Americans can do that."

Nixon deputized Vice President Spiro Agnew to attack the credibility of the media, seeking to undermine the narrative fidelity of media reports. If stories on television and in the liberal press conflicted with the storyline being told by the administration, it was because the media were biased. In contemporary terms, they were presenting "fake news." Vice President Agnew said in a speech on November 13, 1969, "A raised eyebrow, an inflection of the voice, a caustic remark dropped in the middle of a broadcast can raise doubts in a million minds about the veracity of a public official or the wisdom of a Government policy." He further suggested, "Perhaps the place to start looking for a credibility gap is not in the offices of the Government in Washington but in the studios of the networks in New York."[177] In a sense, Agnew and Nixon were "working the refs." Historian Melvin Small claims that accusations of "liberal bias" intimidated the media, especially when backed by the threat of an FCC investigation.[178] True investigative reporting declined and television coverage shifted from the battlefield to stories about programs that benefited the average person in South Vietnam. As American combat troops came home, casualties dropped. Many stories featured returning American soldiers. Broadcasts of combat footage dropped from three to four times weekly to monthly. Media critic Ben Bagdikian claims that the media were becoming a "propaganda arm of the administration in power."[179]

WAR PROTESTS EXPAND

Despite Nixon's attacks on the peace movement, protests against the war grew. On October 15 and November 15 moratoriums attracted more respectable elements of the populace, rather than just "hippies" and radicals. On October 15, a quarter of a million people took part in Washington, D.C., along with sizable crowds in major cities like Boston, New York, and Miami. The next moratorium on November 15 drew even more protestors.[180] On the other side, pro-Nixon rallies were staged in November. Despite the protests, polls showed support for Nixon's policies. "We've got those liberal bastards on the run," boasted Nixon.[181] In addition to attacking his opponents on college campuses and the media, he also devised a strategy that would leave many youthful protestors unconcerned about their personal risk of being drafted. The draft lottery conducted in December 1969 created two classes of young men—those who drew low numbers and were likely to be drafted, and those with higher numbers, who knew they would not go to Vietnam. In 1970, almost half of draft-aged men were in the latter group and could go on with their lives unconcerned about the war, and by the election year of 1972, nearly three-quarters of potential draftees would not be called.[182]

Unfortunately for Nixon, just quieting dissent and appealing to the silent majority were not enough to change the situation on the ground in Vietnam. Herring reports, "By the spring of 1970, the contradictions in Nixon's Vietnamization strategy had become all too apparent." Nevertheless, he cut another 150,000 troops over the coming year.[183] But the effort to silence dissenters was soon overwhelmed by the reaction to Nixon's next escalation, sending troops into neighboring Cambodia. Nixon gave a televised speech on April 30, 1970, justifying his "incursion" as a response to North Vietnam's "aggression." As he so often did, Nixon framed his decision as a way to fight a war for peace: "We take this action not for the purpose of expanding the war into Cambodia but for the purpose of ending the war in Vietnam and winning the just peace we all desire."[184] Again, Nixon was telling the old story of making war to secure the peace.

Nixon could not avoid taking aim at one of the most prevalent sources of protests against his policies, "Even here in the United States, great universities are being systematically destroyed." He warned the nation, "If when the chips are down, the world's most powerful nation, the United States of America, acts like a helpless giant, the forces of totalitarianism and anarchy will threaten free nations and free institutions throughout the world." Nixon then put his decision in the tradition of other presidents who had taken the United States to war:

> In this room, Woodrow Wilson made the great decisions which led to victory in World War I. Franklin Roosevelt made the decisions which led to our victory in World War II. Dwight D. Eisenhower made decisions which ended the war in Korea and avoided war in the Middle East. John F. Kennedy, in his finest hour, made the great decision which removed Soviet nuclear missiles from Cuba and the Western Hemisphere.

Finally, Nixon concluded his speech by playing the same trump card used in so many wars:

> I ask for your support for our brave men fighting tonight halfway around the world—not for territory—not for glory—but so that their younger brothers and their sons and your sons can have a chance to grow up in a world of peace and freedom and justice.

Sadly, U.S. actions in Cambodia, directly or indirectly, led to the North Vietnamese supporting the Khmer Rouge, which eventually prevailed and perpetrated one of the worst genocides in the twentieth century. So, rather than preserving peace and freedom, at least for the people of Cambodia, the U.S. incursion became the catalyst for one of the greatest tragedies of the second half of the twentieth century.

Outrage at Nixon's Cambodia incursion led to protests at colleges around the country, including Kent State University in Ohio. Tragically, Ohio National Guardsmen killed four students. The image of a distraught young woman kneeling by the body of a dead protestor transported Americans to the scene of the tragedy. A number of major universities were closed in protest. Nevertheless, some Americans blamed the protestors, rather than the National Guard. Counter demonstrators shouted slogans like "America: Love it or leave it."[185] In response to the anti-war protests, Herring reports that Nixon "approved one of the most blatant attacks on individual freedom and privacy in American history, the so-called Huston Plan, which authorized the intelligence agencies to open mail, use electronic surveillance methods, and even burglarize to spy on Americans."[186]

At the same time, Nixon continued with his Vietnamization plan, withdrawing another 100,000 troops in 1971, leaving 175,000, of which only 75,000 were combat troops.[187] Yet the protestors were not dissuaded. Among the most powerful protests were those by Vietnam Veterans Against the War, who threw away their medals in a protest at the capitol in April 1971.[188] It was clear that the nation was being torn apart by a war that was becoming widely viewed as a mistake. One of the protest leaders, decorated Vietnam veteran John Kerry, posed the question on many people's minds when he asked the Senate Foreign Relations Committee, "How do you ask a man to be the last man to die for a mistake?"[189]

Adding to the difficulty of defending the war, in the summer of that year, Lt. William Calley was found guilty of multiple murders at My Lai.[190] Nixon intervened and reduced his life sentence to three years.[191] Most of the sentence was served under house arrest, which permitted visits from his girlfriend.[192] Although those who supported the war saw My Lai as an unfortunate exception, war opponents became enraged.

In an effort to counter widespread and well-funded prowar propaganda from the Pentagon, a campaign to "Unsell the War" was begun by moderate anti-war forces and included professionally produced ads. Although major networks declined to run the ads, many local radio and TV stations, as well as print outlets, agreed to use them. According to Mitchell Hall, "Perhaps the most widely distributed print ad was a takeoff of the classic military recruiting poster. It showed Uncle Sam with his head bandaged, hat under his arm, coat torn, and hand out-stretched, captioned 'I Want Out.'"[193] In perhaps the most powerful television ad, "Citizen," World War II veteran and acclaimed actor Henry Fonda spoke out against the war. Research showed that the ad was in the top 7 percent of commercials for next-day recall and was viewed favorably by a margin of 43 to 21 percent.[194] Fonda's daughter Jane visited Hanoi, where she was shown sitting at an anti-aircraft gun of the type used to down American pilots. Supporters of the war deridingly called her Hanoi Jane. Heavyweight champion Muhammad Ali refused to be drafted and was stripped of his title, setting up a legal battle that went all the way to the Supreme Court. Unlike World Wars I and II, where celebrities worked tirelessly to support the war effort, many celebrities used their platform to protest the Vietnam War.[195]

To add to the woes of supporters of the war, in June 1971 the *New York Times* published the *Pentagon Papers*. It took a Supreme Court decision to overcome the administration's objections on national security grounds. Herring summarizes their impact: "The documents confirmed what critics of the war had long been arguing . . . that Kennedy and Johnson had consistently misled the public about their intentions in Vietnam."[196] That summer polls found a record 71 percent agreeing that America had made a mistake sending troops, and 58 percent found the war to be immoral. Nixon's approval rating on Vietnam fell to 31 percent.[197]

Despite the public protests and falling polling, Nixon continued his policies in Vietnam. By early in 1972, he had withdrawn over 400,000 troops and less than ten were dying each week.[198] Nixon was also pursuing his policy of opening the door to China, visiting Beijing in February to meet with Mao and Zhou Enlai. The North Vietnamese feared China would again sell them out, as they had in 1954 at the Geneva Conference.[199] In April and May 1972, they launched an Easter offensive. At that point, only about 6,000 of the remaining 70,000 American forces were combat troops.[200] Thus, a U.S. ground response was out of the question. On May 8, Nixon responded by mining Haiphong harbor, blockading North Vietnam, and launching a large continuous bombing campaign. Despite many protests, a large number of Americans believed his response was justified and his approval rating went up significantly.[201] Nixon, despite the best efforts of the anti-war movement, went on to win an overwhelming victory against anti-war Democrat George McGovern, who carried only one state. It was only after the election that Nixon's efforts to subvert the democratic process were revealed in the Watergate scandal.

There was one issue on which Nixon held the decided advantage over his opponents—Prisoners of War. North Vietnam held about 587 POWs, predominately airmen who had been shot down over North Vietnam. The North frequently used them as propaganda pawns, parading them through the streets and coercing "confessions." By the end of the war, the administration seemed to be making the return of POWs the main rationale for continuing the conflict. POW bracelets became a common item worn by celebrities and ordinary citizens alike.[202]

THE PARIS PEACE ACCORDS

As Nixon was ramping up the pressure on North Vietnam, negotiations were continuing in Paris. By late September, Henry Kissinger and his Vietnamese counterpart, Le Duc Tho, thought they had a deal. Kissinger was planning to initial the settlement on October 22, but was unable to persuade South Vietnam's president Thieu to agree, postponing the peace treaty. Herring writes, "Kissinger attempted to keep alive hopes of an early settlement by stating publicly on October 31 that 'peace is at hand,' but Nixon's support of Thieu ensured the breakdown of the October agreement."[203]

With his re-election secured, Nixon sought to ramp up the pressure on the North Vietnamese to agree to a settlement. From December 18 to 29, he began a brutal bombing campaign against the North in an attempt to bludgeon them into signing the peace agreement. The bombing was focused on the heavily populated area between Haiphong and Hanoi, which drew a rebuke from the Pope.[204] After the attacks, Nixon's approval rating sank to 39 percent. Nixon, offered to stop the bombing if the North resumed peace talks, which it did. Nixon, of course, claimed it was the bombing that brought North Vietnam back to the peace talks. Herring disputes this claim: "Nixon and Kissinger's later claims that the so-called Christmas bombing compelled the North Vietnamese to accept a settlement satisfactory to the United States do not hold up under close scrutiny."[205]

The final settlement was largely the same as that agreed to in October. To ensure South Vietnam's compliance, Nixon promised Thieu that the United States would continue its support and if necessary re-intervene if the North failed to abide by the agreement. At the same time, he threatened Thieu with cutting off aid if he didn't sign. Thieu, ultimately gave in and signed the agreement.[206] Unfortunately, it was less a peace agreement than a prelude to the next phase of the war. At the time, Karnow wrote prophetically that it "may only be an interlude that precedes the beginning of what could become the third Indochina war."[207]

One must ask, did Nixon keep his promise of peace with honor? Herring concludes, "Only by the most narrow definition can the agreement be said to have constituted 'peace with honor.'. . . North Vietnamese troops remained in the south, and the PRG [Provisional Revolutionary Government] was accorded political status."[208] The final price of the war was extraordinary: 107,504 South Vietnamese military died, the NLF lost over 500,000, and 58,320 Americans died. Civilian deaths probably were in the millions. Tragically 20,533 U.S. soldiers died in the last four years of the war, after it had become clear that victory was beyond their grasp.[209]

FALL OF SAIGON

The Paris Accords did not constitute the final chapter of the Vietnam story. The agreement allowed Communist forces and South Vietnamese forces to remain in place as American troops withdrew. Nixon's promises to Thieu emboldened him to violate the peace agreement by attacking areas under Communist control, despite the agreement that each side would keep its existing territory. At the time of the agreement, the South Vietnamese government controlled about 75 percent of the land and 85 percent of the population.[210] But Thieu wasted his advantage by attacking areas controlled by the Communists. During the first three months after the peace agreement,

South Vietnam's army lost over 6,000 men.[211] Nixon used various subterfuges to continue military aid, including keeping 9,000 discharged military personnel in Vietnam and reclassifying them as civilians. He also continued to keep naval and air forces in the area and continued to bomb Cambodia. In short, all parties failed to live up to their commitments under the Paris Accords.[212]

As the Watergate scandal grew, Congress became more assertive, with the House approving a cutoff of funds for air operations and refusing to approve the aid to North Vietnam until MIAs were accounted for, which the North Vietnamese refused to do.[213] Nixon was forced to accept a deadline from Congress to cease all military activities in Indochina by August 15, 1973. By November, Congress passed the War Powers Act over Nixon's veto, which severely restricted the president's power to deploy troops.[214] On August 9, 1974, Nixon resigned. The man who promised to save Thieu's government was gone, succeeded by Gerald Ford, an unelected Vice President.

By the fall of 1974, the North Vietnamese and the NLF had the upper hand.[215] In September Congress cut aid in half, creating a devastating blow to the South Vietnamese government and military.[216] As South Vietnam faced defeat, there was one last effort to save the regime. Kissinger sought congressional aid to South Vietnam, warning that if it fell, the "impact on the United States in the world would be very serious indeed."[217] This plea did no good and all he got from Congress was money to evacuate Americans from Vietnam. Just before Saigon fell, polls showed public support for military intervention virtually anywhere dropping. Barely a third supported sending troops to stop Russia from taking over Berlin. The only intervention supported by a majority was to defend Canada.[218]

The end came even faster than the North Vietnamese had hoped. On May 1, 1975, Saigon fell, fifty-five days after the Communist offensive began. The evacuation was chaotic. The airport was heavily damaged by enemy rockets and mortars, leaving helicopters as the only escape. Again, television images transported viewers to the chaotic scene showing helicopters lifting off the roof of the American embassy. Forty years later, the CIA published a report on the fall of Saigon that described the chaos: "Helicopters landed and took off throughout the day and night of 29 April. At 4:00 a.m. the next morning, President Ford ordered Ambassador Martin to leave the Saigon Embassy, effectively ending the evacuation."[219] Many of the Vietnamese nationals who had worked with the U.S. forces were left behind. Saigon Chief of Station Thomas Polgar recalled, "We had thousands of people in the embassy compound at that time that could not be evacuated."[220]

Chapter 7

PUBLIC OPINION

Narrative coherence and *fidelity* are not inherent in the story itself, but reside in the transaction between storyteller and audience. Because the Vietnam War was the subject of extensive public opinion polls, the public's attitudes can be tracked with some degree of precision. Mueller analyzed public opinion on both the Korean and Vietnam wars and his findings were published in 1971, while the Vietnam War was still raging.[221] William Lunch and Peter Sperlich analyzed public opinion data on the Vietnam War and published their results in 1978.[222] Combining these two extensive reviews of polling leads to several somewhat surprising conclusions. Both studies use the *negative* answer to the question of whether or not the war was a "mistake" as a surrogate for support for the war.

First, it is clear that the public was initially not well informed or interested in Vietnam, although there was an election in 1964 and the Gulf of Tonkin incident happened that year. Lunch and Sperlich report, "Even . . . when the United States stood poised on the verge of major military involvement . . . two-thirds of the American people 'said they paid little or no attention to developments in South Vietnam.'"[223]

Second, opposition to the war increased predictably as U.S. involvement escalated and victory seemed less attainable. According to Mueller's analysis, prowar sentiment exceeded opposition from August 1965 until October 1967. By December, they were essentially tied. After the Tet offensive those who opposed the war narrowly outweighed supporters (46 to 42). From that point on the supporters never exceeded the opponents. By May 1970, 56 percent were opposed and only 36 percent were prowar, with 8 percent who didn't know.[224] Mueller concluded that for Vietnam the decline in public support was directly related to the level of American causalities, just as it had been in Korea.[225]

Nevertheless, it turns out that thinking the war was a mistake in the early years was associated more often with a hawkish viewpoint than a dovish one. Lunch and Sperlich found that "it was not until after the 1968 election that preferences for withdrawal finally broke through the 20 percent level."[226] It took until September 1970 for a majority (55 percent) to prefer withdrawal. By April 1972 support for withdrawal reached a high point of 73 percent.[227] Nixon's Vietnamization strategy was tailored to a public increasingly desirous of an end to the war.

Third, much has been made of the effect of protestors, particularly the young, on undermining support for the war. To this day, there are those who believe that protesters snatched defeat from the jaws of victory. Polling, however, reveals a very different picture. The protestors, particularly the more radical ones, actually undermined their cause. Lunch and Sperlich found,

"Antiwar demonstrations had not convinced most citizens that the United States was morally wrong in being in Vietnam and may have even slowed the development of withdrawal sentiment by acting as a negative reference point."[228] It was only when elites and opinion leaders began questioning the war in 1969 and 1970 that public opinion shifted. Perhaps most surprising, although most of the protestors were young, polling showed, "the striking fact is that the younger a person was during the Vietnam era, the more likely he or she was to support the war."[229] As an example, in February 1968, as overall support for the war was declining, 51 percent of those aged twenty-one to twenty-nine were prowar compared with 44 percent of thirty to forty-nine-year-olds and only 36 percent in the fifty and over age group.[230]

One of the reasons for the perception of youth being the strongest opponents of the war came from the widely covered protests on many college campuses. Until the early part of 1968, those with higher levels of education were more supportive of the war, with the exception of those with advanced degrees. Those with an undergraduate college education were the most supportive, followed by noncollege educated. The least supportive were those with a graduate school degree. However, by 1968, the gap between college and high school graduates disappeared. Among well-educated respondents, the nature of their college experience was crucial in determining support or opposition to the war. Those who attended prestigious schools, such as Berkeley or Harvard, were more likely to oppose the war than those who went to less elite schools. And since the latter group far exceeds the former, that helps explain why the college-educated in general were supportive of the war, while protests raged on campuses such as Berkeley.[231]

Another factor that may have affected college-educated youths' evaluation of the war was their relative unlikelihood of being drafted. Until 1971, any man attending college could obtain a student deferment for up to four years as long as he maintained adequate grades and progress toward a degree.[232] Thus, most college students didn't worry about being drafted during college. The lottery also removed the fear of being drafted for a significant percentage of young men after college. Hence, the ferocity of opposition to the war was tempered. This occurred in conjunction with the Vietnamization strategy, which further reduced the danger of being sent to the war. Thus, it is no surprise that college-educated youth were not as anti-war as was generally thought, except in the elite schools where anti-war sentiment was strongest.

THE LEGACY OF VIETNAM

Measuring the costs of the war to America goes beyond the lives lost, the billions spent, and the crippling inflation that followed the war. Confidence in American institutions was shaken and the military became a less revered institution. For many years, the reluctance to use American military force constrained presidents with what came to be known as the "Vietnam Syndrome." Avoiding another Vietnam became the touchstone of American military policy. Further, the 2.7 million Americans who served in the war were themselves victims. They were often portrayed in television and movies as drug-crazed, violent, and unstable individuals, who had great difficulty adapting to civilian life.[233]

As we look back on a war that ended in defeat nearly a half century ago, there is a sharp division between those who think America should never have intervened and those who blame the policy-makers who failed to apply enough military force to win decisively. As Rambo said in the famous movie line, "Sir, do we get to win *this* time?"[234] Ronald Reagan called it "a noble cause."[235] General H. R. McMaster offers his take on the failure of Vietnam in his seminal book *Dereliction of Duty*:

> The war in Vietnam was not lost in the field, nor was it lost on the front pages of the *New York Times* or on the college campuses. It was lost in Washington, D.C., even before Americans assumed sole responsibility for the fighting in 1965 and before they realized the country was at war; indeed, even before the first American units were deployed. The disaster in Vietnam was not the result of impersonal forces but a uniquely human failure, the responsibility for which was shared by President Johnson and his principal military and civilian advisers.[236]

One of those principal advisers was Robert McNamara, called by some the architect of the war. In his memoir he concedes that the United States had several opportunities to withdraw from the conflict long before it became a quagmire:

> I believe we could and should have withdrawn from South Vietnam either in late 1963 amid the turmoil surrounding Diem's assassination or in late 1964 or early 1965 in the face of increasing political and military weakness in South Vietnam.[237]

Among the lessons McNamara takes from the war are the following:

> We failed to draw Congress and the American people into a full and frank discussion and debate of the pros and cons of a large-scale U.S. military involvement before we initiated the action. . . . After the action got under way . . . we failed to retain popular support in part because we did not explain fully what was happening and why we were doing what we did.[238]

Thus, McNamara attributes the disasters to the failure to level with the American people about the reality of the challenges faced in Vietnam. In other words, the story lacked fidelity to the reality in Vietnam.

What the debate over who lost Vietnam fails to address is the fundamental issue of whether America should have been in Vietnam in the first place. Had the United States supported the Vietnamese nationalists who wanted independence in 1945 or allowed the reunification elections scheduled for 1956 to take place, it is likely there would have been no war involving the United States. Why did a nation built on an anti-colonial foundation support the French in their efforts to reestablish colonial control? When they failed, why did the United States assume their role? The fear of Communism, the Cold War, and the legacy of Munich seemed to blind decision-makers to the unique character of the conflict in Vietnam. Thus, the legacy of Vietnam is not just how poorly the leadership of the U.S. government and military carried out the war, it is also how America chose to go to war in the first place.

One indicator of a war's legacy is the way it is portrayed on film and in song. Few movies were made about the war while it was happening. The one notable exception was *The Green Berets*, starring John Wayne. This 1968 prowar propaganda film portrayed the Viet Cong as rapists and brutalizers, while showing the Americans as brave defenders of their Dodge City fortress. Susan Brewer cites the film as an example of a "conversion narrative," where a liberal reporter who was skeptical of the war is converted to the cause. The film, however, was an outlier and met with little success either with the critics or the public.[239] In fact the hit movie and television series *M*A*S*H* were as much about Vietnam as Korea, and carried anything but a prowar message.

After the war, a number of movies emerged, most with an anti-war theme. Films, such as *The Deer Hunter, Apocalypse Now, Coming Home*, and Vietnam veteran Oliver Stone's *Platoon* and *Born on the Fourth of July*, all put a dark spin on the Vietnam debacle. Spike Lee's *Da 5 Bloods*, released in June 2020, focuses on the racial overtones of the war. As one character says, "We fought in an immoral war that wasn't ours, for rights we didn't have."[240] Even the comedy *Good Morning, Vietnam* had Robin Williams's character sympathetic to a member of the Viet Cong and dismissive of military authority. Unlike World Wars I and II, which continue to inspire movies portraying American soldiers as heroes, Hollywood focused on the tragic aspects of the Vietnam War. Fifteen years after the war ended, polls found that a substantial majority of Americans still believed the war had been a mistake.[241]

Music and hit songs are often created in support of a war. Once America entered World War I, "I Didn't Raise My Boy to be a Soldier" was replaced with "Over There." No Independence Day celebration would be complete without the rousing marches of John Philip Sousa. But the war in Vietnam produced few such musical tributes. Although the hit song "Ballad of the

Green Berets" released in 1966 praised the elite Special Forces corps, most of the music of the late 1960s had a decidedly anti-war theme. From the "Draft Dodger Rag" to "Fortunate Son," musicians focused on the inequity of the draft. Arlo Guthrie's iconic "Alice's Restaurant Massacree" is about the irony of being rejected by the military for having been a convicted litterbug. Edwin Starr's "War (What is it Good For?)" pretty much summed up the attitude of most rock and rollers of the time, when the answer was "absolutely nothing."

ASSESSING THE NARRATIVES

The war in Vietnam was based on a fundamentally flawed narrative: That the North Vietnamese were part of a worldwide monolithic Communist movement that had to be contained. The United States, which had defeated the powerful Nazi and Japanese war machines, stopped the Communist expansion in Europe, and prevented their hostile takeover of South Korea, was the only force capable of stopping the dominoes from falling in Southeast Asia. Only a failure of will would permit the North Vietnamese to succeed. Not only was the United States the superior military force in the world, but it also held the moral high ground. The United States was fighting for the freedom of the people of South Vietnam against a ruthless and cruel aggressor. Finally, U.S. prestige and credibility were on the line in Vietnam. A failure to stand by its commitment to the South Vietnamese would embolden Communist "wars of national liberation" everywhere. Pulling out of Vietnam would be like Munich all over again and the dominoes would fall.

Initially, the story had *narrative coherence* and *fidelity* for the American people. In terms of *structural coherence*, the story that America needed to defeat Communism wherever it threatened free peoples had become the hallmark of U.S. foreign policy ever since the Cold War began. Kennedy's inaugural promise "bear any burden, meet any hardship, support any friend, oppose any foe, in order to assure the survival and the success of liberty" resonated with the nation. The story had *material coherence* in that the failure to stop Communists in China had led to the Korean War and the takeover of Cuba by Communists brought the world to the brink of nuclear war. Finally, the story had *characterological coherence*, as Dr. Tom Dooley and others warned about the ruthless cruelty of godless Communists.

The *narrative fidelity* of the storyline initially resonated with the American people just as the war was heating up. Three events played a key role in giving the story the ring of truth. First, there was Munich—give a dictator an inch and he'll take a mile. To fail to protect the vulnerable Vietnamese from the terror of Communism would be an invitation to wider war. Second, Korea showed that Communists could be stopped if the U.S. military used its might. While some might have questioned why America settled for the status quo in Korea, there was little doubt that the Communist aggressors had been thwarted. Finally, the Cuban Missile Crisis showed Americans that the stakes were incredibly high. Although Communism had to be contained, pushing too hard could lead to Armageddon. Therefore, when Lyndon Johnson adopted a policy of graduated response, sought "no wider war," but refused to "cut and run," that was exactly the sweet spot for the American people in 1964.

Yet, as the war progressed, the stories began to lose their *narrative coherence* and *fidelity*. In terms of *structural coherence*, the story that the United States needed to fight in a far-off Asian jungle so it didn't need to fight the Communists at home became less believable. As the war continued, it became clearer to many that this was not a clear-cut case of Communist aggression, such as had occurred in Korea. Rather, it was actually a civil war. The attacks in the Gulf of Tonkin were the closest events to a clear-cut aggressive action. But with time, the truth started to emerge that they were not what they seemed. Even McNamara concedes the Gulf of Tonkin Resolution was misused to escalate the war. The *characterological coherence* of America's South Vietnamese allies was undermined by what Americans saw on the nightly news. Pictures of Buddhist monks immolating themselves and a police officer shooting a bound Viet Cong prisoner in the head transported viewers to a nation that was anything but free and democratic. America's own claim to moral authority was also undermined by what viewers saw on the nightly news, for example, a young Vietnamese girl running naked to escape napalm. The revelations of the massacre at My Lai were devastating. On the other side, Ho Chi Minh was no Hitler. Allowing the reunification of Vietnam under his leadership was hardly akin to allowing Germany to take over Sudetenland. *Material coherence* was lacking as well. As successive governments of South Vietnam were overthrown by coups and protests often erupted against military leaders, it was hard to portray South Vietnam as a bastion of democracy. Presenting a story that America was in Vietnam to protect freedom was inconsistent with the repressive tactics of a series of regimes instituted by military coups.

The fundamental problem with the stories told by Johnson and later Nixon was they lacked *narrative fidelity*. Because LBJ chose not to tell the American people the truth, when things went badly the dreaded credibility gap emerged. The narrative that the United States was winning the war was destroyed by the events of the Tet offensive. No longer did the narrative have fidelity to what the American people saw nightly on their TVs. The *Pentagon Papers* revealed once and for all how badly the Johnson administration had misled the public. Nixon's promise of "peace with honor" was initially persuasive. However, it ultimately lacked fidelity when Saigon fell and viewers were transported to the chaos of the evacuation of Saigon. Allowing the North's army and Viet Cong to remain in place, while Americans withdrew, led to neither peace nor honor. The credibility of the nation's leaders, both civilian and military, was severely damaged.

The domino theory was disproven because it was based on a flawed premise. VanDeMark criticizes America's leaders,

> whose ignorance and misperception of Southeast Asian history, culture, and politics pulled America progressively deeper into the war. . . . [They] mistakenly viewed Vietnam through the simplistic ideological prism of the Cold War. They perceived a deeply complex and ambiguous regional struggle as a grave challenge to world order and stability, fomented by communist China acting through its local surrogate, North Vietnam.[242]

Although Cambodia and Laos fell into the North Vietnamese orbit, that could be explained by the destabilizing actions taken by the United States as much as Communist aggression. The rest of the dominoes did not fall. Thailand and the Philippines were spared, as were many spots around the world where the Communists attempted to incite revolution. In short, rather than dominoes falling, it was the *domino theory* that fell with a thud.

Finally, the narrative that American prestige and credibility were on the line in Vietnam regardless of the outcome was disproven. As far back as 1964, McMaster reveals that the administration was "planning for failure," having concluded that "losing would be preferable to withdrawing from what they believed was an impossible situation."[243] Rather than enhancing the credibility of the United States, the misadventure in Vietnam led to a decade and a half of an America hamstrung by the Vietnam syndrome. As America lost its first war, its long string of military successes came to an end. The storyline going forward became not one of reliving the successes of prior wars, but avoiding "another Vietnam."

In 1971 John Kerry asked the prophetic question, "How do you ask a man to be the last man to die for a mistake?" We now know the name of that man—Richard Vandegeer. On April 30, 1975, nearly sixteen years after the first American died in Vietnam, Air Force Second Lieutenant Richard Vandegeer was deployed to pilot a helicopter to rescue Americans and Vietnamese as Saigon fell. Fifteen days after the fall of Saigon, on May 15, 1975, Vandegeer piloted a helicopter to rescue the crew of a merchant ship, *Mayaguez*, which the brutal Cambodian Khmer Rouge had captured three days earlier. When his CH-53 helicopter was hit by anti-aircraft fire, it crashed, killing Vandegeer and his crew.[244] The names Dale Buis and Richard Vandegeer are unknown to most Americans. Yet, they are the first and last names engraved on the Vietnam Memorial Wall in Washington, D.C.[245] Visited by some three million people a year, the wall tells the story of the

58,320 Americans who served and died in Vietnam. The uniqueness of the wall is that it is a war memorial that allows visitors to construct their own stories. To some, the wall represents the roster of heroes who died for what Ronald Reagan called a "noble cause." To others, the wall is a roll call of those who tragically lost their lives for what John Kerry called a "mistake." Regardless of how one views the story of Vietnam, it has had a profound impact on America in the more than four-and-a-half decades since the death of Richard Vandegeer and his crew.

NOTES

1. This account is taken from Samantha L. Quigley, "Ceremony Commemorates Vietnam War's First Combat Casualties," *DoD News*, July 8, 2009, https://www.dvidshub.net/news/36136/ceremony-commemorates-vietnam-wars-first-combat-casualties and "South Vietnam: Death at Intermission Time," Togetherweserved.com, July 20, 1959, accessed January 13, 2020, https://army.togetherweserved.com/army/servlet/tws.webapp.WebApp?cmd=ShadowBoxProfile&type=Person&ID=42020.
2. George C. Herring, *America's Longest War: The United States and Vietnam, 1950–1975*, 3rd ed. (New York: McGraw-Hill, 1996), 23.
3. Stanley Karnow, *Vietnam: A History*, revised updated edition (New York: Penguin, 1997), 10–11.
4. Jean Edward Smith, *Eisenhower in War and Peace* (New York: Random House, 2012), 611.
5. John E. Mueller, "Trends in Popular Support for the Wars in Korea and Vietnam," *The American Political Science Review* 65, no. 2 (June, 1971): 365, https://doi.org/10.2307/1954454.
6. "Gulf of Tonkin Resolution," History.com, updated June 7, 2019, accessed January 13, 2020, https://www.history.com/topics/vietnam-war/gulf-of-tonkin-resolution-1.
7. Maggie Bria, "What Did the 1919 Paris Peace Conference Have to Do with the Vietnam War?" Bria Historica, March 30, 2017 and June 4, 2018, accessed June 3, 2020, https://briahistorica.com/2017/03/30/what-did-the-1919-paris-peace-conference-have-to-do-with-the-vietnam-war/.
8. Neil Sheehan, *A Bright Shining Lie: John Paul Vann and America in Vietnam* (New York: Random House, 1988, Modern Library 2009), [page] 148, Kindle.
9. Sheehan, *Bright Shining Lie*, 147.
10. Herring, *Longest War*, 21–23.
11. Herring, *Longest War*, 15–17.
12. Sheehan, *Bright Shining Lie*, 165.
13. Herring, *Longest War*, 44.
14. Quoted in David Halberstam, *The Best and the Brightest* (New York: Modern Library, 2001), 164, Kindle.
15. Quoted in Herring, *Longest War*, 38.
16. Halberstam, *Best and Brightest*, 164.

17. Editors of Encyclopaedia Britannica, "Geneva Accords," Encyclopaedia Britannica, July 14, 2019, https://www.britannica.com/event/Geneva-Accords.
18. Quoted in Sheehan, *Bright Shining Lie*, 138.
19. Herring, *Longest War*, 48.
20. Herring, *Longest War*, 52–55.
21. Sheehan, *Bright Shining Lie*, 138.
22. Karnow, *Vietnam*, 640.
23. Susan A. Brewer, *Why America Fights: Patriotism and War Propaganda from the Philippines to Iraq* (New York: Oxford University Press, 2009), 184.
24. Herring, *Longest War*, 60–61.
25. Halberstam, *Best and Brightest*, 120.
26. Herring, *The Longest War*, 60–62.
27. John F. Kennedy, "America's Stake in Vietnam, American Friends of Vietnam, Washington, D.C." June 1, 1956, Papers of John F. Kennedy, Pre-Presidential Papers, Senate Files, Series 12, Speeches and the Press, Box 895, accessed March 28, 2020, https://www.jfklibrary.org/archives/other-resources/john-f-kennedy-speeches/vietnam-conference-washington-dc-19560601.
28. Diana Shaw, "The Temptation of Tom Dooley: He Was the Heroic Jungle Doctor of Indochina in the 1950s. But He Had a Secret, and to Protect It, He Helped Launch the First Disinformation Campaign of the Vietnam War," *Los Angeles Times*, December 15, 1991, https://www.latimes.com/archives/la-xpm-1991-12-15-tm-868-story.html.
29. Thomas A. Dooley, M.D., *Deliver Us From Evil: The Story Of Viet Nam's Flight To Freedom* (New York: Farrar, Straus & Cudahy, 1956), 181–182, https://archive.org/stream/deliverusfromevi006715mbp/deliverusfromevi006715mbp_djvu.txt.
30. Shaw, "The Temptation of Tom Dooley."
31. Herring, *Longest War*, 74–75.
32. Halberstam, *Best and Brightest*, 172.
33. John F. Kennedy, "Inaugural Address," January 20, 1961. John F. Kennedy Presidential Library and Museum, accessed April 17, 2019, https://www.jfklibrary.org/learn/about-jfk/historic-speeches/inaugural-address.
34. Herring, *Longest War*, 82.
35. Herring, *Longest War*, 86.
36. H. R. McMaster, *Dereliction of Duty: Lyndon Johnson, Robert McNamara, the Joint Chiefs of Staff, and the Lies That Led to Vietnam* (New York: Harper Collins, 1997), 37.
37. Sheehan, *Bright Shining Lie*, 37.
38. Halberstam, *Best and Brightest*, 229.
39. Herring, *Longest War*, 96.
40. Herring, *Longest War*, 103.
41. Halberstam, *Best and Brightest*, 324.
42. Sheehan, *Bright Shining Lie*, 55.
43. Halberstam, *Best and Brightest*, 320.
44. John R. MacArthur, *Second Front: Censorship and Propaganda in the 1991 Gulf War*, 2nd ed. (Berkeley: University of California Press, 2004), 117.
45. Brewer, *Why America Fights*, 185.

46. Brewer, *Why America Fights*, 188 and Herring, *Longest War*, 106.
47. Herring, *Longest War*, 106.
48. Sheehan, *Bright Shining Lie*, 354.
49. Sheehan, *Bright Shining Lie*, 356.
50. Halberstam, *Best and Brightest*, 328.
51. Herring, *Longest War*, 116.
52. McMaster, *Dereliction of Duty*, 61.
53. Bill Moyers, "Bill Remembers LBJ's Road to War," *Bill Moyers Journal*, November 20, 2009, updated August 6, 2014, https://billmoyers.com/content/lbjs-road-to-war/.
54. Robert S. McNamara with Brian VanDeMark, *In Retrospect: The Tragedy and Lessons of Vietnam* (New York: Times Books/Random House, 1995), 96.
55. Halberstam, *Best and Brightest*, 341.
56. Quoted in Herring, *Longest War*, 122.
57. Quoted in Herring, *Longest War*, 122.
58. Herring, *Longest War*, 124.
59. Quoted in Herring, *Longest War*, 126.
60. Herring, *Longest War*, 130–131.
61. Brewer, *Why America Fights*, 190.
62. Quoted in Brewer, *Why America Fights*, 191.
63. Brewer, *Why America Fights*, 196.
64. Halberstam, *Best and Brightest*, 398.
65. Brian VanDeMark, *Into the Quagmire: Lyndon Johnson and the Escalation of the Vietnam War* (New York: Oxford University Press, 1995), 32, Adobe Digital Edition.
66. Karnow, *Vietnam*, 382–383.
67. Karnow, *Vietnam*, 383.
68. Karnow, *Vietnam*, 384.
69. Michael R. Beschloss, ed., *Taking Charge: The Johnson White House Tapes, 1963–1964* (New York: Simon and Schuster, 1997), 498.
70. McNamara, *In Retrospect*, 133.
71. Beschloss, *Taking Charge*, 500.
72. Quoted in Halberstam, *Best and Brightest*, 470.
73. Quoted in Karnow, *Vietnam*, 385.
74. Quoted in Karnow, *Vietnam*, 390.
75. Karnow, *Vietnam*, 389.
76. Quoted in Karnow, *Vietnam*, 390.
77. Keith B. Richburg, "Mission to Hanoi: McNamara Asks Ex-Foes to Join in Search for War's Lessons." *Washington Post* (1974-Current File), November 11, 1995, A21, ProQuest Historical Newspapers.
78. Richburg, "Mission to Hanoi," A21.
79. Richburg, "Mission to Hanoi," A25.
80. "Motion Picture 498; President Johnson's Vietnam Address," August 4, 1964, Lyndon Baines Johnson Library, Austin, TX, accessed March 26, 2020, https://www.docsteach.org/documents/document/johnson-vietnam-address.

81. H. J. Res. 1145, Public Law 88-408, August 10, 1964, https://www.ourdocuments.gov/document_data/pdf/doc_098.pdf.
82. Quoted in Karnow, *Vietnam*, 377.
83. Michael Beschloss, *Presidents of War* (New York: Crown, 2018), [page] 517, Kindle.
84. Quoted in McMaster, *Dereliction of Duty*, 134.
85. Herring, *Longest War*, 137.
86. McNamara, *In Retrospect*, 142 (italics in original).
87. "U.S. Destroyers Open Fire Again In Tonkin Gulf; Targets Vanish; No American Losses in Clash Off Coast of North Vietnam," *New York Times*, September 19, 1964, 1, https://nyti.ms/361MxAp.
88. "Telephone conversation # 5593, sound recording, LBJ and ROBERT MCNAMARA, 9/18/1964, 11:46AM," Recordings and Transcripts of Telephone Conversations and Meetings, LBJ Presidential Library, accessed April 2, 2020, https://www.discoverlbj.org/item/tel-05593. Transcribed by author because official transcriptions not yet digitalized (italics added).
89. Lyndon B. Johnson, "Remarks in Memorial Hall, Akron University, October 21, 1964," *Public Papers of the Presidents of the United States: Lyndon B. Johnson, 1965*, Book II, entry 693 (Washington, DC: Government Printing Office, 1966), 1391, accessed March 29, 2020, https://quod.lib.umich.edu/p/ppotpus/4730949.1964.002/631?page=root;rgn=full+text;size=100;view=image.
90. McMaster, *Dereliction of Duty*, 153.
91. Quoted in Karnow, *Vietnam*, 420.
92. Karnow, *Vietnam*, 396.
93. McMaster, *Dereliction of Duty*, 216.
94. McNamara, *In Retrospect*, 170.
95. Halberstam, *Best and Brightest*, 610.
96. McNamara, *In Retrospect*, 169.
97. Quoted in VanDeMark, *Into the Quagmire*, 42.
98. McNamara, *In Retrospect*, 174.
99. McNamara, *In Retrospect*, 174.
100. McNamara, *In Retrospect*, 206.
101. Halberstam, *Best and Brightest*, 621.
102. Halberstam, *Best and Brightest*, 640.
103. Sheehan, *Bright Shining Lie*, 535.
104. Lyndon B. Johnson, "The President's Address at Johns Hopkins University: Peace Without Conquest, April 7, 1965," *Public Papers of the Presidents of the United States: Lyndon B. Johnson, 1965*, Book I, entry 172 (Washington, DC: Government Printing Office, 1966), 394-399, accessed March 20, 2020, http://www.lbjlibrary.org/exhibits/the-presidents-address-at-johns-hopkins-university-peace-without-conquest (the official transcript uses both spellings—Vietnam and Viet-Nam).
105. Quoted in VanDeMark, *Into the Quagmire*, 160.
106. Herring, *Longest War*, 147.
107. Herring, *Longest War*, 147.
108. Herring, *Longest War*, 155.
109. Quoted in VanDeMark, *Into the Quagmire*, 179.

110. "Ground War in Asia," *New York Times*, June 9, 1965, 46, https://nyti.ms/3wRRfML.
111. Herring, *Longest War*, 170–171.
112. McNamara, *In Retrospect*, 243.
113. Herring, *Longest War*, 168.
114. Sheehan, *Bright Shining Lie*, 6.
115. Sheehan, *Bright Shining Lie*, 617–620.
116. Sheehan, *Bright Shining Lie*, 589.
117. Sheehan, *Bright Shining Lie*, 630 (bracketed word provided by Sheehan).
118. Sheehan, *Bright Shining Lie*, 630.
119. Karnow, *Vietnam*, 603.
120. McNamara, *In Retrospect*, 195.
121. McMaster, *Dereliction of Duty*, 248.
122. Lyndon B. Johnson, "July 28, 1965: Press Conference," Miller Center, University of Virginia, accessed March 25, 2020, https://millercenter.org/the-presidency/presidential-speeches/july-28-1965-press-conference.
123. Directorate for Armed Forces Information and Education, *Why Vietnam*, 1965, accessed March 29, 2020, https://www.youtube.com/watch?v=qEljbPwFQ9M.
124. Warren Weaver, Jr., "Fulbright Scores War 'Propaganda,'" *New York Times*, December 2, 1969, 37, https://nyti.ms/35UzMXX.
125. William Fulbright, "S. 3217-Introduction of a Bill Requiring the Secretary of Defense to Submit Regular Reports With Respect to the Kinds and Amounts of Information Released for Distribution to The Public By The Department Of Defense," *Congressional Record*, 91st Cong. 1st sess., 1969, 115, pt. 28, 37251, 2020, https://www.govinfo.gov/app/details/GPO-CRECB-1969-pt28.
126. Fulbright, "S. 3217," 37261.
127. Fulbright, "S. 3217," 37285.
128. Fulbright, "S. 3217," 37287.
129. Caroline Page, "Introduction," *U.S. Official Propaganda During the Vietnam War, 1965–1973: The Limits of Persuasion* (London: Bloomsbury Academic, 1996), 2, http://dx.doi.org/10.5040/9781474290869.0005.
130. Herring, *Longest War*, 160.
131. Herring, *Longest War*, 165.
132. VanDeMark, *Into the Quagmire*, 131.
133. Herring, *Longest War*, 189.
134. Brewer, *Why America Fights*, 204.
135. Herring, *Longest War*, 198.
136. McMaster, *Dereliction of Duty*, 254–255.
137. Brewer, *Why America Fights*, 204.
138. Brewer, *Why America Fights*, 204.
139. Brewer, *Why America Fights*, 206.
140. Sheehan, *Bright Shining Lie*, 698.
141. Sheehan, *Bright Shining Lie*, 695.
142. Grant Cokeley, "Number of TV Households in America: 1950-1978," *The American Century*, https://americancentury.omeka.wlu.edu/items/show/136.
143. Brewer, *Why America Fights*, 197.

144. Quoted in Beschloss, *Presidents of War*, 553.
145. McNamara, *In Retrospect*, 260.
146. McNamara, *In Retrospect*, 261.
147. McNamara, *In Retrospect*, 294.
148. Herring, *Longest War*, 177.
149. Beschloss, *Presidents of War*, 554.
150. Herring, *Longest War*, 206.
151. Herring, *Longest War*, 209.
152. Kenneth T. Walsh, "50 Years Ago, Walter Cronkite Changed a Nation," U.S. News & World Report, February 27, 2018, https://www.usnews.com/news/ken-walshs-washington/articles/2018-02-27/50-years-ago-walter-cronkite-changed-a-nation.
153. Herring, *Longest War*, 221.
154. Colin Powell with Joseph E. Persico, *My American Journey* (New York: Random House, 1995), 123.
155. Ronald H. Spector, *After Tet: The Bloodiest Year in Vietnam* (New York: The Free Press, 1993).
156. Quoted in Brewer, *Why America Fights*, 207.
157. Brewer, *Why America Fights*, 220 and Herring, *Longest War*, 236.
158. Herring, *Longest War*, 219–221.
159. Lyndon B. Johnson, "The President's Address to the Nation Announcing Steps to Limit the War in Vietnam and Reporting His Decision Not to Seek Reelection," March 31, 1968, *Public Papers of the Presidents of the United States: Lyndon B. Johnson, 1968–1969* (2 vols.; Washington DC, 1970), I, 469–476, accessed March 26, 2020, https://quod.lib.umich.edu/p/ppotpus/.
160. Eric Cortellessa, "Spike Lee Tells a Different Vietnam War History," *Washington Monthly*, June 20, 2020, https://washingtonmonthly.com/2020/06/20/spike-lee-tells-a-different-vietnam-war-history/.
161. William L. Lunch and Peter W. Sperlich, "American Public Opinion and the War in Vietnam," *The Western Political Quarterly* 32, no. 1 (March 1979): 36, https://www.jstor.org/stable/447561.
162. Herring, *Longest War*, 223, 231.
163. John A. Farrell, "When a Candidate Conspired with a Foreign Power to Win An Election," Politico, August 6, 2017, https://www.politico.com/magazine/story/2017/08/06/nixon-vietnam-candidate-conspired-with-foreign-power-win-election-215461.
164. Herring, *Longest War*, 239.
165. Sheehan, *Bright Shining Lie*, 730.
166. Brewer, *Why America Fights*, 212.
167. Sheehan, *Bright Shining Lie*, 730.
168. Sheehan, *Bright Shining Lie*, 741.
169. Herring, *Longest War*, 243.
170. Herring, *Longest War*, 245.
171. Herring, *Longest War*, 248–249.
172. Herring, *Longest War*, 250.
173. Quoted in Karnow, *Vietnam*, 597.

174. Herring, *Longest War*, 247.
175. Brewer, *Why America Fights*, 213.
176. Richard M. Nixon, "Address to the Nation on the War in Vietnam." November 3, 1969, P-691101, accessed March 22, 2020, https://www.nixonlibrary.gov/sites/default/files/2018-08/silentmajority_transcript.pdf (all quotations from this source, italics omitted).
177. "American Rhetoric: Spiro Agnew—Television News Coverage (Nov 13, 1969)," American Rhetoric Top 100 Speeches, https://americanrhetoric.com/speeches/spiroagnewtvnewscoverage.htm.
178. Brewer, *Why America Fights*, 216.
179. Quoted in Brewer, *Why America Fights*, 214–215.
180. Karnow, *Vietnam*, 614–615.
181. Quoted in Herring, *Longest War*, 252.
182. "Vietnam Lotteries," Selective Service System, accessed June 18, 2020. https://www.sss.gov/history-and-records/vietnam-lotteries/.
183. Herring, *Longest War*, 257.
184. Richard M. Nixon, "Address to the Nation on the Situation in Southeast Asia," April 30, 1970, Miller Center, University of Virginia, accessed March 27, 2020, https://millercenter.org/the-presidency/presidential-speeches/april-30-1970-address-nation-situation-southeast-asia.
185. Brewer, *Why America Fights*, 217.
186. Herring, *Longest War*, 263.
187. Herring, *Longest War*, 265.
188. Brewer, *Why America Fights*, 220.
189. John Kerry, "How Do You Ask a Man to Be the Last Man to Die in Vietnam?" [Statement made before the Senate Foreign Relations Committee], April 23, 1971, History News Network, George Washington University, https://hnn.us/articles/3631.html.
190. Herring, *Longest War*, 266.
191. Powell, *My American Journey*, 143.
192. Sheehan, *Bright Shining Lie*, 689.
193. Mitchell Hall, "Unsell the War: Vietnam and Antiwar Advertising," *The Historian* 58, no. 1 (Autumn 1995): 75, https://www.jstor.org/stable/24449611.
194. Hall, "Unsell," 85.
195. Brewer, *Why America Fights*, 220–223.
196. Herring, *Longest War*, 267.
197. Herring, *Longest War*, 267–268.
198. Karnow, *Vietnam*, 651.
199. Karnow, *Vietnam*, 653.
200. Karnow, *Vietnam*, 657.
201. Herring, *Longest War*, 273–274.
202. Brewer, *Why America Fights*, 219.
203. Herring, *Longest War*, 276–278.
204. Karnow, *Vietnam*, 667.
205. Herring, *Longest War*, 280.

206. Herring, *Longest War*, 281.
207. Karnow, *Vietnam*, 669.
208. Herring, *Longest War*, 282.
209. Herring, *Longest War*, 282.
210. Karnow, *Vietnam*, 672.
211. Herring, *Longest War*, 286.
212. Herring, *Longest War*, 288.
213. Herring, *Longest War*, 289.
214. Herring, *Longest War*, 290.
215. Herring, *Longest War*, 291.
216. Herring, *Longest War*, 292–293.
217. Quoted in Herring, *Longest War*, 296.
218. Herring, *Longest War*, 308.
219. Craig R. Gralley, ed., *Voices from the Station: The Evacuation of the US Embassy in Saigon* (Washington, DC: Center for the Study of Intelligence, Central Intelligence Agency, April 2015), 7, accessed June 16, 2021, https://www.cia.gov/static/76218a5483719729a99e7ef716d56b7d/Voices-from-the-Station.pdf (italics omitted).
220. Gralley, *Voices*, 12.
221. Mueller, "Trends."
222. Lunch and Sperlich, "American Public Opinion."
223. Lunch and Sperlich, "American Public Opinion," 22.
224. Mueller, "Trends," 363 (from Table 3).
225. Mueller, "Trends," 366.
226. Lunch and Sperlich, "American Public Opinion," 25–26.
227. Lunch and Sperlich, "American Public Opinion," 27–28.
228. Lunch and Sperlich, "American Public Opinion," 31.
229. Lunch and Sperlich, "American Public Opinion," 34.
230. Lunch and Sperlich, "American Public Opinion," 33.
231. Lunch and Sperlich, "American Public Opinion," 38–39.
232. Peter Shapiro, "Freshman Deferments End As Nixon Signs New Draft Legislation," Harvard Crimson, September 29, 1971, https://www.thecrimson.com/article/1971/9/29/freshman-deferments-end-as-nixon-signs/.
233. Herring, *Longest War*, 306.
234. Quoted in Herring, *Longest War*, 309 (italics in original).
235. Ronald Reagan, "Veterans of Foreign Wars Convention, Chicago, Illinois, Peace: Restoring the Margin of Safety," August 18, 1980, Ronald Reagan Presidential Library and Museum, accessed June 20, 2020, https://www.reaganlibrary.gov/sspeeches/8-18-80.
236. McMaster, *Dereliction of Duty*, 333–334.
237. McNamara, *In Retrospect*, 320. On page 321, McNamara lists several possible withdrawal dates and the corresponding numbers of troops in Vietnam as well as lives lost. In November 1963, the United States had only 16,300 advisers and had lost only 78 KIA. In late 1964 and early 1965, there were 23,300 advisers and 225 KIA. By July 1965, the United States. had increased its forces to 81,400 and had lost

509, still less than 1 percent of those who would eventually die. In December 1965, force levels were up to 184,300 and 1,594 had perished. Finally, the last off ramp McNamara saw was December 1967, when the United States had 485,600 troops and had lost 15,979 KIA.

    238. McNamara, *In Retrospect*, 322.
    239. Brewer, *Why America Fights,* 209.
    240. Quoted in Cortellessa, "Spike Lee."
    241. Herring, *Longest War*, 308.
    242. VanDeMark, *Into the Quagmire*, 249.
    243. McMaster, *Dereliction of Duty*, 180.
    244. "The First and Last Names on the Wall," USO.org, June 18, 2014, accessed March 10, 2018, https://www.uso.org/stories/1715-the-first-and-the-last-names-on-the-wall.
    245. "First and Last Names."

Chapter 8

The Persian Gulf War
Kicking the Vietnam Syndrome

In the early morning of August 1, 1990, President George Bush read the newspapers in bed, as was his custom. Nolan Ryan had won his 300th major league outing the previous day. In the crowd of over 51,000 was Texas Rangers owner George W. Bush, eldest son of the president.[1] Otherwise, the news was bleak. In his diary, the president said, "All in all, it's a wonder the world wakes up . . . with anything other than 'gloom and doom' on their mind."[2] Weighing on the president's mind was the situation on the Iraq-Kuwait border. Saddam Hussein's military had been bringing troops and artillery forward, setting up communications, and reinforcing its supplies. According to Joint Chiefs of Staff Chairman Colin Powell, all of these were "surefire clues that an enemy force is prepared to attack."[3] The Bush administration, however, didn't want to become embroiled in disputes between Arab states. U.S. ambassador to Iraq April Glaspie had told Saddam less than a week earlier that "we have no opinion on the Arab-Arab conflicts like your border disagreement with Kuwait."[4]

Later that same day, after hurting his shoulders hitting golf balls, the president decided to get a deep-heat treatment in the White House basement. At about 8:20 p.m. that evening, National Security Adviser Brent Scowcroft and Middle East expert Richard Haass entered the room. Bush got up, buttoned his shirt, and stepped into the hall. Scowcroft brought disturbing news, "It looks very bad. Iraq may be about to invade Kuwait."[5] Haass briefed the president on the situation and suggested he call Saddam Hussein to dissuade him from invading. Before Bush could make the call, Scowcroft took a call from the State Department and learned that the American Embassy in Kuwait was reporting gunfire. "So much for calling Saddam," said Bush, shaking his head.[6] In the early morning hours of August 2, 1990, Iraq had invaded and occupied the small neighboring state of Kuwait.

THE COLD WAR ENDS: A NEW WORLD ORDER BEGINS

From Truman to Reagan, American foreign policy had been grounded in the narrative of a Cold War with Communists bent on world domination. Truman and Johnson had taken the American people into two very hot wars based on that narrative. President George Bush presided over one of the most dramatic changes in the international landscape in modern history. No longer was containing Communism the fundamental story promoting American involvement in foreign wars. Future wars would need a different enemy and a new narrative. Dubbed the "Evil Empire" by Ronald Reagan, the Soviet Union had ceased to be an adversary and before the end of Bush's term of office it would cease to exist. As Colin Powell mused, what can you do "when you've lost your best enemy?"[7] As we shall see, when Bush needed a new enemy for the Gulf War, he went back to an even older enemy—Adolf Hitler.

The fall of the Berlin Wall symbolized the end of an era. Constructed in 1961 to prevent East Germans from escaping to the west, the Wall had divided the city of Berlin for over a quarter of a century. Ronald Reagan on July 12, 1987, challenged the Soviet leader: "Mr. Gorbachev, tear down this wall!"[8] Mikhail Gorbachev was different than his predecessors. He brought *perestroika* (restructuring) and *glasnost* (openness) to his country and an opportunity for thawing the Cold War to the world. Although the Wall remained through the end of Reagan's term, it finally fell in November 1989.[9] Symbolically, at least, the Cold War was over and the world had been, in the words of the title of Bush and Scowcroft's memoir, "Transformed."

Yet a few short months after the fall of the Berlin Wall, the new world order faced its first test. How would the major powers respond to the naked aggression of one nation against its smaller and weaker neighbor? No longer could the narrative be about the need to respond to Communist aggression. What story would emerge to guide America and the world's response?

OPERATION DESERT SHIELD

At 5:00 a.m. Washington time on the morning of August 2, Brent Scowcroft briefed the president on what was known of the attack on Kuwait. Bush's immediate actions were limited to ordering naval and air forces into the region and freezing Iraqi and Kuwaiti assets. The UN Security Council voted to condemn the action with the Soviet Union's support, something that would have been unimaginable during the Cold War. At an 8:00 a.m. photo op, Bush condemned the invasion, but avoided any threat to use force. He writes, "The truth is, at that moment I had no idea what our options were. I did know for sure that the aggression had to be stopped, and Kuwait's sovereignty restored."[10]

Later that day in Aspen, Colorado, Bush spoke at a joint press conference with British Prime Minister Margaret Thatcher. In response to the question, "Are you still not contemplating military intervention?" Bush replied, "No. . . . And we're not ruling any options in, but we're not ruling any options out."[11] Later Bush addressed the Aspen Institute Symposium. His speech was originally designed to set forth the role of the U.S. military in a post-Cold War world. He used the invasion to illustrate his main point: "The brutal aggression launched last night against Kuwait illustrates my central thesis: Notwithstanding the alteration in the Soviet threat, the world remains a dangerous place."[12]

During the next few days, Bush met at Camp David with Powell, Secretary of Defense Dick Cheney, Undersecretary of Defense Paul Wolfowitz, General Norman Schwarzkopf, and others.[13] Bush spoke on the phone to King Fahd of Saudi Arabia, who compared Saddam to Hitler, a theme Bush would soon employ.[14] Bush assured Fahd that "I am determined that Saddam will not get away with all this infamy."[15] "Infamy" of course, echoes Franklin Delano Roosevelt's "War Message" after the attack on Pearl Harbor.

On August 5, Bush returned to Washington and declared on the south lawn of the White House, "This will not stand, this aggression against Kuwait."[16] Powell had left Camp David under the impression Bush was not yet contemplating the use of military force. He writes, "I sat upright. From 'We're not discussing intervention' to 'This will not stand' marked a giant step. Had the President just committed the United States to liberating Kuwait?"[17]

Three days after the invasion of Kuwait, Secretary of State James Baker and Soviet Foreign Minister Eduard Shevardnadze issued a joint statement condemning the invasion. For the first time in over four decades, the two Cold War adversaries were on the same side. If the old enemy was now on the same side as the United States, how was Bush to convince the Congress and the American people to act and possibly use military force? It was clear that the new storyline needed a new villain. Unlike Truman, Kennedy, Johnson, and Nixon, wars involving American troops could no longer be built on the foundation of containing Communism. Thus, Bush, the veteran of World War II, turned to that conflict's origins to construct his story.

As the United States began a buildup of forces to protect Saudi Arabia from invasion, an operation known as "Desert Shield," Bush planned to address the nation on the morning of August 8. He writes: "As I prepared my speech, I tightened up the language to strengthen the similarity I saw between the Persian Gulf and the situation in the Rhineland in the 1930s."[18] In his speech, the analogy was clear:

> Less than a week ago, in the early morning hours of August 2d, Iraqi Armed Forces, without provocation or warning, invaded a peaceful Kuwait. Facing negligible resistance from its much smaller neighbor, Iraq's tanks stormed in blitzkrieg fashion through Kuwait in a few short hours.[19]

This speech echoes Roosevelt's "War Message." Bush called Saddam's attack "without provocation or warning." Roosevelt said Japan attacked "suddenly and deliberately." Bush said Kuwait was "peaceful." Roosevelt proclaimed the United States was "at peace with" Japan. Bush's uses "blitzkrieg," a word associated with Hitler. He compares Saddam to the Axis powers of the 1930s: "As was the case in the 1930's [sic], we see in Saddam Hussein an aggressive dictator threatening his neighbors." An earlier draft used the word "leader" rather than the more pejorative "dictator" of the final version of the speech.[20]

This speech also set forth four principles that guided the administration's policy throughout the crisis:

> First, we seek the immediate, unconditional, and complete withdrawal of all Iraqi forces from Kuwait. Second, Kuwait's legitimate government must be restored to replace the puppet regime. And third, my administration, as has been the case with every President from President Roosevelt to President Reagan, is committed to the security and stability of the Persian Gulf. And fourth, I am determined to protect the lives of American citizens abroad.[21]

The second principle insists on the restoration of the "legitimate government" of Kuwait, a nominal constitutional monarchy, in which only 10 percent of the citizens are allowed to vote.[22] A return to the status quo was Bush's goal. Although Kuwait might be liberated from the invaders, its people would be no freer than they were before the invasion. And Saddam's own citizens would continue to be ruled by a tyrant whom Bush likened to Hitler.

When he addressed a Joint Session of Congress on September 11, Bush added one more objective: "Out of these troubled times, our fifth objective—a new world order—can emerge: a new era—freer from the threat of terror, stronger in the pursuit of justice, and more secure in the quest for peace."[23] This goal was further developed in Bush's October 1 address to the United Nations, where he declared "an end to the cold war."[24]

SADDAM AS HITLER

One of the most important tests of a story's narrative probability is its *characterological coherence*. Put simply, a good story needs an evil villain. The comparison of Saddam to Hitler was at the heart of Bush's story. At the UN, he argued that the brutality of Iraq's regime violated international laws, and that "Iraq and its leaders must be held liable for these crimes of abuse and destruction." Bush enumerated Saddam's crimes: "Thousands of Iraqis have been executed on political and religious grounds, and even more through a genocidal poison gas war waged against Iraq's own Kurdish villagers."[25] Of course, the flaw in the story was that ending the occupation of Kuwait would not end Saddam's crimes against his own people. Holding Iraq's leaders liable for war crimes would require war trials, something possible only if Saddam were deposed and captured. Painting Saddam as a war criminal against his own people had little to do with the liberation of Kuwait. And the liberation of Iraq from Saddam was not a policy sanctioned by the UN.

John R. MacArthur writes,

> Convincing Americans to fight a war to liberate a tiny Arab sheikhdom ruled by a family oligarchy would require the demonization of Hussein.... It called for a frontal assault on public opinion such as had not been seen since the Spanish-American war.[26]

The people of Kuwaiti were hardly free. Only 65,000 men out of two million people were allowed to vote when there was a National Assembly, which was eliminated by the ruling family in 1986.[27] In 1993, Kuwait was ranked second only to China on the number of journalists it imprisoned (eighteen compared to twenty-seven for the much larger nation).[28] Even Americans serving in the Gulf were not immune to noticing the hypocrisy of fighting one dictator to reinstall another. Dick Runels, a reservist in the Air Force, wrote to his hometown newspaper that he and his fellow soldiers were being "betrayed by their own government, while at the same time being told they are here to 'protect democracy'—protect democracy in countries that have sheikhdoms and absolute despots ruling them."[29]

As Bush's case for war continued to be made, the comparison to Hitler became more explicit. As the last World War II veteran to serve as president, Bush saw Iraq's aggression "not a matter of shades of gray.... It was good versus evil."[30] Bush asked his fellow Veterans of Foreign War, "Think back with me to World War II, when together allies confronted a horror which embodied hell on Earth."[31] He vowed that the mistakes of the 1930s would not be repeated: "Half a century ago, the world had the chance to stop a ruthless aggressor and missed it. I pledge to you: We will not make that mistake again." He also used this opportunity to bring up the idea that Saddam was holding Americans hostage:

> We've been reluctant to use the term "hostage." But when Saddam Hussein specifically offers to trade the freedom of those citizens of many nations he

holds against their will in return for concessions, there can be little doubt that whatever these innocent people are called, they are, in fact, hostages.

Of course, Americans were all too aware of the last time a Middle Eastern country held Americans hostage—the takeover of the U.S. Embassy in Tehran in 1979, humiliating a great power and contributing to the defeat of President Jimmy Carter in 1980.

The surprise attack on Pearl Harbor symbolized the ultimate cost of ignoring the threat of aggression. On October 28, Bush spoke for his entire generation at Pearl Harbor: "No member of that generation can ever forget the clarion call that Pearl Harbor represented."[32] As with World War II, there was no moral ambiguity, "because today, in the Persian Gulf, what we are looking at is good and evil, right and wrong." He added horrific examples of Saddam's evil, including the subsequently discredited incubator story discussed in chapter 2.

In his Pearl Harbor speech Bush promised that Saddam would pay for his crimes, comparing him once again to the Nazis:

> Saddam Hussein will be held accountable. Iraq has waged a war of aggression, plundered a peaceful neighbor, held innocents hostage, and gassed its own people. And all four of those crimes are punishable under the principles adopted by the allies in 1945 and unanimously reaffirmed by the United Nations in 1950. Two weeks ago I made mention of the Nuremberg trials.

The inflammatory charge of gassing his own people was included over the objections of the NSC.[33] By suggesting Saddam should be subject to a war trial, such as that held at Nuremberg, Bush was again raising the expectation that Saddam would be captured and punished, not simply expelled from Kuwait.

Speaking to armed forces stationed in the Gulf at Thanksgiving (figure 8.1), Bush added something new to his case, charging that Saddam might soon develop the ultimate weapon of mass destruction:

> And we understand that we can sacrifice now, or we can pay an even stiffer price later as Saddam moves to multiply his weapons of mass destruction: chemical, biological and, most ominous, nuclear. And we all know that Saddam Hussein has never possessed a weapon that he hasn't used.[34]

This was, of course, a theme that would be repeated by Bush's son as he prepared the nation for yet another war against Saddam.

Bush increasingly demonized Saddam as the crisis deepened. He received the Amnesty International Report in December alleging Iraqi troops' atrocities,

Figure 8.1 President George Bush visits troops in Saudi Arabia on Thanksgiving in November 1990. *Source: Photo courtesy of George Bush Presidential Library and Museum.*

including the later discredited incubator story. Bush biographer Jon Meacham writes, "He cited it frequently, offering it as evidence to support his moral case for war."[35] Scowcroft noticed that Bush's rhetoric was becoming more inflammatory: "It was clear that the President was becoming emotionally involved in the treatment of Kuwait. He was deeply sincere, but the impact of some of his rhetoric seemed a bit counterproductive."[36] Bush acknowledges that "I got into hot water over my strong statements regarding the hostages, and these were the days of my frequent comparisons of Saddam to Hitler."[37] Perhaps nothing expressed his views better than a letter he wrote to his own children, including the future president, George W. Bush: "How many lives might have been saved if appeasement had given way to force earlier on in the late 30s or earliest 40s?"[38] Bush admitted, "I do think that World War II shaped my thinking on the Gulf. I have Saddam Hussein now as clearly bad and evil as Hitler and as the Japanese war machine that attacked Pearl Harbor."[39]

THE SHIELD BECOMES A STORM

Bush secretly approved a large increase of U.S. forces on October 31, but waited until after the midterm election to announce on November 8 "that he was doubling the American forces in Saudi Arabia from 230,000 to more than 500,000 in order to create an 'offensive military option.'"[40] This deployment changed the United States military capability from containing Saddam to liberating Kuwait. The justification for the change of strategy was largely a result of Bush's view of Saddam as Hitler. Greene writes:

> Bush justified his decision . . . on the grounds of saving the world from a brutal bully. By the end of 1990, he was making regular comparisons between Saddam (whose name he continually mispronounced, a serious slight to an Arabic male and one that it is possible Bush did deliberately) and Adolf Hitler. He also frequently used terms like "rapist," "evil," and "madman" to describe the Iraqi leader.[41]

A former ambassador to the United Nations, Bush was committed to establishing a "new world order" and sought UN authority to support offensive military action. On November 29, the Security Council passed resolution 678, the product of intense negotiations between the United States and the Soviet Union, which called for Iraq to withdraw from Kuwait by January 15, 1991. If it failed to meet the deadline, member states would be authorized to "use all necessary means . . . to restore international peace and security in the area."[42] Bush was so convinced of the need to stop Saddam's aggression, that he admits in his memoir that he would have acted, even without UN approval: "If at any point it became clear we could not succeed, we would back away from a UN mandate and cobble together an independent multinational effort built on friendly Arab and allied participation."[43] This strategy is very similar to that adopted by his son in assembling a "coalition of the willing" in 2003.

Bush even considered sending helicopters to resupply the American Embassy hoping to provoke a response that would justify American military action. Bush told Thatcher, "If he shoots down a helo, we clobber him."[44] Bush backed off the plan, but the fact that Bush was willing to send U.S. helicopter pilots to almost certain death shows that he believed Saddam could not be allowed to emerge unscathed.

Despite his private misgivings about a diplomatic resolution, Bush pursued a public policy of going the last mile for peace. Bush offered to set up a meeting with Iraq foreign minister Tariq Aziz in Washington and send Secretary of State James Baker to meet with Saddam between December 15 and January 15.[45] The effect of this offer was to open the door to further manipulation by Saddam, who had an incentive to drag things out to the last minute. Indeed he did delay, and the only meeting held between Baker and Aziz in Geneva on January 9, 1991, made no progress. At the press conference afterward Baker stated: "'Regrettably, ladies and gentlemen, . . . in over six hours I heard nothing that suggested to me any Iraqi flexibility whatsoever on complying with the United Nations Security Council resolutions.'"[46] Baker viewed the meeting as "the turning point in building domestic consensus."[47] He writes that Senator "Sam Nunn . . . would later observe that as soon as I uttered 'regrettably,' any chance of defeating the [congressional] use-of-force resolution was lost."[48]

A congressional resolution was the last step in Bush's efforts to build support for Operation Desert Storm. Although he believed that the constitution empowered the commander-in-chief to engage in military action without congressional approval, he also recognized the importance of sharing the responsibility with Congress. Bush writes that he "wanted to find a way to get Congress on board with an unmistakable show of that support for what we were doing, and what we might have to do."[49] To that end, he looked to Lyndon Johnson's Gulf of Tonkin Resolution, which passed with only two dissenting votes in 1964. Despite the congressional vote, however, Johnson failed to hold on to public support. As a congressman, Bush had visited Vietnam during the war and reported on his observations in a speech delivered in Houston on January 11, 1968. The manuscript of that speech was on display in the Bush Presidential Library in 2003 during the run-up to the second war with Iraq. In his own hand, he penned a line in reference to college students: "and frankly this administration has not *sold* this war to this population."[50] The lesson about selling a war was not forgotten by the future president. Three days before the UN deadline, Congress passed the resolution by 250–183 in the House and only 52–47 in the Senate, a narrower margin than any previous war resolution or declaration of war.[51] Although ten Democratic senators joined Republicans in approving the resolution, future president Joe Biden voted no.[52]

The importance of securing UN and congressional approval in selling the war is confirmed by public opinion polling. "In August, only half the public said that the President had explained clearly his decision to send troops to Saudi Arabia (*NYT*/CBS)," according to Andrew Kohut, who notes that the UN and congressional votes were crucial in building support. "Before those events, in mid-November, 1990, only 37 percent of the public favored United States going to war to drive the Iraqis out of Kuwait, according to Gallup. By January 1991, a 55 percent majority favored taking such steps." As Kohut explained, "[I]t is necessary for the president to sell war as the only alternative that can protect the national interest."[53] There was a sharp racial divide, however, in support for the war. Blacks were less likely to support the war than whites, with only about half in favor versus 80 percent of whites. This might partially be explained by the fact that over a quarter of the troops in the desert were African American, although they were only a little over 10 percent of the population.[54] It appears Bush remembered the lesson from his long-ago visit to Vietnam as a congressman. A president must create a narrative that will resonate with the public, in other words, sell the war.

As the January 15 deadline passed, Bush prepared to announce the beginning of the war to the American people the next day. According to Barbara Bush, to assure that the speech was kept secret, the president wrote it himself.[55] However, this claim is not supported by evidence at the Bush library, where Dan McGroarty's draft can be found.[56] Regardless of who wrote it, the speech laid out the case for immediate action, emphasizing that delay had allowed Saddam's evil to continue. Repeating the refrain, "While the world waited," Bush catalogued Saddam's crimes with inflammatory language: He "raped, pillaged, and plundered a tiny nation, no threat to his own. He subjected the people of Kuwait to unspeakable atrocities—and among those maimed and murdered, innocent children." Furthermore, "Saddam sought to add to the chemical weapons arsenal he now possesses, an infinitely more dangerous weapon of mass destruction—a nuclear weapon."[57] He stressed the liberation of Kuwait, but hinted at an even broader objective:

> Our goal is not the conquest of Iraq. It is the liberation of Kuwait. It is my hope that somehow the Iraqi people can, even now, convince their dictator that he must lay down his arms, leave Kuwait, and let Iraq itself rejoin the family of peace-loving nations.

Such a hope clearly distinguished the people of Iraq from their dictator. Thus, Bush followed in the footsteps of Wilson in making it clear that we were not at war with the citizens of a country, but only its leadership. How the people in a police state might convince a dictator to lay down his arms is left unsaid. Seventy-nine percent of televisions were watching the speech, which made it the biggest television audience up to that point in U.S. history.[58]

Bush's desire to remove Saddam from power stretched clear back to the earliest days of the conflict. According to Woodward's book, *The Commanders*, after an NSC meeting on August 3, 1990, "Bush ordered the CIA to begin planning for a covert operation that would destabilize the regime and, he hoped, remove Saddam from power."[59] Bush made several statements during the early weeks of the war that could be construed as calling for the people of Iraq to take action against Saddam. Bush's diary recorded his reaction to a TV report that Saddam might comply with UN Resolution 660: "But my emotion is not one of elation. We've got some unfinished business. How do we solve it? How do we now guarantee the future peace? I don't see how it will work with Saddam in power."[60] Saddam's offer turned out to be so loaded with conditions that Bush labeled it a "cruel hoax." He then slipped and revealed his hidden goal of removing Saddam. Bush writes, "I impulsively added what I called 'another way for the bloodshed to end': to have the Iraqi people and the military put aside Saddam and rejoin the family of peace-loving nations."[61] It's hard to see how a call to "put aside Saddam" could be taken as anything but a call to revolt, although Scowcroft denies such an implication.

Another example of a not-so-thinly veiled call for Saddam's removal came when Bush spoke on January 23 to the Reserve Officer's Association, quoting British prime minister John Major: "Saddam . . . may yet become a target of his own people . . . . I, for one, will not weep for him." Bush concurred: "No one should weep for this tyrant when he is brought to justice—no one, anywhere in the world."[62] Although Bush never promised aid to rebel groups such as the Kurds, it is clear that his rhetoric encouraged the people of Iraq to take matters into their own hands. Having equated Saddam with Hitler, suggested no one would weep at his ouster, and called for bringing him to justice, Bush created a rhetorical quandary when the war stopped short of removing him from power.

100 HOURS OF GROUND WAR

After five weeks of the air war, Bush set a noon (EST) February 23 deadline for Saddam to begin his unconditional withdrawal from Kuwait. On February 23, Bush addressed the nation, noting that the noon deadline had passed: "The liberation of Kuwait has now entered a final phase."[63] Although there had been much media hype about an amphibious assault and a major frontal assault, in reality, the bulk of Schwarzkopf's forces came from the west, dubbed a "left hook." By day two, Marines surrounded Kuwait City. It was clear the Iraqis were no match for the coalition forces led by the Americans.

One hundred hours after it began, the ground war was over. There was a fear in the administration that media coverage would portray the continued destruction of Saddam's retreating forces as an unnecessary slaughter. In fact, some in the media started calling the only remaining retreat route a "Highway of Death."[64] On February 27, Bush again spoke to the nation. "Kuwait is liberated. Iraq's army is defeated. Our military objectives are met. Kuwait is once more in the hands of Kuwaitis, in control of their own destiny."[65] Nothing was said about liberating the people of Iraq, who were left under the ruthless dictatorship of the man Bush had equated with the most evil villain in history. Nothing was said about allowing the people of Kuwait to choose their government. Instead, the Kuwaiti Royal Family was restored to power. Eight days later, Bush addressed a Joint Session and transported them to the scene of Saddam's defeat:

> Tonight in Iraq, Saddam walks amidst ruin. His war machine is crushed. His ability to threaten mass destruction is itself destroyed. His people have been

lied to, denied the truth. And when his defeated legions come home, all Iraqis will see and feel the havoc he has wrought. And this I promise you: For all that Saddam has done to his own people, to the Kuwaitis, and to the entire world, Saddam and those around him are accountable.[66]

How Saddam, who was still in power, was to be held accountable was left unsaid. Would the Allies have left Hitler in power had his troops been expelled from Poland in 1939? Having painted Saddam as the embodiment of evil, Bush created a rhetorical expectation for his demise that was left unfulfilled—until 2003 when his son fulfilled that pledge in another war against Iraq. Bush himself seemed to realize the discrepancy, telling his diary, "Hitler is alive, indeed, Hitler is still in office and that's the problem."[67]

MUZZLING THE MEDIA

One lasting legacy of the Vietnam War was that many in the military believed that the war had been lost on television and in the newspapers, not on the battlefield. John MacArthur argues that to the contrary, the media were largely supportive of that war. He notes that only about 3 percent of the filmed reports on the evening news during the Vietnam War from August 1965 to August 1970 showed "heavy battle," and from 1968 to 1973 only 2 percent showed pictures of the wounded or dead.[68] Thus, he laments the "speciousness of the press-lost-Vietnam argument" and "the relative docility of most of the press during the Vietnam War."[69]

It should be pointed out, however, that MacArthur's statistics don't tell the whole story. A powerful visual story can outweigh a flood of statistics that seem to contradict it. The images of a police chief shooting a man in the head or a child running from a napalm attack could transport audiences to Vietnam in a way that had more impact than mere statistics indicate. Whether or not the media were in general supportive of that war is less important than the fact that at least some reporters did question the predominant administration narrative that the U.S. was winning the war.

Nevertheless, the misguided belief that the Vietnam War was lost on the front pages of the *New York Times* and the evening news led to an approach that MacArthur deems, "Operation Desert Muzzle" in Iraq.[70] The plan for this muzzling was tested in Grenada and Panama, where reporters were placed in pools and kept away from the action. For the upcoming Gulf War, a secret memorandum called Annex Foxtrot was drafted on August 10. The goal was to avoid the perceived mistakes of Vietnam in dealing with the media, who were relatively free to go anywhere and talk to anyone. The Pentagon sought to assure that reporters would always be under the watchful eye of military escorts. "News media representatives will be escorted at all times. Repeat, at all times."[71] In addition to being closely supervised, the pool reporters would face "security review at the source."[72] In a word—censorship.

Charles Moskos notes that the relationship of media with the military has undergone significant changes over the past several wars:

> During World War II, the American news media were basically incorporated into the armed forces.... In essence, both the media and the military were on the same team. This state of affairs changed during the Vietnam War. The media were subjected to an extraordinary degree of control during the American operations in Grenada, Panama, and the Gulf War.[73]

Abbas Malek and Lisa Leidig went so far as to call the press "a propaganda arm of the government" in the Gulf War.[74] Jowett and O'Donnell explain how this was accomplished:

> [T]he instantaneous technologies available for disseminating news from the battlefields had clashed with the military's need and desire to control what images would actually be seen. The result was that the military denied access to all but a few reporters whom it could control through the use of official "pool" coverage, with military escorts.[75]

CNN, however, provided a different perspective, since Peter Arnett remained in Baghdad after the war began along with the BBC's John Simpson and ITN's Brent Sadler.[76] Colin Powell complains that this was "our first war ... being broadcast live from the enemy capital."[77] These reports drew criticism from American leaders, including a letter signed by twenty-one members of the Congress, accusing Arnett of providing "the demented dictator a propaganda mouthpiece to over one hundred nations."[78] According to Jowett and O'Donnell, "CNN was criticized by some politicians and members of the public for playing into the hands of enemy propaganda, but on the whole, these broadcasts were well received and widely viewed."[79] On the other hand, reporters who violated the pool restrictions and became what were known as "unilaterals" took a big risk. One reporter who strayed away from the pools was Bob Simon of CBS. He ended up captured and held by the Iraqis for forty days.[80] He became a cautionary tale for others who might defy press restrictions.

Those reporters not assigned to pools or remaining in Iraq were forced to rely on the daily briefings of General Norman Schwarzkopf. These briefings often featured videos of U.S. smart weapons hitting their targets with precision. Schwarzkopf emphasized the accuracy and lethality of American weapons. In one memorable briefing, he described a truck driver as "the luckiest man in Iraq," as he played a video of a bridge being targeted for an air strike. He advised reporters, "Keep your eye on the crosshairs." The truck drove across the bridge and through the crosshairs. Schwarzkopf then quipped, "And now, in his rear-view mirror," as the bridge was demolished and the driver escaped with his life.[81] Thus viewers were transported to the war in a sanitized and even humorous way by images that seemed like video games. Yet, less than ten percent of all bombs were so-called smart bombs.[82] Moreover, 10 percent of the precision-guided bombs failed to hit the target and 70 percent of all bombs were off target.[83] Even the vaunted Patriot missiles were actually counterproductive. Because of the debris created when a Scud was intercepted, the damage was actually more widespread (although less severe) than if the Scud hadn't been hit at all.[84] In fact, there were no confirmed Patriot kills according to a report from the Armed Services Committee.[85] Finally, only because of reporters like Peter Arnett did the public learn when U.S. smart weapons went awry as happened when "two bombs . . . killed as many as 1,600 people, mostly women and children."[86]

The information provided in official briefings was not always accurate. On one occasion, Schwarzkopf showed video of what he described as a direct hit on four Scud launchers. But it turns out they were just four fuel trucks at a rest stop. Powell learned of this from his intelligence chief, but Schwarzkopf insisted to Powell they were Scuds. Reconnaissance photos soon established they were in fact fuel trucks. Did Powell or Schwarzkopf correct the record? No, Powell backed up the Scud version so as not to undermine Schwarzkopf. However, CNN eventually got ground photos to prove they were just trucks. Powell claims he learned a lesson, "better to admit a mistake than be caught in one."[87]

Not only did these briefings reach the press in the room in Riyadh, they reached millions at home as they were broadcast on TV. They became such televised pseudo-events that even *Washington Post* TV critic Tom Shales praised them. After a particularly impressive briefing near the end of the war, he wrote, "Gen. H. Norman Schwarzkopf . . . gave a performance as spellbinding as the toniest of Hamlets."[88]

The success of the administration and the military in getting favorable coverage of the war was reflected in the polls. After the war, Powell reports, "80 percent of Americans polled thought press coverage of the Gulf War had been good or excellent."[89] In response to charges of censorship, Powell points out that of over 1,300 stories submitted by print reporters, only 1 was altered for security reasons.[90] This, of course, ignores the limitations on where reporters could go, the use of "minders" to make sure interviews were carefully monitored, and the self-censorship of news media unwilling to buck the popularity of a war supported by the vast majority of their viewers and readers.

Pete Williams, the Pentagon spokesman, claims that of the five stories sent to Washington to be reviewed, only one was stopped, and that was by the news organization itself, not the Pentagon. MacArthur, however, argues there were numerous other types of censorship: "censorship by delay; censorship by direct intimidation of soldiers and interference with pool reporters doing interviews; censorship by outright arrest of unilateral reporters; censorship by preventing reporters from seeing anything interesting; and censorship of pool dispatches."[91] MacArthur specifically calls out:

> the failure, with the exception of Ted Turner, of owners and top executives to take responsibility for their companies . . . the unwillingness of journalists to fight for their lifeblood, the First Amendment; the withdrawal of American reporters from Baghdad; the lack of interest in the matter of the unseen enemy; the inability of anyone to call Pete Williams a liar.[92]

There were almost no actual photos documenting the fighting, except the sanitized versions shown at the military briefings. Robert Schnitzlein, who was a picture editor for Reuters, said "There is no real photographic document [sic] of actual fighting in the Gulf."[93]

THE AFTERMATH

Bush and his advisors believed Saddam would fall after his defeat. Bush predicted, "There will be dancing in the streets, and they will say that he was brutal and a bully, and they will rejoice when he's gone."[94] Scowcroft acknowledges that removing Saddam had been considered and rejected as exceeding "the bounds of the UN resolutions guiding us."[95] America "would be facing an indefinite occupation of a hostile state and some dubious 'nation-building.' Realistically, if Saddam fell, it would not be a democracy emerging but another, perhaps less problematic, strongman."[96] The administration hoped for the collapse of Saddam's regime, but as James Baker wrote, "I'm reminded of something Tariq Aziz said to me in Geneva: 'We will be here long after you're gone.' It was one of the few things he said that proved to be true."[97]

Powell poses the question that was on the minds of so many Americans regarding Saddam: "Why didn't we finish him off? . . . What tends to be forgotten is that while the United States led the way, we were heading an *international* coalition carrying out a clearly defined UN mission."[98] There were thirty-five nations providing support in the form of men, money, or weapons, and 200,000 of the troops were from coalition partners.[99] Powell notes the dissonance between Bush's harsh rhetoric and the reality that Saddam was not deposed: "[T]he President's demonizing of Saddam as the devil incarnate did not help the public understand why he was allowed to stay in power."[100] Bush defends his decision, writing that to have gone to Baghdad would have led to "an unwinnable guerrilla war" and would have "plunge[d] that part of the world into ever greater instability."[101] His wisdom was proven after his son went to Baghdad in the next war with Iraq.

When General Norman Schwarzkopf met with his Iraqi counterparts, Lt. Gen. Sultan Hashim Ahmad and Lt. Gen. Salah Abud Mahmud, they cited the example of General Grant allowing Confederate soldiers to keep their horses and asked to keep their helicopters. Ahmud requested them on the grounds that their infrastructure had been destroyed by the U.S. bombing: "We would like to agree . . . that helicopter flights sometimes are needed to carry officials from one place to the other because the roads and bridges are out."[102] Schwarzkopf agreed, as long as the helos didn't fly over parts the United States was occupying. He even agreed that the helicopters could be armed, a decision that helped Saddam stay in power.

By March, the Iraqi Shiites and Kurds began to rebel. Unfortunately for them, no help was forthcoming from the United States. Powell explains, "Saddam responded by sending his troops to suppress the uprising. . . . Neither revolt had a chance. Nor, frankly, was their success a goal of our policy. President Bush's rhetoric urging the Iraqis to overthrow Saddam, may have given encouragement to the rebels."[103] Meacham writes,

> When the Shiites and Kurds did, in fact, rebel against Saddam . . . everything went wrong. The United States did nothing to support the insurgents, and the uprising was put down in part by Iraqi helicopters that the coalition had allowed Saddam's army to keep.[104]

George Bush left office in 1993 with Saddam still firmly in power. While sanctions, weapons inspectors, and no-fly zones contained the Iraqi dictator, the implied promise of liberation of the Iraqi people was unfulfilled. As Bush learned, it is difficult to paint one's adversary as the embodiment of evil and yet offer no deliverance. So emboldened was Saddam that in 1993 he attempted to have his nemesis assassinated, which brought retaliation from Bill Clinton, who launched cruise missiles at Iraqi intelligence headquarters.[105] Yet, when Clinton left office in 2001, Saddam remained in power and had expelled the UN weapons inspectors.

ENDING THE VIETNAM SYNDROME

Powell served two tours in Vietnam. From his experiences in that war, he offered what some have called the Powell Doctrine:

Have a clear political objective and stick to it. Use all the force necessary, and do not apologize for going in big if that is what it takes. Decisive force ends wars quickly and in the long run saves lives.[106]

As chairman of the Joint Chiefs of Staff under Bush, he applied this principle to the Gulf War. He writes, "I had spent two tours in a war that seemed endless and often pointless."[107] He was not going to let America make that mistake again. Bush was also committed to not allowing the war to become another Vietnam. He followed Powell's doctrine and used overwhelming force to achieve a quick victory. The war reached a successful conclusion after only 100 hours of ground combat. "By God, we've kicked the Vietnam syndrome once and for all," Bush proclaimed.[108] Yet, the Gulf War didn't end in a clear surrender by the enemy. Bush's diary reflects his concern: "It hasn't been clean, there is no Battleship *Missouri* surrender . . . . This is what's missing to make this akin to World War II, to separate it from Korea and Vietnam."[109]

The fear of the Gulf War becoming another Vietnam was reflected in press coverage. A study by the Freedom Forum of around 66,000 media stories during the period of the war found that "Vietnam" was the most frequently appearing word (nearly 7,300 times) and two-thirds of these instances referred to "another Vietnam."[110] The fear of another war becoming a quagmire was deeply embedded in the American psyche as reflected in media coverage.

One of the legacies of Vietnam was that American threats to use force often lacked credibility. Alexander George indicates that the failures in Vietnam may well explain why Saddam did not withdraw from Kuwait despite the threat of facing overwhelming American forces:

[I]t would appear that he was insufficiently impressed with the credibility and/or the potency of U.S. threats of force. He may have been influenced more by an image he had formed of U.S. irresolution, one that attributed to the United States a peculiar reluctance and inability to sustain casualties that stemmed from its catastrophic experience in Vietnam.[111]

Going forward, Bush clearly intended that no one would again doubt America's resolve or willingness to use force.

The change in the public's attitude toward the military as a result of the swift victory was dramatic. After Korea and Vietnam, Powell writes, "[T]he country was hungry for victory. . . . the American people fell in love again with their armed forces."[112] Yellow ribbons became a symbol for supporting the troops, just as they had become a form of support for American hostages during the Iranian hostage crisis in 1979–1980. Powell writes, "The explosion of yellow ribbons . . . recalled a national unity not felt since World War II."[113]

Tom Shales wrote in the *Washington Post* near the end of the war, "People are looking at the military differently than they did six months ago.... Perhaps in the public mind, the tragedy of Vietnam will be erased and replaced by this victory." Shales quotes a retired Admiral, U.S. Grant Sharp, who was asked on CNN if he wished he'd had the sort of authority Schwarzkopf had in the Gulf. "Did I wish it? . . . If I had had the same sort of freedom that General Schwarzkopf has, the Vietnam War would have been over in about 1966."[114] Thus, the Gulf War not only helped kick the Vietnam Syndrome, but it also helped rewrite the history of the only war the United States ever lost—it was not the military's fault. If only the politicians had given the military more freedom, it would have been easily won—a view that stands in sharp contrast to that of Gen. Powell, who wrote, "Given the terrain, the kind of war the NVA and VC were fighting, and the casualties they were willing to take, no defensible level of U.S. involvement would have been enough."[115]

Another implication of "kicking the Vietnam Syndrome" was a restoration in the belief in the superiority and invincibility of the American military machine. Gen. Bolger writes, "Indeed, the scale and speed of the U.S. victory brought a degree of certainty to American military leaders confronted with defining their role in a post-Soviet world." He continues, that with proper investment in the volunteer forces, information technology, and joint operations, "the country would have the capacity to replicate the Gulf War when any threat arose."[116] Of course, overconfidence is deadly in warfare. Assuming that the only remaining superpower could easily win in future wars turned out to be tragically misguided. A decade after the Gulf War triumph, the United States would find itself facing a new enemy very different from Saddam's Republican Guard.

ASSESSING THE NARRATIVE

Bush's war in the Gulf was founded on one unifying narrative: The world needed to stop the next Hitler. This narrative required Bush to convince the American people that this war was the moral equivalent of stopping the Nazis in the 1930s. Had America only done so, millions of Jews and others would have survived and aggression would have been deterred. If the United States failed to stop Saddam, it would be the moral equivalent of appeasing Hitler. Although Saddam was incapable of threatening the United States directly, as Hitler had done, the moral principle was the same.

Looking at the *narrative coherence* of this story, the main method of proof was *characterological*. The comparison of Saddam to Hitler was built on a number of similarities in their character. Both had attacked weak neighbors without warning. The blitzkrieg character of Saddam's conquest was reminiscent of Hitler. He had gassed his own people, just as Hitler had gassed the Jews. He even murdered Kuwaiti babies by stealing their incubators. At first these claims may have been hard for the public to swallow. However, the dramatic testimony of Nayirah, absent fact-checking by the media at the time, was decisive. Not only was the public moved, but also apparently were several crucial senators, whose votes put the war resolution over the top.[117] And, of course, Bush repeated the Hitler comparison ad nauseam.

Once the war began, Americans were transported to a sanitized battlefield that resembled a video game. No images of death and suffering were permitted. Instead, Americans saw a lucky truck driver escape a well-placed smart bomb. Reporters who dared to tell of the suffering of Iraqis were castigated as unpatriotic. War was reduced to a video game, not a life-and-death battle.

The *fidelity* of the Hitler narrative was difficult for the media to disprove. Not only did the revelations about Nayirah's true status come too late to change public opinion, but also the actual coverage of the war was carefully managed. Without great risk (as Bob Simon discovered), there was no way to break away from the pool restrictions on journalists. Further, Schwarzkopf's impressive briefings seemed to confirm that the American way of fighting the war was almost without innocent death and suffering. Videos of smart bombs hitting their targets with precision outweighed reports of civilian casualties from the few journalists still in Iraq. Those journalists also reminded viewers that they were subject to Iraqi censorship. Reporters like Peter Arnett were disparaged as giving aid and comfort to the enemy. Just as Saddam was Hitler, Schwarzkopf was Eisenhower in this story. Thus, it was only after the war was over, and the public no longer particularly interested, that they learned that most bombs were not smart and the vast majority of all bombs missed their targets. The human cost of the war remained largely hidden. It was an easy and seemingly painless victory.

In addition to the Hitler narrative, a secondary narrative developed about a new way of fighting wars and the ending of the disparagement of the American military. This was not another Vietnam. The Powell doctrine worked. Overwhelming force, applied swiftly and decisively, achieved a strictly limited goal. Ending the war with 100 hours of ground combat established the *coherence* of that story. The Vietnam syndrome had been, in Bush's words, "kicked." America stood alone as the world's superpower. In place of the containment narrative of the 1950s through 1980s, a new world order led by America held sway. The *fidelity* of this narrative was confirmed not very long after the Gulf War with the fall of the Soviet Union.

Yet, these two narratives were eventually revealed to be flawed. With respect to the Saddam as Hitler narrative, leaving him in power undermined the narrative *coherence* of the story. If he was really as bad as Hitler, why had he been allowed to remain in power? Why had not his own people overthrown him, as Bush had suggested? How could the job of getting rid of Hitler II have been left unfinished?

Second, the narrative of the United States as the lone invincible superpower in a new world order was to be shattered as well. A decade after the triumph in the Gulf War, America was suddenly and unexpectedly thrust into an entirely different type of war against a shadowy enemy that didn't play by Marquis of Queensberry Rules. The Vietnam syndrome was replaced by overconfidence in American military invincibility. The easy defeat of Saddam's forces led many to assume that round II of war against Saddam would be a cakewalk. As we shall see in the next chapter, the narratives that guided the first Gulf War were instrumental in propelling America into its next great military conflict.

Looking back on the Gulf War, it is worth citing a prophetic statement from Professor Philip Meggs from Virginia Commonwealth University, who spoke in June 1991 at the Broadcast Designers' Association in Baltimore. He advised his colleagues, "It might be good if you kept those Gulf map files; you might need them again in a few years."[118]

NOTES

1. Rick Gano, "Nolan Ryan Wins 300th Game," *Associated Press*, August 1, 1990, https://apnews.com/4ace6196282e3a6ff789d2e40eef59ab. For the sake of clarity, the forty-first president will be referred to as George Bush (omitting his middle initials, H. W.) and the forty-third president will be referred to as George W. Bush.

2. Jon Meacham, *Destiny and Power: The American Odyssey of George Herbert Walker Bush* (New York: Random House, 2015), 420.

3. Colin Powell with Joseph E. Persico, *My American Journey* (New York: Random House, 1995), 461.

4. Quoted in Powell, *My American Journey*, 461.

5. George Bush and Brent Scowcroft, *A World Transformed* (New York: Random House, 1998), 302.

6. Bush and Scowcroft, *A World Transformed*, 303.

7. Taken from the title to chapter 17 of Powell, *My American Journey*.

8. Ronald Reagan, "Remarks on East-West Relations at the Brandenburg Gate in West Berlin," June 12, 1987, accessed May 17, 2020, https://www.reaganlibrary.gov/research/speeches/061287d.

9. Bush and Scowcroft, *A World Transformed*, 148.

10. Bush and Scowcroft, *A World Transformed*, 314–315.

11. George Bush, "Remarks and a Question-and-Answer Session With Reporters in Aspen, Colorado, Following a Meeting With Prime Minister Margaret Thatcher of the United Kingdom," August 2, 1990, accessed May 16, 2020, https://bush41library.tamu.edu/archives/public-papers/2124.

12. George Bush, "Remarks at the Aspen Institute Symposium in Aspen, Colorado," August 2, 1990, accessed May 16, 2020, https://bush41library.tamu.edu/archives/public-papers/2128.

13. Bob Woodward, *The Commanders* (New York: Simon & Schuster, 1991), 247.

14. Bush and Scowcroft, *A World Transformed*, 320.

15. Bush and Scowcroft, *A World Transformed*, 330.

16. George Bush, "Remarks and an Exchange With Reporters on the Iraqi Invasion of Kuwait," August 5, 1990, accessed July 8, 2020, https://bush41library.tamu.edu/archives/public-papers/2138.

17. Powell, *My American Journey*, 466.

18. Bush and Scowcroft, *A World Transformed*, 340.

19. George Bush, "Address to the Nation Announcing the Deployment of United States Armed Forces to Saudi Arabia," August 8, 1990, accessed May 16, 2020, https://bush41library.tamu.edu/archives/public-papers/2147.

20. The change is found in "Oval Office Statement, August 8, 1990, 9:00 A.M." located in speech writer file 8/8/90 [OV 5376] Box 65, George Bush Presidential Library, 4.

21. Bush, "Address to the Nation Announcing the Deployment of United States Armed Forces to Saudi Arabia."

22. CIA, *The World Factbook 2002*, March 19, 2003, accessed August 7, 2003, http://www.cia.gov/cia/publications/factbook/geos/ku.html.

23. George Bush, "Address Before a Joint Session of the Congress on the Persian Gulf Crisis and the Federal Budget Deficit," September 11, 1990, accessed May 16, 2020, https://bush41library.tamu.edu/archives/public-papers/2217.

24. George Bush, "Address Before the 45th Session of the United Nations General Assembly in New York, New York," October 1, 1990, accessed May 16, 2020, https://bush41library.tamu.edu/archives/public-papers/2280. The language on Cold War was taken out of the speech to Congress, but was included here. See memo from McNally to the president in speechwriter files: "The U.N. speech also marks our *last* opportunity—and our *best* opportunity—to say that 'the cold war is over'—a predictable 'headline' likely to resonate clear on into 1992." He adds, "[W]e've [bracketed] for your consideration the 'cold war is over' language that you looked at for the Joint Session of Congress speech." Source: Edward E. McNalley, "Memorandum for the President, Subject: Address to the U.N. General Assembly," September 28, 1990, page 1. Located in Office of Speechwriting Series Speech Files, Drafts, 1989–1993, Box 69, [OA 5377] [1].

25. In earlier drafts of the speech, the language on war crimes was much stronger. For example, on page 5 of draft four, reference is made to the anniversary of the Nuremberg War trials. Deleted sentences included, "Heads of state can be held responsible for crimes against world law—and crimes against world law are liable to punishment." Source: Edward McNally, "Presidential Remarks: United Nations General Assembly, New York City, Monday, October 1, 1990," draft four, page 5. Office of Speechwriting, Series: Speech Files, Drafts, 1989–1993, Box 69 [OA5377] [1]. The paragraphs are crossed out on David Demarest's copy.

26. John R. MacArthur, *Second Front: Censorship and Propaganda in the 1991 Gulf War*, 2nd ed. (Berkeley: University of California Press, 2004), 41–42.
27. MacArthur, *Second Front*, 43.
28. MacArthur, *Second Front*, 234.
29. MacArthur, *Second Front*, 169.
30. Bush and Scowcroft, *A World Transformed*, 375.
31. George Bush, "Remarks at the Annual Conference of the Veterans of Foreign Wars in Baltimore, Maryland," August 20, 1990, accessed May 16, 2020, https://bush41library.tamu.edu/archives/public-papers/2171.
32. George Bush, "Remarks to Officers and Troops at Hickam Air Force Base in Pearl Harbor, Hawaii," October 28, 1990, accessed May 16, 2020, https://bush41library.tamu.edu/archives/public-papers/2369.
33. A White House Staffing Memo dated 10-26-90 from NSC staff under signature of Scowcroft wanted the crime of gassing his own people eliminated. On the manuscript, page 3, there is the following handwritten comment: "The use of CW was years ago. It has nothing to do with this crisis and we were mum about it at the time." Edward McNally and Robert Simon, "Presidential Remarks: Hickam AFB, Hawaii," 10/25/90 response to Chriss Winston signed 10-26-90 by Brent Scowcroft. Office of Speechwriting, Series: Speech Files, Drafts, 1989–1993, Box 73 "Officers & Troops at Hickam Airfield" 10/28/90. [OA 6026].
34. George Bush, "Remarks to United States Army Troops Near Dhahran, Saudi Arabia," November 22, 1990, accessed May 16, 2020, https://bush41library.tamu.edu/archives/public-papers/2483.
35. Meacham, *Destiny and Power*, 453.
36. Bush and Scowcroft, *A World Transformed*, 389.
37. Bush and Scowcroft, *A World Transformed*, 388.
38. Bush and Scowcroft, *A World Transformed*, 435.
39. Quoted in Meacham, *Destiny and Power*, 455.
40. John Robert Greene, *The Presidency of George Bush* (Lawrence, KS: University Press of Kansas, 2000), 122.
41. Greene, *The Presidency*, 122.
42. Quoted in James A. Baker, III with Thomas M. DeFrank, *The Politics of Diplomacy: Revolution, War & Peace, 1989–1992* (New York: Putnam, 1995), 327.
43. Bush and Scowcroft, *A World Transformed*, 356.
44. Bush and Scowcroft, *A World Transformed*, 386.
45. George Bush, "The President's News Conference November 30, 2003," November 30, 1990, accessed May 16, 2020, https://bush41library.tamu.edu/archives/public-papers/2516.
46. Baker, *The Politics of Diplomacy*, 364.
47. Baker, *The Politics of Diplomacy*, 346.
48. Baker, *The Politics of Diplomacy*, 364.
49. Bush and Scowcroft, *A World Transformed*, 371.
50. George Bush, "Congressman Bush's Notes for an Address He Gave Before a Houston Audience on January 11, 1968 Reporting on His Trip to Vietnam." January

11, 1968. On display in the Bush Presidential Library on March 8, 2003 (emphasis in original, underlining replaced by italics).

51. Bush and Scowcroft, *A World Transformed*, 466.

52. Adriel Bettelheim, "Only as a Last Resort," PolitiFact, September 1, 2008, https://www.politifact.com/factchecks/2008/sep/01/lindsey-graham/only-as-a-last-resort/.

53. Andrew Kohut, "Post Cold-War Attitudes toward the Use of Force," in *The Use of Force After the Cold War*, ed. H. W. Brands (College Station: Texas A&M University Press, 2000), 168.

54. Powell, *My American Journey*, 500.

55. Barbara Bush, *A Memoir* (New York: Charles Scribner's Sons, 1994), 389.

56. The WHORM (White House Office of Records Management) files at the Bush library contain a draft of the speech by Dan McGroarty, dated January 15, at 4:40 p.m. In addition, the teleprompter script in the files includes handwritten additions by Richard Haas. SP747, Address to Nation-Persian Gulf War, (War Began), 1/16/91, Case Number 207102 File SP 747, WHITE HOUSE OFFICE OF RECORDS MANAGEMENT Subject File, 1989–1993 SPEECHES (SP Box 150).

57. George Bush, "Address to the Nation Announcing Allied Military Action in the Persian Gulf," January 16, 1991, accessed May 16, 2020, https://bush41library.tamu.edu/archives/public-papers/2625.

58. Bush and Scowcroft, *A World Transformed*, 451.

59. Woodward, *The Commanders*, 237.

60. Bush and Scowcroft, *A World Transformed*, 471.

61. Bush and Scowcroft, *A World Transformed*, 472.

62. George Bush, "Remarks to the Reserve Officers Association," January 23, 1991, accessed May 16, 2020, https://bush41library.tamu.edu/archives/public-papers/2648.

63. George Bush, "Address to the Nation Announcing Allied Military Ground Action in the Persian Gulf," February 23,1991, accessed May 16, 2020, https://bush41library.tamu.edu/archives/public-papers/2734.

64. Powell, *My American Journey*, 520.

65. George Bush, "Address to the Nation on the Suspension of Allied Offensive Combat Operations in the Persian Gulf," February 27, 1991, accessed May 16, 2020, https://bush41library.tamu.edu/archives/public-papers/2746.

66. George Bush, "Address Before a Joint Session of the Congress on the Cessation of the Persian Gulf Conflict," March 6, 1991, accessed May 16, 2020, https://bush41library.tamu.edu/archives/public-papers/2767.

67. Meacham, *Destiny and Power*, 467.

68. MacArthur, *Second Front*, 133.

69. MacArthur, *Second Front*, 138.

70. MacArthur, *Second Front*, 146.

71. Quoted in MacArthur, *Second Front*, 7.

72. Pentagon spokesman Pete Williams, quoted in MacArthur, *Second Front*, 27.

73. Charles Moskos, "The New Cold War: Confronting Social Issues in the Military," in *The Use of Force After the Cold War*, ed. H. W. Brands (College Station: Texas A&M University Press, 2000), 179.

74. Quoted in Phillip Knightley, *The First Casualty: The War Correspondent as Hero and Myth-Maker from the Crimea to Iraq*, 3rd ed. (Baltimore and London: John Hopkins University Press, 2004), 486.
75. Garth S. Jowett and Victoria O'Donnell, *Propaganda and Persuasion*, 7th ed. (Los Angeles: Sage, 2019), 143.
76. Knightley, *The First Casualty*, 492.
77. Powell, *My American Journey*, 507.
78. Quoted in Knightley, *The First Casualty*, 493.
79. Jowett and O'Donnell, *Propaganda and Persuasion*, 143.
80. MacArthur, *Second Front*, 179.
81. Quoted in Mark Thompson, "'Stormin' Norman,' 1934–2012," *Time*, December 27, 2012, https://nation.time.com/2012/12/27/stormin-norman-1934-2012/.
82. Anthony R. DiMaggio, *Mass Media, Mass Propaganda: Examining American News in the "War on Terror"* (Lanham, MD: Lexington Books, 2008), 192.
83. MacArthur, *Second Front*, 161.
84. MacArthur, *Second Front*, 162.
85. Knightley, *The First Casualty*, 496.
86. Knightley, *The First Casualty*, 493.
87. Powell, *My American Journey*, 510–511.
88. Tom Shales, "Stormin' Norman in High Command," *Washington Post*, February 28, 1991, https://www.washingtonpost.com/archive/lifestyle/1991/02/28/stormin-norman-in-high-command/cd526793-85a6-4332-9ad9-61dc1d164b5f/.
89. Powell, *My American Journey*, 530.
90. Powell, *My American Journey*, 528.
91. MacArthur, *Second Front*, 192.
92. MacArthur, *Second Front*, 224.
93. Quoted in MacArthur, *Second Front*, 155.
94. Bush and Scowcroft, *A World Transformed*, 428.
95. Bush and Scowcroft, *A World Transformed*, 433.
96. Bush and Scowcroft, *A World Transformed*, 433.
97. Baker, *The Politics of Diplomacy*, 422.
98. Powell, *My American Journey*, 526 (italics in original).
99. Powell, *My American Journey*, 490.
100. Powell, *My American Journey*, 521.
101. Bush and Scowcroft, *A World Transformed*, 464.
102. Quoted in Daniel P. Bolger, *Why We Lost: A General's Inside Account of the Iraq and Afghanistan Wars* (New York: Houghton Mifflin Harcourt, 2014), xxxiii.
103. Powell, *My American Journey*, 530–531.
104. Meacham, *Destiny and Power*, 467.
105. William G. Hyland, *Clinton's World: Remaking American Foreign Policy* (Westport, CT: Praeger, 1999), 172.
106. Powell, *My American Journey*, 434.
107. Powell, *My American Journey*, 519.
108. Maureen Dowd, "After the War: White House Memo; War Introduces a Tougher Bush to Nation," *New York Times*, March 2, 1991, https://www.nytimes.com

/1991/03/02/world/after-the-war-white-house-memo-war-introduces-a-tougher-bush-to-nation.html.

109. Quoted in Meacham, *Destiny and Power*, 467.

110. Cited by Jowett and O'Donnell, *Propaganda and Persuasion*, 254.

111. Alexander L. George, "The Role of Force in Diplomacy," in *The Use of Force After the Cold War*, ed. H. W. Brands (College Station: Texas A&M University Press, 2000), 87.

112. Powell, *My American Journey*, 532.

113. Powell, *My American Journey*, 495. The idea of tying yellow ribbons around an old oak tree to welcome someone home from prison (or war) originated with the song of the same name by Tony Orlando and Dawn in 1973.

114. Shales, "Stormin' Norman."

115. Powell, *My American Journey*, 147.

116. Bolger, *Why We Lost*, xxxvii.

117. MacArthur, *Second Front*, 70.

118. MacArthur, *Second Front*, 79.

Chapter 9

The War on Terror

America's Forever War

For Chloe and 13,207 other Americans, September 11, 2001, is a day of mixed emotions—the day of their birth and a national tragedy. Nineteen years later, *Politico* interviewed people born on that day about how they responded to the dual meanings of their birthday. Chloe said, "Every single day since I was born, we haven't been in a time where we're at peace." Nicole, also born on 9/11/2001, lamented, "I've heard a lot that people are forgetting about 9/11. I really hope that's not true."[1] On October 21, 2019, *Time's* cover featured Gregory Grammer, who at age seventeenth enlisted to fight a war that *Time* dubbed "American's Forever War."[2] As Elliot Ackerman pointed out, "Never before in our history has an American been able to fight in a war that is older than they are."[3]

The attack was not unexpected. Every day the president receives a daily briefing marked Top Secret. On August 6, 2001, among its headlines was a prophetic one: "Bin Laden Determined to Strike in US."[4] Why was bin Laden so angry at America? Counterterrorism expert Richard Clark traces it back to the American forces that came to Saudi Arabia to expel Saddam from Kuwait: "He could not believe it; letting nonbelievers into the Kingdom of the Two Holy Mosques was against the beliefs of the Wahhabist branch of Islam."[5]

President George W. Bush, who was appearing at an elementary school in Florida the morning of the attack, spoke briefly on television: "Terrorism against our nation will not stand."[6] In his memoir Bush writes, "Later I learned that my words had echoed Dad's promise that 'this aggression will not stand,' after Saddam Hussein invaded Kuwait. The repetition was not intentional. . . . Dad's words must have been buried in my subconscious . . . ."[7]

Bush was shuttled from one secure location to another on *Air Force One* and next spoke from Barksdale Air Force base in Louisiana. He pledged,

"The United States will hunt down and punish those responsible for these cowardly acts."[8] Bush characterized the attack as cowardly, despite the fact that the hijackers sacrificed their own lives on a suicide mission, however misguided. Even his own Secretary of Defense, Donald Rumsfeld, pointed out the incongruity. He writes in his memoir, "I would later offer a suggestion to the President about the word 'cowardly.' The men . . . were many things—evil, ruthless, cruel—but I felt we underestimated and misunderstood the enemy if we considered them cowards."[9] Speechwriter David Frum, writes, "The words were correct and reassuring. The images were not. . . . He looked and sounded like the hunted, not the hunter."[10]

Bush insisted over the objections of Secret Service that he return to the capital. As he flew over the city in *Marine One*, he recalls, "My mind drifted back over history. I was looking at a modern-day Pearl Harbor."[11] Bush wrote in his diary the evening of 9/11 that this was "the Pearl Harbor of the 21 Century."[12] The story of Pearl Harbor and the defeat of the Axis Powers in World War II became the predominant narrative in the rhetoric to follow. That evening Bush delivered his first prepared remarks to the American people from the Oval Office. Frum claims that the hastily crafted speech was nicknamed the "Awful Office Address."[13] After the worst single day loss of life on American soil since the Civil War, the president began his speech with the inappropriate salutation, "Good evening."[14] Bush contrasted the evil committed by the hijackers with the goodness of the American people:

> Today, our nation saw evil, the very worst of human nature. And we responded with the best of America—with the daring of our rescue workers, with the caring for strangers and neighbors who came to give blood and help in any way they could.

Importantly, he not only characterized the attackers as evil, but lumped them together with those who sheltered them: "We will make no distinction between the terrorists who committed these acts and those who harbor them." Bush later wrote, "This new doctrine overturned the approach of the past, which treated terrorist groups as distinct from their sponsors."[15] Frum claims that this speech "upgraded the 'war on terror' from a metaphor to fact."[16]

On that day Bush made two key decisions that would shape his response for the remainder of his presidency. The first, according to Frum, "was to recognize that this war *was* a war."[17] Although he chose to wait to announce this decision publicly, he reached this decision on the day of the attack. He writes in his memoir, "The first plane could have been an accident. The second was definitely an attack. The third was a declaration of war."[18] This was a dramatic departure from the approach of his predecessors, who treated terrorists as criminals, not state actors. As Jean Edward Smith, writes, "The word 'war' carries enormous implications."[19] Rumsfeld was troubled by the word *war*. He writes in his memoir,

> The word "war" left the impression that there would be combat waged with bullets and artillery and then a clean end to the conflict with a surrender—a winner and a loser, and closure—such as the signing ceremony on the battleship USS *Missouri* to end World War II.[20]

Describing the object of the war as *terror* or *terrorism* also troubled Rumsfeld: "Terror was not the enemy, but rather a feeling. Terrorism was also not the enemy but a tactic our enemies were using successfully against us."[21] In fact, in his memoir, Rumsfeld uses a different phrase, "war against *terrorists*," which might have better served the cause.[22] Bush insisted on the "War on Terror" as the fight's moniker.

There were inherent problems with the story Bush was telling. Naming it a *war* created unrealistic expectations. In particular, by using the World War II narrative, Bush should have realized the story would not end with the unconditional surrender of the enemy. Although it is understandable that Bush did not want to label Islamists, even extremist ones, as the enemy, making the object of the war a feeling or tactic, created a problem. Terrorism was as unlikely to be eradicated as tanks and artillery.

Bush's second decision was to hold responsible not just the terrorists themselves but also those who harbored them. This decision broadened the definition of the enemy far beyond those who had attacked the United States. Unlike Roosevelt in his speech after Pearl Harbor, which did not mention Germany or Italy, Bush included allies and enablers of the enemy, even if they had not directly attacked the United States. Bush's second principle opened the door to wars against multiple state actors who may have been even tangentially tied to the hijackers and other terrorists. The seeds of the war in Iraq were sown in those first days after 9/11.

Three days after the attacks, Bush spoke at a memorial service for the victims at the National Cathedral in Washington, D.C. This speech represented a key turning point in the narrative. Bush explicitly adopted the powerful narrative of World War II. He treated these attacks as another Pearl Harbor, just as he had written in his diary. Of course, there were significant differences—no state had attacked the United States, its naval fleet was not disabled, and the survival of the United States was not at risk. Smith writes, "The events of 9/11 were tragic, but scarcely catastrophic. This was not Pearl Harbor."[23] Nevertheless, Bush chose to draw on the story of the "good war." Bush said in his eulogy,

War has been waged against us by stealth and deceit and murder. This nation is peaceful, but fierce when stirred to anger. This conflict was begun on the timing and terms of others. It will end in a way, and at an hour, of our choosing.[24]

He referred to those who attacked the United States as "the evil ones," putting the conflict in moralistic terms. Furthermore, he committed the United States to "rid the world of evil," an unattainable goal. Yet, by framing the goal of America to achieve such a lofty purpose, Bush was committing the nation and himself to a mission of biblical proportions.

The most dramatic words spoken that day by President Bush were not written by any speechwriter. He flew to New York City after the eulogy and went to ground zero. There were no plans for him to speak, but he got up on a damaged fire truck and spoke over a bullhorn (figure 9.1). When someone shouted, "I can't hear you" Bush responded, "I can hear you. (Applause.) I can hear you. The rest of the world hears you. (Applause.) And the people who knocked these buildings down will hear all of us soon."[25] The crowd responded with chants of "U.S.A.! U.S.A.!" If there was any one day that established Bush's leadership, it was September 14, 2001. Not only did he give a prayerful speech at the National Cathedral, he then ad-libbed his way through a difficult situation at the very site of the tragedy. Bush emerged from the confusion of the first days and took the helm of the War on Terror, putting it in moralistic terms not used since the Cold War against "godless

Figure 9.1 President George W. Bush addresses first responders at Ground Zero promising that "the people who knocked these buildings down will hear all of us soon." *Source: Photo courtesy of George W. Bush Presidential Library and Museum. (P7365-23a).*

Communism." It was also on that day that Congress passed an "Authorization for Use of Military Force," with only one dissenting vote. Four days later, it was signed into law by the president.[26]

Bush's strong religious tone was particularly notable in his off-the-cuff remarks, which created trouble when they were framed in terms that were familiar to Protestant evangelicals, but threatening to Muslims. On Sunday, September 16, Bush declared, "This crusade, this war on terrorism is going to take a while."[27] The word "crusade" carries a painful connotation for Muslims, who suffered at the hand of Christian Crusaders. It was quickly banished from Bush's vocabulary. But whether he spoke the word again or not, clearly Bush saw the war on terror in terms of a religious mission. As Smith writes, "Now he was leading the United States on a global crusade, inspired by God, to rid the world of evil. It was a blunder of historic proportions."[28]

All good war stories require a villain, and bin Laden was ready-made for that role. On September 17, Bush invoked a phrase familiar to fans of westerns: "And there's an old poster out West, I recall, that says, 'Wanted: Dead or Alive.'"[29] Rumsfeld writes, "When the President said he was going to get bin Laden 'dead or alive'.... the emphasis on bin Laden concerned me."[30] He adds, "[W]e should have avoided personalizing the war around particular individuals—such as Osama bin Laden and Mullah Omar.... I knew the war would not end with their capture or their deaths."[31] Osama bin Laden may have been a despised villain, but killing him would not end terrorism, as we learned a decade later when he was finally killed in a daring raid.

At the same time, Bush could not allow his war on terror to turn into a war on Islam. At a meeting not long after the attacks, Representative David Bonier expressed concern about retribution against Americans of Arab descent. Looking at Transportation Secretary Norm Mineta, who as a child had been held in an interment camp during World War II, Bush said, "Dave, you're absolutely correct... you *should* be concerned about that because... we don't want what happened to Norm in 1942 to happen again."[32]

This principle was evident when the president visited the Islamic Center in Washington six days after the attacks. He stated, "The face of terror is not the true faith of Islam. That's not what Islam is all about. Islam is peace. These terrorists don't represent peace. They represent evil and war." He spoke respectfully of the worldwide Muslim community: "When we think of Islam we think of a faith that brings comfort to a billion people around the world." And he called on Americans to respect the rights of Muslim Americans: "Women who cover their heads in this country must feel comfortable going outside their homes. Moms who wear cover must be not intimidated in America. That's not the America I know. That's not the America I value."[33] Thus, like Woodrow Wilson, who said he had no quarrel with the German people, Bush distinguished the majority of Muslims from those who had used Islam as an excuse for terrorism.

Despite Bush's efforts, however, demonization of Arabs and Muslims was a predictable outcome of the terrorist attacks of 9/11. The seeds for dehumanizing Arabs had been sown long before 2001. Erin Steuter and Deborah Wills write,

> Films such as *Death Before Dishonor, Black Hawk Down, Executive Decision, Navy Seals, Rules of Engagement, Iron Eagle* and *True Lies*, all produced in partnership with the DoD [Department of Defense] and showing American armed forces personnel killing Arabs and Muslims on a huge scale, solidify Washington's connection with Hollywood.[34]

This negative portrayal of Muslims and Arabs was amplified on conservative talk radio. Steuter and Wills write that Bill O'Reilly "describes Iraqis as 'primitive' and 'prehistoric' and has compared the Muslim holy book, the *Koran*, to Hitler's *Mein Kampf*."[35]

Public attitudes toward Muslims were reflected in opinion polls and increased hate crimes against those thought to be Arab or Muslim (even though some victims were Sikhs wearing turbans). A 2004 Zogby poll found that "75 percent of American Muslims reported that they or someone they know have been subject to harassment and discrimination since 9/11."[36] In an echo of the anti-Japanese sentiment of World War II, an AP poll found that one-in-three respondents "support the creation of internment camps."[37] Perhaps most disturbing was the use of Christianity as an excuse for bigotry. Stauter and Wills write:

> Pat Robertson, for example, equates Muslims with termites "destroying institutions that have been built by Christians.". . . Robertson warns, "the time has arrived for a godly fumigation." Former Southern Baptist Convention president Reverend Jerry Fines blames America's problems on religious pluralism; speaking at a pastor's conference in 2002, he called Islam's founder a "demon-possessed pedophile."[38]

The metaphor of fumigation of pests is not far removed from the gas chambers used to exterminate Jews. Using the term "demon-possessed pedophile," is literally the demonization of the Prophet Muhammad, who is revered by a billion people around the world. Although Bush made an effort to temper anti-Muslim and Arab prejudice, clearly years of propaganda, no doubt heightened by the Iran hostage crisis of 1979–1980 and the Gulf War, fed those very prejudices.

BUSH'S 9/11 NARRATIVE

Bush's narrative had three essential storylines. First, we were at war, just as we had been after Pearl Harbor; the terrorists were the successors of the Nazis of World War II. Second, we were not at war with Islam, but rather with perverters—hijackers—of that religion. Finally, the world was divided into those who supported the evildoers, like the Taliban, and those who supported the righteous—as exemplified by the American heroes who rushed into the Twin Towers. There was no middle ground. This latter point was to become central to Bush's later case for war against a nation that had not attacked nor harbored those who attacked the United States—Iraq.

This story was laid out in the president's September 20 address to a Joint Session of Congress, watched by over eighty million on TV.[39] The decision to use this forum, rather than the Oval Office, was the inspiration of Karl Rove, who proposed that the president "speak not from his solitary desk, but from the rostrum from which Woodrow Wilson and Franklin Roosevelt asked for their declarations of war."[40] The setting emphasized the first storyline—this was another Pearl Harbor. The son of a World War II veteran and former president, Bush recalled that day of infamy: "On September the 11th, enemies of freedom committed an act of war against our country. Americans have known wars—but for the past 136 years, they have been wars on foreign soil, except for one Sunday in 1941."[41] Bush's speech was symbolically a call for a declaration of war as solemn as Roosevelt's. The nation was at war, but who was the enemy? They were "a collection of loosely affiliated terrorist organizations known as al Qaeda." Strengthening the World War II comparison, Bush drew analogies to the tyrannies of the Nazis and other dictators, claiming that "they follow in the path of fascism, and Nazism, and totalitarianism. And they will follow that path all the way, to where it ends: in history's unmarked grave of discarded lies."

Bush's second storyline was designed to avoid alienating the Muslim world, whose cooperation he needed. As he had done three days earlier in his visit to the Islamic Center, he carefully distinguished the religious extremists who had committed the terror from the vast majority of Muslims. Bush proclaimed in a fitting metaphor, "The terrorists are traitors to their own faith, trying, in effect, to hijack Islam itself."

Finally, Bush expanded the enemy list to all who supported terrorists. They were harbored and protected by the Taliban government of Afghanistan. Bush also stressed the Taliban's evil beyond harboring al Qaeda:

> Afghanistan's people have been brutalized—many are starving and many have fled. Women are not allowed to attend school. You can be jailed for owning a television. Religion can be practiced only as their leaders dictate. A man can be

jailed in Afghanistan if his beard is not long enough.... By aiding and abetting murder, the Taliban regime is committing murder.[42]

Bush made a list of demands on the Taliban, warning, "The Taliban must act, and act immediately. They will hand over the terrorists, or they will share in their fate." Bush warned the American people that they "should not expect one battle, but a lengthy campaign, unlike any other we have ever seen." Of course, few could have predicted that the war against the Taliban would continue for nearly two decades.

The scope of the new war on terror would extend, however, far beyond just Afghanistan. Ominously, Bush signaled a much wider net:

> And we will pursue nations that provide aid or safe haven to terrorism. Every nation, in every region, now has a decision to make. Either you are with us, or you are with the terrorists. (Applause.) From this day forward, any nation that continues to harbor or support terrorism will be regarded by the United States as a hostile regime.[43]

This Manichean declaration starkly divided the world into good and evil. While giving past supporters of terrorists an escape clause, "from this day forward," Bush made it clear that the war on terrorism would divide the world into two camps. Bush pledged, "We will not tire, we will not falter, and we will not fail."

The speech was a huge success. According to Gallup, President Bush's approval rating went from 51 percent prior to September 11 to 90 percent after his September 20th speech.[44] This represented the highest approval rating ever achieved by a president in the Gallup poll, besting his father's 89 percent.[45] America was coming together in a way not seen since World War II.

At this point Bush's narrative resonated with the American public. Given the recent events, the story possessed *narrative probability*. The *argumentative and structural coherence* was clear: Evil people who have attacked America must be stopped. Those who knocked down the Twin Towers would hear from us. The *material coherence*—how well it fit with other stories—is crucial to Bush's case. The story on which he relies for comparison is Pearl Harbor and the ensuing "good war." The enemy is likened to the Nazis. The attack was without warning or provocation. Just as evil was defeated in the 1940s, it must be confronted and defeated again. Finally the *characterological coherence* is rooted in a perversion of Islam. These are not typical Muslims, but rather a crazed set of radicals who have, in Bush's terms, hijacked an otherwise peaceful religion. Thus, it is not Islam that is the source of the evil, but those who would pervert it to their own ends and those who would harbor or encourage them.

The *fidelity* of Bush's narrative was persuasive to the American people in the days after 9/11. The events had been witnessed by the entire world with the collapsing towers replayed incessantly on TV, transporting viewers to that horrific scene. However, there was one element of Bush's narrative that, on later scrutiny, was problematic. Were all those who supported or condoned terrorists equally guilty? Initially, the Taliban in Afghanistan were the target. But eventually, that target would widen. The Manichean division of the world into those who were with us versus those who were against us, created a dualism that would be difficult to sustain in the years to come. The designation of the target of this war as terror, rather just a specific group of terrorists, al Qaeda, opened the door to what has proved to be a forever war.

Despite the similarities to World War II, there were two crucial differences that ultimately led to public disillusionment. First, as Rumsfeld noted, there was no clear ending in sight—no surrender on the battleship *Missouri*. Ridding the world of terrorism was not akin to defeating Hitler and the Japanese Empire. No one could expect bin Laden to acknowledge defeat. Furthermore, the Taliban would simply slip away, only to regroup later. Second, in World War II, the entire nation was mobilized to fight the enemy. As FDR put it, it was a war for survival. But 9/11, despite its horror, did not threaten the end of America or freedom. Instead, it was a horrific act that required an appropriate response. Americans (except those who were in the military or military families) were not asked to sacrifice. In fact, they were encouraged by Bush and others to resume their normal lives. Richard Clark laments, "After September 11, Americans were asked to shop, not to sacrifice."[46] Engles and Sass write, "Bush neither received nor requested civic sacrifice. Yet it seems to us that the absence of civic sacrifice is, in fact, a desired outcome of the new war rhetoric."[47] Rumsfeld admits, "We also could have engaged and asked more of the American people in the war effort."[48] This contrasts dramatically with what Roosevelt asked of the American people after Pearl Harbor.

OPERATION ENDURING FREEDOM

Naming an operation is an important part of any war narrative. Initially, the invasion of Afghanistan was to be known as Operation Infinite Justice. As Bob Woodward points out, that name was "criticized for its insensitivity to the Muslim faith, which holds that only Allah can mete out infinite justice."[49] Perhaps the original title reflected the fundamental war between good and evil that lay at the heart of Bush's narrative. However, needing support from Muslim nations, and not wanting the war to be seen as a crusade (despite his earlier slip of the tongue), Bush named the operation "Enduring Freedom," which broadened the purpose of the war in Afghanistan to bringing freedom to the people oppressed by the Taliban, rather than simply avenging the attacks on America.

The attacks of 9/11 also led to an unprecedented response from NATO under Article V of its charter. This was the first time in NATO history that the collective defense provisions of that article had been enforced. Thus, the United States stood with allies in its response to the attacks. In fact, the United States was supported by sixty-nine other nations in its actions in Afghanistan.[50]

Less than four weeks after the United States was attacked, military action began in Afghanistan. At 1:00 p.m. on October 7, Bush spoke to the nation from the White House Treaty Room. As he had done in his address to Congress, Bush emphasized that he had no quarrel with the people of Afghanistan, or the vast majority of Muslims:

> The United States of America is a friend to the Afghan people, and we are the friends of almost a billion worldwide who practice the Islamic faith. The United States of America is an enemy of those who aid terrorists and of the barbaric criminals who profane a great religion by committing murder in its name.[51]

Again, Bush stressed the separation of the enemy from mainstream Islam, even to the extent of claiming they had profaned their religion, a harsh charge, particularly coming from a Christian.

Bush writes about the fall of the Taliban in his memoir, "The remaining Taliban officials fled Kandahar. The city fell on December 7, 2001, the sixtieth anniversary of Pearl Harbor . . . ."[52] Again, the parallel to the "good war" was embedded in his thinking. Rumsfeld writes, "By any measure, it was an impressive military success."[53] He even quotes a soldier who recalled the Spanish-American War, asking "What more can you ask for than a splendid little war over here?"[54] Bob Gates, who served as Secretary of Defense under both Bush and Obama, writes, "The challenges we have faced in Afghanistan over the past dozen years obscure the memory that things actually went pretty well there between 2002 and 2005."[55] He also notes that the number of troops there was relatively small, "During this period, there were never more than 15,000 U.S. troops in the country."[56]

As we now know, however, the victory in Afghanistan proved pyrrhic. We have learned from an extensive collection of documents obtained through the Freedom of Information Act by the *Washington Post*, "[S]enior U.S. officials failed to tell the truth about the war in Afghanistan throughout the 18-year campaign, making rosy pronouncements they knew to be false and hiding unmistakable evidence the war had become unwinnable."[57] The *Post* reports, "The documents also contradict a long chorus of public statements from U.S. presidents, military commanders and diplomats who assured Americans year after year that they were making progress in Afghanistan and the war was worth fighting."⁵⁸ It quotes John Sopko, the head of the agency responsible for what they call the *Afghanistan Papers* (in homage to the Vietnam era *Pentagon Papers*), "[T]he American people have constantly been lied to."⁵⁹

One person who, in retrospect, recognized the danger of getting into a war in Afghanistan is Lt. General Daniel P. Bolger, who commanded troops in both Iraq and Afghanistan. After retiring in 2013, he wrote a scathing book on U.S. failures in both wars, titled, *Why We Lost*. In his view, Osama bin Laden actually *wanted* the United States to invade Afghanistan, hoping to destroy American infidels, just as the Soviets had been destroyed in their occupation of Afghanistan. Bolger writes, "If al-Qaeda could lure the United States to the same killing ground, that might well cripple the far enemy . . . . So that was the plan: a baited ambush to lure, snare, and then shred the American eagle."⁶⁰ Bolger continues, "Thus, in the days after 9/11, America decided to go into Afghanistan . . . . Isn't this just what Osama bin Laden wanted?"⁶¹ Richard Clark faults Bush for not making a greater effort to finish the job: "When the Taliban and al Qaeda leaders escaped, he dispatched additional forces but less than one full division equivalent, fewer U.S. troops for all of Afghanistan than the number of NYPD assigned to Manhattan."⁶²

In April 2002, Secretary of Defense, Donald Rumsfeld stated, "The war is over."⁶³ Of course, it was really only beginning as the Taliban bided its time. What appeared to be an easy victory in Afghanistan was later to become a quagmire that would prolong the war into the longest in American history. Soon the war in Afghanistan was no longer front-page news in the story of the war on terror as Bush focused on another familiar villain—Saddam Hussein.

EXPANDING THE WAR ON TERROR

A fundamental principle of Bush's war was to hold all those harboring or supporting terrorists equally responsible for their acts. Where might Iraq fit into this equation? Shortly after the attacks of 9/11, there had been debate within the administration as to whether to include Iraq among those targeted for supporting terrorists. In the early morning hours after 9/11, Richard Clark discovered that discussions were already beginning about invading Iraq. He writes,

> Then I realized . . . that Rumsfeld and Wolfowitz were going to try to take advantage of this national tragedy to promote their agenda about Iraq. . . . My friends in the Pentagon had been telling me that the word was we would be invading Iraq sometime in 2002.⁶⁴

Clark's recollections are supported by Woodward who reports that at a NSC meeting on September 12, "Rumsfeld raised the question of Iraq. Why shouldn't we be against Iraq, not just al Qaeda?"[65] Although urged by others, including Paul Wolfowitz to invade Iraq, on September 17 Bush "ended the debate," saying, "I believe Iraq was involved, but I'm not going to strike them now. I don't have the evidence at this point."[66] Iraq was mentioned only once in the September 20 speech.

Nevertheless, Bush was thinking about a war in Iraq almost immediately after 9/11. On September 26, just over two weeks after the attacks, Bush met privately in the Oval Office with Rumsfeld, who writes that Bush "asked that I take a look at the shape of our military plans on Iraq."[67] Woodward reports,

> On November 21, the day before Thanksgiving, 71 days after the 9/11 attacks, Bush asked Rumsfeld to start updating the war plan for Iraq. . . . He also wondered if this planning could be done so it would be kept secret.[68]

Finally, Woodward reports, "In the fall of 2002, [CIA Director George] Tenet and Bush had a 30-second conversation in which Bush made it clear that war with Iraq was necessary and inevitable."[69]

With the situation in Afghanistan appearing (wrongly as it turned out) to be under control, Bush turned his attention to other nations deemed "against us." Although he had rejected the original advice of Rumsfeld and Wolfowitz, by the time he presented his State of the Union Address in January 2002, Iraq had become Bush's next target. Christopher Scheer and his colleagues point out, "To wage war, the American public needs to feel an immediate sense of clear and present danger . . . . U.S. presidents know that to sell a war to the American people, they need at least two basic ingredients: self-defense and moral duty."[70]

To meet that need, David Frum was asked to draft the speech. Frum has taken credit for coining the phrase, "axis of hatred," which became "axis of evil." Although Frum's draft had mentioned only Iraq, Iran and Korea were added by head speechwriter Michael Gerson and the "axis of hatred" became the "axis of evil."[71] This echoed the Axis powers of Germany, Italy, and Japan in World War II. The story of the war on terror became framed as another World War II. After detailing the actions of Iran, North Korea, and Iraq in sponsoring terrorists Bush stated:

> States like these, and their terrorist allies, constitute an axis of evil, arming to threaten the peace of the world. By seeking weapons of mass destruction, these regimes pose a grave and growing danger. They could provide these arms to terrorists, giving them the means to match their hatred. They could attack our

allies or attempt to blackmail the United States. In any of these cases, the price of indifference would be catastrophic.[72]

Although North Korea and Iran were named with Iraq, it was the latter nation that received the strongest condemnation from Bush:

> Iraq continues to flaunt its hostility toward America and to support terror. The Iraqi regime has plotted to develop anthrax, and nerve gas, and nuclear weapons for over a decade. This is a regime that has already used poison gas to murder thousands of its own citizens—leaving the bodies of mothers huddled over their dead children. This is a regime that agreed to international inspections—then kicked out the inspectors. This is a regime that has something to hide from the civilized world.

Bush made it clear he would not wait for another 9/11 to protect the nation's security:

> I will not wait on events, while dangers gather. I will not stand by, as peril draws closer and closer. The United States of America will not permit the world's most dangerous regimes to threaten us with the world's most destructive weapons.

The president and vice president thought that war with Iraq would be easy. Dick Cheney proclaimed, "They're going to welcome us. It'll be like the American army going through the streets of Paris."[73] On May 16, Cheney stated on *Meet the Press*, "My belief is we will, in fact, be greeted as liberators."[74] Ken Adelman, who had been an assistant to Rumsfeld when he was Secretary of Defense from 1975 to 1977, wrote an opinion piece in the *Washington Post* titled "Cakewalk In Iraq."[75] Those who were familiar with the Middle East and particularly Iraq were not so sanguine about starting another war. In February, there was a meeting of American ambassadors to countries in the Middle East. According to Robert Draper, "Richard Jones, America's Ambassador to Kuwait, was seized by an awful premonition. 'I hope we avoid a Vietnam situation . . . . We'll be in there at least five years.'" Another diplomat predicted, "Within two years, there'll be an insurgency! Don't you know Iraq's history?"[76]

Beginning in April 2002, Bush began using the phrase "regime change" in reference to Iraq.[77] Interestingly, that had been the official U.S. policy since 1998.[78] How to change the regime, however, was up for debate. After much discussion within the administration, it was decided to involve the UN. Bush addressed the United Nations a year and a day after the attack on the World Trade Center and Pentagon. He challenged the UN to finally deal with the threat posed by Saddam Hussein some twelve years after his invasion of

Kuwait: "To suspend hostilities, to spare himself, Iraq's dictator accepted a series of commitments. The terms were clear, to him and to all. And he agreed to prove he is complying with every one of those obligations." Bush claimed Saddam "has proven instead only his contempt for the United Nations, and for all his pledges. By breaking every pledge—by his deceptions, and by his cruelties—Saddam Hussein has made the case against himself." Specifically, Bush cited violations of Iraq's commitment to renounce terrorism, including the rarely mentioned attempt on his father's life: "In 1993, Iraq attempted to assassinate the Emir of Kuwait and a former American President."[79] Bush credits Secretary of State Powell with the insistence on a new UN resolution, "He told me a UN resolution was the only way to get any support from the rest of the world. He went on to say that if we did take out Saddam, the military strike would be the easy part. Then, as Colin put it, America would 'own' Iraq."[80] The latter became known, inaccurately, as the Pottery Barn Rule—"you break it, you own it."

Although the essential argument of the speech revolves around enforcing the UN resolutions that Saddam had violated, Bush also makes the case that the people of Iraq deserved liberation. The speech details the savagery of the regime toward its own citizens:

> Tens of thousands of political opponents and ordinary citizens have been subjected to arbitrary arrest and imprisonment, summary execution, and torture by beating and burning, electric shock, starvation, mutilation, and rape. Wives are tortured in front of their husbands, children in the presence of their parents—and all of these horrors concealed from the world by the apparatus of a totalitarian state.[81]

While not explicitly calling for the overthrow of Saddam, Bush clearly implies that it would be a moral victory: "Liberty for the Iraqi people is a great moral cause, and a great strategic goal. The people of Iraq deserve it; the security of all nations requires it."

Beyond the moral imperative of ending Saddam's reign of terror, Bush also made the argument that he posed an imminent threat to the world. Nearly four years earlier, the UN inspectors had been expelled from Iraq. Bush stated,

> We know that Saddam Hussein pursued weapons of mass murder even when inspectors were in his country. Are we to assume that he stopped when they left? The history, the logic, and the facts lead to one conclusion: Saddam Hussein's regime is a grave and gathering danger.

Bush got his resolution number 1441.

Bush's next major speech on the Iraqi threat was given in Cincinnati on October 7. In addition to UN support, unlike Truman in Korea, he sought a congressional resolution authorizing the use of force in Iraq. This speech is important for what it says about the threat of Saddam and the implication that he was somehow linked to the event of September 11. Communication consultant Frank Luntz, advised Bush to make the link of Iraq to 9/11 repeatedly. As Steuter and Wills write, "His advice was to connect the war on terror to the war in Iraq by ensuring that 'no speech about homeland security or Iraq should begin without a reference to 9/11.'"[82] For example, Bush constantly refers to eleven years having passed since the Gulf War, which differs from the speech to the United Nations, which set the time frame at *twelve* years. The repetition of the word *eleven* helps cement a relationship of Iraq to the terror of 9/11. For example,

> *Eleven* years ago, as a condition for ending the Persian Gulf War, the Iraqi regime was required to destroy its weapons of mass destruction, to cease all development of such weapons, and to stop all support for terrorist groups. The Iraqi regime has violated all of those obligations. . . . The entire world has witnessed Iraq's *eleven*-year history of defiance, deception and bad faith.
>
> We also must never forget the most vivid events of recent history. On September the *11th*, 2001, America felt its vulnerability—even to threats that gather on the other side of the earth.[83]

In the space of a few sentences the word *eleven* is used three times. Although Bush does not directly say Saddam was linked to the September 11th attacks, he invites the audience to complete the enthymeme.

In the Cincinnati speech, the Bush doctrine is fully developed. Whether or not an enemy was responsible for 9/11 isn't the issue. Rather, action is called for whenever a threat is obvious. One of the most memorable lines of the speech became a mantra for the administration in selling the war: "Facing clear evidence of peril, we cannot wait for the final proof—the smoking gun—that could come in the form of a mushroom cloud." Smith attributes the mushroom cloud line to speechwriter Michael Gerson noting, it "would become the battle cry of the administration."[84] This image transports listeners to a world where Iraq had the bomb and could kill thousands instantly. This was a less direct accusation than the original draft, which included

> an alarming claim about a potential Saddam nuclear program, by charging that Iraq had been caught trying to buy uranium oxide in Africa. "You need to take this fucking sentence out because we don't believe it," Tenet told [Deputy National Security Advisor Stephen J.] Hadley when he read the draft.[85]

That claim was to reappear in a later speech and became one of the most disputed parts of Bush's war narrative.

Bush's story resonated with the American people. Rampton and Stauber report,

> In an October 2002 opinion poll by the Pew Research Center for the People and the Press, 66 percent of Americans said that they believed Saddam Hussein was involved in the September 11 attacks on the United States, while 79 percent believed that Iraq already possessed, or was close to possessing, nuclear weapons.[86]

After the Cincinnati speech, the Gallup poll showed 53 percent support for invading Iraq, and forty-six believed Bush had done all he could diplomatically. However, a unilateral invasion only garnered 38 percent support.[87] The speech clearly pressured Congress to support Bush's war plans, particularly with a midterm election on the horizon. Nine days later, on October 16, the president signed a joint congressional resolution authorizing the use of force in Iraq.[88] It passed the House by a vote of 296 to 133 and the Senate by 77 to 23, a more comfortable margin than the elder Bush had received in the Gulf War.[89] Following George W. Bush's lead in the Cincinnati speech, the resolution made five references to September 11.[90]

On January 28, 2003, the forty-third president delivered his State of the Union Address, which contained sixteen controversial words that were later recanted by the White House.[91] Bush alleged, "The British government has learned that Saddam Hussein recently sought significant quantities of uranium from Africa."[92] These sixteen disputed words were technically correct, illustrating the point that propaganda need not always be based on lies. British intelligence had made the report in question, but U.S. intelligence agencies doubted its credibility. The CIA had previously warned the Bush White House that British intelligence charges that Saddam had tried to purchase yellowcake uranium were shaky, and it was omitted from his earlier speech in Cincinnati. In fact, the so-called "yellowcake" uranium contract was forged.[93]

Eight days after Bush addressed the nation, Powell carried the U.S. case for war to the world when he addressed the UN Security Council. Powell was one of the most trusted men in America and the world when it came to matters of war and peace. In this speech, Powell laid out in great detail the alleged evidence for Saddam's possession of WMD, omitting the reference to attempting to purchase uranium in Africa for which the intel was shaky. He also tried to demonstrate links to al Qaeda. Powell claimed, "These are not assertions. What we're giving you are facts and conclusions based on solid intelligence."[94] Bush writes in his memoir that George Tenet had assured him that the case that Saddam had WMD was "a slam dunk."[95] In a Los Angeles public forum Tenet later admitted, "Those are the two dumbest words I ever said."[96] A poll found nearly four of five respondents thought Powell's case for invading Iraq was a strong one.[97] The speech earned rave reviews in the press, with the *Washington Post* judging Powell's case "irrefutable."[98]

It turned out that Powell's speech was actually based on flawed intelligence and that he was skeptical of going to war to remove Saddam. Draper writes, "Nearly all the intelligence Powell presented to the world in his speech turned out to be false."[99] U.S. diplomat John Brady Kiesling resigned from the Foreign Service in February 2003, writing, "We have not seen such systematic distortion of intelligence, such systematic manipulation of the American people, since the war in Vietnam."[100] O'Shaughnessy writes that the British intelligence on which the WMD case relied "had borrowed parts of an old PhD thesis without acknowledgement to help create a public dossier on Saddam Hussein. . . . Such was the extent of the plagiarism that not even grammatical errors were corrected."[101]

Believing that there was little doubt Saddam possessed WMD, the administration was not particularly concerned if their intelligence rested on unreliable sources and conjecture. Once weapons were found, no one would care about the original intelligence. Clark, who was in a position to know how to interpret intelligence reports, explains what was wrong with the intelligence and that those flaws were concealed:

> As studies by the Senate Intelligence Committee and the Carnegie Endowment have made clear, both the CIA and the President failed to tell the Congress and the American people that they were making judgments about the Iraqi WMD threat based on dated information.[102]

Clark also argues that possession of WMD is not, in and of itself, a reason for war: "Over two dozen nations possess WMD, according to unclassified CIA testimony to Congress."[103] Why not attack a different member of the axis of evil? Maureen Dowd wrote in the *New York Times*,

> It still confuses many Americans that, in a world full of vicious slimeballs, we're about to bomb one that didn't attack us on 9/11 (like Osama); that isn't intercepting our planes (like North Korea); that isn't financing Al Qaeda (like Saudi Arabia); that isn't home to Osama and his lieutenants (like Pakistan); that isn't a host body for terrorists (like Iran, Lebanon and Syria).[104]

William Greider wrote in the *Nation*, "As a bogus rallying cry, 'Remember 9/11' ranks with 'Remember the Maine' of 1898 for war with Spain or the Gulf of Tonkin resolution of 1964 for justifying the US escalation in Vietnam."[105]

Saddam eventually caved and allowed inspectors into Iraq. Now there was a way to determine if the U.S. intelligence was sound. As Bush beat the drums for war, the inspectors on the ground found no evidence that Saddam had restarted his WMD programs. On February 14, head weapons inspector Hans Blix told the UN Security Council that "his inspectors had visited over three hundred sites and had found no evidence of WMD."[106] Director General of the International Atomic Energy Agency Mohamed ElBaradei reported that "We have to date found no evidence of ongoing prohibited nuclear or nuclear-related activities in Iraq."[107] On March 7, according to Smith, "Blix and ElBaradei gave their fourth and what would be their final inspection report to the Security Council. Once again the inspectors could find nothing to substantiate American charges."[108] As the UN inspectors in Iraq continued to find no WMD, Bush ignored their findings and continued the rush toward war. Scheer and his colleagues asked, "What was the rush? Couldn't the inspectors be given another four months—the time they said it would take to complete their work?"[109]

Lacking proof that Saddam had restarted his WMD program, by March it became clear that the Security Council would not pass a second UN resolution. Bush, however, kept up the pressure for war, with or without UN support. When France promised to veto a second resolution, Bush abandoned his effort to get a UN vote. Instead, he held a summit with sympathetic leaders, such as Britain's Tony Blair. The statement they released contained a line that paralleled what Bush had said about the perpetrators of 9/11 and Islam: "Iraq's talented people, rich culture, and tremendous potential have been hijacked by Saddam Hussein."[110] Without UN support, Bush was forced to assemble what was called the "Coalition of the Willing." However, Rampton and Stauber write, "The so-called 'coalition of the willing' was almost entirely a U.S.-British campaign, with virtually no military contribution from any other country except Australia."[111]

SELLING THE WAR: THE MEDIA BUY BUSH'S STORY

Bill Moyers, who served as Lyndon Johnson's press secretary during the period of the Vietnam War's dramatic escalation, knows something about selling a war. Moyers has gone on to become a fierce critic of the selling of subsequent wars. In 2007, *Bill Moyers Journal* featured an episode titled "Buying the War." It focused on how the media, with few exceptions, bought the narrative the Bush White House was selling prior to the invasion of Iraq.[112] The pressure on the media to accept the administration's narrative was immense. Walter Isaacson, who was head of CNN at the time, told Moyers, "There was a patriotic fervor and the Administration used it so that if you challenged anything you were made to feel that there was something wrong with that." The pressure to support the war caused broadcasters to avoid showing civilian casualties. Once the war began, this pressure was intensified. Isaacson, "ordered his reporters and anchors to balance the images of civilian devastation with reminders of September 11th."

Moyers also interviewed the *Washington Post's* Walter Pincus. He asked about the White House Iraq Group, known as WHIG, which was in charge of "selling the war." Pincus characterized it as a marketing group:

> And the link was a two-fold link. One, he had weapons of mass destruction. And two, he supported terrorists. And they repeated it everyday. Anybody who watches television these days knows you sell a product . . . by saying it over and over again with new spokesmen two, three times a day and it sinks into the public.

Not only did the administration directly promote the war, it used leaks to the press, particularly the *New York Times*, and then quoted those stories to support the case for war. Vice President Cheney did exactly that on Tim Russert's *Meet the Press* on September 8. Moyers points out in his interview with Russert, "Someone in the Administration plants a dramatic story in the *New York Times*[.] And then the Vice President comes on your show and points to the *New York Times*. It's a circular, self-confirming leak."

Journalists also bought the story about Saddam's atrocities. James Fallows wrote in 2018 about prominent writers for his own publication, the *Atlantic*:

> Two of the writers who were most eloquent in making their case for the war— Christopher Hitchens . . . and Michael Kelly, who was then our editor-in-chief— based much of their case on the evils Saddam Hussein had gotten away with after the original Gulf War.[113]

The Bush administration emphasized these atrocities when they named Saddam Hussein "the Butcher of Baghdad."[114]

Even though there were occasional critical pieces, the dominant story in the press was the administration's narrative for war. According to Howard Kurtz, the *Washington Post*'s media critic, between August 2002 and the start of the war only a handful of the approximately 140 stories about Iraq on the front page of his paper made the case against the war.[115] Similarly, Rampton and Stauber report, "Journalism professor Todd Gitlin tabulated editorials that appeared in the *Washington Post* during a 12-week period shortly before the onset of war and found that 'hawkish op-ed pieces numbered 39, dovish ones 12—a ratio of more than 3-to-1.'"[116] It was not as if the evidence for WMD was undisputed. Deepa Kumar writes, "Despite abundant evidence to the contrary, such as the interviews with former weapons inspector Scott Ritter who had stated repeatedly that Iraq was 90-95 percent disarmed, the media chose to bury questions about WMDs deep inside a story or to ignore it all together."[117]

Thus, forty years after Bill Moyers helped sell the Vietnam War for the Johnson administration, he criticized the media for its credulity in buying Bush's argument for war: "Four years after shock and awe, the press has yet to come to terms with its role in enabling the Bush administration to go to war on false pretenses."[118] As an example of how the press promoted the war while concealing doubts about its justification, Pulitzer Prize-winning journalist James Risen writes,

> Before the invasion of Iraq, my stories that revealed that CIA analysts had doubts about the prewar intelligence on Iraq were held, cut, and buried deep inside the *Times*, even as stories . . . loudly proclaiming the purported existence of Iraqi weapons of mass destruction were garnering banner headlines on page one.[119]

The television networks were no better. Susan Brewer writes, "From September 2002 to February 2003, more than 90 percent of the stories on the rationale for war on ABC, NBC, and CBS originated from the White House."[120] In March, polling "showed that 53 to 70 percent of Americans thought that Saddam Hussein was personally behind the attacks and that 50 percent thought that some of the hijackers had been Iraqis."[121] Although all the networks shared a prowar stance, Fox stood out as most likely to present a one-sided portrayal of the war. A 2003 study found that although most respondents had significant misperceptions about the war in Iraq, "Those who receive most of their news from Fox News are more likely than average to have misperceptions. Those who receive most of their news from NPR or PBS are less likely to have misperceptions."[122] Fox was not alone in its prowar bias: Steuter and Wills write, "In a study during a two-week period prior to the Iraq war, NBC, CBS, ABC, and PBS recorded 393 interviews on the conflict, of which only three reported the anti-war movement."[123] The media indeed bought the narrative George W. Bush was peddling, leading America into the very quagmire that George H. W. Bush had avoided when he stopped the First Gulf War without going to Baghdad. Not only were the TV networks complicit in promoting the war, but also Hollywood did its part. Paul Achter writes, "Over three hundred films and television programs have been made about the Iraq War alone, some of which (*The Hurt Locker, The Messenger*) won major awards."[124] Not all movies were supportive of the war, of course, as shown by Michael Moore's award-winning, anti-war documentary, *Fahrenheit 9/11*.

OPERATION IRAQI FREEDOM

On March 19, a little after 10:00 p.m., Bush addressed the nation from the Oval Office to announce the beginning of combat operations in Iraq. The purposes of the attack were stated succinctly: "to disarm Iraq, to free its people and to defend the world from grave danger."[125] Bush put the war in the context of avoiding another terrorist attack: "We will meet that threat now, with our Army, Air Force, Navy, Coast Guard and Marines, so that we do not have to meet it later with armies of fire fighters and police and doctors on the streets of our cities." This echoed Truman, who had argued we were fighting in Korea so we wouldn't have to fight in Wichita and similar claims used to defend the Vietnam War. Transporting Americans back to 9/11, Bush clearly assumed the link between Saddam and terrorism was believed by the American people. In fact a poll, taken in January had shown that less than one in five respondents knew that none of the hijackers were Iraqi.[126]

The war began with striking television pictures that came to be known as "shock and awe," as American bombs lit up the night sky in Iraq, transporting viewers to a battlefield dominated by American firepower. According to Woodward, Rumsfeld explained to the president that the phrase "meant building up so much force and conducting various 'spiking' operations and bombing that it might in itself trigger regime change." Bush thought it was a good slogan.[127]

Operation Iraqi Freedom was an opportunity for the Pentagon to perfect the strategies for managing the media it had tried out in past conflicts. According to Phillip Knightley, "[I]nstead of managing the media, the Pentagon incorporated the media into the national war effort—enlisting its vast resources in the service of the country as it had done in the Second World War."[128] This process was known as embedding, through which journalists were assigned to a specific unit for the duration of the conflict. They even went through basic training with their unit.[129] Nicholas O'Shaughnessy writes, "[T]he embedded journalist was probably a successful propaganda slight-of-hand. Since the embedded reporter by definition shares the hardship of the troops . . . the bias will inevitably be towards the military."[130] In Knightley's words, "The correspondents were merely extras in a piece of theatre."[131] This role, however, was not without risk. Rumsfeld reveals, "From 2003 to 2009, seven embedded reporters were killed in Iraq, and several others were wounded."[132]

American media downplayed the damage inflicted on innocent Iraqis by American forces. Even highly acclaimed reporters who were critical of U.S. efforts faced retribution. Kumar notes, "Peter Arnett, the Pulitzer Prize winning journalist, was fired from MSNBC for admitting on Iraqi television that things were not going as planned for the US."[133] The networks became virtual cheerleaders for the war. Rampton and Stauber describe how they used graphics to frame their stories:

> Networks quickly scrambled to give names to their war coverage, with corresponding graphic logos that swooshed and gleamed in 3-D colors accompanied by mood-inducing soundtracks. CBS chose "America at War." CNN went with "Strike on Iraq." CNBC used "The Price of War," while NBC and MSNBC both went with "Target: Iraq"—a choice that changed quickly as MSNBC joined Fox in using the Pentagon's own code name for the war—"Operation Iraqi Freedom."[134]

Two events stood out in the media coverage of the early days of the war. The heroism of Pvt. Jessica Lynch and the toppling of Saddam's statue were key stories told to the American public that were not what they seemed.[135] Pvt. Jessica Lynch was heralded as a war hero for fighting off Iraqis before she was captured on March 23. Rumsfeld writes, "A nineteen-year-old private named Jessica Lynch was captured by the enemy and extravagant reports about her resistance to capture flooded the media."[136] However,

> The reality was different from the media storyline. . . . Lynch's unit had become lost after taking a wrong turn, and in a firefight she had been wounded and captured. Lynch's captors took her to a local hospital, where a courageous Iraqi reported her whereabouts to U.S. forces.[137]

It turns out Lynch never fired her weapon because it jammed.[138] Of course, the propaganda value of the courageous Pvt. Lynch fighting off her captors and the supposedly cruel treatment she received far outweighed the truth, which Rumsfeld relegates to a footnote in his memoirs.

On April 9, a statue of Saddam was toppled in Firdos Square in the center of Baghdad. A Marine put an American flag over Saddam's head, but it was quickly removed in recognition that this was supposed to be a liberation not an occupation.[139] The toppling of the statue was reminiscent of the toppling of statues of Lenin and Stalin when the Soviet Union fell, transporting viewers to the scene of Iraq's "liberation." Smith writes,

> The toppling of Saddam's statute was the high mark of the invasion. CNN replayed the incident every 7.5 minutes on April 9, and Fox News every 4.4 minutes. . . . Bush's public approval rating surged from 57 to 77 percent.[140]

In reality, the statue falling was not a spontaneous Iraqi response, but rather the result of American tanks pulling down the statue in front of a small group of Iraqis.[141]

However, the euphoria of toppling Saddam was soon overshadowed by the emergence of looting and chaos in Iraq. Instead of liberation, viewers were transported to a chaotic scene in the streets of Baghdad. Scheer and his colleagues write, "Within weeks, the U.S. cakewalk began melting in the 120-degree oven of Iraqi anger. The images of celebration were quickly replaced by those of looting, as roving bands of marauders indiscriminately pillaged hospitals, museums, embassies, and government buildings."[142] Part of the problem was that U.S. troops were only assigned to protect oil resources, contributing to the perception that this was a war for oil, not the liberation of the people of Iraq.[143] The focus of press coverage quickly turned sour. In a press conference on April 11, Rumsfeld lamented, "I picked up a newspaper today and I couldn't believe it . . . . I read eight headlines that talked about chaos, violence, and unrest. . . . And here is a country that is being liberated . . . and they're free."[144]

MISSION ACCOMPLISHED?

Bush delivered the most dramatic speech of the war on May 1 from the deck of the USS *Abraham Lincoln*. Elisabeth Bumiller describes that memorable event "as one of the most audacious moments of presidential theater in American history." The staging of the event was carefully planned, as Bumiller recounts:

> Media strategists noted afterward that Mr. Sforza and his aides had choreographed every aspect of the event, even down to the members of the Lincoln crew arrayed in coordinated shirt colors over Mr. Bush's right shoulder and the "Mission Accomplished" banner placed to perfectly capture the president and the celebratory two words in a single shot. The speech was specifically timed for what image makers call "magic hour light," which cast a golden glow on Mr. Bush.[145]

Although an earlier speech draft had contained the words "mission accomplished," they were stricken at the insistence of Secretary Rumsfeld, who told Woodward, "I took Mission Accomplished out . . . They fixed the speech but not the sign."[146] The opening paragraph of Bush's speech conveyed the same message as the banner: "Major combat operations in Iraq have ended. In the battle of Iraq, the United States and our allies have prevailed."[147] Bush refers to the "battle of Iraq," not the war in Iraq, putting it in the context of the larger war on terror:

> The battle of Iraq is one victory in a war on terror that began on September the 11, 2001—and still goes on. That terrible morning, 19 evil men—the shock

troops of a hateful ideology—gave America and the civilized world a glimpse of their ambitions. They imagined, in the words of one terrorist, that September the 11th would be the "beginning of the end of America."

Clark notes that calling the invasion of Iraq part of the war that began on September 11, helped explain why "70 percent of the American people believed that Saddam Hussein had attacked the Pentagon and the World Trade Center."[148]

The story of the War on Terror combined the World War II metaphor of liberation with an ongoing struggle against evil. Only liberation of the oppressed could ultimately deliver us from the evil of terrorism. Bush drives home the message by transporting his audience back to September 11: "the last phone calls, the cold murder of children, the searches in the rubble. With those attacks, the terrorists and their supporters declared war on the United States. And war is what they got."[149]

Bush drove home the point that the war was not over, a somewhat contradictory message from the "Mission Accomplished" banner. He reminded his audience on the carrier and at home, "The war on terror is not over; yet it is not endless. We do not know the day of final victory, but we have seen the turning of the tide." Finally, Bush put the war in the context of the struggle against the darkness of evil, quoting Isaiah, "To the captives, 'come out,'— and to those in darkness, 'be free.'"

As late as April 2006, Bush told his Chief of Staff, Andy Card, that he "still believed that Saddam had possessed weapons of mass destruction."[150] The failure to find them did not immediately cost Bush public support. A Gallup poll taken May 30–June 1, 2003, revealed that most respondents did not believe Bush misled them about weapons of mass destruction and even if no weapons were ever found, the war on Iraq was justified.[151] In 2006, half of Americans still thought Iraq had WMD when they were invaded.[152] Because the American people had long ago concluded that Saddam was Hitler reincarnated, it was not difficult to believe that Bush spoke truthfully when he asserted that Saddam posed a threat. That demonstrates the importance of the groundwork laid by the senior Bush. Fareed Zakaria explains, "Saddam was assumed to be working on a vast weapons program because he was an evil man."[153]

Ironically, in fulfilling the promise implied by his father to liberate the people of Iraq, the son was faced with his own unfulfilled promise. The banner proclaiming, "Mission Accomplished" suggested that liberation from Saddam's rule was an end in itself. American troops would be welcomed as heroes, not resisted as occupiers. Despite such widely publicized events as the fall of the statue of Saddam in Baghdad, American troops were not universally hailed as liberators. They faced escalating attacks and growing resistance. By late August 2003, the American people were expressing dissatisfaction with the continuing difficulties in Iraq. One poll found that "nearly 70 percent of Americans feel the United States will be bogged down in the country for years without achieving its goals."[154] On August 25, the postwar death toll matched the total of those killed prior to Bush's May 1 carrier speech.[155] During the Bush's re-election bid in 2004, Woodward reports, "The violence was now 10 times worse than it had been when Bush landed on the aircraft carrier in May 2003 and declared that major combat was over."[156] The senior George Bush had recognized the difficulty of occupying Iraq and chose not to go to Baghdad. His son failed to heed his father's warning.

Another consequence of Bush's speech, according to Smith, was that it "changed the military's mission in Iraq . . . when he announced . . . that the United States was going to bring democracy to that country. . . . They did not anticipate that American troops would become occupiers."[157] Although at the time, the story of the war in Iraq seemed over, there were those who questioned the broader narrative. Rampton and Stauber asked back in 2003,

> But in the wake of this conflict, we should ask ourselves whether we have made the mistake of believing our own propaganda, and whether we have been fighting the war on terror against the wrong enemies, in the wrong places, with the wrong weapons.[158]

In due time, that same question would be asked by many Americans as the situation in Iraq became more troubling.

IRAQ BECOMES A QUAGMIRE

Lt. Gen. Bolger points out,

> As the war soured in late 2003, the debate grew quite heated. The former consensus evaporated. A new one arose: Saddam had no WMD. . . . And Saddam had no ties to al-Qaeda, none at all. . . . The opposition boiled it down to a pithy, angry slogan: Bush lied, thousands died.[159]

In his memoir, Bush calls the slogan "illogical," asserting, "Nobody was lying. We were all wrong."[160] Paul Krugman disagrees, writing in 2015,

> The Iraq war wasn't an innocent mistake, a venture undertaken on the basis of intelligence that turned out to be wrong. America invaded Iraq because the Bush administration wanted a war. The public justifications for the invasion were

nothing but pretexts, and falsified pretexts at that. We were, in a fundamental sense, lied into war.[161]

To some extent, Bush may have been deceived by his own propaganda. Woodward reports on an interview December 11, 2003, in his aptly named third book on the Bush Wars, *State of Denial*, "It had taken five minutes and 18 seconds for Bush simply to acknowledge the *fact* that we hadn't found weapons of mass destruction."[162] The final sentence of that book sums up the lack of *fidelity* in the president's narrative: "With all Bush's upbeat talk and optimism, he had not told the American people the truth about what Iraq had become."[163]

The situation in Iraq soon developed into a quagmire. Draper reports, "Signs of a growing insurgency had appeared as far back as early April, just after Saddam's fall."[164] When confronted with questions about the apparent insurgency in Iraq on July 2, Bush's response was, "bring 'em on."[165] Of course, such a response only encouraged the insurgents and increased the risks to American troops who had to confront them. Woodward reports, "Classified reports showed that the insurgent attacks had jumped to 1,000 in the month of October [2003], more than 30 a day.... The numbers were kept secret."[166] By the end of the year, Saddam had been captured hiding in his spider hole near Tikrit. He was hanged on December 30, 2006.[167] Yet that did not end the insurgency, which had far broader support than just Saddam's loyalists.

The central premise of Bush's case for war in Iraq was that it would make America safer and deny al Qaeda an ally. However, in his memoir, Bush's own words show that the result was the opposite. Noting that Iraq was in some ways a better location for al Qaeda than Afghanistan, he writes:

> When al Qaeda lost its safe haven in Afghanistan, the terrorists went searching for a new one. After we removed Saddam in 2003, bin Laden exhorted his fighters to support the jihad in Iraq.... Over time, the number of extremists affiliated with al Qaeda in Afghanistan declined to the low hundreds, while the estimated number in Iraq topped ten thousand.[168]

Ironically, the removal of Saddam, whose tyranny would have crushed any al Qaeda cells, opened the way for al Qaeda in Iraq to directly confront Americans on turf that was suited to asymmetrical warfare. In fact, a National Intelligence Estimate showed that the invasion of Iraq *increased* terrorism.[169] Clark writes, "Bush handed the enemy precisely what it wanted and needed, proof that America was at war with Islam, that we were the new Crusaders come to occupy Muslim land."[170] He also writes, "In Muslim countries, the U.S. invasion of Iraq increased support for al Qaeda and radical anti-Americanism."[171]

Bolger identifies one of the great problems fighting the insurgency in Iraq, "Who was the enemy?" His answer was "everybody."[172] Difficulty identifying the enemy inevitably leads to the killing of innocents and civilians. In the April attack on Fallujah U.S. firepower ended up backfiring.

> [T]he insurgents invited reporter Ahmed Mansour of Al Jazeera into the city.... Ahmed Mansour's cameramen sent out a steady stream of dead babies, mangled elders, bloodied children, wailing mothers, and thin, pathetic, still corpses in civil dress.... But it did not play well in Peoria, let alone in Baghdad, Riyadh, Amman, or Washington.[173]

Bolger acknowledges the U.S. success on the battlefield,

> Yet in April of 2004, the propaganda front proved to be the only one that counted. As Marine commander Jim Conway summarized, "Al Jazeera kicked our butts." . . . Placing a cherry on the crap sundae, the Abu Ghraib detainee-abuse story broke worldwide on April 28.[174]

In one particularly disturbing photo, a hooded prisoner is forced to stand on a box hooked up to wires (figure 9.2). Bolger summarizes the situation, "The great, liberating march upcountry of 2003 had degenerated into the heat, squalor, and blood of Iraqi resentment, prisoner abuse, and baby-killing in 2004."[175]

The treatment of prisoners at Abu Ghraib became one of the most sordid stories of a war built on the alleged savagery of Saddam. Zachary Justus argues that the distinction between abuse and torture was critical to the administration's efforts to distinguish the actions of Americans at Abu Ghraib from those of Saddam:

> The importance of naming the events at Abu Ghraib abuse rather than torture cannot be overstated. The characterization of abuse limits the culpability of the US government. In addition to the legal implications the act of naming . . . reframes the discussion another way. Limiting the scope of the events at Abu Ghraib makes the fact that previous indicators of torture fell on deaf ears more reasonable. It seems terrible that the administration ignored cries of torture, but what if what happened was only abuse? The semantic difference seems to absolve the relevant parties of guilt on multiple levels.[176]

In many ways, the Abu Ghraib fiasco was a logical result of the abandonment of normal strictures against mistreatment of prisoners of war during the war on terror. According to Woodward, "Bush decided on January 18, 2002, that the protections of the Geneva Convention would not apply to terrorist suspects detained from al Qaeda and the Taliban."[177] As prisoners of war, detainees

Figure 9.2 The hooded prisoner at Abu Ghraib, standing on the box with wires attached, was told that he would be electrocuted if he fell off the box. The release of this photo and others like it was a source of propaganda for America's enemies. *Source*: Photo was taken on November 4, 2003 by Sabrina Harman and was seized by U.S. Army / Criminal Investigation Command (CID).

would have been entitled to certain protections. As unlawful combatants, they were subject to so-called "enhanced interrogation" and over 700 were held at Guantanamo Bay at some point, with about 40 remaining as of June 2020.[178] Woodward contends, "Lost in the entire torture controversy is the fact that none of those interrogated ever gave up the major intelligence priority—the location of bin Laden."[179] Former CIA Chief and Defense Secretary Leon Panetta, however, indicates some useful information did come from these practices, although he agreed with Obama's decision to end them.[180]

Regarding torture, Risen writes, "The United States is now relearning an ancient lesson, dating back to the Roman Empire. Brutalizing an enemy only serves to brutalize the army ordered to do it. Torture corrodes the mind of the torturer."[181] He continues, "Bush's decision to abandon the Geneva Conventions changed everything."[182] Rumsfeld dismisses prisoner abuse at Abu Ghraib as "the senseless crimes of a small group of prison guards who ran amok in the absence of adequate supervision."[183] In echoes of My Lai, therefore, the military chose to blame a few bad apples and ignore the broader question of how the enemy was treated. Justus writes,

> The Administration's strategy of placing blame entirely on the soldiers involved accomplished the task of rebuilding ties with foreign governments and absolving

the Administration of guilt. The choice to ignore alternative representations disqualifies their existence. This is not an alternative representation of events, it is a complete departure from the truth.[184]

Aside from the moral aspects of the Abu Ghraib revelations, the photos were a huge propaganda defeat for the United States. Risen writes,

> The global release of the photographs did what nothing else could—bring sudden and intense pressure on the White House, Pentagon, and CIA for an accounting of how the United States had been treating prisoners captured in the global war on terror.[185]

Woodward reports that according to Middle East intelligence expert Derek Harvey, Abu Ghraib

> had inflamed Iraqis. Photographs of smiling U.S. soldiers alongside naked, hooded, manacled and leashed inmates had flooded newspapers, television screens and the Internet. They had spread like a lightning bolt throughout Iraqi society and sent a devastating message: The U.S. occupation was the new oppressor.[186]

Abu Ghraib was not the lone American misdeed in Iraq. Blackwater contractors murdered fourteen civilians in September 2007. According to the *Guardian*, "FBI investigators who visited the scene in the following days described it as the 'My Lai massacre of Iraq.'"[187] The perpetrators were eventually convicted, but in December 2020, President Trump issued pardons. The *Washington Post* reported, "[F]or many Iraqis, it seemed only a restatement of their decades-long experience with U.S. power."[188] Thus one more effect of the war in Iraq was to undermine faith in America's commitment to justice and democracy in the Middle East.

THE FREEDOM AGENDA

After winning a second term, Bush decided to expand his rhetoric to include what he called the Freedom Agenda. In his second inaugural, he declared, "So it is the policy of the United States to seek and support the growth of democratic movements and institutions in every nation and culture, with the ultimate goal of ending tyranny in our world."[189] Bush mentioned "freedom" as well as "liberty" a total of forty-four times.[190] This promise elicited a response from Iraq's al Qaeda leader Abu Musab Al-Zarqawi: "We have declared a fierce war on this evil principle of democracy and those who follow this wrong ideology."[191]

Although the situation in Iraq was getting worse, the administration continued its policy of denial. Appearing on CNN on May 30, 2005, Vice President Cheney declared, "I think they're in the last throes, if you will, of the insurgency."[192] Yet, the public was not fooled. The ABC/*Wall Street Journal* poll had Bush's favorables at 38 percent and his unfavorables at 57 percent by November 2005.[193] On January 1, 2006, he stood for a press availability after visiting the wounded at Brooke Army Medical Center in Texas. Answering a question about how it felt to confront the wounded soldiers, Bush said:

> There's horrible consequences to war—that's what you see in this building.... On the other hand, we also see people who say, "I'd like to go back in, Mr. President, what we're doing is the right thing." Because many of these troops understand that by defeating the enemy there, we don't have to face them here. And they understand that by helping the country and the Middle East become a democracy, we are, in fact, laying the foundation for future peace. And I, as the commander in chief, am resolved to make sure that those who have died in combat's sacrifice are not in vain.[194]

There are three common war propaganda techniques here (1) we have to fight them over there so we don't have to fight them here; (2) we're fighting a war for peace; (3) our soldier's deaths can't be in vain. Although hardly new (one can find traces of these in Korea and Vietnam, to name just two), it is rare to find so much propaganda in the space of five sentences. Still, some progress in the war was being made. As Draper reports, "On June 7, the American military scored a major victory when Al Qaeda's brutal leader in Iraq, the Jordanian Abu Musab Al-Zarqawi, was killed by two five-hundred pound bombs."[195]

THE SURGE IN IRAQ

A key event in promoting sectarian violence was the bombing of a Shia holy site in early 2006. Bush writes, The Askariya shrine at the Golden Mosque of Samarra is considered one of the holiest sites in Shia Islam. . . . On February 22, 2006, two massive bombs destroyed the mosque. . . . By early April, sectarian violence had exploded.[196] Rumsfeld admits, "By the spring of 2006, al-Qaida had seized the initiative in Iraq."[197] By late 2006-early 2007, the public had grown increasingly skeptical of the administration's conduct of the war. According to Rumsfeld, "In one poll, only 44 percent had confidence that we could leave behind a stable Iraqi government. More than 80 percent believed Iraq was engulfed in a civil war."[198] Even General John Abizaid, who headed up the U.S. Central Command, reportedly "had concluded that the United States' armed presence in Iraq on such a large scale for so many years was doing more harm than good. In private, he put it bluntly: 'We need to get the fuck out.'"[199]

Yet Bush continued to double down on his policy in Iraq. On September 11, 2006, the president returned to the same theme of protecting America from terrorists that had led him into the quagmire that Iraq had become:

> Whatever mistakes have been made in Iraq, the worst mistake would be to think that if we pulled out, the terrorists would leave us alone. They will not leave us alone. They will follow us. The safety of America depends on the outcome of the battle in the streets of Baghdad.[200]

A month later, at a press conference October 11, 2006, Bush again tied the Iraq war to protecting America from terrorists: "If we were to abandon that country before the Iraqis can defend their young democracy, the terrorists would take control of Iraq and establish a new safe haven from which to launch new attacks on America."[201]

Bush ended up supporting a surge in Iraq of 21,500 additional troops.[202] In a January 10, 2007, prime time address Bush announced, "The situation in Iraq is unacceptable to the American people — and it is unacceptable to me. . . . So I've committed more than 20,000 additional American troops to Iraq."[203] At the peak of the surge, U.S. troops exceeded 170,000.[204] Draper writes,

> In opting for the Surge/Reinforcement, Bush was ignoring the advice of the bipartisan Iraq Study Group. . . . A Gallup poll taken after his speech indicated that only 38 percent of the American public approved of his new strategy. And for the first time in Gallup's surveying of the matter, a plurality of Americans 47–49 percent, believed that the Untied States was likely to lose the war.[205]

That was only the beginning of what Bush acknowledges was the most difficult time of his presidency. He writes in his memoir:

> The summer of 2006 was the worst period of my presidency. . . . I was deeply concerned that the violence was overtaking all else. An average of 120 Iraqis a day were dying. The war had stretched to more than three years and we had lost more than 2,500 Americans. By a margin of almost two to one, Americans said they disapproved of the way I was handling Iraq.[206]

Bush claims that the surge was a huge success. He writes in his memoir,

> Iraqi civilian deaths had declined 70 percent in Baghdad and 45 percent across the country. Deaths from sectarian violence had plunged 80 percent in Baghdad

and 55 percent across the country. IED attacks had dropped by a third, and car bombings and suicide attacks had declined by almost 50 percent.

In short, Bush contends, "The surge was working."[207]

Smith relates that Bush started drawing down troops after the "surge" appeared successful.

> Bush's willingness to begin the withdrawal of U.S. forces dampened public interest in Iraq. . . .[T]elevision networks devoted roughly 25 percent of the news coverage to the war [until the drawdown was announced]. By mid-2008, it was down to 3 percent.[208]

Just as Nixon's Vietnamization strategy helped dampen media interest in that war, Bush's drawdown was having the desired effect. "He also concluded an agreement with Iraqi prime minister Houri al-Maliki to withdraw all forces by 2011."[209] There was an obstacle to keeping a small contingent of U.S. troops in Iraq, with the United States insisting its soldiers not be subject to the Iraqi justice system. In June 2008, the Iraqi prime minister,

> announced that negotiations over the status of U.S. forces in Iraq had "reached a dead end." Though talks would continue, he said, "We could not give amnesty to a [U.S.] soldier carrying arms on our ground. We will never give it."[210]

This failure to reach a Status of Forces agreement with Iraq ultimately led to the complete withdrawal of U.S. troops under Bush's successor, a fact which some believe led to the rise of ISIS.

While the surge in Iraq seemed to be working, Afghanistan was unraveling. Although touted as a model of Bush's Freedom Agenda, in reality the Taliban was regrouping. Rumsfeld claims, "Afghanistan experienced relatively few incidents of violence until the summer of 2005."[211] However, he acknowledges, "By early 2006, a reorganized Taliban insurgency had emerged in Afghanistan's east and south."[212] As Bolger put it, "In Afghanistan, only the dead really surrender. . . . For Afghans, giving up is a time-out, not a game-over."[213] What happened, in Bolger's view, is that "the continued presence of thousands of infidels . . . offered the most likely catalyst to a Taliban resurgence. In other words, over time the outsiders' staying might actually engender more instability."[214] Scheer and his colleagues write, "Less than a year after a rousing military victory, the U.S. troops were no longer in control of major parts of the countryside and the Taliban were already regrouping and regaining their strength."[215] Near the end of Bush's term in 2008 Smith reports, "The Taliban was operating in thirty-three of Afghanistan's thirty-four provinces, and IED . . . attacks had risen to 7,200 annually—as opposed to 80 in 2003."[216]

ASSESSING BUSH'S IRAQ NARRATIVE

Bush's narrative after 9/11 was straightforward. It was grounded in the story of the good war—World War II. Clearly, this story resonated with the shell-shocked American public. However, after what was mistakenly thought to be a resounding victory in Afghanistan, Bush turned his sights on Iraq. He told three major narratives. First Saddam was somehow linked to 9/11. Second, he possessed and would possibly provide WMD to terrorists to use against the United States. Finally, he was an evil and cruel tyrant who oppressed his people. The United States would be welcomed by the Iraqi people as liberators, just as the French welcomed Americans in World War II. It would be a "cakewalk."

Although the first two stories seemed to have *narrative coherence*—after all Saddam's past actions and his character had been thoroughly demonstrated in the Gulf War, it eventually become clear that they lacked *fidelity*. We now know that Saddam was not linked to al Qaeda or the September 11th attacks and no significant WMD were ever found in Iraq after the war. Two of the three pillars of Bush's story fell fairly soon after the war began. Only the "liberation" of the people of Iraq from a tyrant remained. When it couldn't find WMDs, the administration shifted the rationale for the war to democracy.[217] However, that story soon lost *fidelity* in the face of a growing insurgency. It is little wonder that "Bush lied, people died" came to be the "Hey, Hey LBJ" chant of the opponents of the war in Iraq.

OBAMA INHERITS TWO WARS

At the time the war in Iraq began, Barack Obama was an obscure state senator from Illinois. Ben Rhodes, who was deputy national security adviser in the Obama administration, writes,

> Obama would not have been elected as the 44th president of the United States were it not for 9/11, which set in motion the chain of events that led to the Iraq War. His pre-invasion opposition to the war and pledge to end it provided his core contrast with Hillary Clinton in the Democratic primary.[218]

On October 2, 2002, Obama, spoke prophetically:

> I know that even a successful war against Iraq will require a U.S. occupation of undetermined length, at undetermined cost, with undetermined consequences. I

know that an invasion of Iraq without a clear rationale and without strong international support will only fan the flames of the Middle East, and encourage the worst, rather than best, impulses of the Arab world, and strengthen the recruitment arm of al-Qaida. I am not opposed to all wars. I'm opposed to dumb wars.[219]

Once he took office, Obama faced multiple crises. Not only was the nation facing an economic catastrophe unseen since the Great Depression, 161,000 American troops remained in Iraq and the 38,000 in Afghanistan were unable to defeat the growing Taliban insurgency.[220] Obama writes in his memoir, *The Promised Land*:

> The collapse of Iraq into sectarian violence, and the Bush administration's decision to reinforce our presence with a sustained troop surge, had siphoned military and intelligence capabilities out of Afghanistan.... The shift in focus had allowed the Taliban ... to go on the offensive, and that summer the monthly U.S. casualties in Afghanistan would exceed those in Iraq.[221]

Ending these wars was a central objective of the Obama administration, which, as we now know, was less than completely successful.

Despite his desire to end the wars he inherited, Obama suffered, as had Bush, from a lack of understanding of the real situation in Afghanistan. Woodward writes, "The U.S. remained dangerously ignorant about the Afghan insurgency. Basic questions had gone unasked over the course of the war: Who is the enemy? Where are they? How do they see the fight? What are their motivations?"[222] Just killing the Taliban was no way to defeat the insurgency. Woodward adds, "High body counts alone cannot end an insurgency. The deaths often had the opposite effect, swelling an insurgency's ranks as recruits joined to avenge what they deemed to be a family member's murder."[223]

Bush had commissioned the NSC to review the strategy and they recommended adding 20,000 troops. Although he agreed with their recommendation, Bush "decided the new strategy would have a better chance of success if we gave the new team an opportunity to revise it as they saw fit and then adopt it as their own."[224] Even Army Chief of Staff George Casey admitted, "It is not possible to defeat the Taliban in the classic sense."[225] Based on the Bush NSC Report, Obama increased American troop strength by 17,000, an increase of almost 50 percent.[226] This was done before the review of policy he had commissioned was completed. That review ended up becoming a source of conflict between the military leadership and new president. When General Stanley McChrystal delivered his report, Obama was surprised at how much he was asking for. Then, what was supposed to be an internal document, suddenly started leaking to the media, as Obama recounts:

Just two days after I received the report, *The Washington Post* published an interview with David Petraeus in which he declared that any hope for success in Afghanistan would require substantially more troops and a "fully resourced, comprehensive" COIN [counter-insurgency] strategy. . . . [O]n September 21, the *Post* published a synopsis of McChrystal's report that had leaked to Bob Woodward, under the headline MCCHRYSTAL: MORE FORCES OR "MISSION FAILURE.". . . Rahm [Emanuel] remarked that in all his years in Washington, he'd never seen such an orchestrated, public campaign by the Pentagon to box in a president. Biden was more succinct: "It's fucking outrageous."[227]

It seemed clear that the Pentagon brass were trying to box in the young, inexperienced president, forcing him to ramp up the military's war in Afghanistan, and setting him up to be roasted in the media if he didn't follow their advice.

Feeling the pressure to add more troops, but not wanting an open-ended escalation of the war, Panetta writes,

In the end, Obama accepted [Secretary of Defense] Gates's recommendation, settling on thirty thousand new troops with an emergency reserve of three thousand more, and more important, moving away from the notion that our mission was to destroy or eliminate the Taliban. Rather, he adopted the formula that our mission was to "disrupt, dismantle, and defeat" Al Qaeda.[228]

Woodward claims that Panetta made it clear that Obama really had no choice but to give the military what it wanted, asserting, "No Democratic president can go against military advice, especially if he asked for it."[229] Gates points out, "It is a measure of the deterioration in Afghanistan after 2006 that in just three years the number of U.S. military personnel in Afghanistan had more than quadrupled to nearly 100,000."[230] Not wanting the military to later blame him if the strategy failed, Obama took the unusual action of preparing a document that the military leaders had to sign, agreeing to his policy. He writes "that having the Pentagon brass look me in the eye and commit to an agreement laid out on paper was the only way to avoid their publicly second-guessing my decision if the war went south."[231]

Obama laid out the new strategy in a speech at West Point on December 9, 2009. In planning for his West Point Speech Obama told his speechwriter Ben Rhodes, "We need to remind people why we went into Afghanistan in the first place . . . . We need to tell the story of how we got up to where we are today."[232] Indeed he did exactly that, transporting Americans back to 9/11:

On September 11, 2001, 19 men hijacked four airplanes and used them to murder nearly 3,000 people. They struck at our military and economic nerve centers.

They took the lives of innocent men, women, and children without regard to their faith or race or station. Were it not for the heroic actions of passengers onboard one of those flights, they could have also struck at one of the great symbols of our democracy in Washington, and killed many more.[233]

He went on to link the problems in Afghanistan to the resources devoted to the Iraq War that he had opposed:

It's enough to say that for the next six years, the Iraq war drew the dominant share of our troops, our resources, our diplomacy, and our national attention—and that the decision to go into Iraq caused substantial rifts between America and much of the world.

He then stressed that American troops would be withdrawn by 2011, the date agreed to by his predecessor. All the while, the situation in Afghanistan had grown more dire. After citing the complete review of the policy in Afghanistan, Obama announced,

This review is now complete. And as Commander-in-Chief, I have determined that it is in our vital national interest to send an additional 30,000 U.S. troops to Afghanistan. After 18 months, our troops will begin to come home. These are the resources that we need to seize the initiative, while building the Afghan capacity that can allow for a responsible transition of our forces out of Afghanistan.

Gates rates the surge a temporary success, but acknowledges that a fixed ending date allowed the Taliban to just wait it out, writing,

Thanks to the "Obama surge" in 2010, we actually made significant headway in improving security in the south and east of Afghanistan. But the progress was temporary because, thanks to Obama's deadline, the Taliban knew we would begin pulling out the following year.[234]

In retrospect, Gates believes that the United States should not have remained in Afghanistan in a nation-building capacity in the first place. He writes, "I believe we—and the Afghans—would have been better served had our military departed in 2002 and had we thereafter relied on our nonmilitary instruments of national power, and patience."[235]

Despite its limited scope, the surge was a costly one with a price tag of almost $50 billion yearly,[236] and yet, the Obama surge failed to have a lasting effect. As the *Washington Post* reports:

In 2014, as evidence piled up that Obama's plan was faltering, a senior State Department official told government interviewers that the mission had been unfocused from the start. "I am sick of Obama saying, 'We're sick of war,'" the senior diplomat said. "Only 5 percent of Americans are involved in the war; it doesn't affect most Americans." "If I were to write a book, its [cover] would be: 'America goes to war without knowing why it does,'" she added. "We went in reflexively after 9/11 without knowing what we were trying to achieve. I would like to write a book about having a plan and an endgame before you go in."

The *Post* article also documents that failure to plan for the endgame:

> In March 2011, when he was commander of U.S. and NATO forces, Petraeus estimated there were "somewhere around 25,000 Taliban," according to testimony he gave to Congress. Today, the U.S. military estimates the number has more than doubled—to about 60,000.[237]

KILLING BIN LADEN

Bush's call to take bin Laden "dead or alive" was accomplished on the watch of his successor. Perhaps no military mission was more dramatic or more important to Obama's re-election than the raid on Abbottabad, Pakistan, on May 2, 2011 (May 1 in the United States). There were great risks in undertaking the raid, not the least of which was that the Pakistan government was not informed in advance, given the concern that bin Laden would be tipped off. Obama was mindful of the failed attempt to rescue hostages in Iran in 1980, where helicopters collided and burned, costing Carter his re-election in the opinion of many. According to Panetta, it was Obama who added "two backup helicopters to the mission."[238] It turned out the backups were needed when one of the helicopters was downed and another deviated from the plan. The raid succeeded and the mission's commander, Bill McRaven reported, "Geronimo.... EKIA," shorthand for "Enemy Killed in Action."[239]

That night, at 11:35 in Washington (where it was still May 1), Obama announced the death of bin Laden and transported Americans back to the origin of the war:

> It was nearly 10 years ago that a bright September day was darkened by the worst attack on the American people in our history. The images of 9/11 are seared into our national memory—hijacked planes cutting through a cloudless September sky; the Twin Towers collapsing to the ground; black smoke billowing up from the Pentagon; the wreckage of Flight 93 in Shanksville,

Pennsylvania, where the actions of heroic citizens saved even more heartbreak and destruction.[240]

Obama called on Americans to never forget and sought to bring back, at least for a moment, the unity that had prevailed back on that dark day in September 2001. Of course, the death of bin Laden was more important as a symbol rather than a coda to the "War on Terror." In fact, many of the most difficult days were ahead.

THE RISE OF ISIS

While Afghanistan was once again a major concern of the administration, the war in Iraq was far from over. As noted earlier, Bush had concluded an agreement with the Iraqis to withdraw American forces by 2011 without concluding a Status of Forces agreement to allow some American troops to remain. Gates reports, "Lacking any new agreement, the last 500 American troops crossed the border from Iraq into Kuwait on December 18, 2011. We thought our military involvement in Iraq was over. We were wrong."[241] The failure to keep a significant number of American troops in Iraq is believed by some to be a major factor in the rise of ISIS (also known as ISIL) and their acquiring control over significant parts of Iraq. According to Panetta:

> Over the course of the following two and a half years, the situation in Iraq slowly deteriorated. . . . Meanwhile, with the conflict in Syria raging, an Al Qaeda offshoot—ISIS—or the Islamic State in Iraq and Syria—gained strength. . . . [I]t began to move into Iraq in 2014 . . . . Perhaps most distressing, Iraqi military units cut and ran, unable or unwilling to defend their own country from this new Sunni extremist element.[242]

In early January 2014, ISIS took over Fallujah and Ramadi. Within six months, they also took over the second-largest city, Mosul. Gates writes, "[T]he Iraqi army essentially disintegrated, leaving behind huge quantities of American military equipment."[243] The former Defense Secretary continues,

> Shortly thereafter, on June 19, President Obama sent hundreds of American military advisers back into Iraq, mainly to help plan air strikes. . . . By the time Obama left office in January 2017, the American military presence in Iraq had grown to more than 5,000.[244]

Thus, the man who secured his nomination for president largely because of his opposition to a "dumb war," was compelled to re-engage in that very war.

Although the conventional wisdom is that the withdrawal of American troops is what led to the rise of ISIS, a different narrative is told by William McCants, who served as a State Department senior advisor on countering violent extremism. Relying on primary sources in Arabic, he traces the rise in ISIS to the U.S. invasion of Iraq, which radical Sunnis saw as fulfilling an apocalyptic prophecy: "The U.S. invasion of Iraq and the stupendous violence that followed dramatically increased the Sunni public's appetite for apocalyptic explanations of a world turned upside down."[245] Many Muslim scholars believe in an end-of-times apocalypse. Iraq was prophesized to be the site of the fight between true Muslims and infidels. The founders of ISIS believed "the Shi'a had untied with the Jews and Christians under the banner of the Antichrist to fight against the Sunnis. The Final Hour must be approaching, to be heralded by the rebirth of the caliphate . . . whose return was prophesized."[246] According to McCants, "References to the End Times fill Islamic State propaganda. It's a big selling point with foreign fighters, who want to travel to the lands where the final battles of the apocalypse will take place."[247]

As Obama ended his presidency, he left behind a difficult situation in the Middle East. Despite his efforts to end both wars, neither Afghanistan nor Iraq was at peace. Even one of his signature campaign promises was left unfulfilled. He had vowed to close the prison at Guantanamo Bay, viewed by some as a recruiting tool for terrorists, but congressional restrictions stopped him. He reduced the number of prisoners from 242 to 55, but failed to close the prison.[248]

ASSESSING OBAMA'S NARRATIVE

The Obama narrative required the merging of two conflicting storylines. In his prepresidential years, particularly in his campaign for the Democratic nomination, Obama made it clear that he did not oppose all wars, just "dumb wars." Taking out al Qaeda and its state sponsor, the Taliban, was not a dumb war to Obama, but the war in Iraq was. He writes in his memoir, "Unlike the war in Iraq, the Afghan campaign had always seemed to me a war of necessity."[249] In terms of narrative probability, the *coherence* was clear. We were attacked and taking action against the nation from which those attacks emanated was fair and just. There was little distance between his narrative regarding Afghanistan and Bush's. However, on the subject of Iraq, by the time he was running for president, the war had lost public support. The coherence of his story was in sync with the views of most Americans. In terms of *fidelity* to events on the ground, it appeared America's mission there was ready to end. Obama was helped by Bush's announced agreement to withdraw U.S. forces by the end of 2011, which conveniently was just in time for Obama to begin his re-election bid. However, the need to leave residual troops there was glossed over. One might argue that his administration was not particularly interested in doing so, and thus failure to secure a Status of Forces agreement was actually welcomed, allowing him to proclaim the end of the "dumb war" he had opposed.

In Afghanistan, however, the re-emergence of the Taliban created a different narrative. Unable to withdraw as he had in Iraq, Obama adopted the narrative promoted by his predecessor—a surge of American forces would tame the insurgency and pave the way for America to end its war. The story had *structural and material coherence*—after all it had supposedly worked in Iraq and the same general, David Petraeus, would be in charge. Given his success in Iraq, this also evidenced *characterological coherence*—after all he was a hero of the Iraq war, who had led the surge.

Obama's story regarding Afghanistan reached a dramatic climax when bin Laden was captured and killed. The contrast between the *character* of bin Laden—an admitted mass murderer—and the brave Navy SEALs who killed him was stark. Movie viewers were transported to that triumph in the movie *Zero Dark Thirty*. Obama's narrative seemed on track to finally end the endless war on terror. As he approached his re-election campaign, Obama's story seemed complete—he'd finished the wars started by Bush and restored American supremacy over the terrorists.

Unfortunately for Obama, the *fidelity* of his story was soon to be undone by actual events on the ground. In both Iraq and Afghanistan, the enemy returned. In Iraq, it came in the form of a new group of Islamic extremists—ISIS. In Afghanistan, it came in the return of the supposedly defeated Taliban. As Obama left office after eight years, the wars continued.

Obama clearly was deeply troubled by the costs in human terms of the wars he inherited. He made a habit of visiting the wounded at military hospitals. In his memoir he writes that some criticized his visits as clouding his judgment, but he found them critical to his understanding of the reality of war:

> I was never more clear-eyed than on the flights back from Walter Reed and Bethesda. Clear about the true costs of war, and who bore those costs. Clear about war's folly, the sorry tales we humans collectively store in our heads and pass on from generation to generation—abstractions that fan hate and justify cruelty and force even the righteous among us to participate in carnage. Clear that by virtue of my office, I could not avoid responsibility for lives lost or shattered, even if I somehow justified my decisions by what I perceived to be some larger good.[250]

ENDING FOREVER WARS

When Donald J. Trump took office, he reluctantly added troops and increased the authority of the local commanders in Iraq. As 2017 came to an end, ISIS had lost control of its strongholds.[251] However, as McCants predicted in 2015, "[T]he disappearance of a jihadist statelet doesn't mean the disappearance of the jihadists."[252] Gates acknowledges that ISIS, "remains an enduring threat."[253] The impossibility of defeating terror once and for all demonstrates how Bush's story of the War on Terror could never end in victory. It is ironic that in an effort to fight terrorists, Bush's invasion of Iraq actually encouraged the development of ISIS.

One of the underlying appeals of Trump's "America First" narrative was to those who were tired of forever wars. He had difficulty seeing why the United States was staying in Afghanistan so many years after 9/11. According to Woodward, Trump complained, "There is too much emphasis on terrorism and fighting the old Bush wars." His Secretary of Defense James Mattis answered, "That is so the terrorists can't come after the United States here . . . as happened with the 9/11 attacks."[254] Trump reluctantly kept troops in Afghanistan.

The cost of the Afghanistan War has been great. The *Washington Post* reported at the end of 2019, "Over the past 18 years, more than 775,000 U.S. troops have deployed to Afghanistan, many repeatedly. Of those, 2,300 died there and 20,589 came home wounded, according to Defense Department figures."[255] Finally, on September 12, 2020, nineteen years and a day after the terrorist attacks on New York and the Pentagon, the two sides in the Afghanistan war sat down for peace talks. The negotiations were only possible after Trump agreed to withdraw American troops. The *Washington Post* reports that Trump's own former National Security Advisor H. R. McMaster, "has publicly said that Trump's Afghanistan policy is a 'travesty,' and that his deal with the Taliban constitutes appeasement similar to Europe's accommodation with Adolf Hitler in the Munich agreement of 1938."[256] The belief that appeasement leads to war has continued to resonate, testimony to the enduring impact of the World War II narrative.

On November 3, 2020, Trump lost his bid for re-election and in his final weeks in office, he moved to fulfill his promise to end forever wars. After firing the Defense Secretary, who opposed his action, he announced a dramatic drawdown of troops in both Afghanistan and Iraq. The *New York Times* reported, "The Defense Department recently announced troop withdrawals by Jan. 15 that will reduce American forces in Iraq and Afghanistan to 2,500 each from their one-time highs of some 170,000 and 100,000 troops, respectively."[257] On January 15, the promised reduction to 2,500 troops in Iraq and Afghanistan was completed.[258] However, there were actually about

1,000 more troops in Afghanistan than officially acknowledged, and the *New York Times* reported the total was about 3,500.[259] The *Times* also reported on January 29, 2021, "A report from the U.S. Treasury Department earlier this month indicated that Al Qaeda had only gained strength in Afghanistan and continued its ties with the Taliban throughout 2020."[260]

What Joe Biden would do in Iraq and Afghanistan was not initially clear and a review of U.S. policy options was ordered. Due to a terrible pandemic, a resulting recession, and civil unrest, foreign policy was but a footnote in his campaign. His website vaguely promised, "Biden will end the forever wars in Afghanistan and the Middle East, which have cost us untold blood and treasure."[261] After opposing the first Gulf War, Joe Biden voted in favor of the 2002 resolution to invade Iraq, a war he later came to oppose. As vice president, he argued against Obama's surge of troops in Afghanistan, preferring to concentrate on counter-terrorism rather than counter-insurgency and nation building. In mid-April, shortly before the deadline negotiated by Trump, Biden's plan was finally announced. The *Washington Post* reported,

> President Biden will withdraw all American troops from Afghanistan over the coming months, people familiar with the plans said, completing the military exit by the 20th anniversary of the Sept. 11, 2001, attacks that first drew the United States into its longest war.[262]

In fact, the withdrawal came even sooner. The *New York Times* reported on May 25 that United States and NATO troops would fully withdraw ahead of Biden's deadline.[263] Thus, twenty years after the attacks that led to the invasion and occupation of Afghanistan, America's longest war finally ended.

ARE THE FOREVER WARS REALLY OVER?

Although President Biden withdrew the last troops from Afghanistan as this book is written, the end of the forever wars is not certain. Just as he learned as vice president, it is difficult for a president to withstand public opposition from the military. In fact, that lesson was probably as true for Truman in firing MacArthur as for Obama in trying to resist the call for a surge in Afghanistan. The last U.S. commander in Afghanistan, General Austin Miller, stated at a press conference on June 29, 2001, "Civil war is certainly a path that can be visualized if it continues on the trajectory it's on . . . . That should be a concern for the world." The *New York Times* goes on to report, "With some intelligence estimates saying that the Afghan government could fall in six months to two years after a final American withdrawal, General

Miller's comments were a window into recent tension between the White House and the Pentagon."[264] Intelligence estimates were overly optimistic, and the Taliban prevailed in mid-August.

In Iraq itself, the United States continues to face military challenges for its remaining 2,500 troops. As of mid-2021, there had been at least five drone attacks on U.S. military personnel. On June 27, according to the *Washington Post*, "U.S. forces launched airstrikes on facilities on both sides of the Iraq-Syria border, the Pentagon said Sunday, in response to recent drone attacks on U.S. troops in the region carried out by Iran-backed militias."[265] Thus, the future of the "War on Terror" remains uncertain. Whether America's forever wars have finally ended is a story that remains to be told.

CONCLUSION

George W. Bush did not enter office with any particular agenda to take out Saddam Hussein. But in the wake of September 11, it was no longer enough to deter enemies; Bush believed they had to be defeated before they could attack. In a battle between good and evil, there could be no compromise. So when the Taliban government of Afghanistan was ousted and the people rejoiced at their liberation, Bush turned his attention to other sources of evil. Because of his father's successful demonization of Saddam, it was not difficult to persuade the American people the Iraqi dictator posed a threat.

As he proclaimed the end of major combat in Iraq, however, Bush faced a contradiction. If the mission was accomplished, why were Americans continuing to die? If U.S. soldiers were liberators, why were they greeted by IEDs instead of celebrations in the streets? Bush created a rhetorical expectation that failed to be fulfilled in the months that followed his carrier landing. It was not the lack of weapons of mass destruction that vexed the second Bush regime, but the unfulfilled promise of its own rhetoric. Was going to war in Iraq a mistake? Jean Edward Smith argues that it was "easily the worst foreign policy decision ever made by an American president."[266]

As new challenges such as the Covid-19 pandemic and the associated recession have arisen, 9/11 seems a distant memory even for those alive at the time. The *Washington Post's* Ishaan Tharoor has suggested that the era of 9/11 is over. He writes on the eve of the nineteenth anniversary of the attacks, "But in many ways, 9/11—and the epochal conflagration that followed—feels distant." A RAND Corporation study found, "These multiple missions strained the capacity of the United States. None was completed satisfactorily."[267] This view seems to be similar to that expressed by former deputy national security advisor Ben Rhodes, writing in the *Atlantic*, "[I]t is time to finally end the chapter of our history that began on September 11, 2001."[268] Few families are affected by war because of the volunteer military. Risen writes, "Only a small slice of society . . . fight and die."[269] In fact, by 2018, only about one percent of the U.S. population had served in either war.[270] Thus, these wars have slipped to near the bottom of the public's agenda.

Another reason for the public's lack of interest in the war is the lack of U.S. casualties, which is partly the result of the lethality of drone attacks. Risen writes, "The drone is the ultimate imperial weapon, allowing a superpower almost unlimited reach while keeping its own soldiers far from the battle."[271] Jessy J. Ohl agrees,

> Drone technologies and boring visual rhetoric lubricate the gears of war by compressing the need for sophisticated forms of public reception, participation, and approval. By asking less and less of the citizenry, the low level yet unending violence of light war is ultimately free to do much more.[272]

Of course, that is a double-edged sword, as drones and airstrikes often cause casualties beyond the intended targets. According to the *Washington Post*, "Civilian deaths at the hands of U.S. forces have been a powerful rallying cry for anti-American and anti-Afghan government sentiment during the two decades of war."[273]

It seems obvious that it was not the war George W. Bush's narrative promised. There has been no ultimate victory—no surrender on the battleship *Missouri*. The attacks of 9/11 may have resembled Pearl Harbor, but the ensuing wars have been nothing like World War II. Hopefully, the American public has learned from these wars that, as George Ball warned about Vietnam, "Once on the tiger's back we cannot be sure of picking the place to dismount."[274]

NOTES

1. Garrett M. Graff, "The Children of 9/11 Are About to Vote," *Politico Magazine*, September 11, 2020, https://www.politico.com/news/magazine/2020/09/11/september-eleven-children-vote-410829.

2. *Time*, October 21–28, 2019, cover.

3. Elliot Ackerman, "Born Into War," *Time*, October 21–28, 2019, 45.

4. Quoted in Bob Woodward, *Rage* (New York: Simon & Shuster, 2020), [page] 260, Kindle.

5. Richard A. Clark, *Against All Enemies: Inside America's War on Terror* (New York: Free Press, 2004), 59.

6. George W. Bush, "Remarks by the President After Two Planes Crash Into World Trade Center," September 11, 2001, accessed August 10, 2020, https://georgewbush-whitehouse.archives.gov/news/releases/2001/09/20010911.html.

7. George W. Bush, *Decision Points* (New York: Crown Publishers, 2010), 128.

8. George W. Bush, "Remarks by the President upon Arrival at Barksdale Air Force Base," September 11, 2001, accessed August 10, 2020, https://georgewbush-whitehouse.archives.gov/news/releases/2001/09/text/20010912-2.html.

9. Donald Rumsfeld, *Known and Unknown: A Memoir* (New York: Sentinel, 2011), 342.

10. David Frum, *The Right Man: The Surprise Presidency of George W. Bush* (New York: Random House, 2003), 119.

11. Bush, *Decision Points*, 137.

12. Robert Draper, *Dead Certain: The Presidency of George W. Bush* (New York: Free Press, 2007), 147.

13. Frum, *Right Man*, 133.

14. George W. Bush, "Statement by the President in His Address to the Nation," September 11, 2001, accessed August 8, 2020, https://georgewbush-whitehouse.archives.gov/news/releases/2001/09/20010911-16.html.

15. Bush, *Decision Points*, 137.

16. Frum, *The Right Man*, 142.

17. Frum, *The Right Man*, 141 (italics in original).

18. Bush, *Decision Points*, 128.

19. Jean Edward Smith, *Bush* (New York: Simon and Shuster, 2016), 229.

20. Rumsfeld, *Known and Unknown*, 352–353.

21. Rumsfeld, *Known and Unknown*, 353.

22. Rumsfeld, *Known and Unknown*, 351 (italics added).

23. Smith, *Bush*, 231.

24. George W. Bush, "President's Remarks at National Day of Prayer and Remembrance," September 14, 2001, accessed August 10, 2020, https://georgewbush-whitehouse.archives.gov/news/releases/2001/09/20010914-2.html.

25. George W. Bush, "President Bush Salutes Heroes in New York," September 14, 2001, accessed August 10, 2020, https://georgewbush-whitehouse.archives.gov/news/releases/2001/09/20010914-9.html.

26. Richard F. Grimmett, "Authorization for Use of Military Force in Response to the 9/11 Attacks (P.L. 107-40): Legislative History," CRS Report for Congress, January 16, 2007, https://fas.org/sgp/crs/natsec/RS22357.pdf.

27. George W. Bush, "Remarks by President Upon Arrival [at the South Lawn]," September 16, 2001, accessed August 10, 2020, https://georgewbush-whitehouse.archives.gov/news/releases/2001/09/20010916-2.html.

28. Smith, *Bush*, 229.

29. "Bush: Bin Laden Wanted Dead or Alive," *ABC News*, September 17, 2001, updated January 7, 2006, accessed October 15, 2020, https://abcnews.go.com/US/story?id=92483&page=1.

30. Rumsfeld, *Known and Unknown*, 402–403.

31. Rumsfeld, *Known and Unknown*, 360.

32. Draper, *Dead Certain*, 147 (italics in original).
33. George W. Bush, "'Islam is Peace' Says President," September 17, 2001, accessed August 10, 2020, https://georgewbush-whitehouse.archives.gov/news/releases/2001/09/20010917-11.html.
34. Erin Steuter and Deborah Wills, *At War with Metaphor: Media, Propaganda, and Racism in the War on Terror* (Lanham, MD: Lexington Books, 2008, pb edition 2009), 100.
35. Steuter and Wills, *At War with Metaphor*, 136 (Koran spelling in original).
36. Steuter and Wills, *At War with Metaphor*, 191.
37. Quoted in Steuter and Wills, *At War with Metaphor*, 192.
38. Steuter and Wills, *At War with Metaphor*, 192.
39. Bob Woodward, *Bush at War* (New York, Simon & Schuster, 2002), 107.
40. Frum, *The Right Man*, 135.
41. George W. Bush, "Address to a Joint Session of Congress and the American People," 20 September 20, 2001, accessed August 8, 2020, https://georgewbush-whitehouse.archives.gov/news/releases/2001/09/20010920-8.html.
42. Bush, "Address to a Joint Session of Congress and the American People."
43. Bush, "Address to a Joint Session of Congress and the American People."
44. Gallup, "Presidential Approval Ratings—George W. Bush," accessed August 21, 2020, https://news.gallup.com/poll/116500/presidential-approval-ratings-george-bush.aspx.
45. Jeffery M. Jones, "Who Had the Highest Gallup Presidential Job Approval Rating?" Gallup, December 17, 2019, https://news.gallup.com/poll/271628/highest-gallup-presidential-job-approval-rating.aspx.
46. Clark, *Against All Enemies*, 286.
47. Jeremy Engels and William O. Saas, "On Acquiescence and Ends-Less War: An Inquiry into the New War Rhetoric," *Quarterly Journal of Speech* 99, no. 2 (May 2013): 227, https//doi.org/10.1080/00335630.2013.775705.
48. Rumsfeld, *Known and Unknown*, 360.
49. Woodward, *Bush at War*, 134–135.
50. Rumsfeld, *Known and Unknown*, 374.
51. George W. Bush, "Presidential Address to the Nation," October 7, 2001, accessed August 10, 2020, https://georgewbush-whitehouse.archives.gov/news/releases/2001/10/20011007-8.html.
52. Bush, *Decision Points*, 201.
53. Rumsfeld, *Known and Unknown*, 400.
54. Quoted in Rumsfeld, *Known and Unknown*, 408.
55. Robert M. Gates, *Exercise of Power: American Failures, Successes, and a New Path Forward in the Post-Cold War World* (New York: Alfred A. Knopf, 2020), loc. 3041 of 7416, Kindle.
56. Gates, *Exercise of Power*, loc. 3047 of 7416.
57. Craig Whitlock, "At War with the Truth," *Washington Post*, December 9, 2019, https://www.washingtonpost.com/graphics/2019/investigations/afghanistan-papers/afghanistan-war-confidential-documents/?wpisrc=pw_ret_afghanistan_20191210.

58. Whitlock, "At War."
59. Whitlock, "At War."
60. Daniel P. Bolger, *Why We Lost: A General's Inside Account of the Iraq and Afghanistan Wars* (New York: Houghton Mifflin Harcourt, 2014), 19.
61. Bolger, *Why We Lost*, 45.
62. Clark, *Against All Enemies*, 245.
63. George F. Will, "We've been in Afghanistan for 6,000 days. What are we doing?" *Washington Post*, March 9, 2018, https://www.washingtonpost.com/opinions/can-someone-please-explain-what-were-doing-in-afghanistan/2018/03/09/a6a6e91e-230c-11e8-86f6-54bfff693d2b_story.html.
64. Clark, *Against All Enemies*, 30.
65. Woodward, *Bush at War*, 49.
66. Woodward, *Bush at War*, 99.
67. Rumsfeld, *Known and Unknown*, 425.
68. Bob Woodward, *State of Denial* (New York: Simon & Schuster, 2006), 81.
69. Woodward, *State of Denial*, 89.
70. Christopher Scheer, Robert Scheer, and Lakshimi Chaudhry, *The Five Biggest Lies Bush Told Us About Iraq* (New York: Akashic Books and Seven Stories Press, 2003), 30.
71. Frum, *The Right Man*, 238.
72. George W. Bush, "President Delivers State of the Union Address," January 29, 2002, accessed August 10, 2020, https://georgewbush-whitehouse.archives.gov/news/releases/2002/01/20020129-11.html.
73. Quoted in Draper, *Dead Certain*, 178.
74. Quoted in Woodward, *State of Denial*, 151.
75. Ken Adelman, "Cakewalk in Iraq," *Washington Post*, February 13, 2002, https://www.washingtonpost.com/archive/opinions/2002/02/13/cakewalk-in-iraq/cf09301c-c6c4-4f2e-8268-7c93017f5e93/.
76. Draper, *Dead Certain*, 176.
77. Woodward, *Bush at War*, 330.
78. Sheldon Rampton and John Stauber, *Weapons of Mass Deception: The Uses of Propaganda in Bush's War on Iraq* (New York: Tarcher/Penguin, 2003), [page] 48, Kindle.
79. George W. Bush, "President's Remarks at the United Nations General Assembly," September 12, 2002, accessed August 11, 2020, https://georgewbush-whitehouse.archives.gov/news/releases/2002/09/20020912-1.html.
80. Bush, *Decision Points*, 238.
81. Bush, "President's Remarks at the United Nations General Assembly."
82. Steuter and Wills, *At War with Metaphor*, 14.
83. George W. Bush, "President Bush Outlines Iraqi Threat," October 7, 2002, accessed August 11, 2020, https://georgewbush-whitehouse.archives.gov/news/releases/2002/10/20021007-8.html (italics added).
84. Smith, *Bush*, 316.
85. Woodward, *State of Denial*, 97.
86. Rampton and Stauber, *Weapons of Mass Deception*, 78.

87. Smith, *Bush*, 323.

88. George W. Bush, "President Signs Iraq Resolution," October 16, 2002. accessed August 11, 2020, https://georgewbush-whitehouse.archives.gov/news/releases/2002/10/20021016-1.html.

89. Woodward, *Bush at War*, 351.

90. Office of the Press Secretary, "Joint Resolution to Authorize the Use of United States Armed Forces Against Iraq," October 2, 2002, accessed August 11, 2020, https://georgewbush-whitehouse.archives.gov/news/releases/2002/10/20021002-2.html.

91. Walter Pincus, "Bush Recantation of Iraq Claim Stirs Calls for Probes," *Washington Post (1974-Current File)*, July 09, 2003, accessed August 10, 2020, http://mantis.csuchico.edu/login?url=https://search-proquest-com.mantis.csuchico.edu/docview/2267467562?accountid=10346.

92. George W. Bush, "State of the Union Address by President George W. Bush," January 28, 2003, accessed August 11, 2020, https://georgewbush-whitehouse.archives.gov/news/releases/2003/01/20030128-19.html.

93. Smith, *Bush*, 351.

94. Colin Powell, "U.S. Secretary of State Colin Powell Addresses the U.N. Security Council," February 5, 2003, accessed August 9, 2020, https://georgewbush-whitehouse.archives.gov/news/releases/2003/02/20030205-1.html.

95. Bush, *Decision Points*, 242.

96. Quoted in Woodward, *State of Denial*, 304.

97. Susan A. Brewer, *Why America Fights: Patriotism and War Propaganda from the Philippines to Iraq* (New York: Oxford University Press, 2009), 245.

98. Smith, *Bush*, 344.

99. Robert Draper, "Colin Powell Still Wants Answers," *New York Times Magazine*, July 16, 2020, https://www.nytimes.com/2020/07/16/magazine/colin-powell-iraq-war.html.

100. Quoted in Scheer, Scheer, and Chaudhry, *Five Biggest Lies*, 81.

101. O'Shaughnessy, *Politics and Propaganda*, 221.

102. Clark, *Against All Enemies*, 267.

103. Clark, *Against All Enemies*, 267.

104. Maureen Dowd, "The Xanax Cowboy," *New York Times*, March 9, 2003, https://www.nytimes.com/2003/03/09/opinion/the-xanax-cowboy.html?searchResultPosition=1.

105. William Greider, "Washington Post Warriors," *Nation*, March 6, 2003, https://www.thenation.com/article/archive/washington-post-warriors/.

106. Smith, *Bush*, 345.

107. Quoted in Smith, *Bush*, 345.

108. Smith, *Bush*, 250.

109. Scheer, Scheer, and Chaudhry, *Five Biggest Lies*, 104.

110. "Statement of the Atlantic Summit: A Vision for Iraq and the Iraqi People," March 16, 2003, accessed August 11, 2020, https://georgewbush-whitehouse.archives.gov/news/releases/2003/03/20030316-1.html.

111. Rampton and Stauber, *Weapons of Mass Deception*, 117.

112. Bill Moyers, "Buying the War: How Big Media Failed Us," *Bill Moyers Journal*, April 25, 2007, June 19, 2014 [Transcript], https://billmoyers.com/content/buying-the-war/.

113. James Fallows, "The Iraq War and the Inevitability of Ignorance," *Atlantic*, March 20, 2018, https://www.theatlantic.com/international/archive/2018/03/iraq-war-anniversary-fifty-first-state/555986/.

114. Rumsfeld, *Known and Unknown*, 459.

115. Bill Moyers, "Buying the War."

116. Rampton and Stauber, *Weapons of Mass Deception*, 171.

117. Deepa Kumar, "Media, War, and Propaganda: Strategies of Information Management During the 2003 Iraq War," *Communication and Critical/Cultural Studies* 3, no.1 (2006): 59, https://doi.org/10.1080/14791420500505650.

118. Moyers, "Buying the War."

119. James Risen, *Pay Any Price: Greed, Power, and Endless War* (New York: Houghton Mifflin Harcourt, 2014), 271.

120. Brewer, *Why America Fights*, 248.

121. Brewer, *Why America Fights*, 244.

122. Steven Kull, "Misperceptions, the Media and the Iraq War," The Pipa/Knowledge Networks Poll, October 2, 2003, https://worldpublicopinion.net/wp-content/uploads/2017/12/IraqMedia_Oct03_rpt.pdf.

123. Steuter and Wills, *At War with Metaphor*, 175.

124. Paul Achter, "Rhetoric and the Permanent War," *Quarterly Journal of Speech* 102, no. 1 (February 2016): 89, https://doi.org/10.1080/00335630.2016.1135544.

125. George W. Bush, "President Bush Addresses the Nation," March 19, 2003, accessed August 11, 2020, https://georgewbush-whitehouse.archives.gov//news/releases/2003/03/20030319-17.html.

126. Frank Davis, "Many Confused on Weapons and Terror, Polls Find," *Sacramento Bee*, June 15, 2003, A18.

127. Bob Woodward, *Plan of Attack* (New York: Simon & Schuster, 2004), 102.

128. Phillip Knightley, *The First Casualty: The War Correspondent as Hero and Myth-Maker from the Crimea to Iraq*, 3rd ed. (Baltimore and London: John Hopkins University Press, 2004), 531.

129. Knightley, *The First Casualty*, 531.

130. Nicholas Jackson O'Shaughnessy, *Politics and Propaganda: Weapons of Mass Seduction* (Ann Arbor: University of Michigan Press, 2004), 212.

131. Knightley, *The First Casualty*, 535.

132. Rumsfeld, *Known and Unknown*, 465.

133. Kumar, "Media, War, and Propaganda," 63.

134. Rampton and Stauber, *Weapons of Mass Deception*, 180.

135. Knightley, *The First Casualty*, 543–545.

136. Rumsfeld, *Known and Unknown*, 462–463.

137. Rumsfeld, *Known and Unknown*, 463.

138. "Jessica Lynch: I'm No Hero," ABC News, November 6, 2003, updated January 6, 2006, https://abcnews.go.com/Primetime/story?id=132434.

139. Rumsfeld, *Known and Unknown*, 468–469.

140. Smith, *Bush*, 361.
141. Rampton and Stauber, *Weapons of Mass Deception*, 3.
142. Scheer, Scheer, and Chaudhry, *Five Biggest Lies*, 126.
143. Scheer, Scheer, and Chaudhry, *Five Biggest Lies*, 130.
144. Quoted in Woodward, *State of Denial*, 164.
145. Elisabeth Bumiller, "Keepers of Bush Image Lift Stagecraft to New Heights," *New York Times*, May 16, 2003, http://www.nytimes.com/2003/05/16/politics/16IMAG.html.
146. Quoted in Woodward, *State of Denial*, 186.
147. George W. Bush, "President Bush Announces Combat Operations in Iraq Have Ended," May 1, 2003, accessed August 11, 2020, https://georgewbush-whitehouse.archives.gov/news/releases/2003/05/20030501-6.html.
148. Clark, *Against All Enemies*, 268.
149. Bush, "President Bush Announces Combat Operations in Iraq Have Ended."
150. Draper, *Dead Certain*, 388.
151. David W. Moore, "Little Concern About Lack of WMD in Iraq," Gallup News Service, June 4, 2003, https://news.gallup.com/poll/8566/little-concern-about-lack-wmd-iraq.aspx.
152. John Stauber, "Half of Americans Still Believe In WMDs—They Saw Them on TV," *PR Watch*, August 8, 2006, https://www.prwatch.org/news/2006/08/5067/half-americans-still-believe-wmds-they-saw-them-tv.
153. Fareed Zakaria, "Exaggerating the Threats," *Newsweek*, June 16, 2003, 33.
154. "Most Expect U.S. to Be Bogged Down in Iraq, Poll Says," *Greensboro News and Record*, August 23, 2003, updated January 24, 2015, https://greensboro.com/most-expect-u-s-to-be-bogged-down-in-iraq/article_1dead32a-96b3-5145-ba9b-f3388c847abc.html.
155. "U.S. Postwar Deaths Equal Iraq Combat Toll," *Sacramento Bee*, August 26, 2003, A1.
156. Woodward, *State of Denial*, 336.
157. Smith, *Bush*, 589.
158. Rampton and Stauber, *Weapons of Mass Deception*, 204.
159. Bolger, *Why We Lost*, 117.
160. Bush, *Decision Points*, 262.
161. Paul Krugman, "Errors and Lies," *New York Times*, May 18, 2015, https://www.nytimes.com/2015/05/18/opinion/paul-krugman-errors-and-lies.html?_r=0.
162. Woodward, *State of Denial*, 489 (italics in original).
163. Woodward, *State of Denial*, 491.
164. Draper, *Dead Certain*, 209.
165. Quoted in Draper, *Dead Certain*, 209.
166. Woodward, *State of Denial*, 261.
167. Rumsfeld, *Known and Unknown*, 711.
168. Bush, *Decision Points*, 358–359.
169. Mark Mazzetti, "Spy Agencies Say Iraq War Worsens Terrorism Threat," *New York Times*, September 24, 2006, https://www.nytimes.com/2006/09/24/world/middleeast/24terror.html.

170. Clark, *Against All Enemies*, 246.
171. Clark, *Against All Enemies*, 273.
172. Bolger, *Why We Lost*, 157.
173. Bolger, *Why We Lost*, 177.
174. Bolger, *Why We Lost*, 179.
175. Bolger, *Why We Lost*, 182.
176. Zachary Justus, "Torture as Text: The Rhetoric of Abu Ghraib," (Master's thesis, California State University, Chico, 2005), 67.
177. Woodward, *State of Denial*, 86.
178. "Guantanamo Bay Fast Facts," CNN, October 7, 2020, accessed October 17, 2020, https://www.cnn.com/2013/09/09/world/guantanamo-bay-naval-station-fast-facts/index.html.
179. Bob Woodward, *Obama's Wars* (New York: Simon & Shuster, 2010), 106.
180. Leon Panetta with Jim Newton, *Worthy Fights: A Memoir of Leadership in War and Peace* (New York: Penguin Press, 2014), 222.
181. Risen, *Pay Any Price*, 165.
182. Risen, *Pay Any Price*, 168.
183. Rumsfeld, *Known and Unknown*, 545.
184. Justus, "Torture as Text," 73.
185. Risen, *Pay Any Price*, 173.
186. Bob Woodward, *The War Within: A Secret White House History 2006–2008* (New York, Simon & Schuster, 2008), 19.
187. Michael Safi, "Trump Pardons Blackwater Contractors Jailed for Massacre of Iraq Civilians," *Guardian*, December 23, 2020, https://www.theguardian.com/world/2020/dec/23/trump-pardons-blackwater-contractors-jailed-for-massacre-of-iraq-civilians.
188. Mustafa Salim and Louisa Loveluck, "In Iraq, Trump's Blackwater Pardons Meet With Cynicism, Fatigue," *Washington Post*, December 23, 2020, https://www.washingtonpost.com/world/middle_east/iraq-blackwater-military-contractors-pardons/2020/12/23/062ee814-44bb-11eb-ac2a-3ac0f2b8ceeb_story.html.
189. George W. Bush, "Inaugural Address by President George W. Bush," January 20, 2005, accessed August 28, 2020, https://georgewbush-whitehouse.archives.gov/news/releases/2005/01/20050120-3.html.
190. Woodward, *State of Denial*, 378.
191. Quoted in Draper, *Dead Certain*, 289.
192. Quoted in Woodward, *State of Denial*, 397.
193. Woodward, *State of Denial*, 421.
194. George W. Bush, "President Visits Troops at Brooke Army Medical Center," January 1, 2006, accessed August 28, 2020, https://georgewbush-whitehouse.archives.gov/news/releases/2006/01/20060101.html.
195. Draper, *Dead Certain*, 383.
196. Bush, *Decision Points*, 361.
197. Rumsfeld, *Known and Unknown*, 692.
198. Rumsfeld, *Known and Unknown*, 693.
199. Woodward, *The War Within*, 5.

200. George W. Bush, "President's Address to the Nation," September 11, 2006, accessed August 28, 2020, https://georgewbush-whitehouse.archives.gov/news/releases/2006/09/20060911-3.html.
201. George W. Bush, "Press Conference by the President," October 11, 2006, accessed August 28, 2020, https://georgewbush-whitehouse.archives.gov/news/releases/2006/10/20061011-5.html.
202. Draper, *Dead Certain*, 409.
203. George W. Bush, "President's Address to the Nation," January 10, 2007, accessed August 28, 2020, https://georgewbush-whitehouse.archives.gov/news/releases/2007/01/20070110-7.html.
204. Gates, *Exercise of Power*, loc. 3648 of 7416.
205. Draper, *Dead Certain*, 410.
206. Bush, *Decision Points*, 367.
207. Bush, *Decision Points*, 385.
208. Smith, *Bush*, 597.
209. Smith, *Bush*, 645.
210. Woodward, *The War Within*, 428 (brackets in original).
211. Rumsfeld, *Known and Unknown*, 682.
212. Rumsfeld, *Known and Unknown*, 687.
213. Bolger, *Why We Lost*, 52.
214. Bolger, *Why We Lost*, 95.
215. Scheer, Scheer, and Chaudhry, *Five Biggest Lies*, 124.
216. Smith, *Bush*, 603.
217. Rumsfeld, *Known and Unknown*, 500.
218. Ben Rhodes, "The 9/11 Era Is Over," *Atlantic*, April 6, 2020, https://www.theatlantic.com/ideas/archive/2020/04/its-not-september-12-anymore/609502/.
219. Barack Obama, "Transcript: Obama's Speech Against The Iraq War," October 2, 2002, posted January 20, 2009 on NPR website, https://www.npr.org/templates/story/story.php?storyId=99591469.
220. Woodward, *Obama's Wars*, 3.
221. Barack Obama, *A Promised Land*, (New York: Crown, 2020), [page] 154, Kindle.
222. Woodward, *Obama's Wars*, 77.
223. Woodward, *Obama's Wars*, 83.
224. Quoted in Smith, *Bush*, 604.
225. Quoted in Woodward, *Obama's Wars*, 259.
226. Helene Cooper, "Putting Stamp on Afghan War, Obama Will Send 17,000 Troops," *New York Times*, February 17, 2009, https://www.nytimes.com/2009/02/18/washington/18web-troops.html.
227. Obama, *Promised Land*, 434.
228. Panetta, *Worthy Fights*, 255.
229. Quoted in Woodward, *Obama's Wars*, 247.
230. Gates, *Exercise of Power*, loc. 3069 of 7416.
231. Obama, *Promised Land*, 443.

232. Whitlock, "Stranded."
233. Barack Obama, "Remarks by the President in Address to the Nation on the Way Forward in Afghanistan and Pakistan," December 1, 2009, accessed September 19, 2020, https://obamawhitehouse.archives.gov/photos-and-video/video/president-obama-way-forward-afghanistan-and-pakistan#transcript.
234. Gates, *Exercise of Power*, loc. 3124 of 7416.
235. Gates, *Exercise of Power*, loc. 3292 of 7416.
236. Panetta, *Worthy Fights*, 370.
237. Craig Whitlock, "Stranded Without a Strategy," *Washington Post*, December 9, 2019, https://www.washingtonpost.com/graphics/2019/investigations/afghanistan-papers/afghanistan-war-strategy/?tid=bottom_nav (brackets in original).
238. Panetta, *Worthy Fights*, 315.
239. Panetta, *Worthy Fights*, 324.
240. Barack Obama, "Osama Bin Laden Dead," May 2, 2011, accessed September 21, 2020, https://obamawhitehouse.archives.gov/blog/2011/05/02/osama-bin-laden-dead.
241. Gates, *Exercise of Power*, loc. 3763 of 7416.
242. Panetta, *Worthy Fights*, 394.
243. Gates, *Exercise of Power*, loc. 3764 of 7416.
244. Gates, *Exercise of Power*, loc. 3769 of 7416.
245. William McCants, *The ISIS Apocalypse: The History, Strategy, and Doomsday Vision of the Islamic State* (New York: St. Martin's Press, 2015), 145.
246. McCants, *ISIS Apocalypse*, 146.
247. McCants, *ISIS Apocalypse*, 147.
248. "Why Obama Failed to Close Guantanamo," PBS Newshour, January 14, 2017, https://www.pbs.org/newshour/show/obama-failed-close-guantanamo.
249. Obama, *Promised Land*, 315.
250. Obama, *Promised Land*, 325.
251. Gates, *Exercise of Power*, loc. 3774 of 7416.
252. McCants, *ISIS Apocalypse*, 158.
253. Gates, *Exercise of Power*, loc. 6448 of 7416.
254. Bob Woodward, *Rage*, 109.
255. Whitlock, "Stranded."
256. Josh Rogin, "McMaster Says Trump's Taliban Deal Is Munich-Like Appeasement," *Washington Post*, October 19, 2020, https://www.washingtonpost.com/opinions/2020/10/19/mcmaster-says-trumps-taliban-deal-is-munich-like-appeasement/.
257. Timothy Kudo, "Two Costly Wars, and a Legacy of Shame," *New York Times*, November 24, 2020, https://www.nytimes.com/2020/11/24/opinion/iraq-afghanistan-troop-withdrawal.html?campaign_id=9&emc=edit_nn_20201124&instance_id=24415&nl=the-mornin%E2%80%A6.
258. "US Downsizes Its Troops in Afghanistan to 2500," *Aljazeera* [English], January 15, 2021, https://www.aljazeera.com/news/2021/1/15/us-meets-its-goal-of-downsizing-in-afghanistan-to-2500-troops.

259. Thomas Gibbons-Neff, Helene Cooper, and Eric Schmitt, "U.S. Has 1000 More Troops in Afghanistan Than It Disclosed," *New York Times*, March 14, 2021, https://www.nytimes.com/2021/03/14/world/asia/us-troops-afghanistan.html.

260. Adam Nossiter and Thomas Gibbons-Neff, "Violence May Delay U.S. Troop Withdrawal from Afghanistan," *New York Times*, January 29, 2021, https://www.nytimes.com/2021/01/29/world/asia/afghanistan-withdrawal-ghani-biden.html.

261. "The Power of America's Example: The Biden Plan for Leading the Democratic World to Meet the Challenges of the 21st Century," accessed November 7, 2020, https://joebiden.com/americanleadership/.

262. Missy Ryan and Karen DeYoung, "Biden Will Withdraw All U.S. Forces from Afghanistan by September 11, 2021," *Washington Post*, April 13, 2021, https://www.washingtonpost.com/national-security/biden-us-troop-withdrawal-afghanistan/2021/04/13/918c3cae-9beb-11eb-8a83-3bc1fa69c2e8_story.html.

263. Thomas Gibbons-Neff, Eric Schmitt, and Helene Cooper, "Pentagon Accelerates Withdrawal from Afghanistan," *New York Times*, May 25, 2021, https://www.nytimes.com/2021/05/25/us/politics/us-afghanistan-withdrawal.html.

264. Thomas Gibbons-Neff and Eric Schmitt, "Security in Afghanistan Is Decaying, U.S. General Says as Forces Leave," *New York Times*, June 29, 2021, updated June 30, 2021, https://www.nytimes.com/2021/06/29/world/asia/afghanistan-civil-war-miller.html.

265. Alex Horton, Louisa Loveluck, and John Hudson, "U.S. Targets Iran-Backed Militias in Iraq, Syria Strikes," *Washington Post*, June 28, 2021, https://www.washingtonpost.com/national-security/2021/06/27/us-airstrike-iraq-syria/.

266. Smith, *Bush*, 660.

267. Ishaan Tharoor, "Is the 9/11 Era Over?" *Washington Post*, September 10, 2020, https://www.washingtonpost.com/world/2020/09/11/is-911-era-over/.

268. Rhodes, "The 9/11 Era Is Over."

269. Risen, *Pay Any Price*, xv.

270. Fallows, "The Iraq War."

271. Risen, *Pay Any Price*, 130.

272. Jessy J. Ohl, "Nothing to See or Fear: Light War and the Boring Visual Rhetoric of U.S. Drone Imagery," *Quarterly Journal of Speech* 101, no. 4 (November 2015): 625, https://doi.org/10.1080/00335630.2015.1128115.

273. Susannah George, "As U.S. Air War in Afghanistan Surged, Investigations into Civilian Harm Plunged," *Washington Post*, September 4, 2020, https://www.washingtonpost.com/world/2020/09/04/afghanistan-civilian-casualties-us-airstrikes/?arc404=true.

274. Quoted in Stanley Karnow, *Vietnam: A History*, revised updated edition (New York: Penguin, 1997), 420.

Chapter 10

Conclusion

Recurring War Stories

Over 120 years ago, the explosion that rocked the USS *Maine* in Havana not only provided the war that William Randolph Hearst sought, it ushered in a new era in American war propaganda. Although there had been multiple wars on American and adjacent soil, this was the first to take Americans halfway around the world. And as America defeated the Spanish, it also became a colonial power, acquiring the Philippines, Puerto Rico, Guam, and Hawaii. A nation founded by a revolution against the colonial power of Britain joined the empires of Europe in waging war to gain control of distant territories. Thus began over a century of wars and the propaganda campaigns that sold them to America.

People are transported by the stories they find probable and that ring true to their own experiences and beliefs. Stories that have *narrative probability* and *fidelity* are the propagandist's best friend. Sometimes the stories are self-evidently true—the Japanese Empire attacked the U.S. fleet moored at Pearl Harbor on December 7, 1941. The enemy was obvious, and when Germany and Italy joined the war on the side of the Japanese, Roosevelt didn't need to convince Americans that they were in a war for survival. Yet, the story was retold through propaganda such as Capra's *Why We Fight* films. Additionally, the story of the war became a staple not just of that era's cinema but also films to this very day—from *Saving Private Ryan* to *Schindler's List* to *Dunkirk*. World War II became the "good war" fought by the "greatest generation." It also became the template for several subsequent wars. Both Presidents Bush recast the role of Hitler as Saddam Hussein. For George W. Bush, Pearl Harbor was replaced with the attacks of 9/11. The story that sold America on these wars was lifted directly from the plot and cast of characters in World War II.

The narratives underlying America's wars typically have strong *narrative probability*. There is almost always a *structural coherence* that rests on some pivotal event—the sinking of the *Maine* or the *Lusitania*, the attacks on Pearl Harbor and American destroyers in the Gulf of Tonkin, and the hijacked airliners crashing into the World Trade Center and Pentagon. Such events are widely known, and there is a predisposition to believe the propagandist's story of who committed such unthinkable acts. *Material coherence* is often grounded in similar acts by the same villains. For example, it was not hard to believe that Saddam was involved in 9/11 after his ruthless invasion of Kuwait a decade earlier and his long war against Iran. Hitler's attacks on Germany's weaker neighbors were reminiscent of the Kaiser's World War I invasion of Belgium. And so it goes, the public has very little reason to doubt the official version of events when the *characterological coherence* of the story's villain is well established. The Kaiser, Hitler, the Communists, Saddam, and Osama bin Laden all were villains of the first order. Hitler became the archetypical villain in subsequent wars. Truman, Johnson, and both Bushes demonized the enemy by comparing them to the Nazis. Avoiding another Munich, which came to be seen as the proximate cause of World War II, became the rationale for war after war—first against the Communists in Korea and Vietnam and later against terrorists and their alleged supporters, such as Saddam.

It is not difficult, therefore, to understand why the narrative probability of most stories that lead to war is, at least initially, persuasive. However, the *narrative fidelity* of a war story is a different matter. Narrative fidelity is a product of the knowledge, experience, and beliefs of those being told a story and their understanding of the reality of the events portrayed. To understand how different people often inhabit different realities, one need look no further than the 2020 election, where roughly a third of voters thought the election was rigged, while a majority accepted the outcome. How can two such divergent stories coexist in the same universe? The reason can be partially explained by where those stories are told. Those who relied on so-called "mainstream media" largely believed that the 2020 election was fair. Those who turned to more conservative media or the loser's tweets were more likely to think the reverse. When events are far away, as they are in foreign wars, the reality for citizens is almost entirely a product of their media consumption unless they are personally affected by the war. As noted in chapter 9, beliefs about the second war in Iraq varied by media usage. Those who watched some news sources (Fox in particular) were more likely to believe things that were not true (such as that WMD had been found or that Iraq was involved in 9/11). No matter what the war—from the war against Spain to the War on Terror—most Americans have had to rely on the era's primary media to form their opinions about the wars.

The fidelity of the narrative is difficult to maintain when facts emerge that contradict the official storyline. This does not always happen during a war, but even if revealed after the war, it can have an effect on the storyline of the next conflict. We see this in the aftermath of World War I, when the atrocity stories told about the Germans were later discredited. Rigorous censorship and propaganda from the Committee on Public Information dampened down any negative news about the war and even the flu pandemic, which was ravaging the nation in 1918–1919. However, we now know from public opinion polling that after the war most Americans believed they had been duped by propaganda into joining World War I. Thus, the next war faced a skeptical public.

Roosevelt, despite his desire to help the Allies in Europe, was constrained by the lack of fidelity of the story that led to World War I. Even when a U-boat sank an American vessel (the very act that eventually triggered the United States joining World War I), he held off asking for a declaration of war. He promised no foreign wars in his 1940 re-election campaign, but added the caveat that if America was attacked it wasn't a foreign war. When that attack came, there was virtually no dissent to the United States entering World War II—in fact, there really was no choice. The fidelity of the story was unquestioned as Americans were transported by images of the devastation of their fleet. One of the hallmarks of Roosevelt's presidency was that he used his fireside chats to level with the American people about the difficulty ahead. Virtually all Americans were involved in the war effort—either because they were in military service, had family members at war, worked in a defense plant, or simply planted a victory garden. It is noteworthy that the atrocity stories of German concentration camps were downplayed, largely because in the prior war such stories were later disproven. It is no small tribute to Harry S. Truman that he insisted on the Nuremburg war crime trials after the war, documenting the inhumanity of the Holocaust. Although there exist deniers to this day, they are outliers. The fidelity of the story of the atrocities perpetrated by the Nazis and their Axis partners was exceptionally high. Therefore, the lessons from that war—particularly that appeasement feeds aggression—were learned, perhaps too well. Korea, Vietnam, and the Gulf War all rested on the premise that aggression had to be stopped and that appeasement would only lead to more aggression.

The next two American wars—Korea and Vietnam—both started with high levels of public support and apparent fidelity to what was happening on the ground. But before they were over, both wars suffered from revelations that all was not as it seemed and that the public had been lied to. In Korea, the belief that China would not intervene and the troops would be home by Christmas was shattered by the wave of Chinese volunteers that drove MacArthur back below the 38th parallel. The war ended in a stalemate, ended only by a new president who fulfilled his promise to go to Korea. Unfortunately, the armistice was the prelude to a dispute that continues to this day. With North Korea now armed with nuclear weapons and missiles capable of delivering them to U.S. territory, it's hard to claim with any fidelity that the Korean War was a victory for the United States and the UN.

Vietnam became the prime example of how a lack of fidelity destroyed an initially persuasive war narrative. A war that escalated due to an attack that didn't happen—which Senator Wayne Morse compared to the sinking of the USS *Maine*—eventually was lost, despite constant assurances there was light at the end of the tunnel. When LBJ lamented that having lost Walter Cronkite, he had lost middle America, what he was really saying was that the "most trusted man in America," who told his viewers everyday "That's the way it is," had exposed the lack of fidelity of the official story of Vietnam.

Two wars against Saddam Hussein were shaped by the conflicting legacies of World War II and Vietnam. In the First Gulf War, George H. W. Bush adopted the World War II narrative—if a brutal dictator were appeased, he would keep expanding his wars and eventually threaten the free world. Saddam was repeatedly compared to Hitler—he gassed his own citizens, threw babies out of their incubators, and possessed weapons of mass destruction. At the same time Bush had to deal with the legacy of Vietnam—the so-called Vietnam Syndrome. Could the United States actually carry out a successful military action against a significant foe, who possessed the fourth largest military in the world at the time? The war was an apparent success, with ground combat ending after 100 hours. Former secretary of defense Bob Gates places it alongside World War II as one of only two wars that were supported by most Americans.[1] However, the Gulf War narrative contained the seeds of its own destruction. Bush created an unrealistic expectation that the new Hitler would be overthrown by his own people and eventually brought to justice. Saddam stayed in power, and there was no Nuremberg trial for his war crimes. A decade later, Bush's son was president and sought to rectify the mistake of his father.

That brings us to the story of the wars in Iraq and Afghanistan. That the United States was attacked on 9/11 is as true as the attack on Pearl Harbor. Unfortunately as with the attack on the *Maine*, the public was misled about who was responsible. From the very outset, George W. Bush set in motion plans for a war against Iraq. But his first concern was going after the group of extremists who masterminded the plot. In the process, the mission grew from merely taking out al Qaeda, to removing the Taliban government that harbored them, and ultimately to nation-building in a place that neither the British nor the Soviets were able to conquer. As this book is being written, the very group that harbored bin Laden and his band of extremists has reclaimed power far more rapidly than anyone predicted and the United States and its allies have left. The American-supported Afghan government has collapsed and the war in Afghanistan certainly has not accomplished Bush's goal of defeating terrorism.

Iraq was unconnected to 9/11 and didn't possess WMD, two of the three pillars of the administration's war story. The connection to the attack on 9/11 was a fiction repeated often enough to be convincing. The WMD rationale also turned out to be false. Nevertheless, most Americans initially believed the WMD narrative—it was a "slam dunk" according to the experts. Bush 43 was the beneficiary of Bush 41's casting of Saddam in the role of a modern Hitler. It was not much of a stretch for most Americans to believe that Iraq constituted a real threat and it had been involved in the shocking terrorist attacks of September 11. George W. Bush adopted not just the story of World War II, but the setting as well, delivering his war message from the same rostrum that FDR had used to proclaim December 7 a day of infamy.

The fidelity of the younger Bush's narrative was eventually shattered. There were no WMD, there was no connection to 9/11, and most disappointingly, Iraqis did not welcome the U.S. soldiers as liberators, but fell into sectarian violence. Once the United States left Iraq in 2011, the fidelity of Obama's story that the United States had accomplished its goals in Iraq and left a working democracy in its wake was shattered by the rise of ISIS, which paradoxically was driven by the U.S. invasion, fulfilling an apocalyptic prophesy for radical Sunnis.

What are we to make of these stories and how several of them ended up lacking fidelity—at least for many Americans—by the end of the wars? Where do people get their information—the "pictures in their heads" as Walter Lippmann called them? We know from audience research that where people get their news matters. How could readers of Hearst's *New York Journal* doubt the Spanish blew up the *Maine*? How could viewers of Fox News doubt that Saddam had WMD and helped carry out terrorist attacks on the United States? Even readers of supposedly liberal newspapers, such as the *Washington Post*, were led to believe that Colin Powell had presented a compelling case for war at the UN. Learning the truth requires readers or viewers to step out of their comfort zone and confront facts that are dissonant with their prior beliefs. The theory of cognitive dissonance would suggest that few are likely to do so.

During the Vietnam War, there were only three television network news sources and television was king. When the most prominent and trusted TV anchor declared Vietnam a stalemate after the Tet offensive, the cracks started to show in the administration's narrative. Light at the end of the tunnel was no longer a believable narrative for large segments of the population. Viewers were transported by the horrific pictures on the evening news of children running from napalm and Vietnamese police shooting captives in plain sight. Furthermore, with millions serving in Vietnam, the number of Americans with first or second-hand knowledge of the reality of the war grew. Journalists, such as Neil Sheehan, reported the experiences of soldiers who doubted the official story of the war. Although the war was not lost in the media, as some have claimed, it is clear that the fidelity of the story told by the Pentagon was ultimately shattered by the bright light shined by journalists on the reality of the war. The lessons learned in Vietnam became a story that kept America out of significant military conflict for a decade and a half. And the next war was fought with overwhelming force and limited objectives, just as officers such as Colin Powell had advised in the wake of the Vietnam debacle.

Today, Americans have the most fragmented media environment in history. It is a far cry from the era when three networks told essentially the same story every evening. There are numerous cable TV outlets—some with very specific partisan agendas. There are innumerable Internet sources. From QAnon to Politifact—there is something out there for every political persuasion. As George Lakoff lamented, "The most startling finding is that, in considering whether a statement is a lie, the *least* important consideration for most people is whether it is true!"[2] That is something that needs to change if we are to avoid more unnecessary wars and loss of lives and treasure. When the next war story is told, it is difficult to know how the average person is to determine the fidelity of the story. "Fool me once, shame on you—fool me twice, shame on me," may be a convenient motto, but how are citizens to know if they are being fooled? Prior to the second war in Iraq, even the most "liberal" media sources, such as the *New York Times*, bought the story the administration was selling. The *Times* printed leaks from administration sources as hard news, which were later cited as evidence by the very administration that leaked them.

There is no easy way to judge the fidelity of a future war narrative. The seven propaganda techniques put forth by the IPA were a primitive attempt to try to alert citizens to propaganda, but they were at best superficial clues as to when to be skeptical. Based on the wars that were examined in this study, it is clear that certain stories are retold again and again. It is wise for citizens to exercise a healthy skepticism when these narratives are used to justify a war. Moreover, it is incumbent upon the news media to learn from past mistakes and not simply accept these narratives at face value.

REOCCURRING WAR STORIES

We Were Attacked—We Are Already at War

Whether it was the sinking of the USS *Maine*, the U-boat attacks in World War I, Pearl Harbor, Gulf of Tonkin, or 9/11, most American wars were precipitated by an alleged attack on the United States or its assets. That the Germans U-boats sank ships with Americans on board, even those flying the American flag, was not seriously disputed. Rather the real issue was whether or not such attacks justified involvement in a war that didn't really threaten the American homeland. That Wilson had to broaden his rhetoric beyond the mere loss of lives at sea to include fourteen points is evidence that the story needed to be about more than just protecting the sea-lanes. On the other hand, the Japanese attack on Pearl Harbor was indisputable—and there was no doubt that the survival of the United States was at stake.

In some cases, the identity of the attackers or even the veracity of the story of the attacks was at issue. According to the last official naval report commissioned by Admiral Rickover, the USS *Maine* was the victim of an internal explosion, not a Spanish mine. Even Robert McNamara now admits the second attack in the Gulf of Tonkin never occurred, and 9/11 was perpetrated by al Qaeda, not Saddam Hussein. Yet, the public, primed by a compliant press, initially supported a war story that lacked fidelity to the facts.

We Must Avoid Another Munich

Of course, it is not always an attack on the United States or its assets that propels the storyline of a war. North Korea didn't attack the United States in 1950, North Vietnam didn't attack America, and Saddam Hussein never attacked the United States. What story justified such wars? The narrative only resonated if the American people believed that failure to defend against aggression would eventually threaten the U.S. proper. This was the lesson of Munich—appeasement only begets more aggression. If we don't fight them over there, we'll be fighting them in the streets of Wichita or some other American city.

This prompts one to ask—does the Munich narrative have fidelity to the actual cause of World War II? Tim Reuter claims that "the Munich Agreement did not cause World War II. That dubious distinction belongs to an odious deal struck between Hitler and Stalin on August 23, 1939."[3] That deal permitted Hitler to avoid a two-front war. One can never know for sure if Hitler would have taken Czechoslovakia if Chamberlain had not agreed to his demands. After all, Hitler complained after the Munich pact, "That fellow Chamberlain has spoiled my entry into Prague."[4] So perhaps he would have done so anyway.

Therefore, the lesson of Munich may have been learned too well. The power of the World War II narrative cannot be overstated. Many wars since then were portrayed as avoiding another Munich. As George H. W. Bush made clear, he believed if only Hitler had been stopped earlier, millions of lives could have been saved. After 9/11, the invulnerability of the American homeland was shattered. George W. Bush drew on the analogy to Pearl Harbor and suggested a war on terror that would rival World War II in eventually defeating evil. As we look to the future, we should be skeptical of the narrative that we must fight in some far off land to avoid another Munich.

The Enemy is Less Than Human

The demonization of the enemy is, of course, a staple of all war stories. Sometimes it's the leaders, such as the Kaiser, Hitler, Ho, Saddam or Osama bin Laden. However, it is not hard for the demonization to spread to an entire race or religion. After Pearl Harbor, all Japanese were suspect regardless of where they were born. That thousands were placed in relocation camps is a stain on American history. That almost all went willingly and most professed their patriotism from behind barbed wire speaks volumes. George W. Bush did his best to avoid demonizing all Muslims after 9/11, but he was fighting anti-Arab and anti-Muslim stereotypes that were deeply ingrained by years of negative rhetoric and media portrayals. Michael J. Lee writes,

> Storeowners were shot in three states "as an anti-Muslim backlash broke out across the country." Over 700 reports of hate crimes targeting Arab Americans were issued in just thirty days. . . . Wide majorities of Americans believed that Islam was a violent religion.[5]

When Donald Trump was elected, while calling for a ban on all Muslim immigration, the deep roots of Islamophobia were laid bare. When the enemy is "not like us" it is a recipe for racism and ethnocentrism.

It Will Be a Cakewalk and There's Light at the End of the Tunnel

Unlike FDR, who leveled with the American people after Pearl Harbor and throughout the war, his successors sugarcoated their narratives. Truman called Korea a mere "police action." LBJ and the Pentagon promised "light at the end of the tunnel" so often that the term became meaningless. After 9/11, Americans were promised that the invasion of Iraq would be a "cakewalk." The banner over Bush proclaimed "Mission Accomplished" and Cheney claimed the insurgency was in its last throes. Even successful military actions, like the First Gulf War, created expectations that were unfulfilled—Saddam remained in power for over a decade after his defeat and was not held accountable for his actions until after another war. War stories that promise easy victory should immediately be suspect. There are no "splendid little wars" in today's world. And once a war has begun, the narratives that victory is near and the troops will be home by Christmas usually have little fidelity to the reality on the battlefield.

One of the most troubling legacies of this narrative is that presidents in recent years, particularly after the end of military conscription, have asked little in the way of sacrifice from the general public. Americans were urged to go shopping after 9/11. The brunt of the wars in Afghanistan and Iraq were born by a tiny percentage of the public. Those serving in the military faced multiple deployments, while their peers got on with their lives. Unlike World War II, where the entire population was involved in the war effort in ways large and small, in contemporary America, 99 percent of the population is not directly affected by war. If there's one important lesson to be learned from Franklin Roosevelt, it's that American leaders need to level with the American public rather than minimizing the costs of war. If citizens know the price to be paid, they are better equipped to assess the narrative that calls for war. American citizens need to be treated as adults who can take the truth, not as children who need to be told fairy tales.

We Must Support Our Military

Going back to McKinley, virtually every war president has rallied support for his war by calling out opponents for not supporting America's brave troops. In some wars, this was not a hard case to make. Few would have spoken out against World War II once millions of Americans were fighting in both Europe and the Pacific. Buying war bonds, supporting the USO, and placing gold stars on homes told a story of a nation united as never before or since.

It wasn't until Vietnam that the line between supporting the war and the troops fighting it was broken. Many men returned from the war only to be vilified by its opponents. Stories of returning soldiers being called "baby killers" and being spat on enraged not just supporters of the war, but many of its opponents as well. Nixon learned how to change the narrative by celebrating returning soldiers as heroes and especially honoring the POWs once they returned.

Sometimes it is not the president calling on Americans to support their military. Often military leaders have blamed civilians for hamstringing them and thus losing a war that could have been won. The most obvious example was Vietnam, where the mythology developed that if LBJ had just given the military what it wanted, it would have easily prevailed. Recall from chapter 8 that retired Admiral Sharp claimed the U.S. military could have won the Vietnam War easily had they had the same authority as Schwarzkopf had in the Gulf War.[6] During the Korean conflict, MacArthur's public dispute with Truman was grounded in the president's failure to give him what he believed was needed for victory. As Barack Obama learned, it can be hazardous to one's political health to go against military advice, particularly when that advice is leaked to the media.

We Are Fighting a War for Peace

The oxymoron that a conflict is a war for peace is at least as old as Wilson's "war to end all wars" storyline. Anyone familiar with the classic film, *Dr. Strangelove*, may recall that "Peace is our profession" was the motto of the Strategic Air Command, which kept bombers loaded with nuclear weapons in the air at all times. In Vietnam, Nixon alleged that the United States was fighting for "peace with honor." George H. W. Bush promised a new world order, enforced by the coalitions such as he assembled for the Gulf War. And his son believed that bringing democracy to nations like Afghanistan and Iraq would usher in a more peaceful world. Of course, the narrative fidelity of the story that war can bring an era of peace has been disproven time after time in the twentieth and early twenty-first century. Only a few years after the war to end all wars, the world was again plunged into an even more destructive war. After World War II, it was but a short five years later that the new enemy—Communism—was confronted in North Korea. That nation, supposedly defeated in 1953, now threatens the United States with nuclear-armed missiles. Barack Obama acknowledged the danger of portraying war as a fight for peace in his acceptance speech for the Nobel Peace Prize, delivered in Oslo, Norway, December 10, 2009:

> So yes, the instruments of war do have a role to play in preserving the peace. And yet this truth must coexist with another—that no matter how justified, war promises human tragedy. The soldier's courage and sacrifice is full of glory, expressing devotion to country, to cause, to comrades in arms. But war itself is never glorious, and we must never trumpet it as such.[7]

ASSESSING THE NARRATIVES FOR WAR

It is clear from the preceding chapters that several presidents and their administrations have led the United States into war by either misleading, omitting important facts, or outright lying to the Congress and public. Although one might think this is a recent phenomenon, Louis Fisher has traced such presidential dissembling back to the earliest days of the republic. He concludes, "At least since the Mexican-American War of 1846, presidents have had a record of making misleading statements to justify wars."[8]

The ultimate question for all citizens to ask when war is threatened is one of *narrative fidelity*. Keep in mind Fisher's five tests of fidelity: *fact, relevance, consequence*, *consistency*, and *transcendental issue*. First, is the story true? Unfortunately, average Americans cannot answer that question themselves. The current media environment is one that leads to multiple realities existing simultaneously, often in dramatic opposition. The best advice one can offer is that credulous belief in either the official government story or any particular type of media's reporting is dangerous to democracy. Seeking out as many divergent sources of information and applying a healthy dose of skepticism to stories that fit the above storylines is necessary to get to the truth. Second, have relevant facts been omitted? Yes, British intelligence did produce a report suggesting Saddam sought to buy uranium, but the report was known by the CIA to be flawed. Third, what will be the consequences of acting on the narrative? Future President Obama foresaw the dangers of what he called "dumb wars," including destabilization of the Middle East. Fourth, are stories consistent? Keep in mind that the United States armed and supported the very dictator both Bushes called Hitler when his enemy was Iran. Finally, what are the transcendental issues raised by a proposed war? Here Americans must ask themselves what values they hold in the highest regard. Certainly self-defense against an enemy that has attacked the nation or its allies is a value embedded in the constitution. Beyond that, however, each war narrative must be judged critically in terms of the values it embraces.

In addition to each citizen thinking critically about war narratives, the media have a unique responsibility under the First Amendment to find and report the truth. Fortunately, since World War I, the government has allowed at least some measure of press freedom. Vietnam probably represented the pinnacle of media vigilance and digging for the truth. Sadly, prior to the second Iraq War, the media largely failed to ask the necessary questions or listen to those who knew the intelligence was flawed. It is not as if no one knew the truth—former ambassador Joe Wilson, for example, exposed the falsehood about Saddam trying to buy yellowcake uranium.[9] But the story *for* the war was so compelling, the narrative about Saddam being another Hitler so embedded in people's minds, that media executives bowed to the pressure to gloss over any doubts about the administration's story. When the widely admired Colin Powell presented the administration's case to the United Nations, the march to war was unstoppable.

It is not surprising that at the same time the nation was being led to war by a questionable narrative, so-called fact checkers began to emerge. In December 2003, the Annenberg School for Communication at the University of Pennsylvania founded the website Factcheck.org in preparation of the upcoming election in 2004. Brooks Jackson and Kathleen Hall Jamieson report, "FactCheck.org got nine million visits during its first two years of operation from citizens seeking help to sort through the deception and confusion in U.S. politics."[10] By the 2008 election cycle, Factcheck.org was joined by Politifact.com, originally sponsored by the *Tampa Bay Times*, which gives ratings on a "truth-o-meter" ranging from "true" to "pants on fire." The 2008 election also saw the *Washington Post* began its own fact-checking column, awarding four Pinocchios to the most deceptive ads. Of course, fact checkers only have influence if citizens seek them out and perceive them as credible sources. In the next crisis, it remains to be seen how much they can affect the narrative proposed for going to war or if they will choose to challenge the official narrative.

The rise of nontraditional media as a primary source of information further complicates learning the truth for the average citizen. Cyber security expert Chris Bronk writes, "Information controls, disinformation, and computer hacking represent important tools for today's cyber propagandist."[11] It is clear that social media now play an oversized role in shaping public discourse. For example, conspiracy theories such as QAnon now flourish with little to restrain them. Deep fakes that appear to be legitimate photos and videos are frequently found online. When leaders, including even the president, retweet or like stories found on the Internet, the power of the stories are amplified. What will war propaganda look like in the years to come? To what extent will hackers from America's adversaries be able to create dissention and discord when the United States faces a real threat to its security? And to what extent will political actors use these new tools to promote military adventures that are of questionable value? As was pointed out in chapter 2, false Twitter stories travel faster and reach more people than true ones. Thus, one important lesson should be to look skeptically upon stories found on such sources unless they are independently confirmed by reliable sources. Social media companies such as Facebook are just now recognizing that they have a responsibility to maintain some modicum of control over disinformation, even extending to banning accounts that spread egregious and dangerous lies.

Beyond the media, it is also the responsibility of academics and other scholars to challenge prowar propaganda. Deepa Kumar writes, "In this context of growing public skepticism, the failure of the media to meet the democratic needs of this society, and the absence of significant anti-war and anti-imperialist voices in the public sphere, intellectuals bear an enormous responsibility."[12] It is hoped that this book will make a small contribution to that effort by alerting readers to the dangers of uncritically accepting prowar narratives as truthful.

German chancellor Otto von Bismarck once prophetically said, "You know where a war begins but you never know where it ends."[13] Had Kaiser Wilhelm listened to his sage advice, perhaps the twentieth century would have been a far more peaceful one. But it is good advice for all of us. Beware of the rush to war. The story may seem on the surface to have narrative probability and fidelity. But it is important to recall how often the story that brought America to war turned out to be a horror story.

NOTES

1. Robert M. Gates, *Exercise of Power: American Failures, Successes, and a New Path Forward in the Post-Cold War World* (New York: Alfred A. Knopf, 2020), loc. 6463 of 7416, Kindle.
2. Quoted in Christopher Scheer, Robert Scheer, and Lakshimi Chaudhry, *The Five Biggest Lies Bush Told Us About Iraq* (New York: Akashic Books and Seven Stories Press, 2003), 167 (italics in original).
3. Tim Reuter, "The Munich Agreement Did Not Cause World War II, The Nazi-Soviet Nonaggression Pact Did," *Forbes*, May 8, 2015, https://www.forbes.com/sites/timreuter/2015/05/08/the-munich-agreement-did-not-cause-world-war-ii-the-nazi-soviet-nonaggression-pact-did/?sh=155dc3dc44c7.
4. Roger Moorhouse, *The Devils' Alliance* (New York: Basic Books, 2014), loc. 554 of 5745, Kindle.
5. Michael J. Lee, "Us, Them, and the War on Terror: Reassessing George W. Bush's Rhetorical Legacy," *Communication and Critical/Cultural Studies* 14, no. 1 (2017): 4, https://doi.org/10.1080/14791420.2016.1257817.
6. Tom Shales, "Stormin' Norman in High Command," *Washington Post*, February 28, 1991, https://www.washingtonpost.com/archive/lifestyle/1991/02/28/stormin-norman-in-high-command/cd526793-85a6-4332-9ad9-61dc1d164b5f/.
7. Barack Obama, "Remarks by the President at the Acceptance of the Nobel Peace Prize," December 10, 2009, accessed September 19, 2020, https://obamawhitehouse.archives.gov/the-press-office/remarks-president-acceptance-nobel-peace-prize.
8. Louis Fisher, "The Law: When Wars Begin: Misleading Statements by Presidents," *Presidential Studies Quarterly* 40, no. 1 (March 2010): 171–184, https://doi.org/10.1111/j.1741-5705.2009.03739.x.
9. Joseph C. Wilson 4th, "What I Didn't Find in Africa," *New York Times*, July 6, 2003, https://www.nytimes.com/2003/07/06/opinion/what-i-didn-t-find-in-africa.html.
10. Brooks Jackson and Kathleen Hall Jamieson, *unSpun: Finding Facts in a World of Disinformation* (New York: Random House, 2007), xi.
11. Chris Bronk, "Appendix: Cyber Propaganda," in *Propaganda and Persuasion*, 7th ed., by Garth S. Jowett and Victoria O'Donnell (Thousand Oaks, CA: Sage, 2019), 325.
12. Deepa Kumar, "Media, War, and Propaganda: Strategies of Information Management During the 2003 Iraq War," *Communication and Critical/Cultural Studies* 3, no.1 (2006): 65, https://doi.org/10.1080/14791420500505650.
13. Robert K. Massie, *Dreadnought: Britain, Germany, and the Coming of the Great War* (New York: Ballantine Books, 1991), 76.

Bibliography

"1941: Germany and Italy Declare War On US." *BBC On This Day*. Accessed May 25, 2019. http://news.bbc.co.uk/onthisday/hi/dates/stories/december/11/newsid_3532000/3532401.stm.

Achter, Paul. "Rhetoric and the Permanent War." *Quarterly Journal of Speech* 102, no. 1, (February 2016): 79–94. https://doi.org/10.1080/00335630.2016.1135544.

Ackerman, Elliot. "Born Into War." *Time*, October 21–28, 2019: 45–57.

Adelman, Ken. "Cakewalk in Iraq." *Washington Post*, February 13, 2002. https://www.washingtonpost.com/archive/opinions/2002/02/13/cakewalk-in-iraq/cf09301c-c6c4-4f2e-8268-7c93017f5e93/.

Allen, Thomas B. "Remember the Maine?" *National Geographic* 193, no. 2 (February, 1998): 92–111.

"American Rhetoric: Spiro Agnew—Television News Coverage (November 13, 1969)." American Rhetoric Top 100 Speeches. https://americanrhetoric.com/speeches/spiroagnewtvnewscoverage.htm.

Associated Press. "U.S. Casualties Rise in Korea to 33,878." *New York Times*, December 28, 1950, 11. https://nyti.ms/34OCJsP.

"Attack at Pearl Harbor, 1941." Eyewitness to History, www.eyewitnesstohistory.com, 1997. Accessed October 11, 2019. http://www.eyewitnesstohistory.com/pfpearl.htm.

"Author Interview: The History of American Intervention and the 'Birth of the American Empire.'" *Fresh Air with Terry Gross*. NPR, January 24, 2018. https://www.npr.org/2017/01/24/511387528/the-history-of-u-s-intervention-and-the-birth-of-the-american-empire.

Baker, James A., III with Thomas M. DeFrank. *The Politics of Diplomacy: Revolution, War & Peace*, 1989–1992. New York: Putnam, 1995.

Baron Stanley J. and Dennis K. Davis, *Mass Communication Theory*. Belmont, CA: Wadsworth, 1995.

Berg, A. Scott. *Wilson*. New York: G. P. Putnam's Sons, 2013.

Beschloss, Michael. *Presidential Courage: Brave Leaders and How They Changed America 1789–1989*. New York: Simon & Schuster, 2007.

Beschloss, Michael. *Presidents of War*. New York: Crown, 2018. Kindle.

Beschloss, Michael R., ed., *Taking Charge: The Johnson White House Tapes, 1963–1964*. New York: Simon and Schuster, 1997.

Bettelheim, Adriel. "Only as a Last Resort." PolitiFact, September 1, 2008. Accessed November 7, 2020. https://www.politifact.com/factchecks/2008/sep/01/lindsey-graham/only-as-a-last-resort/.

Biser, Margaret. "The Fireside Chats: Roosevelt's Radio Talks: The White House Speaks to America." The White House Historical Association, August 19, 2016. https://www.whitehousehistory.org/the-fireside-chats-roosevelts-radio-talks.

Boissoneault, Lorraine. "What Did President Wilson Mean When He Called for 'Peace Without Victory' 100 Years Ago?" Smithsonian.com, January 23, 2017. https://www.smithsonianmag.com/history/what-did-president-wilson-mean-when-he-called-peace-without-victory-100-years-ago-180961888/.

Bolger, Daniel P. *Why We Lost: A General's Inside Account of the Iraq and Afghanistan Wars*. New York: Houghton Mifflin Harcourt, 2014.

Borenstein, Seth, Associated Press. "False Stories Travel Way Faster on Twitter Than True Ones Do, Study Finds." *USA Today*, March 9, 2018. Accessed March 9, 2019. https://www.usatoday.com/story/tech/news/2018/03/09/false-stories-travel-way-faster-twitter-than-true-ones-do-study-finds/409872002/.

Brewer, Susan A. *Why America Fights: Patriotism and War Propaganda from the Philippines to Iraq*. New York: Oxford University Press, 2009.

Bria, Maggie. "What Did the 1919 Paris Peace Conference Have to Do with the Vietnam War?" Bria Historica, March 30, 2017 and June 4, 2018. Accessed June 3, 2020. https://briahistorica.com/2017/03/30/what-did-the-1919-paris-peace-conference-have-to-do-with-the-vietnam-war/.

Brokaw, Tom. *The Greatest Generation*. New York: Random House, 1998.

Bronk, Chris. "Appendix: Cyber Propaganda." In *Propaganda and Persuasion*. 7th ed. by Garth S. Jowett and Victoria O'Donnell, 320–25. Thousand Oaks, CA: Sage, 2019.

Brown, Robert L. "Manzanar—Relocation Center." *Common Ground* 3, no. 1 (Autumn 1942): 27–32. https://www.unz.com/print/CommonGround-1942q3-00027/.

Bumiller, Elisabeth. "Keepers of Bush Image Lift Stagecraft to New Heights." *New York Times*, May 16, 2003. http://www.nytimes.com/2003/05/16/politics/16IMAG.html.

Burke, Kenneth. *A Grammer of Motives and A Rhetoric of Motives*. Cleveland: Meridian Books, 1962.

Burke, Kenneth. "The Rhetoric of Hitler's 'Battle.'" In *The Philosophy of Literary Form: Studies in Symbolic Action*, edited by Kenneth Burke, 164–189. New York: Vintage, 1957.

Bush, Barbara. *A Memoir*. New York: Charles Scribner's Sons, 1994.

"Bush: Bin Laden Wanted Dead or Alive." ABC News, September 17, 2001, updated January 7, 2006. Accessed October 15, 2020. https://abcnews.go.com/US/story?id=92483&page=1.

Bush, George. "Address Before the 45th Session of the United Nations General Assembly in New York, New York." October 1, 1990. Accessed May 16, 2020. https://bush41library.tamu.edu/archives/public-papers/2280.

Bush, George. "Address Before a Joint Session of the Congress on the Cessation of the Persian Gulf Conflict." March 6, 1991. Accessed May 16, 2020. https://bush411ibrary.tamu.edu/archives/public-papers/2767.

Bush, George. "Address Before a Joint Session of the Congress on the Persian Gulf Crisis and the Federal Budget Deficit." September 11, 1990. Accessed May 16, 2020. https://bush41library.tamu.edu/archives/public-papers/2217.

Bush, George. "Address to the Nation Announcing Allied Military Action in the Persian Gulf." January 16, 1991. Accessed May 16, 2020, https://bush41library.tamu.edu/archives/public-papers/2625.

Bush, George. "Address to the Nation Announcing Allied Military Ground Action in the Persian Gulf." February 23,1991. Accessed May 16, 2020. https://bush41library.tamu.edu/archives/public-papers/2734.

Bush, George. "Address to the Nation Announcing the Deployment of United States Armed Forces to Saudi Arabia." August 8, 1990. Accessed May 16, 2020. https://bush41library.tamu.edu/archives/public-papers/2147.

Bush, George. "Address to the Nation on the Suspension of Allied Offensive Combat Operations in the Persian Gulf." February 27, 1991. Accessed May 16, 2020. https://bush41library.tamu.edu/archives/public-papers/2746.

Bush, George. "Congressman Bush's Notes for an Address He Gave Before a Houston Audience on January 11, 1968 Reporting on His Trip to Vietnam." January 11, 1968. On display in the Bush Presidential Library on March 8, 2003.

Bush, George. "The President's News Conference November 30, 2003." November 30, 1990. Accessed May 16, 2020. https://bush41library.tamu.edu/archives/public-papers/2516.

Bush, George. "Remarks at the Annual Conference of the Veterans of Foreign Wars in Baltimore, Maryland." August 20, 1990, accessed May 16, 2020. https://bush41library.tamu.edu/archives/public-papers/2171.

Bush, George. "Remarks at the Aspen Institute Symposium in Aspen, Colorado." August 2, 1990. Accessed May 16, 2020. https://bush41library.tamu.edu/archives/public-papers/2128.

Bush, George. "Remarks and an Exchange with Reporters on the Iraqi Invasion of Kuwait." August 5, 1990. Accessed July 8, 2020. https://bush41library.tamu.edu/archives/public-papers/2138.

Bush, George. "Remarks at a Fundraising Luncheon for Gubernatorial Candidate Clayton Williams in Dallas, Texas." October 15, 1990. Accessed May 21, 2021. https://bush41library.tamu.edu/archives/public-papers/2328.

Bush, George. "Remarks to Officers and Troops at Hickam Air Force Base in Pearl Harbor, Hawaii." October 28, 1990. Accessed May 16, 2020. https://bush41library.tamu.edu/archives/public-papers/2369.

Bush, George. "Remarks and a Question-and-Answer Session with Reporters in Aspen, Colorado, Following a Meeting with Prime Minister Margaret Thatcher of the United Kingdom." August 2, 1990 Accessed May 16, 2020. https://bush41library.tamu.edu/archives/public-papers/2124.

Bush, George. "Remarks to the Reserve Officers Association." January 23, 1991. Accessed May 16, 2020. https://bush41library.tamu.edu/archives/public-papers/2648.

Bush, George. "Remarks to United States Army Troops Near Dhahran, Saudi Arabia." November 22, 1990. Accessed May 16, 2020. https://bush41library.tamu.edu/archives/public-papers/2483.

Bush, George and Brent Scowcroft. *A World Transformed*. New York: Random House, 1998.

Bush, George W. "Address to a Joint Session of Congress and the American People." September 20, 2001. Accessed August 8, 2020. https://georgewbush-whitehouse.archives.gov/news/releases/2001/09/20010920-8.html.

Bush, George W. *Decision Points*. New York: Crown Publishers, 2010.

Bush, George W. "Inaugural Address by President George W. Bush." January 20, 2005. Accessed August 28, 2020. https://georgewbush-whitehouse.archives.gov/news/releases/2005/01/20050120-3.html.

Bush, George W. "'Islam is Peace' Says President." September 17, 2001. Accessed August 10, 2020, https://georgewbush-whitehouse.archives.gov/news/releases/2001/09/20010917-11.html.

Bush, George W. "President Bush Addresses the Nation." March 19, 2003. Accessed August 11, 2020. https://georgewbush-whitehouse.archives.gov//news/releases/2003/03/20030319-17.html.

Bush, George W. "President Bush Announces Combat Operations in Iraq Have Ended." May 1, 2003. Accessed August 11, 2020, https://georgewbush-whitehouse.archives.gov/news/releases/2003/05/20030501-6.html.

Bush, George W. "President Bush Outlines Iraqi Threat." October 7, 2002. Accessed August 11, 2020, https://georgewbush-whitehouse.archives.gov/news/releases/2002/10/20021007-8.html.

Bush, George W. "President Bush Salutes Heroes in New York." September 14, 2001. Accessed August 10, 2020, https://georgewbush-whitehouse.archives.gov/news/releases/2001/09/20010914-9.html.

Bush, George W. "President Delivers State of the Union Address." January 29, 2002. Accessed August 10, 2020, https://georgewbush-whitehouse.archives.gov/news/releases/2002/01/20020129-11.html.

Bush, George W. "President Signs Iraq Resolution." October 16, 2002. Accessed August 11, 2020. https://georgewbush-whitehouse.archives.gov/news/releases/2002/10/20021016-1.html.

Bush, George W. "President Visits Troops at Brooke Army Medical Center." January 1, 2006. Accessed August 28, 2020. https://georgewbush-whitehouse.archives.gov/news/releases/2006/01/20060101.html.

Bush, George W. "Presidential Address to the Nation." October 7, 2001. Accessed August 10, 2020. https://georgewbush-whitehouse.archives.gov/news/releases/2001/10/20011007-8.html.

Bush, George W. "President's Address to the Nation." September 11, 2006. Accessed August 28, 2020. https://georgewbush-whitehouse.archives.gov/news/releases/2006/09/20060911-3.html.

Bush, George W. "President's Address to the Nation." January 10, 2007. Accessed August 28, 2020. https://georgewbush-whitehouse.archives.gov/news/releases/2007/01/20070110-7.html.

Bush, George W. "President's Remarks at National Day of Prayer and Remembrance." September 14, 2001. Accessed August 10, 2020, https://georgewbush-whitehouse.archives.gov/news/releases/2001/09/20010914-2.html.

Bush, George W. "President's Remarks at the United Nations General Assembly." September 12, 2002. Accessed August 11, 2020. https://georgewbush-whitehouse.archives.gov/news/releases/2002/09/20020912-1.html.

Bush, George W. "Press Conference by the President." October 11, 2006. Accessed August 28, 2020. https://georgewbush-whitehouse.archives.gov/news/releases/2006/10/20061011-5.html.

Bush, George W. "Remarks by the President After Two Planes Crash Into World Trade Center." September 11, 2001. Accessed August 10, 2020. https://georgewbush-whitehouse.archives.gov/news/releases/2001/09/20010911.html.

Bush, George W. "Remarks by the President Upon Arrival at Barksdale Air Force Base." September 11, 2001. Accessed August 10, 2020. https://georgewbush-whitehouse.archives.gov/news/releases/2001/09/text/20010912-2.html.

Bush, George W. "Remarks by President Upon Arrival [at the South Lawn]." September 16, 2001. Accessed August 10, 2020, https://georgewbush-whitehouse.archives.gov/news/releases/2001/09/20010916-2.html.

Bush, George W. "State of the Union Address by President George W. Bush." January 28, 2003. Accessed August 11, 2020. https://georgewbush-whitehouse.archives.gov/news/releases/2003/01/20030128-19.html.

Bush, George W. "Statement by the President in his Address to the Nation." September 11, 2001. Accessed August 8, 2020. https://georgewbush-whitehouse.archives.gov/news/releases/2001/09/20010911-16.html.

"Business in Evacuation Centers." *Business Week*, July 18, 1942, 19–21.

"Camp Food Quality Comparable to the Average Standards." *Manzanar Free Press*. (Manzanar, CA), Sep. 10 1943, 8. https://www.loc.gov/item/sn84025948/1943-09-10/ed-1/.

Carey James W. and Albert L. Kreiling. "Popular Culture and Uses and Gratifications: Notes Toward an Accommodation." In *The Uses of Mass Communications: Current Perspectives on Gratifications Research*, edited by Jay G. Blumler and Elihu Katz, 225–248. Beverly Hills: Sage, 1974.

Choe Sang-Hun and Charles J. Hanley. "Ex-GIs Tell AP of Korea Killing Associated Press Writers." *Washington Post Archives*, September 30, 1999. https://www.washingtonpost.com/wp-srv/aponline/19990930/aponline010625_000.htm.

Choe Sang-Hun. "Kim Jong-un Vows to Boost North Korea's Nuclear Capability as Leverage With Biden." *New York Times*, January 8, 2020. https://www.nytimes.com/2021/01/08/world/asia/kim-nuclear-north-korea.html.

CIA. *The World Factbook 2002*, March 19, 2003. Accessed August 7, 2003. http://www.cia.gov/cia/publications/factbook/geos/ku.html.

Clark, Richard A. *Against All Enemies: Inside America's War on Terror*. New York: Free Press, 2004.

Cogan, Charles G. "He Kept Us Out of War." *The World Post* [Huffington Post]. Updated November 13, 2013. https://www.huffingtonpost.com/dr-charles-g-cogan/he-kept-us-out-of-war_b_3931495.html.

Cohen, Zachary and Barbara Starr. "North Korea Promises Nuclear Strike on US if Regime Is Threatened." CNN, July 25, 2017. https://www.cnn.com/2017/07/25/politics/north-korea-threatens-nuclear-strike-us.

Cokeley, Grant. "Number of TV Households in America: 1950–1978." *The American Century*. https://americancentury.omeka.wlu.edu/items/show/136.

Cooper, Helene. "Putting Stamp on Afghan War, Obama Will Send 17,000 Troops." *New York Times*, February 17, 2009. https://www.nytimes.com/2009/02/18/washington/18web-troops.html.

Cortellessa, Eric. "Spike Lee Tells a Different Vietnam War History." *Washington Monthly*, June 20, 2020. https://washingtonmonthly.com/2020/06/20/spike-lee-tells-a-different-vietnam-war-history/.

Cowen, Tyler [Bloomberg]. "Middle East Resembles the Situation before World War I." *Japan Times*, April 16, 2018. Accessed April 16, 2018. https://www.japantimes.co.jp/opinion/2018/04/16/commentary/world-commentary/middle-east-resembles-situation-world-war/#.WtUqldPwaRs.

Cull, Nicholas John. *Selling War: The British Propaganda Campaign Against American "Neutrality" in World War II*. New York: Oxford, 1995. Adobe Digital Edition.

Curtiz, Michael, dir. *Casablanca*. Burbank, CA: Warner Home Video, 1999. DVD.

Davis, Frank. "Many Confused on Weapons and Terror, Polls Find." *Sacramento Bee*. June 15, 2003, A18.

D'Haeseleer, Brian and Roger Peace. "The War of 1898 and U.S.-Filipino War." United States Foreign Policy History and Resource Guide. Accessed January 30, 2018. http://peacehistory-usfp.org/1898-1899.

"December 8, 1941 - Franklin Roosevelt Asks Congress for a Declaration of War with Japan." Accessed May 25, 2019. http://docs.fdrlibrary.marist.edu/tmirhdee.html.

Diamond, Jeremy. "Donald Trump: Ban All Muslim Travel to U.S." CNN. December 8, 2015. Accessed March 9, 2018. https://www.cnn.com/2015/12/07/politics/donald-trump-muslim-ban-immigration/index.html.

DiMaggio, Anthony R. *Mass Media, Mass Propaganda: Examining American News in the "War on Terror"*. Lanham, MD: Lexington Books, 2008.

Directorate for Armed Forces Information and Education. *Why Vietnam*. 1965. Accessed March 29, 2020. https://www.youtube.com/watch?v=qEljbPwFQ9M.

Dooley, Thomas A., M.D. *Deliver Us From Evil: The Story of Viet Nam's Flight to Freedom*. New York: Farrar, Straus & Cudahy, 1956. https://archive.org/stream/deliverusfromevi006715mbp/deliverusfromevi006715mbp_djvu.txt.

Dowd, Maureen. "After the War: White House Memo; War Introduces a Tougher Bush to Nation." *New York Times*, March 2, 1991. https://www.nytimes.com/1

991/03/02/world/after-the-war-white-house-memo-war-introduces-a-tougher-bush-to-nation.html.

Dowd, Maureen. "The Xanax Cowboy." *New York Times*, March 9, 2003. https://www.nytimes.com/2003/03/09/opinion/the-xanax-cowboy.html?searchResultPosition=1.

Dower, John W. *War without Mercy: Race and Power in the Pacific War*. New York: Pantheon Books, 1993. https://hdl-handle-net.mantis.csuchico.edu/2027/heb.02403. EPUB.

Downing, John, Ali Mohammadi, and Annabelle Sreberny-Mohammadi, eds. *Questioning the Media: A Critical Introduction*, 2nd ed. Thousand Oaks, CA: Sage, 1995,

Draper, Robert. "Colin Powell Still Wants Answers." *New York Times Magazine*, July 16, 2020. https://www.nytimes.com/2020/07/16/magazine/colin-powell-iraq-war.html.

Draper, Robert. *Dead Certain: The Presidency of George W. Bush*. New York: Free Press, 2007.

Dunning, Brian. "Why was Pearl Harbor so Vulnerable?" *Reader's Digest*, May 2019, 104–105.

Editors of Encyclopaedia Britannica. "Geneva Accords." *Encyclopaedia Britannica*, July 14, 2019. https://www.britannica.com/event/Geneva-Accords.

Editors of Encyclopaedia Britannica. "United States Presidential Election of 1940." *Encyclopedia Britannica*, October 29, 2019. https://www.britannica.com/event/United-States-presidential-election-of-1940.

Edwards, Bob. "Edward R. Murrow Broadcast from London (September 21, 1940)." Added to the National Registry, 2004. http://www.loc.gov/static/programs/national-recording-preservation-board/documents/murrow.pdf.

"Election of 1916: Now Just Two Parties, but Same Results as 1912." United States History. Accessed December 7, 2018. https://www.u-s-history.com/pages/h888.html.

Ellul, Jacques. *Propaganda: The Formation of Men's Attitudes*. Translated by Konrad Kellen and Jean Lerner. New York: Vintage, 1973.

Engels, Jeremy and William O. Saas., "On Acquiescence and Ends-Less War: An Inquiry into the New War Rhetoric." *Quarterly Journal of Speech* 99, no. 2 (May 2013): 225–232. https//doi.org/ 10.1080/00335630.2013.775705.

Fallows, James. "The Iraq War and the Inevitability of Ignorance." *Atlantic*, March 20, 2018. https://www.theatlantic.com/international/archive/2018/03/iraq-war-anniversary-fifty-first-state/555986/.

Farrell, John A. "When a Candidate Conspired With a Foreign Power to Win An Election." Politico, August 6, 2017. https://www.politico.com/magazine/story/2017/08/06/nixon-vietnam-candidate-conspired-with-foreign-power-win-election-215461.

Fearon, James D. "The Big Problem with the North Koreans Isn't That We Can't Trust Them. It's That They Can't Trust Us." *Washington Post*, April 16, 2017. https://www.washingtonpost.com/news/monkey-cage/wp/2017/08/16/the-big-problem-with-north-korea-isnt-that-we-cant-trust-them-its-that-they-cant-trust-us/.

Festinger. Leon. *A Theory of Cognitive Dissonance.* Stanford, CA: Row, Peterson, 1957.

"The First and Last Names on the Wall." USO.org, June 18, 2014. Accessed March 10, 2018. https://www.uso.org/stories/1715-the-first-and-the-last-names-on-the-wall.

Fisher, Louis. "Destruction of the Maine (1898)." Law Library of Congress, August 4, 2009. accessed April 17, 2021, https://www.loc.gov/law/help/usconlaw/pdf/Maine.1898.pdf.

Fisher, Louis. "The Law: When Wars Begin: Misleading Statements by Presidents." *Presidential Studies Quarterly* 40, no. 1 (March 2010): 171–184. https://doi.org/10.1111/j.1741-5705.2009.03739.x.

Fisher, Walter R. "Clarifying the Narrative Paradigm." *Communication Monographs* 56 (1989): 55–58. https://doi.org/10.1080/03637758909390249.

Fisher, Walter R. *Human Communication as Narration: Toward a Philosophy of Reason, Value, and Action.* Columbia: University of South Carolina Press, 1987.

Frum, David. *The Right Man: The Surprise Presidency of George W. Bush.* New York: Random House, 2003.

Fulbright, William. "S. 3217-Introduction of a Bill Requiring the Secretary of Defense to Submit Regular Reports With Respect to the Kinds and Amounts of Information Released for Distribution to The Public By The Department Of Defense." *Congressional Record*, 91st Cong. 1st sess., 1969, 115, pt. 28, 37251. https://www.govinfo.gov/app/details/GPO-CRECB-1969-pt28.

Fyne, Robert. *Long Ago and Far Away: Hollywood and the Second World Wa*r. Lanham, Maryland, The Scarecrow Press, 2008.

Gallup, "Presidential Approval Ratings—George W. Bush." Accessed August 21, 2020. https://news.gallup.com/poll/116500/presidential-approval-ratings-george-bush.aspx.

Gano, Rick. "Nolan Ryan Wins 300th Game." *Associated Press*, August 1, 1990. https://apnews.com/4ace6196282e3a6ff789d2e40eef59ab.

Gates, Robert M. *Exercise of Power: American Failures, Successes, and a New Path Forward in the Post-Cold War World.* New York: Alfred A. Knopf, 2020. Kindle.

George, Alexander L. "The Role of Force in Diplomacy." In *The Use of Force After the Cold War*, edited by H.W. Brands, 59–92. College Station: Texas A&M University Press, 2000.

George, Susannah. "As U.S. Air War in Afghanistan Surged, Investigations into Civilian Harm Plunged." *Washington Post*, September 4, 2020. https://www.washingtonpost.com/world/2020/09/04/afghanistan-civilian-casualties-us-airstrikes/?arc404=true.

Gerbner, George, Larry Gross, Michael Morgan, and Nancy Signorielli, "Growing Up with Television: The Cultivation Perspective." In *Media Effects: Advances in Theory and Research*, edited by Jennings Bryant and Dolf Zillmann, 17–41. Hillsdale, NJ: Lawrence Erlbaum Associates, 1994.

Gibbons-Neff, Thomas, Helene Cooper, and Eric Schmitt. "U.S. Has 1,000 More Troops in Afghanistan Than It Disclosed." *New York Times*, March 14, 2021. https://www.nytimes.com/2021/03/14/world/asia/us-troops-afghanistan.html.

Gibbons-Neff Thomas and Eric Schmitt. "Security in Afghanistan Is Decaying, U.S. General Says as Forces Leave." *New York Times*, June 29, 2021, updated June 30, 2021. https://www.nytimes.com/2021/06/29/world/asia/afghanistan-civil-war-miller.html.

Gibbons-Neff, Thomas, Eric Schmitt, and Helene Cooper, "Pentagon Accelerates Withdrawal from Afghanistan." *New York Times*, May 25, 2001. https://www.nytimes.com/2021/05/25/us/politics/us-afghanistan-withdrawal.html.

Gladstone, Rick "Threats Sow Concern Over Korean Armistice." *New York Times*, March 9, 2013. https://www.nytimes.com/2013/03/10/world/asia/threats-sow-concerns-over-korean-armistice.html.

Graff, Garrett M. "The Children of 9/11 Are About to Vote." Politico Magazine, September 11, 2020. https://www.politico.com/news/magazine/2020/09/11/september-eleven-children-vote-410829.

Gralley, Craig R., ed., *Voices from the Station: The Evacuation of the US Embassy in Saigon*. Washington, DC: Center for the Study of Intelligence, Central Intelligence Agency, April 2015. Accessed June 16, 2021. https://www.cia.gov/static/76218a54 83719729a99e7ef716d56b7d/Voices-from-the-Station.pdf.

"The Great War." PBS. July 3, 2018. [Transcript]. Accessed February 8, 2020. https://www.pbs.org/wgbh/americanexperience/films/great-war/#transcript.

Greene, John Robert. *The Presidency of George Bush*. Lawrence, KS: University Press of Kansas, 2000.

Green, Melanie C. "Narratives and Cancer Communication." *Journal of Communication* 56 (2006): S163–S183. https://doi:10.1111/j.1460-2466.2006.00288.x.

Green, Melanie C. and Timothy C. Brock. "The Role of Transportation in the Persuasiveness of Public Narratives." *Journal of Personality & Social Psychology* 79, no. 5 (November 2000): 701–721. https://doi: 10.1037//0022-3514.79.5.701.

Greider, William. "Washington Post Warriors." *Nation*, March 6, 2003. https://www.thenation.com/article/archive/washington-post-warriors/.

Grimmett, Richard F. "Authorization for Use of Military Force in Response to the 9/11 Attacks (P.L. 107-40): Legislative History." *CRS Report for Congress*, January 16, 2007. https://fas.org/sgp/crs/natsec/RS22357.pdf.

"Ground War in Asia," *New York Times*, June 9, 1965, 46. https://nyti.ms/3wRRfML.

"Guantanamo Bay Fast Facts." CNN, October 7, 2020. Accessed October 17, 2020. https://www.cnn.com/2013/09/09/world/guantanamo-bay-naval-station-fast-facts/index.html.

"Gulf of Tonkin Resolution," History.com, updated June 7, 2019. Accessed January 13, 2020. https://www.history.com/topics/vietnam-war/gulf-of-tonkin-resolution-1.

Gwertzman, Bernard. "U.S. Papers Tell of '53 Policy To Use A-Bomb In Korea." *New York Times*, June 8, 1984. http://www.nytimes.com/1984/06/08/world/us-papers-tell-of-53-policy-to-use-a-bomb-in-korea.html.

Halberstam, David. *The Best and the Brightest*. New York: Modern Library, 2001. Kindle.

Hall, Mitchell. "Unsell the War: Vietnam and Antiwar Advertising." *The Historian* 58, No. 1 (Autumn 1995): 69–86. https://www.jstor.org/stable/24449611.

"Hanging My Hat in Manzanar." *Manzanar Free Press* (Manzanar, CA), Sep. 10 1943, 16. https://www.loc.gov/item/sn84025948/1943-09-10/ed-1/.

Hansen, Gregory. "Kenneth Burke's Rhetorical Theory within the Construction of the Ethnography of Speaking." *Folklore Forum* 27, no. 1 (1996): 50–59. https://scholarworks.iu.edu/dspace/bitstream/handle/2022/2207/27(1)%2050-59.pdf?sequence=1.

Harmetz, Aljean. "Murray Burnett, 86, Writer of Play Behind 'Casablanca'." *New York Times*, September 29, 1997. https://www.nytimes.com/1997/09/29/arts/murray-burnett-86-writer-of-play-behind-casablanca.html.

Harris, Mark. *Five Came Back: A Story of Hollywood and the Second World War.* New York: Penguin Press, 2014.

Heider, Fritz. *The Psychology of Interpersonal Relations.* New York: Wiley, 1958.

Herring, George C. *America's Longest War: The United States and Vietnam, 1950–1975*, 3rd ed. New York: McGraw-Hill, 1996.

History.com editors. "Hitler Appeased at Munich." *History*, last updated July 28, 2010. https://www.history.com/this-day-in-history/hitler-appeased-at-munich.

H.J. Res. 1145, Public Law 88-408, August 10, 1964. https://www.ourdocuments.gov/document_data/pdf/doc_098.pdf.

Hobsbawm, Eric. *Age of Extremes: The Short Twentieth Century 1914–1991.* London: Abacus, 1994 [1995 edition]. http://libcom.org/files/Eric%20Hobsbawm%20-%20Age%20Of%20Extremes%20-%201914-1991.pdf.

Hong, Jane. "Immigration Act of 1952." *Densho Encyclopedia*. Accessed February 29, 2020. https://encyclopedia.densho.org/Immigration%20Act%20of%201952/.

Horton, Alex, Louisa Loveluck, and John Hudson. "U.S. Targets Iran-Backed Militias in Iraq, Syria Strikes." *Washington Post*, June 28, 2021. https://www.washingtonpost.com/national-security/2021/06/27/us-airstrike-iraq-syria/.

Houston, Jeanne Wakatsuki and James D. Houston, *Farewell to Manzanar.* Boston: Houghton Mifflin, 1973, 2002 edition. Kindle.

Hyland, William G. *Clinton's World: Remaking American Foreign Policy.* Westport, CT: Praeger, 1999.

Immerwahr, Daniel. *How to Hide an Empire: A History of the Greater United States.* New York: MacMillan, 2019. Kindle.

"Inch'ŏn landing," *Encyclopaedia Britannica*, September 8, 2019. https://www.britannica.com/event/Inchon-landing.

Jackson, Brooks and Kathleen Hall Jamieson. *unSpun: Finding Facts in a World of Disinformation.* New York: Random House, 2007.

Jacobellis v. Ohio, 378 U.S. 184 (1964), https://caselaw.findlaw.com/us-supreme-court/378/184.html.

"Jessica Lynch: I'm No Hero." *ABC News*, November 6, 2003, updated January 6, 2006. https://abcnews.go.com/Primetime/story?id=132434.

Johnson, Lyndon B. "July 28, 1965: Press Conference." Miller Center, University of Virginia. Accessed March 25, 2020. https://millercenter.org/the-presidency/presidential-speeches/july-28-1965-press-conference.

Johnson, Lyndon B. "The President's Address at Johns Hopkins University: Peace Without Conquest, April 7, 1965." *Public Papers of the Presidents of the United*

States: Lyndon B. Johnson, 1965*, Book I, entry 172. Washington, D. C.: Government Printing Office, 1966, 394–399. Accessed March 20, 2020. http://www.lbjlibrary.org/exhibits/the-presidents-address-at-johns-hopkins-university-peace-without-conquest.

Johnson, Lyndon B. "The President's Address to the Nation Announcing Steps to Limit the War in Vietnam and Reporting His Decision Not to Seek Reelection." March 31, 1968. *Public Papers of the Presidents of the United States: Lyndon B. Johnson, 1968–1969* (2 vols.; Washington DC: Government Printing Office, 1970, Book I, 469–476). Accessed March 26, 2020, https://quod.lib.umich.edu/p/ppotpus/.

Johnson, Lyndon B. "Remarks in Memorial Hall, Akron University, October 21, 1964." *Public Papers of the Presidents of the United States: Lyndon B. Johnson, 1965*, Book II, entry 693. Washington, DC: Government Printing Office, 1966, 1387–1393. Accessed March 29, 2020. https://quod.lib.umich.edu/p/ppotpus/4730949.1964.002/631?page=root;rgn=full+text;size=100;view=image.

Jones, Jeffery M. "Who Had the Highest Gallup Presidential Job Approval Rating?" Gallup, December 17, 2019. https://news.gallup.com/poll/271628/highest-gallup-presidential-job-approval-rating.aspx.

Jowett, Garth S. and Victoria O'Donnell. *Propaganda and Persuasion*, 7th ed. Thousand Oaks, CA: Sage, 2019.

Justus, Zachary. "Torture as Text: The Rhetoric of Abu Ghraib." Master's thesis, California State University, Chico, 2005.

Karnow, Stanley. *Vietnam: A History*, revised updated edition. New York: Penguin, 1997.

Kazin, Michael. "Five Myths About World War I." *Washington Post*, April 6, 2017. https://www.washingtonpost.com/opinions/2017/04/06/06a8bcae-1597-11e7-9e4f-09aa75d3ec57_story.html?utm_term=.03a04afe0839.

Kazin, Michael. "If the U.S. Had Not Entered World War I, Would There Have Been a World War II?" *New Republic*, July 6, 2014. https://newrepublic.com/article/118435/world-war-i-debate-should-us-have-entered.

Kazin, Michael. *War Against War: The American Fight for Peace, 1914–1918*. New York: Simon & Schuster, 2017. Kindle.

Keegan, John. *The First World War*. New York: Vintage, 2012.

Kellen, Konrad. "Introduction." In *Propaganda: The Formation of Men's Attitudes*, by Jacques Ellul. Translated by Konrad Kellen and Jean Lerner, v–xviii. New York: Vintage, 1973.

Keller, Allan. *The Spanish-American War: A Compact History*. New York: Hawthorn, 1969.

Kennedy, John F. "America's Stake in Vietnam, American Friends of Vietnam, Washington, D.C." June 1, 1956. Papers of John F. Kennedy, Pre-Presidential Papers, Senate Files, Series 12, Speeches and the Press, Box 895. Accessed March 28, 2020. https://www.jfklibrary.org/archives/other-resources/john-f-kennedy-speeches/vietnam-conference-washington-dc-19560601.

Kennedy, John F. "Inaugural Address." January 20, 1961. John F. Kennedy Presidential Library and Museum. Accessed April 17, 2019. https://www.jfklibrary.org/learn/about-jfk/historic-speeches/inaugural-address.

Kerry, John. "How Do You Ask a Man to Be the Last Man to Die in Vietnam?" [Statement made before the Senate Foreign Relations Committee], April 23, 1971. History News Network, George Washington University. https://hnn.us/articles/3631.html.

Kinzer, Stephen. *The True Flag: Theodore Roosevelt, Mark Twain, and the Birth of American Empire.* New York: Henry Holt and Co., 2017. Kindle.

Kirk, Donald. "One of Biden's First Acts as President-Elect Was to Antagonize Kim Jong Un." Daily Beast, November 16, 2020. https://www.thedailybeast.com/one-of-joe-bidens-first-acts-as-president-elect-was-to-antagonize-kim-jong-un?source=articles&via=rss.

Knightley, Phillip. *The First Casualty: The War Correspondent as Hero and Myth-Maker from the Crimea to Iraq*, 3rd ed. Baltimore and London: John Hopkins University Press, 2004.

Kohut, Andrew. "Post Cold-War Attitudes toward the Use of Force." In *The Use of Force After the Cold War*, edited by H.W. Brands, 165–177. College Station: Texas A&M University Press, 2000.

"Korean War." *Encyclopaedia Britannica*, January 3, 2020. Accessed January 22, 2020. https://www.britannica.com/event/Korean-War.

"Korean War Fast Facts." CNN, last modified June 10, 2019. Accessed December 2, 2019. https://www.cnn.com/2013/06/28/world/asia/korean-war-fast-facts/index.html.

Kraus, Sidney and Dennis Davis. *The Effects of Mass Communication on Political Behavior.* University Park: Pennsylvania State University Press, 1976.

Krauss, Clifford. "The World; Remember Yellow Journalism." *New York Times*, February 15, 1998. https://www.nytimes.com/1998/02/15/weekinreview/the-world-remember-yellow-journalism.html.

Krugman, Paul. "Errors and Lies." *New York Times*, May 18, 2015. https://www.nytimes.com/2015/05/18/opinion/paul-krugman-errors-and-lies.html?_r=0.

Kudo, Timothy. "Two Costly Wars, and a Legacy of Shame." *New York Times*, November 24, 2020. https://www.nytimes.com/2020/11/24/opinion/iraq-afghanistan-troop-withdrawal.html?campaign_id=9&emc=edit_nn_20201124&instance_id=24415&nl=the-mornin%E2%80%A6.

Kull, Steven. "Misperceptions, the Media and the Iraq War." The Pipa/Knowledge Networks Poll, October 2, 2003. https://worldpublicopinion.net/wp-content/uploads/2017/12/IraqMedia_Oct03_rpt.pdf.

Kumar, Deepa. "Media, War, and Propaganda: Strategies of Information Management During the 2003 Iraq War." *Communication and Critical/Cultural Studies* 3, no. 1 (2006): 48–69. https://doi.org/10.1080/14791420500505650.

Kuper, Glenn G. "Review of Narrative Persuasion in Legal Settings: What's the Story?" *The Jury Expert* 23, no. 3 (May 2011): 37–38. https://www.thejuryexpert.com/2011/05/narrative-persuasion/.

Lambert, Andrew. "Jutland: Why World War I's Only Sea Battle Was So Crucial to Britain's Victory." *The Conversation*, May 27, 2016. Accessed August 27, 2019, http://theconversation.com/jutland-why-world-war-is-only-sea-battle-was-so-crucial-to-britains-victory-59415.

Langewiesche, William. "The Reporter Who Told the World About the Bomb." *New York Times*, August 4, 2020. https://www.nytimes.com/2020/08/04/books/review/fallout-hiroshima-hersey-lesley-m-m-blume.html.

Lasswell, Harold D. "The Theory of Political Propaganda." *The American Political Science Review* 21, no. 3 (August, 1927): 627–631.

Lee, Michael J. "Us, Them, and the War on Terror: Reassessing George W. Bush's Rhetorical Legacy." *Communication and Critical/Cultural Studies* 14, no. 1 (2017): 3–30, https://doi.org/10.1080/14791420.2016.1257817.

"A Lie Can Travel Halfway around the World While the Truth Is Putting on Its Shoes." Quote Investigator. Accessed March 9, 2019. https://quoteinvestigator.com/2014/07/13/truth/.

Link, Arthur Stanley. *Wilson: The Struggle for Neutrality, Vol. 3*. Princeton, NJ: Princeton University Press, 1947. https://hdl-handle-net.mantis.csuchico.edu/2027/heb.01547. EPUB.

Lippmann, Walter. *Public Opinion*. New York: Harcourt Brace & Co., 1922.

Little, Becky. "Inside America's Shocking WWII Propaganda Machine." National Geographic, December 19, 2016. https://news.nationalgeographic.com/2016/12/world-war-2-propaganda-history-books/.

Lunch, William L. and Peter W. Sperlich. "American Public Opinion and the War in Vietnam." *Western Political Quarterly* 32, no. 1 (March 1979): 21–44. https://www.jstor.org/stable/447561.

MacArthur, Douglas. "Address of the General of the Army, Douglas MacArthur." *Congressional Record—House*. April 19, 1951, 4123–4125. https://www.govinfo.gov/app/details/GPO-CRECB-1951-pt3/GPO-CRECB-1951-pt3-18-.

MacArthur, John R. "Remember Nayirah, Witness for Kuwait?" *New York Times*, January 6, 1992. https://www.nytimes.com/1992/01/06/opinion/remember-nayirah-witness-for-kuwait.html?searchResultPosition=1.

MacArthur, John R. *Second Front: Censorship and Propaganda in the 1991 Gulf War*, 2nd ed. Berkeley: University of California Press, 2004.

Maggio, John (writer and producer). *Korea: The Never Ending War*. PBS Video, 2019.

Martí, José. "Letter to Manuel Mercado," May 18, 1895. History of Cuba.com. http://www.historyofcuba.com/history/marti/mercado.htm.

Massie, Robert K. *Dreadnought: Britain, Germany, and the Coming of the Great War*. New York: Ballantine Books, 1991.

Masterson, Julia, "Chronology of U.S.-North Korean Nuclear and Missile Diplomacy." Arms Control Association. Accessed January 24, 2020. https://www.armscontrol.org/factsheets/dprkchron.

Mazzetti, Mark. "Spy Agencies Say Iraq War Worsens Terrorism Threat." *New York Times*, September 24, 2006. https://www.nytimes.com/2006/09/24/world/middleeast/24terror.html.

Mazzocco, Philip J. and Melanie C. Green. "Narrative Persuasion in Legal Settings: What's the Story?" *The Jury Expert* 23, no. 3 (May 2011): 27–34. https://www.thejuryexpert.com/2011/05/narrative-persuasion/.

McCants, William. *The ISIS Apocalypse: The History, Strategy, and Doomsday Vision of the Islamic State*. New York: St. Martin's Press, 2015.

"McCarthy Says Communists Are in State Department." History.com, last updated July 17, 2019. Accessed January 14, 2020. https://www.history.com/this-day-in-history/mccarthy-says-communists-are-in-state-department.

McCombs, Maxwell. "News Influence on Our Pictures of the World." In *Media Effects: Advances in Theory and Research*, edited by Jennings Bryant and Dolf Zillmann, 1–16. Hillsdale, NJ: Lawrence Erlbaum Associates, 1994.

McCullough, David. *Truman*. New York: Simon & Schuster, 1992.

McKinley, William. "Inaugural Address," March 4, 1897. The American Presidency Project. Accessed February 28, 2020, https://www.presidency.ucsb.edu/node/205278.

McKinley, William. "Message to Congress Requesting a Declaration of War with Spain." April 11, 1898. The American Presidency Project. https://www.presidency.ucsb.edu/documents/message-congress-requesting-declaration-war-with-spain.

McKinley, William. *Speeches and Addresses of William McKinley*. New York: Doubleday & McClure, 1900. Google Books. https://play.google.com/books/reader?id=iOh2AAAAMAAJ&hl=en&pg=GBS.PP1.

McMaster, H. R. *Dereliction of Duty: Lyndon Johnson, Robert McNamara, the Joint Chiefs of Staff, and the Lies That Led to Vietnam*. New York: Harper Collins, 1997.

McNamara, Robert S. with Brian VanDeMark. *In Retrospect: The Tragedy and Lessons of Vietnam*. New York: Times Books/Random House, 1995.

McWilliams, Carey. "Japanese Evacuation: Policy and Perspectives." *Common Ground* 2, no. 4 (Summer 1942): 65–72. https://www.unz.com/print/CommonGround-1942q2-00065/.

Meacham, Jon. *Destiny and Power: The American Odyssey of George Herbert Walker Bush*. New York: Random House, 2015.

"Memories of Manzanar." *Manzanar Free Press* (Manzanar, CA), Sep. 10 1943, 2. https://www.loc.gov/item/sn84025948/1943-09-10/ed-1/.

Merritt, Robert P. "The Spirit of Manzanar." *Manzanar Free Press* (Manzanar, CA), Sep. 10, 1943, 2. https://www.loc.gov/item/sn84025948/1943-09-10/ed-1/.

Miller, Daniel A. (producer, writer, and director) *Crucible of Empire*. PBS Video [Transcript], 1999. Accessed May 6, 2021, https://www.pbs.org/crucible/frames/_journalism.html.

Mock, James R. and Cedric Larson. *Words That Won the War: The Story of The Committee on Public Information 1917–1919*. Princeton: Princeton University Press, 1939. http://www.archive.org/details/wordsthatwonwars00mockrich.

Moore, David W. "Little Concern about Lack of WMD in Iraq." Gallup News Service, June 4, 2003. https://news.gallup.com/poll/8566/little-concern-about-lack-wmd-iraq.aspx.

Moorhouse, Roger. *The Devils' Alliance*. New York: Basic Books, 2014. Kindle.

Moskos, Charles. "The New Cold War: Confronting Social Issues in the Military." In *The Use of Force After the Cold War*, edited by H.W. Brands, 178–198. College Station: Texas A&M University Press, 2000.

"Most Expect U.S. To Be Bogged Down In Iraq, Poll Says." *Greensboro News and Record*, August 23, 2003, updated January 24, 2015. https://greensboro.com/mo

st-expect-u-s-to-be-bogged-down-in-iraq/article_1dead32a-96b3-5145-ba9b-f33 88c847abc.html.

"Motion Picture 498; President Johnson's Vietnam Address." August 4, 1964. Lyndon Baines Johnson Library, Austin, TX. Accessed March 26, 2020. https://www.docsteach.org/documents/document/johnson-vietnam-address.

Moyers, Bill. "The 30-Second President." *A Walk Through the 20th Century*, September 19, 1984 [Transcript]. https://billmoyers.com/content/30-second-president/.

Moyers, Bill. "Bill Remembers LBJ's Road to War." *Bill Moyers Journal*, November 20, 2009, updated August 6, 2014. https://billmoyers.com/content/lbjs-road-to-war/.

Moyers, Bill. "Buying the War: How Big Media Failed Us." *Bill Moyers Journal*, April 25, 2007, June 19, 2014 [Transcript]. https://billmoyers.com/content/buying-the-war/.

Moyers, Bill "The Image Makers." *A Walk Through the 20th Century*, April 14, 1983 [Transcript]. https://billmoyers.com/content/image-makers/.

Moyers, Bill. "WWII: The Propaganda Battle." *A Walk Through the Twentieth Century*, May 9, 1984 [Transcript]. https://billmoyers.com/content/wwii-propaganda-battle/.

Mueller, John E. "Trends in Popular Support for the Wars in Korea and Vietnam." *The American Political Science Review* 65, no. 2 (June, 1971): 358–375. https://doi.org/10.2307/1954454.

Mukawa, Tomoko. "Making the Unacceptable Seem Acceptable: Narrative Rhetoric and the Japanese American Internment of World War II." Master's thesis, California State University, Chico, 1999.

National Parks Service Presidio of San Francisco. "The Philippine War—Suppressing An Insurrection." Accessed March 15, 2018. https://www.nps.gov/prsf/learn/historyculture/the-philippine-war-suppressing-an-insurrection.htm.

Nixon, Richard M. "Address to the Nation on the Situation in Southeast Asia." April 30, 1970. Miller Center, University of Virginia. Accessed March 27, 2020. https://millercenter.org/the-presidency/presidential-speeches/april-30-1970-address-nation-situation-southeast-asia.

Nixon, Richard M. "Address to the Nation on the War in Vietnam." November 3, 1969, P-691101. Accessed March 22, 2020. https://www.nixonlibrary.gov/sites/default/files/2018-08/silentmajority_transcript.pdf.

Nossiter, Adam and Thomas Gibbons-Neff. "Violence May Delay U.S. Troop Withdrawal from Afghanistan." *New York Times*, January 29, 2021. https://www.nytimes.com/2021/01/29/world/asia/afghanistan-withdrawal-ghani-biden.html.

Obama, Barack. "Osama Bin Laden Dead." May 2, 2011. Accessed September 21, 2020. https://obamawhitehouse.archives.gov/blog/2011/05/02/osama-bin-laden-dead.

Obama, Barack. *A Promised Land*. New York: Crown, 2020. Kindle.

Obama, Barack. "Remarks by the President at the Acceptance of the Nobel Peace Prize." December 10, 2009. Accessed September 19, 2020. https://obamawhitehouse.archives.gov/the-press-office/remarks-president-acceptance-nobel-peace-prize.

Obama, Barack. "Remarks by the President in Address to the Nation on the Way Forward in Afghanistan and Pakistan." December 1, 2009. Accessed September 19, 2020. https://obamawhitehouse.archives.gov/photos-and-video/video/president-obama-way-forward-afghanistan-and-pakistan#transcript.

Obama, Barack. "Transcript: Obama's Speech Against The Iraq War." October 2, 2002. Posted January 20, 2009 on NPR website. https://www.npr.org/templates/story/story.php?storyId=99591469.

Office of the Historian, Bureau of Public Affairs, United States Department of State. "A Guide to the United States' History of Recognition, Diplomatic, and Consular Relations, by Country, since 1776: Cuba." Accessed March 1, 2018. https://history.state.gov/countries/cuba.

Office of the Historian, Foreign Service Institute, U.S. Department of State. "The Philippine-American War, 1899–1902." Accessed March 6, 2018. https://history.state.gov/milestones/1899-1913/war.

Office of the Historian, Foreign Service Institute, United States Department of State. "The Spanish-American War, 1898." Accessed June 21, 2021. https://history.state.gov/milestones/1866-1898/spanish-american-war.

Office of the Press Secretary. "Joint Resolution to Authorize the Use of United States Armed Forces Against Iraq." October 2, 2002. Accessed August 11, 2020. https://georgewbush-whitehouse.archives.gov/news/releases/2002/10/20021002-2.html.

Ohl, Jessy J. "Nothing to See or Fear: Light War and the Boring Visual Rhetoric of U.S. Drone Imagery." *Quarterly Journal of Speech* 101, no. 4 (November 2015): 612–632, https://doi.org/10.1080/00335630.2015.1128115.

O'Shaughnessy, Nicholas Jackson. *Politics and Propaganda: Weapons of Mass Seduction*. Ann Arbor: University of Michigan Press, 2004.

Owen, J. "Pearl Harbor Ships on the Morning of the Attack." Pearl Harbor Visitors Bureau, October 12, 2012. https://visitpearlharbor.org/pearl-harbor-ships-on-december-7th/.

Page, Caroline. "Introduction," *U.S. Official Propaganda During the Vietnam War, 1965–1973: The Limits of Persuasion*. London: Bloomsbury Academic, 1996. http://dx.doi.org/10.5040/9781474290869.0005.

Panetta, Leon with Jim Newton. *Worthy Fights: A Memoir of Leadership in War and Peace*. New York: Penguin Press, 2014.

Parrott, Lindesay. "M'Arthur Reports 450,000 of Enemy Are Now in Korea." *New York Times*, December 28, 1950, 1–2. https://nyti.ms/3fRhlt4.

Perse, Elizabeth M. *Media Effects and Society*. Mahwah, NJ: Lawrence Erlbaum Associates, 2001.

Pew Research Center. "Social Media Usage: 2005–2015." October 8, 2015. https://www.pewresearch.org/internet/2015/10/08/social-networking-usage-2005-2015/.

Pincus, Walter. "Bush Recantation of Iraq Claim Stirs Calls for Probes," *Washington Post* (1974-Current File), Jul 09, 2003. http://mantis.csuchico.edu/login?url=https://search-proquest-com.mantis.csuchico.edu/docview/2267467562?accountid=10346.

Ponting, Clive. *1940: Myth and Reality*. Chicago: Ivan R. Dee, Inc., 1990.

Potter, W. James. *Digital Media Effects*. Lanham, MD: Rowman & Littlefield, 2021. Kindle.
Powell, Colin with Joseph E. Persico. *My American Journey*. New York: Random House, 1995.
Powell, Colin. "U.S. Secretary of State Colin Powell Addresses the U.N. Security Council." February 5, 2003. Accessed August 9, 2020. https://georgewbush-whitehouse.archives.gov/news/releases/2003/02/20030205-1.html.
"The Power of America's Example: The Biden Plan for Leading the Democratic World to Meet The Challenges Of The 21st Century." Accessed November 7, 2020. https://joebiden.com/americanleadership/.
"The Press: I'll Furnish the War." *Time*, October 27, 1947. http://content.time.com/time/magazine/article/0,9171,854840,00.html.
Preston, Richard. "First World War Centenary: The Assassination of Franz Ferdinand, As It Happened." *Telegraph*, June 27, 2014. https://www.telegraph.co.uk/history/world-war-one/10930863/First-World-War-centenary-the-assassination-of-Franz-Ferdinand-as-it-happened.html.
Quigley, Samantha L. "Ceremony Commemorates Vietnam War's First Combat Casualties." *DoD News*, July 8, 2009. https://www.dvidshub.net/news/36136/ceremony-commemorates-vietnam-wars-first-combat-casualties.
Rampton, Sheldon and John Stauber. *Weapons of Mass Deception: The Uses of Propaganda in Bush's War on Iraq*. New York: Tarcher/Penguin, 2003. Kindle.
Reagan, Ronald. "Remarks on East-West Relations at the Brandenburg Gate in West Berlin." June 12, 1987. Accessed May 17, 2020. https://www.reaganlibrary.gov/research/speeches/061287d.
Reagan, Ronald. "Veterans of Foreign Wars Convention, Chicago, IL, Peace: Restoring the Margin of Safety." August 18, 1980. Ronald Reagan Presidential Library and Museum. Accessed June 20, 2020, https://www.reaganlibrary.gov/sspeeches/8-18-80.
Redmond, Caroline. "'It Was War': 33 Photos of the Pearl Harbor Attack That Changed History Forever," *ATI* [All That's Interesting], Published December 7, 2018, Updated February 28, 2019. Accessed October 11. 2019. https://allthatsinteresting.com/pearl-harbor-attack-pictures.
Reuter, Tim. "The Munich Agreement Did Not Cause World War II, The Nazi-Soviet Nonaggression Pact Did." *Forbes*, May 8, 2015. https://www.forbes.com/sites/timreuter/2015/05/08/the-munich-agreement-did-not-cause-world-war-ii-the-nazi-soviet-nonaggression-pact-did/?sh=155dc3dc44c7.
Rhodes, Ben. "The 9/11 Era Is Over." *Atlantic*, April 6, 2020. https://www.theatlantic.com/ideas/archive/2020/04/its-not-september-12-anymore/609502/.
Richburg, Keith B. "Mission to Hanoi: McNamara Asks Ex-Foes to Join in Search for War's Lessons." *Washington Post* (1974-Current File), Nov 11, 1995, A21. ProQuest Historical Newspapers.
Rickover, H. G. *How the Battleship Maine Was Destroyed*. Washington, DC: Naval History Division, Department of the Navy, 1976. https://www.ibiblio.org/hyperwar/NHC/NewPDFs/USN/USN%20Manuals%20and%20Reports/USN.HOW%20.THE.BATTLESHIP.MAINE.WAS.DESTROYED.Rickover.pdf.

Ridgway, Mathew B. *The Korean War*. Garden City, NY: Doubleday and Co., 1967.

Risen, James. *Pay Any Price: Greed, Power, and Endless War*. New York: Houghton Mifflin Harcourt, 2014.

Rogin, Josh. "McMaster Says Trump's Taliban Deal Is Munich-Like Appeasement." *Washington Post*, October 19, 2020. https://www.washingtonpost.com/opinions/2020/10/19/mcmaster-says-trumps-taliban-deal-is-munich-like-appeasement/.

Roosevelt, Franklin D. "Address by the President." *Congressional Record—House*. December 8, 1941, 9519–9520. Accessed February 3, 2020, https://www.govinfo.gov/content/pkg/GPO-CRECB-1941-pt9/pdf/GPO-CRECB-1941-pt9-9-2.pdf.

Roosevelt, Franklin D. "Fireside Chat 19: On the War with Japan." December 9, 1941. Miller Center, University of Virginia. https://millercenter.org/the-presidency/presidential-speeches/december-9-1941-fireside-chat-19-war-japan.

Rothman, Lily. "Why the United States Controls Guantanamo Bay." *Time*, January 22, 2015. http://time.com/3672066/guantanamo-bay-history/.

Ruane, Michael E. "The U.S. Was Looking for the Enemy Near Pearl Harbor—But It Was Looking in the Wrong Direction." *Washington Post*, December 7, 2018. https://www.washingtonpost.com/history/2018/12/07/us-was-looking-enemy-near-pearl-harbor-it-was-looking-wrong-direction/?utm_term=.106d476a76d3.

Rumsfeld, Donald. *Known and Unknown: A Memoir*. New York: Sentinel, 2011.

Ryan, Missy and Karen DeYoung. "Biden Will Withdraw All U.S. Forces From Afghanistan by Sept. 11, 2021." *Washington Post*, April 13, 2021. https://www.washingtonpost.com/national-security/biden-us-troop-withdrawal-afghanistan/2021/04/13/918c3cae-9beb-11eb-8a83-3bc1fa69c2e8_story.html.

Safi, Michael. "Trump Pardons Blackwater Contractors Jailed for Massacre of Iraq Civilians." *Guardian*, December 23, 2020. https://www.theguardian.com/world/2020/dec/23/trump-pardons-blackwater-contractors-jailed-for-massacre-of-iraq-civilians.

Salim, Mustafa and Louisa Loveluck. "In Iraq, Trump's Blackwater Pardons Meet with Cynicism, Fatigue." *Washington Post*, December 23, 2020. https://www.washingtonpost.com/world/middle_east/iraq-blackwater-military-contractors-pardons/2020/12/23/062ee814-44bb-11eb-ac2a-3ac0f2b8ceeb_story.html.

Sanger, David E. and William J. Broad. "Trump Inherits a Secret Cyberwar Against North Korean Missiles." *New York Times*, March 4, 2017. https://www.nytimes.com/2017/03/04/world/asia/north-korea-missile-program-sabotage.html?_r=0.

Scheer, Christopher, Robert Scheer, and Lakshimi Chaudhry. *The Five Biggest Lies Bush Told Us About Iraq*. New York: Akashic Books and Seven Stories Press, 2003.

Schwartz, Tony. *The Responsive Chord*. New York: Anchor Press/Doubleday, 1974.

Senate Subcommittee on Korean War Atrocities. *Korean War Atrocities*. January 11, 1954. https://www.loc.gov/rr/frd/Military_Law/pdf/KW-atrocities-Report.pdf.

Shales, Tom. "Stormin' Norman in High Command." *Washington Post*, February 28, 1991. https://www.washingtonpost.com/archive/lifestyle/1991/02/28/stormin-norman-in-high-command/cd526793-85a6-4332-9ad9-61dc1d164b5f/.

Shapiro, Peter, "Freshman Deferments End As Nixon Signs New Draft Legislation." *Harvard Crimson*, September 29, 1971. https://www.thecrimson.com/article/1971/9/29/freshman-deferments-end-as-nixon-signs/.

Shaw, Diana. "The Temptation of Tom Dooley: He Was the Heroic Jungle Doctor of Indochina in the 1950s. But He Had a Secret, and to Protect It, He Helped Launch the First Disinformation Campaign of the Vietnam War." *Los Angeles Times*, December 15, 1991. https://www.latimes.com/archives/la-xpm-1991-12-15-tm-868-story.html.

Sheehan, Neil. *A Bright Shining Lie: John Paul Vann and America in Vietnam*. New York: Random House, 1988, Modern Library, 2009. Kindle.

Smith, Jean Edward. *Bush*. New York: Simon and Shuster, 2016.

Smith, Jean Edward. *Eisenhower in War and Peace*. New York: Random House, 2012.

"South Vietnam: Death at Intermission Time." Togetherweserved.com, July 20, 1959. Accessed January 13, 2020. https://army.togetherweserved.com/army/servlet/tws.webapp.WebApp?cmd=ShadowBoxProfile&type=Person&ID=42020.

Spector, Ronald H. *After Tet: The Bloodiest Year in Vietnam*. New York: The Free Press, 1993.

Spiller, James. "This is War! Network Radio and World War II Propaganda in America." *Journal of Radio Studies* 11, no. 1 (June 2004): 55–72. https://doi.org/10.1207/s15506843jrs1101_6.

Sproule, J. Michael. *Channels of Propaganda*. Bloomington, IN: ERIC Clearinghouse on Reading, English, and Communication, 1994. https://files.eric.ed.gov/fulltext/ED372461.pdf.

Sproule, J. Michael. *Propaganda and Democracy: The American Experience of Mass Media and Mass Persuasion*. New York: Cambridge University Press, 1997.

Sreberny-Mohammadi, Annabelle. "Global News Media Cover the World." in *Questioning the Media: A Critical Introduction*, 2nd ed. edited by John Downing, Ali Mohammadi, and Annabelle Sreberny-Mohammadi, 428–443. Thousand Oaks, CA: Sage, 1995.

"Statement of the Atlantic Summit: A Vision for Iraq and the Iraqi People." March 16, 2003. Accessed August 11, 2020. https://georgewbush-whitehouse.archives.gov/news/releases/2003/03/20030316-1.html.

Stauber, John. "Half of Americans Still Believe in WMDs—They Saw Them on TV." *PR Watch*, August 8, 2006. https://www.prwatch.org/news/2006/08/5067/half-americans-still-believe-wmds-they-saw-them-tv.

Stelzner, Hermann G. "'War Message,' December 8, 1941: An Approach to Language." *Speech Monographs* 33, no. 4 (1966): 419–437. https://doi.org/10.1080/03637756609375508.

Steuter, Erin and Deborah Wills. *At War with Metaphor: Media, Propaganda, and Racism in the War on Terror*. Lanham, MD: Lexington Books, 2008, pb edition 2009.

"Telephone conversation # 5593, sound recording, LBJ and ROBERT MCNAMARA, 9/18/1964, 11:46AM." Recordings and Transcripts of Telephone Conversations and Meetings, LBJ Presidential Library. Accessed April 2, 2020. https://www.discoverlbj.org/item/tel-05593.

Tharoor, Ishaan. "75 Years after Auschwitz's Liberation, the Ghosts of the Past Loom Large." *Washington Post*, January 27, 2020. https://www.washingtonpost.com/world/2020/01/28/75-years-after-auschwitzs-liberation-ghosts-past-loom-large/.

Tharoor, Ishaan. "Is the 9/11 Era Over?" *Washington Post*, September 10, 2020. https://www.washingtonpost.com/world/2020/09/11/is-911-era-over/.

Thompson, Mark. "'Stormin' Norman,' 1934–2012." *Time*, December 27, 2012. https://nation.time.com/2012/12/27/stormin-norman-1934-2012/.

Time. October 21–28, 2019. Cover.

"Timeline of the Cold War." Harry S. Truman Library and Museum. Accessed January 12, 2020. https://www.trumanlibrary.gov/public/TrumanCIA_Timeline.pdf.

Truman, Harry S. "Address in the Oakland Auditorium." October 4, 1952. Harry S. Truman Library and Museum. Accessed January 15, 2020. https://www.trumanlibrary.gov/library/public-papers/279/address-oakland-auditorium.

Truman, Harry S. "Address in Tullahoma, Tenn., at the Dedication of the Arnold Engineering Development Center." June 25, 1951. Harry S. Truman Library and Museum. Accessed January 21, 2020. https://www.trumanlibrary.gov/library/public-papers/138/address-tullahoma-tenn-dedication-arnold-engineering-development-center.

Truman, Harry S. *Memoirs, Vol. 1: Year of Decisions*. Garden City, NY: Doubleday, 1955.

Truman, Harry S. *Memoirs, Vol. 2: Year of Trial and Hope*. Garden City, NY: Doubleday, 1956.

Truman, Harry S. "The President's Press Conference." November 30, 1950, Harry S. Truman Library and Museum. Accessed January 20, 2020. https://www.trumanlibrary.gov/library/public-papers/295/presidents-news-conference.

Truman, Harry S. "Special Message to the Congress on Greece and Turkey: The Truman Doctrine." March 12, 1947. Harry S. Truman Library and Museum. Accessed January 14, 2020. https://www.trumanlibrary.gov/library/public-papers/56/special-message-congress-greece-and-turkey-truman-doctrine.

Truman, Harry S. "Statement by the President on the Situation in Korea." June 27, 1950. Harry S. Truman Library and Museum. Accessed January 15, 2020. https://www.trumanlibrary.gov/library/public-papers/173/statement-president-situation-korea.

Tuchman, Barbara. *The Guns of August*. New York: MacMillan, 1962.

Tye, Larry. *The Father of Spin*. New York: Crown, 1998.

United Press, "War is Declared by North Koreans; Fighting on Border." *New York Times*, June 25, 1950, 1, 21. https://nyti.ms/3z5DQ59.

"U.S. Destroyers Open Fire again in Tonkin Gulf; Targets Vanish; No American Losses in Clash Off Coast of North Vietnam." *New York Times*, September 19, 1964, 1. https://nyti.ms/361MxAp.

"US Downsizes Its Troops in Afghanistan to 2,500." *Aljazeera* [English], January 15, 2021. https://www.aljazeera.com/news/2021/1/15/us-meets-its-goal-of-downsizing-in-afghanistan-to-2500-troops.

"U.S. Postwar Deaths Equal Iraq Combat Toll." *Sacramento Bee*, August 26, 2003, A1.

"USS Pueblo Captured." History.com, July 20, 2010, last updated January 22, 2020. https://www.history.com/this-day-in-history/uss-pueblo-captured.

VanDeMark, Brian. *Into the Quagmire: Lyndon Johnson and the Escalation of the Vietnam War*. New York: Oxford University Press, 1995. Adobe Digital Edition.

"Victory at Sea." IMDb. Accessed January 22, 2020, https://www.imdb.com/title/tt0046658/.

"Vietnam Lotteries." Selective Service System. Accessed June 18, 2020. https://www.sss.gov/history-and-records/vietnam-lotteries/.

Vogel, Steve. "The Maine Attraction." *Washington Post*, April 23, 1998. https://www.washingtonpost.com/archive/local/1998/04/23/the-maine-attraction/19167d57-2116-401c-922c-96cc2067349c/.

Waggoner, Walter H. "Acheson Tells Bitter Marine to Have Faith in U.S. Ideals." *New York Times*, March 4, 1951, 1, 5. https://nyti.ms/3ikzHV5.

Walsh, Kenneth T. "50 Years Ago, Walter Cronkite Changed a Nation." *U.S. News & World Report*, February 27, 2018. https://www.usnews.com/news/ken-walshs-washington/articles/2018-02-27/50-years-ago-walter-cronkite-changed-a-nation.

Watzlawick, Paul. *How Real is Real? Confusion, Disinformation, Communication*. New York: Vintage, 1977.

Weaver, Jr., Warren. "Fulbright Scores War 'Propaganda.'" *New York Times*, December 2, 1969, 37. https://nyti.ms/35UzMXX.

West, Darrell M. *The Rise and Fall of the Media Establishment*. Boston: Bedford/St. Martin's, 2001.

"What Happened at Manzanar." *Common Ground* 3, no. 3 (Spring 1943): 83–86. https://www.unz.com/print/CommonGround-1943q1-00083/.

Wheatcroft, Geoffrey. "The War to End All Wars: The Ardent but Flawed Movement Against World War I." *Nation*, October 5, 2017. https://www.thenation.com/article/the-war-to-end-all-wars/.

White, Robert A. "Mass Communication and Culture: Transition to a New Paradigm." *Journal of Communication* 33 (Summer 1983): 279–301.

Whitlock, Craig. "At War with the Truth." *Washington Post*, December 9, 2019. https://www.washingtonpost.com/graphics/2019/investigations/afghanistan-papers/afghanistan-war-confidential-documents/?wpisrc=pw_ret_afghanistan_20191210.

Whitlock, Craig. "Stranded Without a Strategy." *Washington Post*, December 9, 2019. https://www.washingtonpost.com/graphics/2019/investigations/afghanistan-papers/afghanistan-war-strategy/?tid=bottom_nav.

"Why Obama Failed to Close Guantanamo." *PBS Newshour*, January 14, 2017. https://www.pbs.org/newshour/show/obama-failed-close-guantanamo.

"'Why We Fight'—America's World War Two Propaganda Masterpiece." *Military History Now*, November 21, 2014. https://militaryhistorynow.com/2014/11/21/why-we-fight-americas-world-war-two-propaganda-masterpiece/.

Will, George F. "We've been in Afghanistan for 6,000 days. What are we doing?" *Washington Post*, March 9, 2018. https://www.washingtonpost.com/opinions/can-someone-please-explain-what-were-doing-in-afghanistan/2018/03/09/a6a6e91e-230c-11e8-86f6-54bfff693d2b_story.html.

Wilson, Joseph C. 4th. "What I Didn't Find in Africa." *New York Times*, July 6, 2003. https://www.nytimes.com/2003/07/06/opinion/what-i-didn-t-find-in-africa.html.

Wilson, Woodrow. "Address of the President of the United States to the Senate." January 22, 1917. Accessed February 23, 2020. https://wwi.lib.byu.edu/index.php?title=Address_of_the_President_of_the_United_States_to_the_Senate&oldid=8374.

Wilson, Woodrow. "Message to Congress, 63rd Cong., 2d Sess., Senate Doc. No. 566." August 19, 1914, 3–4. Accessed February 23, 2020. https://wwi.lib.byu.edu/index.php/President_Wilson%27s_Declaration_of_Neutrality.

Wilson, Woodrow. "Message Regarding German Actions." April 19, 2016. Accessed February 27, 2020. https://millercenter.org/the-presidency/presidential-speeches/april-19-1916-message-regarding-german-actions.

Wilson, Woodrow. "Message Regarding Safety of Merchant Ships." February 26, 1917, UVA Miller Center. Accessed February 26, 2020. https://millercenter.org/the-presidency/presidential-speeches/february-26-1917-message-regarding-safety-merchant-ships.

Wilson, Woodrow. "President Wilson's Address to Both Houses of Congress in Joint Session." February 3, 1917. Accessed February 23, 2020. https://wwi.lib.byu.edu/index.php/President_Wilson%27s_Address_to_Both_Houses_of_Congress_in_Joint_Session,_February_3,_1917.

Wilson, Woodrow. "President Wilson's Fourteen Points." January 9, 1918. Accessed February 27, 2020. https://wwi.lib.byu.edu/index.php/President_Wilson%27s_Fourteen_Points.

Wilson, Woodrow. "Second Inaugural Address." March 5, 1917, UVA Miller Center. Accessed February 26, 2020. https://millercenter.org/the-presidency/presidential-speeches/march-5-1917-second-inaugural-address.

Wilson, Woodrow. "War Message to Congress." April 2, 1917. Accessed December 1, 2019. https://wwi.lib.byu.edu/index.php/Wilson's_War_Message_to_Congress.

Wong, Julia Carrie and Liz Barney. "Hawaii Ballistic Missile False Alarm Results in Panic." *Guardian*, January 14, 2018. Accessed August 9, 2019. https://www.theguardian.com/us-news/2018/jan/13/hawaii-ballistic-missile-threat-alert-false-alarm.

Woodward, Bob. *Bush at War.* New York: Simon & Schuster, 2002.

Woodward, Bob. *The Commanders.* New York: Simon & Schuster, 1991.

Woodward, Bob. *Obama's Wars.* New York: Simon & Shuster, 2010.

Woodward, Bob. *Plan of Attack.* New York: Simon & Schuster, 2004.

Woodward, Bob *Rage.* New York: Simon & Shuster, 2020. Kindle.

Woodward, Bob. *State of Denial.* New York: Simon & Schuster, 2006.

Woodward, Bob. *The War Within: A Secret White House History 2006–2008.* New York: Simon & Schuster, 2008.

"The World of 1898: The Spanish American War Rough Riders." Hispanic Division of Library of Congress. https://www.loc.gov/rr/hispanic/1898/roughriders.html.

Xiong, Jack. "The Fake News in 1990 That Propelled the US into the First Gulf War." *Citizen Truth*, May 7, 2018. https://citizentruth.org/fake-news-1990-that-ignited-gulf-war-sympathy/.

Zakaria, Fareed. "Exaggerating the Threats." *Newsweek*, June 16, 2003, 33.

Index

Abizaid, John, 234–35
Abu Ghraib revelations, 231–33
Acheson, Dean, 25, 99, 103, 110
Achter, Paul, 224
Ackerman, Elliot, 205
Adelman, Ken, 217
Advanced Marine Enterprises (AME), 33
Afghanistan, 211–15, 236–45, 263
Afghanistan war, 6, 213–15, 236–45
agenda setting, 4
Agnew, Spiro, 155
Ahmad, Sultan Hashim, 193
Alger, Philip R., 31
Alison, Joan, 83
al-Maliki, Houri, 236
al Qaeda, 211–13, 215–16, 220–21, 229–34, 237, 239, 242–43, 246, 262, 265
al-Sabah, Saud Nasir, 23
Al-Zarqawi, Abu Musab, 233–34
AME. *See* Advanced Marine Enterprises (AME)
American Society of Trial Consultants, 20–21
America's Longest War: The United States and Vietnam, 1950–1975 (Herring), 130
Anglo-German alliance, 49
Annex Foxtrot, 190
Apocalypse Now, 165

AP poll, 210
Army of the Republic of Vietnam (ARVN), 133–35
Arnett, Peter, 191
artifacts, 25–26
ARVN. *See* Army of the Republic of Vietnam (ARVN)
atomic bomb, 90–91
Auschwitz liberation, 85–86
Austria, 50
Austria-Hungary, 51
"Awful Office Address," 206
Axis Powers, 79, 89, 93, 182, 206, 216
Aziz, Tariq, 186, 193

Bagdikian, Ben, 156
Baker, James, 181, 186–87, 193
Ball, George, 141
Baron, Stanley J., 4
The Battle of Britain, 3
Battle of Kosovo (1389), 50
Battle of Las Guásimas, 35
Battle Report—Washington, 107
Beast of Berlin, 83
Belgium, 50, 51
Belgrade, 50, 51
Bennett, Murray, 83
Berg, A. Scott, 55, 62
Berlin, 102

Berlin Wall, fall of, 180
Bernays, Edward, 10
Beschloss, Michael, 66, 85, 103–5, 138–39, 151
Biden, Joe, 121, 187, 246
bin Laden, Osama, 11, 205, 209, 213, 215, 230, 232, 241–42, 244, 260, 262, 266
Black Hand, 51
Black Hawk Down, 210
Blair, Tony, 222
Blix, Hans, 222
Boissoneault, Lorraine, 56
Bolger, Daniel P., 215, 231, 236
Bonesteel, Charles, 101
Bonier, David, 209
Born on the Fourth of July, 165
Bosnia, 50
Brewer, Susan A., 25, 38–39, 58–59, 65–66, 165, 224
Bright Shining Lies (Sheehan, Neil), 135
Brinkley, David, 108–9
British Empire, 30, 49–68
British-German alliance, 49–51
Brock, Timothy C., 20
Brown, Robert, 88–89
Bryce, James, 53–54
Bryce Report, 7
Buddhists, 134
Buis, Dale, 129, 168
Bumiller, Elisabeth, 227
Bundy, McGeorge, 150
Burke, Kenneth, 12, 21, 79
Bush, George H. W., 11, 23–24, 26, 93, 179–98, 259
Bush, George W., 1, 6, 11, 59, 93, 142, 179, 185, 205–48, 259
Business Week, 88–89

"Cakewalk In Iraq" (Adelman), 217
Calhoun, John C., 37
Calley, William, 152
Cambodia, 154–58, 161, 168
Capra, Frank, 3, 80–82, 86, 107, 147
Card, Andy, 228

Carey, James W., 6
Carter, Jimmy, 184
Casablanca, 62, 83, 93
Casey, George, 238
Castro, Fidel, 37–38
Central Powers of Germany, 51–54, 59, 65
Chamberlain, Neville, 76
Chancellor, John, 24
Chaney, Lon, 62
Chaplin, Charlie, 83, 92
Cheney, Dick, 11, 181, 217
"Chennault affair," 153
Chiang Kai-shek, 102, 104
China, 111–15
Chou En-lai, 108
Churchill, Winston, 76–77, 101
Ciccolella, R. G., 148
Clark, Richard, 205, 213, 215–16, 221, 228, 230
Clinton, Bill, 194
"Coalition of the Willing," 222
Cohan, George M., 61
Cold War, 93, 100–103, 107, 132, 134, 143, 145, 154, 165–66, 180–82
Coming Home, 165
The Commanders (Woodward), 188
Committee on Public Information (CPI), 60–62
Communism, 93, 99, 102–3, 105, 110–12, 117, 121, 131–34, 143, 146–48, 154, 165–67, 180–81, 208, 268
Communists, 93, 100, 102–15, 122, 129, 131–51, 155, 160, 166–68, 260
conditional effects model, 3
Confessions of a Nazi Spy, 83
consequence, 23–24
consistency, 23–24
Cowen, Tyler, 66
CPI. *See* Committee on Public Information (CPI)
Crane, Stephen, 35–36
Creel, George, 8, 60
Creel Committee, 10, 64
critical theory, 5

Cronkite, Walter, 151–52
Cuban Missile Crisis (1962), 38, 143, 146, 148, 167
Cuba war, 35–36; colony/protectorate, 37–38; Rough Riders, 35–36, 40; stories from, 35–36
Cull, Nicholas, 77
cultivation theory, 4–5, 11
cumulative effects model, 4–5; agenda setting, 4; critical theory, 5; cultivation theory, 4–5
Czechoslovakia, 102

Da 5 Bloods, 165
Dagan, Batsheva, 86
Daily Express, 91
"Daisy Girl" television ad, 141
Davis, Dennis K., 4
Davis, Richard Harding, 35–36
Death Before Dishonor, 210
Death of a Salesman, 23
Debs, Eugene, 64
December 7, 1941, 1
The Deer Hunter, 165
Deliver Us from Evil (Dooley), 133
Democratic People's Republic of Korea (DPRK), 101
Dereliction of Duty (McMaster), 164
"Desert Shield" operation, 180–82, 185–89
Dewey, George, 34–35
D'Haeseleer, Brian, 39–40
Diem, Ngo Dinh, 132, 134–37
digital *versus* analog media, 7
DiMaggio, Anthony R., 4, 6
Diplomatic Pouch, 107
direct effects model, 2–3
Dooley, Tom, 133, 166
Dowd, Maureen, 221
Dower, John, 82
Downing, John, 9
DPRK. *See* Democratic People's Republic of Korea (DPRK)
Draper, Robert, 217, 221
Dunkirk, 259

education *versus* propaganda, 10
Edwards, Bob, 85
Eisenhower, Dwight, 82, 115–16, 129–32, 155, 157, 197
ElBaradei, Mohamed, 222
Ellul, Jacques, 11–13
Espionage Act, 61–62, 64
European War (1914), 7
Executive Decision, 210

fact, 23–24
The Facts We Face, 107
Fahrenheit 9/11, 224
fake news, 2
Fallows, James, 223
Farewell to Manzanar (Houston), 89
Farrell, John A., 153
Fearon, James D., 120–21
Ferdinand, Archduke Franz, 50–51
fidelity, tests of, 22–25, 43; of Bush's narrative, 212–13; consequence, 23–24; consistency, 23–24; fact, 23–24; relevance, 23–24; transcendental issue, 23–24
films, 62, 80, 83–84
"Fireside Chats," 85
Fisher, Jacky, 52
Fisher, Louis, 31–33
Fisher, Walter, 20–26
Five O'Clock Follies, 138
Flags of Our Fathers, 84
Flying Tigers, 83
Follette, Robert La, 53
Four-Minute Men program, 60–61, 67
framing, 6
France, 30, 49–50, 131
Frank, Anne, 86
Freedom Agenda, 233–34
Freedom of Information Act, 214
Frum, David, 206, 216
Fulbright, William J., 147–48
Fyne, Robert, 83–84

Gallup Poll, 66, 79, 109, 112, 212, 220, 228

Gates, Bob, 120, 214
Geneva Accord, 132–33
George, Alexander, 195
Gerbner, George, 5
Germany, 30, 49–68, 76
Gerson, Michael, 216, 219
Gitlin, Todd, 223
Glaspie, April, 179
Global War on Terror, 37
The Glory Brigade, 113
Golden Mosque of Samarra, 234
Goldstein, Robert, 64
Goldwater, Barry, 139, 149
Good Morning, Vietnam, 165
Gorbachev, Mikhail, 180
Grammer, Gregory, 205
gratifications, 6
Great Britain, 49–68, 77
The Great Dictator (Chaplin), 83, 92
The Great Gatsby, 23
Great War (1914), 7
Greece, 101
Green, Melanie, 20–21, 26
Green, Wallace, 144
The Green Berets, 165
Greene, John Robert, 186
Greider, William, 221
Griffith, D. W., 62
Groves, Leslie, 91
Guadalcanal Diary, 83
Guam, 37
Guantanamo Bay Naval Station, 37
Gulf of Tonkin incidents, 130, 138–41, 143–44, 147, 167, 187
Guthrie, Arlo, 166

Haass, Richard, 179
Halberstam, David, 132, 134
Haldeman, H. R., 154
Hallet, Jack, 129
Harkens, Paul D., 135
Harper's Weekly, 43
Harris, Mark, 80
Harvey, Derek, 233
Haughland, Vernon, 82

Hawaii, 1, 37
Hay, John, 36
H-bomb, 119
Hearst, William Randolph, 2, 29–31, 35, 52, 259
Heart of Humanity, 62
"He kept us out of war" campaign (1916), 55
Helms, Dick, 151
Herrick, John J., 138
Herring, George C., 130
Hersey, John, 87, 91
Herzegovina, 50
Higgins, Marguerite, 82
Hill 303 massacre, 117
Hiroshima, 90
Hitler, Adolf, 2, 8, 10–12, 24, 76, 79, 82–83, 92–93, 113, 115, 122, 131, 145–48, 180
Hoar, George, 42
Hobsbawm, Eric, 65
Ho Chi Minh, 68, 129–32
Hollywood movies, 83–84
Houston, Jeanne Wakatsuki, 89
How to Understand Propaganda (Lee), 9
Hughes, Robert P., 39
Humphrey, Hubert, 153
Hungry, 50
Huns, 12, 58–59
Hussein, Saddam, 11–12, 19, 23–24, 179–98, 205, 215, 217–31, 237, 247, 259–60, 262–66, 269

Institute for Propaganda Analysis (IPA), 8
Iran, 216–17
Iraq: operation freedom, 225–27; as quagmire, 229–33; surge in, 234–37; war, 3, 6, 9, 11, 179–98
Iron Eagle, 210
Isaacson, Walter, 222–23
ISIS, rise of, 242–43
Islam, 209

Japan, 77–78; attack on Pearl Harbor, 77–78; empire, 78–79; United States

with, 78–79; war against, declaration of, 78–79
Japanese Americans, 79–82, 87–88
Jefferson, Thomas, 131
Johnson, Hiram, 22, 25, 101
Johnson, Lyndon, 11, 137–55, 164, 167, 180–81, 187, 222, 224, 260, 262, 266–67
Jones, Richard, 217
Jowett, Garth S., 9, 86, 191
Justus, Zachary, 231

The Kaiser, the Beast of Berlin, 62
Karnow, Stanley, 138
Katzenbach, Nicholas, 139
Kazin, Michael, 52, 57–58, 60, 63–66
Keegan, John, 65
Kellen, Konrad, 11
Keller, Allen, 30–31, 35–36, 40
Kennedy, John F., 101, 131–37, 157–59
Kennedy, Joseph, 76, 93
Kennedy, Robert F., 153
Khanh, Nguyen, 137, 141
Kiesling, John Brady, 221
Kim Il Sung, 100, 103–4
Kim Jong-un, 1–2, 120
King, Martin Luther, Jr., 153
Kinzer, Stephen, 31, 33, 39
Kissinger, Henry, 145
Knightley, Philip, 106
Knightley, Phillip, 54, 82–83, 106–7, 225
Know Your Enemy—Japan, 82
Kohut, Andrew, 187
Koran, 210
Korean War, 1–2, 84, 99–123; armistice (no peace treaty), 116–17; atrocities, 117–19; China intervention, 109–11; Cold War and containment, 100–103; crimes, 117–19; government/media propaganda, 106–7; Ike's "go to Korea" promise, 115–16; Macarthur's Inchon miracle, 106; narrative assessment, 121–23; North to Pyongyang, 107–9; nuclear threat in twenty-first century, 119–21; South Korea's security, 103–4; truce talks, 114–15; United States in, 99–123; UN "police action," 104–5; victory/limited war narratives, 111–14; Yalu and, 107–9
Korean War Memorial, 118–19
Krieling, Albert L., 6
Krugman, Paul, 229–30
Krulak, Victor H. "Brute," 145
Kumar, Deepa, 223–25
Kuper, Glenn G., 21
Kurtz, Howard, 223
Kuwait, 179–98, 205–6
Ky, Nguyen Cao, 141, 151

Lakoff, George, 264
Langewiesche, William, 91–92
Larson, Cedric, 60–64
Lasswell, Harold, 9, 60
Laszlo, Victor, 83
League of Nations, 65
Lee, Alfred, 9
Lee, Spike, 165
Leidig, Lisa, 191
Lie, Trygve, 114
limited effects model, 3
Link, Arthur Stanley, 54
Lippmann, Walter, 7
Little, Becky, 80
Lodge, Henry Cabot, 30
Lunch, William, 162
Luntz, Frank, 219
Lynch, Charles, 82
Lynch, Jessica, 225

MAAG. *See* Military Assistance and Advisory Group (MAAG)
MacArthur, John R., 9, 19, 23–24, 103–4, 106–13, 135, 183, 190, 193
Mahmud, Salah Abud, 193
Major, John, 189
Malek, Abbas, 191
Malik, Jacob, 114
Manichean declaration, 212
Manzanar, 87–88

Manzanar Free Press, 87
Mao Zedong, 102
Martin, John, 24
M*A*S*H, 165
mass communications, 3
Massie, Robert, 50
mass media, 3
Matar, Mohammed, 24
Mayaguez, 168
Mazzocco, Philip, 20–21
McCants, William, 243
McCarthy, Eugene, 152
McCarthy, Joe, 111
McCarthy, Joseph, 102–3, 117, 131
McChrystal, Stanley, 238
McCloskey, Bob, 144
McCullough, David, 106, 113
McGroarty, Dan, 188
McKinley, William, 29–30, 33–34, 36–42, 267
McMaster, H. R., 136, 141–42, 146, 149–50, 164
McNamara, Robert, 135–36, 139–40, 144–45, 150–51, 164–65, 167
McNaughton, John, 142
McWilliams, Carey, 88–89
Meacham, Jon, 185, 194
media effects, 2–7; cumulative effects, 4–5 (agenda setting, 4; critical theory, 5; cultivation theory, 4–5); direct effects, 2–3; limited and conditional effects, 3; transactional model, 5–7 (framing, 6; gratifications, 6; priming, 6; social media, 6–7; uses, 6); on war propaganda, 7–14
Meet the Press (Russert), 107, 223
Mein Kampf (Hitler), 12, 210
Melville, George W., 31
Memoirs (Truman), 89, 91, 99, 101
"Memories of Manzanar" (Merritt), 87–88
Merritt, Ralph P., 87
Mexican-American War (1846–1848), 37
Middle East, 6, 24, 59, 66, 157, 179, 184, 217, 233–34, 238, 243, 246, 269

Middleton, Drew, 82
Military Assistance and Advisory Group (MAAG), 129
Miller, Robert, 107
Mineta, Norm, 209
"Mission Accomplished," 222–29
Mock, James R., 60–64
Montenegro, 50
Moore, Michael, 224
Morse, Wayne, 139–40
Moskos, Charles, 191
Moyers, Bill, 10, 80, 222
Mueller, John E., 109–11, 130
Mukawa, Tomoko, 87–88
Munich Pact, 76
Murrow, Edward R., 83, 85, 113–14, 118
Muslim: Americans, 209–10; Bush's narrative on, 209–13; negative portrayal of, 209–10; public attitudes toward, 210; and terrorist attacks of 9/11, 209–10

Nagasaki, 90
narrative fidelity, tests of, 22–25
narrative paradigm, 21–25
narratives of war, 19–26, 268–71; artifacts selection, 25–26; Korean War, 121–23; paradigm, 21–25; Persian Gulf War (1991), 196–98; Spanish-American War (1898), 40–43; transportation theory, 20–21; Vietnam War, 166–69; World War I, 66–68; World War II, 92–94
National Defense Act, 55
National Geographic Society, 33
National Liberation Front (NLF), 134
National Security League, 53
Navy Seals, 210
Nazis, 10, 82–84, 86, 92, 184, 196, 211–12, 260–61
Nebraska Volunteer infantry, 38
Nhu, Ngo Dinh, 136
Night (Wiesel), 86
Nightingale, E. C., 75

9/11 narrative, 205–48, 263. *See also* war on terror
Nixon, Richard M., 153–57
NKPA. *See* North Korean People's Army (NKPA)
NLF. *See* National Liberation Front (NLF)
North Korea, 1–2, 99–123, 216–17. *See also* Korean War
North Korean People's Army (NKPA), 99–100

Obama, Barack, 214, 237–41, 243–44
obscenity, 9
obtrusive issues, 4
O'Donnell, Victoria, 9, 86, 191
Office of Facts and Figures program, 85
Office of War Information (OWI), 80
Ogburn, Charlton Jr., 90
Omar, Mullah, 209
One Minute to Zero, 113
Operation Desert Muzzle, 190–93
Operation "Desert Shield," 180–82, 185–89
Operation Enduring Freedom, 213–15
Operation Infinite Justice, 213
Operation Iraqi Freedom, 3, 82, 225–27
Operation Maximum Candor, 137–38
Operation Rolling Thunder, 142
O'Reilly, Bill, 210
Osborne, Robert, 118
O'Shaughnessy, Nicholas Jackson, 9–10, 12, 221, 225
Ovnand, Chester, 129
OWI. *See* Office of War Information (OWI)

Page, Caroline, 148
Panetta, Leon, 87, 232, 242
Paris Peace Accords, 159–60
partipulation, 13
Peace, Roger, 39–40
"peace with honor," 154–56
Pearl Harbor attack, 75, 77–78, 81–86, 91–94, 184, 206, 259–60

People's Republic of China, 102
Perse, Elizabeth, 2–5
Persian Gulf War (1991), 19, 179–98, 262; aftermath, 193–94; "Desert Shield" operation, 180–82, 185–89; ground war, 189–90; media and, 190–93; narrative assessment, 196–98; post-Cold War world, 180; Saddam as Hitler in, 182–85; Vietnam syndrome, ending of, 194–96
persuasion, 3; narrative *versus* rhetorical, 21; *versus* propaganda, 13–14
Philippines, 100; falls, 36–37, 42; insurgency in, 38–40
pictorial propaganda, 62
Pincus, Walter, 223
Platoon, 165
Platt Amendment, 37
Politics and Propaganda: Weapons of Mass Seduction (O'Shaughnessy), 9
posters, 62–63, 80–81, 89, 158, 209
Potter, W. James, 7
Pottery Barn Rule, 218
Powell, Colin, 152, 179–80, 191, 193–95, 220–21, 264
Powell Doctrine, 194–95
Prelude to War, 80–82
presidential campaign (1940), 76–78
priming, 6
"Progress Campaign," 149–50
The Promised Land (Obama), 238
propaganda, war: analysis, 8; channel of communication in, 12–13; Creel Committee, 10; critics of, 13; definition of, 8–10; *versus* education, 10; Ellul's view of, 11–13; films for, 62; Korean War, 106–7; narratives paradigm, 21–25; perspectives on, 7–9; *versus* persuasion, 13–14; pictorial, 62; recognition, 9–14; references to, 9; techniques, 8; transportation theory, 20–21; war on terror, 234; World War I, 60–65; World War II, 79–82

Propaganda and Democracy: The American Experience of Media and Mass Persuasion (Sproule), 7
Propaganda and Persuasion (Sproule, Jowett, and O'Donnell), 9
Prophet Muhammad, 210
psychological manipulations, 12
Public Opinion (Lippmann), 7
Puerto Rico, 33, 36–38
Pulitzer, Joseph, 29–30

Quang Duc, 135
Queen Victoria, 49

racism, 82
radio, 80, 84–85
Rampton, Sheldon, 220–23, 226, 229
Reagan, Ronald, 180
reconcentration policy, 29
Red Scare, 103
relevance, 23–24
Remington, Frederick, 29, 31, 40
Republic of Vietnam (RVN), 132
The Responsive Chord (Schwartz), 13
Rhee, Syngman, 103, 116–17
Rhodes, Ben, 237, 239, 247–48
Richard Nixon: The Life (Farrell), 153
Rickover, H. R., 33
Ridgway, Matthew, 99, 104
Riefenstahl, Leni, 80–81
Risen, James, 224, 233, 248
Ritter, Scott, 224
Rogers, Richard, 113
Roosevelt, Franklin Delano, 1, 8, 22, 66, 68, 76–78, 84–85, 100, 211, 213, 264, 266
Roosevelt, Theodore, 29–30, 34–35, 40–41, 43, 53
"Rosie the Riveter" poster, 80–81
Rough Riders, Cuba, 35–36, 40, 43
Rove, Karl, 211
Ruane, Michael E., 77–78
Rules of Engagement, 210
Rumsfeld, Donald, 206–7, 209, 213–16, 225–27, 234, 236

Runels, Dick, 183
Rusk, Dean, 101
Russert, Tim, 223
Russia, 30, 49–51, 100–102
RVN. *See* Republic of Vietnam (RVN)

Sacra Congregatio de Propaganda Fide, 9
Sadler, Brent, 191
Saigon, fall of, 160–61
Sands of Iwo Jima, 84
San Juan Hill, battle for, 35
Sarajevo, 50
Saudi Arabia, 181–86, 205
Saving Private Ryan, 84, 259
Scheer, Christopher, 216
Schindler's List, 86, 259
Schnitzlein, Robert, 193
Schrecklichkeit, 61
Schwartz, Tony, 13
Schwarzkopf, Norman, 181, 191–94
Scowcroft, Brent, 179–80
Second Front: Censorship and Propaganda in the 1991 Gulf War (MacArthur), 9
Sedition Act, 64
Serbia, 50–51
Shafter, William, 35
Shales, Tom, 192, 196
Shangri-La. *See* Manzanar
Sheehan, Neil, 87, 135–36, 145, 264
Shevardnadze, Eduard, 181
Shia Islam, 234
Sidle, William, 150
Simon, Bob, 191
Simpson, John, 191
Sino-Japanese war (1894–1895), 100
Small, Melvin, 156
Smith, Jacob H., 40
Smith, Jean Edward, 207, 209, 236
Smith, Kim, 1
social media, 6–7
Sousa, John Philip, 165
South Korea, 99–123. *See also* Korean War

Soviet Union, 84, 89, 93, 100–101, 129, 180, 186, 197, 226
Spanish-American War (1898), 25, 29–43, 89; Cuba (colony/protectorate, 37–38; Rough Riders, 35–36; war stories from, 35–36); narrative assessment, 40–43; origins of, 30–34; Philippines (falls, 36–37; insurgency in, 38–40); prelude to, 30–34; reconcentration policy, 29; Spanish fleet, Dewey destroys, 34–35; yellow journalism in, 30
Spector, Ronald, 152
Sperlich, Peter, 162
The Spirit of '76, 64
Sproule, J. Michael, 7–9, 53–54, 64, 83
Sreberny-Mohammadi, Annabelle, 5
Stalin, Joseph, 89–90, 100–101, 103–4, 116, 122, 131, 226, 265
Starr, Edwin, 166
State of Denial (Woodward), 230
Stauber, John, 220–23, 226, 229
The Steel Helmet, 113
Stelzner, Hermann, 79
Steuter, Erin, 210, 224
Stevenson, Adlai, 115
Stewart, Potter, 9
Stimson, Henry, 77
Stockdale, James, 139
Stone, Oliver, 165
St. Vitus's Day, 50
Syngman Rhee, 114

Taft, William Howard, 42
Taliban, 211–15, 236–38, 244
The Tattered Dress, 129
Taylor, Maxwell, 135
television, 4–6, 23, 107–9, 113–14, 147, 150–58, 161, 164–65, 188, 190, 224–26, 263
Teller Amendment, 36–37
Tenet, George, 220–21
Tenth Pennsylvania Regiment, 42–43
terrorism, 205–48
Tet offensive, 151–54

Tharoor, Ishaan, 247
Thatcher, Margaret, 181
Thieu, Nguyen Van, 151
Thirty Seconds Over Tokyo, 83
torture, 39, 41, 133, 231–32
transactional model, 5–7, 19; framing, 6; gratifications, 6; priming, 6; social media, 6–7; uses, 6
transcendental issue, 23–24
transportation theory, 20–21, 62
Trask, Ashly, 1
Treaty of London (1839), 50
Treaty of Paris, 38
Triumph of the Will, 80–81
True Lies, 210
Truman, Harry S., 22, 89–92, 99–115, 121–23, 129, 131, 142–43, 225, 246, 260–61, 266–67
Trump, Donald, 1–2, 119–21, 157, 233, 245–46, 266
Tuchman, Barbara, 49–50
Tumulty, Joseph, 56
Tuohy, William, 138
Turkey, 101
Twain, Mark, 25, 42
two-step flow of influence, 3

United States, 50; actions in Cambodia, 154–58, 161, 168; anti-Semitism in, 86; foreign policy, 180; Hollywood movies, 83–84; Japan, declaration of war against, 78–79; with Japan, 78–79; in Korean War, 99–123; neutrality in World War I, 51–55; radio, 84–85; in Vietnam War, 137–69; war on terror, 205–48
USS *Abraham Lincoln*, 227
USS *Maddox*, 138
USS *Maine*, 29–33, 40–41, 55, 79, 259, 262
USS *Pueblo*, 119
USS *Turner Joy*, 138

Vandegeer, Richard, 168
VanDeMark, Brian, 149, 168

Vanderbilt, Cornelius, 53
Vann, John Paul, 135
Victory at Sea, 113
Viet Minh, 131–33
Vietnamization strategy, 154–58, 162–63, 236
Vietnam Memorial, 129–30
Vietnam War, 11, 39–40, 84, 129–69, 190, 262–64; of attrition, 144–45; escalation, 141–44; Gulf of Tonkin incidents, 138–41; Johnson, Lyndon and, 137–38; legacy of, 163–66; narrative assessment, 166–69; Nixon, Richard M. and, 154–56; Paris Peace Accords and, 159–60; "peace with honor," 154–56; prelude to, 130–34; protests, 156–59; prowar propaganda, 145–48; public opinion on, 162–63; as quagmire, 148–51; Saigon, fall of, 160–61; Tet offensive, 151–54; United States in, 137–69
von Bismarck, Otto, 51, 66, 270
von Clausewitz, Carl, 152
von Stroheim, Erich, 62

Wallace, George, 154
war on terror, 205–48; bin Laden, killing of, 241–42; Bush's 9/11 narrative, 205–13; ending forever wars, 245–47; expansion of, 215–22; Freedom Agenda, 233–34; Iraq (operation freedom, 225–27; as quagmire, 229–33; surge in, 234–37); ISIS, rise of, 242–43; media buy Bush's story, 222–24; mission accomplishment, 222–29; Obama, Barack and, 237–41, 243–44; Operation Enduring Freedom, 213–15; Operation Iraqi Freedom, 225–27; propaganda, 234; selling, 222–24
war stories, reoccurring, 264–68
Watzlawick, Paul, 26
Wayne, John, 93, 165

Webb, Peter, 106
Westmoreland, William, 137, 144, 150
Wheatcroft, Geoffrey, 53
Wheeler, Earle, 141
WHIG. *See* White House Iraq Group (WHIG)
White House Iraq Group (WHIG), 223
Why Korea, 107
Why Vietnam, 147
Why We Fight series, 3, 80, 86, 92–93, 147, 259
Why We Lost (Bolger), 215
Wiesel, Elie, 86
William, Kaiser, 49–50, 58–59, 62–63
Williams, Pete, 193
Williams, Robin, 165
Wills, Deborah, 210, 224
Wilson, Woodrow, 56–68, 78–79, 130, 157, 209–11, 265, 268–69
Wolfowitz, Paul, 181, 216
Woodward, Bob, 119–20, 216, 225, 229–31, 238
A World Transformed (Bush and Scowcroft), 23
World War I, 2, 8, 10, 12, 49–68; American in, 51–68; declaration, 58–60; Germany in, 49–68; "He kept us out of war" campaign (1916), 55; legacy of, 65–66; narrative assessment, 66–68; propaganda/silencing dissent, 60–65; Wilson and, 56–68
World War II, 3, 10, 22, 62, 65–66, 75–94, 262; Axis Powers of, 79, 89, 93, 182, 206, 216; correspondents, 82–83; ends, 89–92; Germans, portraying, 85–86; Hollywood movies and, 83–84; Japan (declaration of war, 78–79; portraying of, 86–89); narrative assessment, 92–94; presidential campaign (1940) and, 76–78; propaganda, 79–82; radio in, 84–85; United States in, 75–94

Yalta conference, 89–90
Yalu, 107–9
yellow journalism, 30
"Yellow Kid," 30
York, Alvin, 65

Youssef, Fayeza, 24
Zakaria, Fareed, 228
Zimmerman telegram, 57, 59, 67
Zogby poll (2004), 210

About the Author

Steven R. Brydon is professor emeritus at California State University, Chico, where he taught courses in persuasion, public speaking, argumentation, political communication, and public opinion and propaganda. He received his PhD from the University of Southern California. He has coauthored three books and has published in the areas of political communication, argumentation, and debate.

www.ingramcontent.com/pod-product-compliance
Lightning Source LLC
Chambersburg PA
CBHW071402300426
44114CB00016B/2148